Red Shadows: Memories and I
Cultural Revo

Red Shadows: Memories and Legacies of the Chinese Cultural Revolution

The China Quarterly Special Issues
New Series, No. 12

Edited by

PATRICIA M. THORNTON, PEIDONG SUN

and

CHRIS BERRY

CAMBRIDGE
UNIVERSITY PRESS

CAMBRIDGE
UNIVERSITY PRESS

University Printing House, Cambridge CB2 8BS, United Kingdom

Cambridge University Press is part of the University of Cambridge.

It furthers the University's mission by disseminating knowledge in the pursuit of education, learning and research at the highest international levels of excellence.

www.cambridge.org
Information on this title: www.cambridge.org/9781316604755

First published 2016 (The China Quarterly 227 September 2016)
This edition 2016

Printed in the United Kingdom at Bell & Bain Ltd, Glasgow

A catalogue record for this publication is available from the British Library

ISBN 978-1-316-60475-5 Paperback

Contents

Acknowledgements   vii

Preface
The Once and Future Tragedy of the Cultural Revolution
RODERICK MACFARQUHAR   1

Introduction
The Cultural Revolution: Memories and Legacies 50 Years On
CHRIS BERRY, PATRICIA M. THORNTON AND PEIDONG SUN   6

Bending the Arc of Chinese History: The Cultural Revolution's Paradoxical
   Legacy
ANDREW G. WALDER   15

The Cultural Revolution and Its Legacies in International Perspective
JULIA LOVELL   34

Mummifying the Working Class: The Cultural Revolution and the
   Fates of the Political Parties of the 20th Century
ALESSANDRO RUSSO   55

Debates on Constitutionalism and the Legacies of the Cultural Revolution
WU CHANGCHANG   76

The Cultural Revolution as a Crisis of Representation
PATRICIA M. THORNTON   99

Cultural Revolution as Method
MICHAEL DUTTON   120

Whodunnit? Memory and Politics before the 50th Anniversary of the
   Cultural Revolution
SUSANNE WEIGELIN-SCHWIEDRZIK AND CUI JINKE   136

Restricted, Distorted but Alive: The Memory of the "Lost Generation" of
   Chinese Educated Youth
MICHEL BONNIN   154

The Collar Revolution: Everyday Clothing in Guangdong as Resistance
   in the Cultural Revolution
PEIDONG SUN   175

The Silent Revolution: Decollectivization from Below during the Cultural
   Revolution
FRANK DIKÖTTER   198

Index   214

Cover Illustration: Waitresses from the countryside perform a Cultural
Revolution dance for the customers of the "Old Rusticated Youth" restaurant in
Chongqing. Photograph courtesy of Michel Bonnin (2008)

Acknowledgements

The editors would like to thank *The China Quarterly* and its staff for their support throughout the process of putting together the collection, as well as the authors for their efforts and cooperation, and the anonymous reviewers for their hard work. We would also like to thank our colleagues at SOAS and the International Center for Studies of Chinese Civilization at Fudan University for hosting the workshops we held in the process of developing this volume.

Acknowledgements

Preface

The Once and Future Tragedy of the Cultural Revolution

Roderick MacFarquhar*

Let me start with a personal experience. Over many years at Harvard, I taught a course in the core programme on the Cultural Revolution. During the 1980s and 1990s, the students were mainly Americans, but in the new millennium, Harvard, like other US schools, began to admit undergraduates from China. Although some of them avoided my course because they reportedly feared I might insult Mao Zedong 毛泽东, quite a few risked this possibility. Many of those Chinese students came up to me at the end of the course to thank me for opening their eyes to the events of 1966–1976; mum and dad/grandma and grandpa had told them nothing about the Cultural Revolution.

My reaction to these revelations was that their ignorance must in part be owing to the vigorous attempt by the regime to consign the Cultural Revolution to the dustbin of history by discouraging research and teaching on the subject. Under those circumstances, parents and grandparents could be forgiven for not igniting their children's curiosity and perhaps exposing them to sanctions. But, other possibilities also occurred to me. Since most of the Harvard cohort of Chinese undergraduates are from bourgeois families, their relatives are unlikely to have escaped involvement in the Cultural Revolution: either they were beaten up, had their houses trashed, their books burned, their valuables confiscated, or they were among the beaters and looters. Either way, these would be deeply shaming experiences: would one really want to dwell on them with one's children? Louisa Lim entitled her book about Tiananmen *The People's Republic of Amnesia.*[1] The title could be equally well applied to the Cultural Revolution.

The dangers of inducing national amnesia is encapsulated in George Santayana's famous dictum: "Those who cannot remember the past are condemned to repeat it." Or, as the Nobel Prize-winning author Gao Xingjian 高行健 put it when discussing the Cultural Revolution:

Furthermore, it is very likely that when people have forgotten about it, it will make a comeback, and people who have never gone crazy will go crazy, and people who have never been oppressed will oppress or be oppressed. This is because madness has existed since the birth of humanity, and it is simply a question of when it will flare up again.[2]

That is why the enterprise enshrined in this volume on the Cultural Revolution is well judged. There are still so many important questions, events and subjects that

---

* Harvard University. Email: macfarq@fas.harvard.edu.
1 Lim 2014.
2 Gao 2002, 195, quoted in MacFarquhar and Schoenhals 2006, 450.

© The China Quarterly, 2016   doi:10.1017/S0305741016000400

need to be explored further, and Fudan and *The China Quarterly* are to be congratulated on recruiting Chinese and Western scholars to tackle them together.

For most observers of contemporary China, the very obvious legacy of the Cultural Revolution is Deng Xiaoping's 邓小平 reform and opening up. As Chairman Mao was wont to say, although he would have refrained on this topic, "out of bad things come good things." The desperate plight of China in 1976, left far behind in the race for development by other peoples in the old Chinese cultural area, woke up the survivors of Mao's last folly to the need for new ideas and new directions. Fortunately, Deng Xiaoping had the courage and the clout to start crossing the river by feeling for the stones, to embrace any method which contributed to economic progress by calling it "socialism with Chinese characteristics," to proclaim that "practice is the sole criterion of truth" and not ideology, and to permit the widespread use of a slogan that was the very antithesis of the Cultural Revolution: "To get rich is glorious." As a result, over the past 35 years, the Chinese people have transformed their nation into the workshop of the world, and hundreds of millions of them have become prosperous to an extent undreamt of in the Maoist era. So, how likely is it that amnesia about the Cultural Revolution could bring about a repeat as Santayana and Gao would predict? What were the basic ingredients of the Cultural Revolution that might be replicable?

First, no Mao, no Cultural Revolution. One needs a supreme leader with a cult so pervasive that he can act with little danger of being questioned. Second, the supreme leader must sense danger so great – either to the system or to himself or to both – that he must take extraordinary measures to ward it off. Mao did not launch a cultural revolution in the 1950s, because he was only beginning to develop his obsession with the concept of revisionism, i.e. Soviet "abandonment" of Leninist doctrine. And, while Khrushchev's denunciation of Stalin in 1956 may have caused Mao to fear that his own doctrines might be abandoned after his death, it was only when Khrushchev was dismissed in 1964 that he may have begun to fear that his colleagues might unseat him even before his death.

Third, the leader must have a bulwark of support for any drastic measures like a cultural revolution. In Mao's case it was the PLA. Fourth, the leader must also have a gang of "trusties" who can be counted on to do his bidding, even in the face of a hostile party and society. Could those elements be reproduced today?

First, no Chinese leader can be Mao, revolutionary victor and founder of the People's Republic, and its leader for 27 years. But, Josif Dzhugashvili did not have to be Lenin in order to be Stalin. Within a leader-friendly system like Leninism, new supreme leaders can arise. Already, it is widely recognized that in a brief three and a half years, Xi Jinping 习近平 has become more powerful than his two predecessors. A healthy cult of Xi *dada* 习大大 ("Uncle" Xi) is being developed. Seven major books with his writings and anecdotes, etc. have been published. There is a compendium entitled *Approachable: The Charm of Xi Jinping's Words* which, though large and yellow, apparently conjures up memories of Mao's "little red book." There is a song entitled "Xi Dada loves Mama Peng," and perhaps most significantly, an amulet which has Mao on one side and Xi on the other.[3]

Second, are there system-threatening dangers in China? The Party and state have been described by Jiang Zemin 江泽民, Hu Jintao 胡锦涛 and Xi Jinping as in danger of collapse because of corruption. This is what has aroused Xi Jinping to launch his hard-driving anti-corruption campaign. The campaign is to target Party officials, high and low, "tigers" and "flies." Unlike Mao's Cultural Revolution, in which the violence was often random and gratuitous, this campaign will zero in on known corrupt officials.

Third, Xi has also emulated Mao in indicating that the PLA is his bulwark by getting 18 senior generals to pledge their allegiance. Finally, Xi Jinping has no "gang of four," but he has far more powerful weapons: the Party secretariat and the Central Discipline Inspection Commission (CDIC), led by his old friend and colleague, Wang Qishan 王岐山.

And yet, surely there is no possibility of a repeat of the Cultural Revolution. What leader with any knowledge of the killing and chaos of that period would want to repeat it? What leader would be so confident as to feel his leadership would not be challenged if he tried to? Xi Jinping is, above all, the trumpeter of the "Chinese dream," the rejuvenation of the Chinese nation. He has no interest in throwing the country into confusion, as Mao did. His obsession is how to avoid what happened to the Soviet Union and the Soviet Communist Party. He seeks to do that by ridding the Chinese Communist Party (CCP) of corruption.

But, there's the rub. Mao wanted to make China's leaders revolutionary, whereas Xi seeks to make them pure. The aims may be different, but in a very real sense what Xi is attempting is also a cultural revolution. It may not be a "great revolution that touches people to their very souls,"[4] but the anti-corruption campaign touches their families, their wealth and their positions. Everything that Party members have worked for or schemed for over the past 35 years is at risk. As in Mao's Cultural Revolution, the highest in the land are not to be spared. Zhou Yongkang 周永康, a member of the ruling Politburo Standing Committee (PSC) and the boss of the security apparatus and law enforcement until he retired at the last Party congress, is the biggest tiger to have been brought down so far. The rumoured convention that PSC members are sacrosanct even in retirement has been breached. Zhou is not a Liu Shaoqi 刘少奇, but he was a formidable figure, even after leaving office. General Xu Caihou 徐才厚, a former Politburo member and vice-chairman of the Party's Military Affairs Commission, was not spared from indictment even though he was dying of cancer. Again, Xu was no Lin Biao 林彪 but he was as senior a military officer as one can find these days.

---

3 See Phillips, Tom. 2014. "Xi Jinping: the growing cult of 'Big Daddy Xi'," *The Telegraph*, 8 December, http://www.telegraph.co.uk/news/worldnews/asia/china/11279204/Xi-Jinping-the-growing-cult-of-Chinas-Big-Daddy-Xi.html. Accessed 28 April 2016.
4 The quote is from the 16-point decision on the Cultural Revolution passed at the Central Committee's 11th Plenum in August 1966.

The CDIC strategy used against tigers is designed to cut away all defences before striking, like cutting down small trees and clearing undergrowth before felling a giant sequoia or a Douglas fir. Zhou's associates from the various places where he had worked and developed loyalty to himself were arrested first. Doubtless, officials under pressure will reveal all about the corruption of their bosses, friends or colleagues if it means a lighter punishment for themselves.

But, how long can this process continue? In Mao's Cultural Revolution, nobody dared even to try to rein in the chairman. Xi has not reached that eminence yet, and there must be some current colleagues or retired grandees like Jiang Zemin who feel the campaign is getting out of hand, or more basically, that they may be the next tiger for indictment. Will they really sit quietly and do nothing to stop Xi and Wang before it is too late?

And what about the flies? During the Cultural Revolution, the Party machine was trashed and, if they were lucky, lower officials only lost their jobs, but many were publicly denounced, beaten, maimed or even killed. There is no solid evidence as to whether torture is being used in the anti-corruption campaign, and certainly there is no repetition of the Red Guard rampages. But already thousands of officials have been brought to book and the whole campaign cannot but be demoralizing for those who fear they may be next. And, if corruption is as pervasive as CCP leaders claim, then they probably will be next!

In Mao's Cultural Revolution, up to 1.5 million people may have been killed according to Andrew Walder's research, but 100 million people were affected according to post-Mao official accounts. Similarly, in Xi's cultural revolution, the collateral damage will be far greater than the number of officials indicted. As the revelations of the CDIC and the investigations of *Bloomberg News* and *New York Times* reporters have confirmed, for every cadre officially designated as corrupt, there is quite possibly also a spouse, a child, a sibling or an in-law deeply involved. So, the social devastation of Xi's campaign, if carried through firmly to the end as he has promised, would be massive, going far beyond whatever proportion of the CCP's 85 million members are corrupt.

Will the leaders and the led of the CCP put up with that prospect? That is the considerable risk that Xi Jinping is taking with his cultural revolution.

Biographical note

Roderick MacFarquhar is the Leroy B. Williams Research Professor of History and Political Science at Harvard University. His works on China include three volumes of *The Origins of the Cultural Revolution*, two volumes of the *Cambridge History of China* (edited with John K. Fairbank), and *Mao's Last Revolution* (co-authored with Michael Schoenhals). In previous personae, he was a journalist (print, radio and TV), founding editor of *The China Quarterly*, and an MP.

References

Gao, Xingjian. 2002. *One Man's Bible*. New York: Harper Collins.

Lim, Louisa. 2014. *The People's Republic of Amnesia: Tiananmen Revisited*. New York: Oxford University Press.

MacFarquhar, Roderick, and Michael Schoenhals. 2006. *Mao's Last Revolution*. Harvard: Harvard University Press and Belknap Press.

Introduction

The Cultural Revolution: Memories and Legacies 50 Years On

Chris Berry[*], Patricia M. Thornton[†] and Peidong Sun[‡]

The year 2016 marks the 50th anniversary of the launch of the Cultural Revolution in China, where controversy continues to rage over its meaning and its legacies. The Communist Party's unequivocal condemnatory labelling of the entire movement as "a grave 'left' error … responsible for the most severe setback and the heaviest losses suffered by the Party, the state and the people since the founding of the People's Republic" has remained in place since 1981.[1] Yet, even decades after the Party's official resolution, the Cultural Revolution remains a lightning rod for contention, particularly in Chinese cyberspace.[2] As a result, in March 2016, with the anniversary of the start of the Cultural Revolution still months away, the Party tabloid, *Global Times* (*Huanqiu shibao* 环球时报), issued an ominous warning against "small groups" that might seek to generate "a totally chaotic misunderstanding of the Cultural Revolution." The editorial sternly reminded *Global Times* readers that "discussions strictly should not depart from the Party's decided politics or thinking,"[3] a prohibition that appears to have short-circuited both popular discussion and scholarly reflection on this critical watershed in 20th-century Chinese politics.

This issue of *The China Quarterly* is not concerned with further excavation into what happened during that tumultuous decade; that has been amply covered in a wealth of new scholarship.[4] Instead, we focus on how the Cultural Revolution is remembered today and what its legacies are, both in the People's Republic of China (PRC) as well as elsewhere across the globe. Five decades after Mao declared the beginning of a new movement to "touch people to their very

* King's College London. Email: chris.berry@kcl.ac.uk (corresponding author).
† University of Oxford. Email: patricia.thornton@politics.ox.ac.uk.
‡ Fudan University: spd@fudan.edu.cn.
1 "Resolution on certain questions in the history of our Party since the founding of the People's Republic of China." Adopted by the sixth plenary session of the 11th Central Committee of the Communist Party of China on 27 June 1981. See https://www.marxists.org/subject/china/documents/cpc/history/01.htm. Accessed 29 June 2016.
2 Yang 2007.
3 "Mao Zedong wannian weihe youlü 'wenge' zhe yi yichan bei xiuzheng?" (Why did Mao worry in his later years that the legacy of the Cultural Revolution would be altered?), *Huanqiu shibao*, 29 March 2016, http://history.huanqiu.com/china/2016-03/8788346_3.html. Accessed 21 June 2016.
4 MacFarquhar and Schoenhals 2006; Andreas 2009; Walder 2009; Wu 2014; Dikötter 2016; Mittler 2013; Clark 2008; Leese 2013.

© The China Quarterly, 2016   doi:10.1017/S0305741016000758

souls," how are we to assess its relevance for China today? In this special issue of *The China Quarterly*, we offer a range of contemporary perspectives on the Cultural Revolution as reflected in memory – both individual and collective – and through a range of historical legacies that continue to exert impact on China's contemporary social, political and economic realities.

Engaging with the Cultural Revolution is fraught with difficulty. The Xi Jinping 习近平 regime's statements on the socialist past have been taken by some as signs of a softening in the regime's position on the Mao era, but not one that enables or encourages scholarly enquiry into the topic. Only months after assuming power, in January 2013 Xi summed up the spirit of the 18th Party Congress by drawing a clear distinction between two periods of PRC history: before Deng Xiaoping's 邓小平 "reform and openness," and after. Despite acknowledging profound ideological and policy differences, Xi argued that the two periods form an indivisible whole, with each period playing an indispensable role in the construction of Chinese socialism: "One cannot use the historical period following reform and opening to negate the historical period prior to reform and opening, and one cannot use the historical period prior to reform and opening to negate the historical period following reform and opening."[5]

This theme of simultaneously recognizing the fundamental differences between the two periods and denying the power of the inherent contradiction between them was reiterated again in March 2013, in the infamous Document No. 9, an internal notice promulgated by the General Office of the Party Central Committee.[6] Further instruction from the Party leadership on this thorny issue came in November, on the day before the third plenum opened, in the form of a full-page article placed by the CCP Central Party History Research Office in the *People's Daily* (*Renmin ribao* 人民日报) entitled, "Correctly view the historical periods, before and after reform and opening." Repeating the condemnatory language laid down in the "1981 Resolution on certain questions in the history of our Party since the founding of the People's Republic of China," the *People's Daily* article noted that the Cultural Revolution "brought untold disasters to the Party, state, and the people of all nationalities," but nevertheless warned against "deliberately negating Comrade Mao Zedong's mistakes in his later years, much less completely negating Comrade Mao Zedong and Mao Zedong Thought." On the contrary, the "two historical periods" (i.e. before and after reform) "are never separated from each other, let alone fundamentally opposed to each other."[7]

---

5 "Haobu dongyao jianchi he fazhan Zhongguo tese shehui zhuyi zai shijian zhong buduan yousuo faxian yousuo chuangzao yousuo qianjin" (Unhesitatingly uphold and develop socialism with Chinese characteristics; have some new discoveries, some new innovations, and some advances in the course of practice), *Renmin ribao*, 6 January 2013.

6 Document No. 9 was published on 19 August 2013 in *Mingjing yuekan*; the above translation appeared in Fewsmith 2014, 5.

7 Central Party History Research Office. 2013. "Zhengque kandai gaige kaifang qianhou liangge lishi shiqi" (Correctly view the two historical periods prior to and after reform and opening up), *Renmin ribao*, 8 November.

Xi's new directive, along with the restrictions that have since followed on public and scholarly discussion of the meaning and import of the Mao era in the present, has greatly hampered reflection on the pivotal event in the final decade of Mao's life, the Chinese Cultural Revolution. The "case closed" official line on the post-1949 past provoked Chinese scientist Fang Lizhi 方励之 to write his essay "The Chinese amnesia" whilst sheltering in the American embassy in Beijing in 1989.[8] Indeed, the sustained official effort to produce, maintain and police a certain type of cultural amnesia can itself be claimed as one of the legacies of the Cultural Revolution, even as individual and collective memories of the late Mao era persistently break out of the confinement imposed upon them by the officially constructed "master narrative" laid out in the 1981 Resolution.[9]

Among social scientists who seek to explain precisely how history matters, legacies are understood to represent deeper underlying historical continuities that continue to shape contemporary realities in profound and complex ways. Yet, while continuity and change have long been central in the study of politics and society, it is clear that we do not yet fully understand the criteria by which claims of such continuity can be made. How are we to understand and investigate the difference between continuity and change from the past? Historical legacies have emerged as a key social science variable in many explanations of contemporary outcomes in authoritarian, transitional and hybrid regimes, although there is still no clear understanding of what a legacy is or how legacy arguments actually work.

Many political scientists have chosen to hone in on "communist legacies," including cultural practices, encompassing attitudes, beliefs, and shared knowledge and experience acquired during the communist period. Anna Grzymała-Busse, for example, has recently drawn attention to the skills developed and retained by communist parties over several decades that have allowed them to weather the transition to new political environments and demands.[10] Jan Kubik has argued that the hybrid mix of nationalism and socialism that proved inimical to liberal values has slowed the progress of reform in post-communist regimes, and Phineas Baxandall has traced how beliefs and expert knowledge about how centrally planned markets work continue to affect economic planning in post-communist countries attempting to undertake market reform.[11]

Yet, as we attempt to identify how legacies continue to affect contemporary outcomes, a number of important analytic and conceptual distinctions emerge. First, and perhaps most clearly, not all outcomes that appear at the end of causal chains can be construed as legacies. Social scientists agree that there is a need to establish the existence of a measurable outcome or influence on the present that is rooted in the past. It also follows that a necessary (although not sufficient)

---

8   Fang 1990.
9   Yang 2005, 14–15.
10 Grzymała-Busse 2003.
11 Kubik 2003; Baxandall 2004.

condition for a phenomenon to be considered as a legacy is that it has to exist in at least two time periods, and that it must refer *explicitly* to the past and, at the same time, *implicitly* to the present. Jason Wittenberg identifies various sorts of legacies, including cultural legacies (which may include political beliefs or proclivities that are collectively held as a result of past experiences), material legacies (for example, a lack of infrastructure), and institutional legacies (i.e. the persistence of old regime institutions such as centralized economic planning), all of which keep vestiges of the past alive in the present day.[12] With respect to the Cultural Revolution, Hong Yung Lee has argued that its most immediate political legacies have included the rise of the political influence of the PLA, the decentralization and devolution of political power to local leaders, and the waxing influence of mass groups previously allied with conservative forces.[13] Writing in 1985, Thomas Gold argued that the Cultural Revolution "left a deleterious economic, political and moral legacy for personal relations" that paved the way for the instrumentalization and commodification of social life early in the reform era.[14] Six years later, Chen Yizi noted that, insofar as the original proposal for rural reform had been developed by a group of young scholars who had been dispatched to the countryside during the Cultural Revolution, post-Mao rural reforms must be counted as one of the more salient legacies of the sent-down movement.[15]

Turning to memory, it is clear that although it overlaps in some cases with legacy, not all memory can be regarded as legacy. Memory is far more fluid and mutable, admitting no clear boundaries between past and present, but most often presents as a fusion of the two. Pierre Nora, for example, argues that memory "remains in permanent evolution, open to the dialectic of remembering and forgetting, unconscious of its successive deformations, vulnerable to manipulation and appropriation, susceptible to being long dormant and periodically revived. Memory is a perpetually actual phenomenon, a bond tying us to the eternal present."[16]

To also qualify as legacy, memory has to have an effect in and on the present, and on social, cultural and historical features of the present that go beyond the individual. Recently, an older contestant on a Chinese reality show sang about his memories of his family's suffering during the Cultural Revolution.[17] As long as Yang Le 杨乐 kept those memories to himself, few would consider them to be a legacy. But does injecting them into the public domain through his performance qualify them as a "legacy"? Certainly, the performance visibly moved many of the listeners in the television studio and commanded a lot of media attention; however, perhaps even in these circumstances, we can say that

12 Wittenberg 2013.
13 Lee 1980, 10.
14 Gold 1985.
15 Chen 1991.
16 Nora 1989, 8.
17 Phillips 2016.

by putting personal memories into public space and culture in this way, Yang Le invoked the broader collective memory from his audience, thereby creating the potential for them to become a recognizable cultural legacy.

Distinctions like these between different analytical categories and types of memory underpin the field of memory studies, although the issue of legacy itself is not often directly discussed in the field. All the scholars who work on memory understand it as something that is constructed and sustained through various practices of telling and retelling. However, for the major writers in the field as it has developed over the years, a primary distinction is between informal and often unrecorded memory and official memory. For example, this distinction is often taken to characterize the key difference between the approaches of the two scholars now understood to be the founding fathers of the field. On the one hand, Maurice Halbwachs' "collective memory" stands in contrast to both the discipline of history's interest in times beyond the reach of memory and the interest of his contemporaries such as Freud and Bergson in individual memory. Halbwachs stressed the social nature of collective memory as something sustained in various ways, but especially in those ways that are dependent on informal and taken-for-granted interactions.[18] On the other hand, where Halbwachs' interest leads to a focus on the ephemeral, Nora's work on memory sites, or *lieux de memoire*, focuses more on material sites, which of course are generally more formal and often officially endorsed.[19]

Jan Assmann makes a similar distinction in his discussion of "cultural memory" and "communicative memory." The way in which he understands cultural memory positions it as similar to Nora's concept, because it emphasizes memories that are material, ritualized, and so on. Communicative memory, on the other hand, comprises memories that come into being and are sustained through everyday interactions and can be seen as part of the larger field of oral history.[20] To this we could also add John Bodnar's distinction between "vernacular" and "official" memory, and William Hirst and David Manier's distinction between "lived" and "distant" memory.[21]

In the case of the Cultural Revolution, to adopt Assmann's terminology, the state attempts to police both communicative memories disseminated through gatherings of former Red Guards or sent-down youth, and cultural memory in terms of the absence of official memorials. Many of the essays collected here analyse not only what gets remembered but also where and how that memory is circulated and sustained. Various issues are at stake in these contestations and negotiations around memory, and in particular efforts to not only sustain communicative memory but also produce cultural memory. Recognition of various wrongs in the past would not only imply acknowledgment by the state but also

18 Halbwachs 1992.
19 Nora 1996–98.
20 Assman 2008.
21 Bodnar 1992, 13–20; Hirst and Manier 2008, 183–200.

carries with it the possibility of financial compensation and the pursuit of justice through the legal system. Concerns such as these subtend the efforts of former sent-down youth, as discussed in Michel Bonnin's essay in this volume, and the efforts to determine and discuss killings, as discussed in Susanne Weigelin-Schwiedrzik and Cui Jinke's essay.

For scholars, we need to recognize that writing about memories of the Cultural Revolution also participates in their production. Although this is usually moti-vated by scholarly aims concerning the pursuit of deeper knowledge and under-standing of what happened during the Cultural Revolution, we need to acknowledge that scholarship is in this way implicated in extending the impact of the Cultural Revolution into the present, and therefore plays a role, however small or unintended, in the production of legacy.

These issues are reflected in the range of contributions we have assembled here. Broadly speaking, after Roderick MacFarquhar's timely foreword, the essays move from considerations of legacy and the international impact of the Cultural Revolution (Andrew Walder, Julia Lovell, and Alessandro Russo), to Chinese politics (Changchang Wu, Patricia M. Thornton, and Michael Dutton), and then on to everyday life, the archive, and memory (Michel Bonnin, Peidong Sun, and Frank Dikötter). However, all the essays engage with memory and legacy to lesser and greater degrees.

On the one hand, Michel Bonnin's article documents a resurgence of latent *zhiqing* memory and nostalgia in the wake of the massacre on 4 June 1989 that in turn gave rise to the phenomenon of *zhiqing* restaurants and other "places where memory sits," which participated in remaking the shared past in the pre-sent. Nora reminds us that, "at the heart of history is a critical discourse that is antithetical to spontaneous memory. History is perpetually suspicious of mem-ory, and its true mission is to suppress and destroy it."[22] And, of course, this is particularly and spectacularly true of the contemporary party-state, which is ac-tively engaged in tightly controlling, if not eliminating altogether, unofficial dis-cussion of the Cultural Revolution era. Susanne Weigelin-Schwiedrzik and Cui Jinke's examination of the apologies offered by former Red Guards and the lar-ger context of the absence of prosecution further illustrates the ongoing nature of these tensions around history and memory.

Both Changchang Wu and Patricia M. Thornton touch upon the contradictions inherent in the Party's struggle to suppress debate regarding the alternative pos-sible futures contained within the radical Maoist past. As Wu demonstrates, the key tension within the debate turns on concepts raised by the liberal and reform-minded constitutionalists on the one hand, and "the Maoist constitutional move-ment" on the other. Likewise, Thornton concurs that one chief historical legacy is the unresolved struggle between the liberal bourgeois model of constitutional and parliamentary democracy, and the unrealized potential of radical alternatives.

22 Nora 1989, 8.

By contrast, Michael Dutton proposes that rather than focusing on questions of representation, the concept of the Maoist political "on the ground" raises the possibility of a new dynamic at work: a question of politico-affective flows and the technologies devised "to harness affective energy flows and channel them towards a productive intensity" as the "basis of a particular and unique mode of being political." Alessandro Russo agrees that the Maoist political offered unique but largely unrealized possibilities, but also sees three inter-twined legacies at work: a radical impasse in the practices of modern egalitarian politics, a significant but also less visible alteration in the sphere of the government, and an even more profound change in the overall organization of knowledge.

Finally, the actual working of a historical legacy may – as both Andrew Walder and Frank Dikötter demonstrate – be hidden or counter-intuitive, and alter the historical trajectory of a nation, a party-state and a people, as the adoption of market reform under the reconsolidated rule of the CCP has done. What all of the papers seem to show is that the chief legacies of the Cultural Revolution were either unintended by Mao and his supporters at the time, or very nearly the exact opposite of what the initiators of the movement were attempting to achieve at the time. Walder goes so far as to assert that "China today is the very definition of what the Cultural Revolution was intended to forestall. It is a caricature of a genuine Maoist's worst nightmare: the degeneration of the Party into a capitalist oligarchy with unprecedented levels of corruption and inequality"; whereas Dikötter's portrait of a paralysed Party machine presiding over a restive and re-siliently entrepreneurial peasantry produces a "silent revolution" by default. Peidong Sun also discovers deep roots for today's more individualist China in her research data revealing the huge variety of everyday resistance to power in the form of clothing choices. Julia Lovell casts a wider net to show that the original enthusiasm for the Cultural Revolution experienced across Western Europe, the United States and parts of South-East Asia helped to splinter the radical left, thereby facilitating the consolidation of the political power of the right through the 1980s and beyond.

We have attempted to ensure that the widest possible range of disciplines and positions on the Cultural Revolution are included in this special issue. To diversify the academic milieux the scholars contributing to the volume are drawn from, we have held workshops in Shanghai and London and invited scholars from around the world to contribute. We hope the result constitutes a stimulating and thought-provoking set of reflections and engagements with the topic of memory and legacy. Certainly, the positions taken here are diverse to the extent of being sometimes mutually incompatible. While that may increase the likelihood that no reader will agree with every essay, we hope that although, of course, not everything is covered, most readers will feel satisfied with the variety.

References

Andreas, Joel. 2009. *Rise of the Red Engineers: The Cultural Revolution and the Origins of China's New Class*. Stanford, CA: Stanford University Press.

Assman, Jan. 2008. "Communicative and cultural memory." In Astrid Erll and Ansgar Nünning (eds.), *Cultural Memory Studies: An International and Interdisciplinary Handbook*. Berlin: Walter de Gruyter, 109–118.

Baxandall, Phineas. 2004. *Constructing Unemployment: The Politics of Joblessness in East and West*. Aldershot: Ashgate.

Bodnar, John E. 1992. *Remaking America: Public Memory, Commemoration, and Patriotism in the Twentieth Century*. Princeton, NJ: Princeton University Press.

Chen, Yizi. 1991. *Zhongguo: shinian gaige yu bajiu minyun* (*China: The Ten-Year Reform and the 1989 Pro-Democracy Movement*). Taipei: Lianjing Publisher.

Clark, Paul. 2008. *The Chinese Cultural Revolution: A History*. New York: Cambridge University Press.

Dikötter, Frank. 2016. *The Cultural Revolution: A People's History, 1962–1976*. London: Bloomsbury.

Fang, Lizhi. 1990. "The Chinese amnesia" (Perry Link (trans.)), *New York Review of Books*, 27 September, http://www.nybooks.com/articles/1990/09/27/the-chinese-amnesia/. Accessed 22 April 2016.

Fewsmith, Joseph. 2014. "Mao's shadow." *China Leadership Monitor* 43(Spring), www.hoover.org/publications/China-leadership-monitor.

Gold, Thomas B. 1985. "After comradeship: personal relations in China since the Cultural Revolution." *The China Quarterly* 104, 657–675.

Grzymała-Busse, Anna. 2003. *Redeeming the Communist Past*. Cambridge: Cambridge University Press.

Halbwachs, Maurice. 1992. *On Collective Memory* (Lewis A. Coser (trans.)). Chicago: University of Chicago Press.

Hirst, William, and David Manier. 2008. "Towards a psychology of collective memory." *Memory* 16 (3), 183–200.

Kubik, Jan. 2003. "Cultural legacies of state-socialism: history making and cultural-political entrepreneurship in postcommunist Poland and Russia." In G. Ekiert and S. Hanson (eds.), *Capitalism and Democracy in Central and Eastern Europe: Assessing the Legacy of Communist Rule*. Cambridge: Cambridge University Press, 317–351.

Lee, Hong Yung. 1980. *The Politics of the Chinese Cultural Revolution: A Case Study*. Berkeley, CA: University of California Press.

Leese, Daniel. 2013. *Mao Cult: Rhetoric and Ritual in China's Cultural Revolution*. New York: Cambridge University Press.

MacFarquhar, Roderick, and Michael Schoenhals. 2006. *Mao's Last Revolution*. Cambridge, MA: Harvard University Press.

Mittler, Barbara. 2013. *Continuous Revolution: Making Sense of the Cultural Revolution*. Cambridge, MA: Harvard University Press.

Nora, Pierre. 1989. "Between memory and history: les lieux de mémoire." *Representations* 26, 4–24.

Nora, Pierre. 1996–98. *Realms of Memory* (3 vols.). New York: Columbia University Press.

Phillips, Tom. 2016. "Reality show singer breaks China's Cultural Revolution taboo," *The Guardian*, 1 April, http://www.theguardian.com/world/2016/mar/30/reality-show-singer-china-cultural-revolution-taboo. Accessed 23 April 2016.

Walder, Andrew G. 2009. *Fractured Rebellion: The Beijing Red Guard Movement*. Cambridge, MA: Harvard University Press.

Wittenberg, Jason. 2013. "What is a historical legacy?" Paper presented at American Political Science Association 2013 Annual Meeting, http://ssrn.com/abstract=2303391. Accessed 21 June 2016.

Wu, Yiching. 2014. *The Cultural Revolution at the Margins: Chinese Socialism in Crisis*. Cambridge: Harvard University Press.

Yang, Guobin. 2005. "Days of old are not puffs of smoke: three hypotheses on collective memories of the Cultural Revolution." *The China Review* 5(2), 13–41.

Yang, Guobin. 2007. "'A portrait of the martyr Jiang Qing': the Chinese Cultural Revolution on the internet." In Ching Kwan Lee and Guobin Yang (eds.), *Re-envisioning the Chinese Revolution: The Politics and Poetics of Collective Memories in Reform China*. Palo Alto, CA: Stanford University Press, 287–316.

Bending the Arc of Chinese History: The Cultural Revolution's Paradoxical Legacy

Andrew G. Walder[*]

Abstract
Contrary to its initiators' intentions, the Cultural Revolution laid political
foundations for a transition to a market-oriented economy whilst also creating circumstances that helped to ensure the cohesion and survival of China's
Soviet-style party-state. The Cultural Revolution left the Chinese
Communist Party and civilian state structures weak and in flux, and drastically weakened entrenched bureaucratic interests that might have blocked
market reform. The weakening of central government structures created a
decentralized planned economy, the regional and local leaders of which
were receptive to initial market-oriented opportunities. The economic and
technological backwardness fostered by the Cultural Revolution left little
support for maintaining the status quo. Mao put Deng Xiaoping in charge
of rebuilding the Party and economy briefly in the mid-1970s before purging
him a second time, inadvertently making him the standard-bearer for post-
Mao rebuilding and recovery. Mutual animosities with the Soviet Union
provoked by Maoist polemics led to a surprising strategic turn to the
United States and other Western countries in the early 1970s. The resulting
economic and political ties subsequently advanced the agenda of reform and
opening. China's first post-Mao decade was therefore one of rebuilding and
renewal under a pre-eminent leader who was able to overcome opposition to
a new course. The impact of this legacy becomes especially clear when con-
trasted with the Soviet Union in the 1980s, where political circumstances
were starkly different, and where Gorbachev's attempts to implement similar
changes in the face of entrenched bureaucratic opposition led to the collapse
and dismemberment of the Soviet state.

Keywords: Chinese Cultural Revolution; post-Mao reform; Deng Xiaoping;
Gorbachev

There are two ways of thinking about historical legacies. The first and most common refers to surviving practices or ways of thought that reflect the continuing
influence, whether conscious or unconscious, of an earlier period. The second
is less common, and refers to legacies that are hidden or counter-intuitive. In

* Department of Sociology, Stanford University. Email: walder@stanford.edu.

© The China Quarterly, 2016   doi:10.1017/S0305741016000709

this second sense, a prior period can shape subsequent ones by altering a country's historical trajectory, leading to present circumstances that are very different than would otherwise have been the case. Thus, the present can be the product of the past in ways that do not directly reflect earlier practices or ways of thought. This essay is about the latter type of legacy. The argument, in brief, is that the Cultural Revolution made it more likely that the Chinese Communist Party (CCP) would turn away from a Soviet-inspired development model, implement reforms in a deep and sustained fashion, and do so while maintaining CCP cohesion and stability – in fact strengthening and revitalizing its Soviet-inherited political institutions. This is in sharp contrast to the final years of the Soviet Union, where belated initial attempts to implement economic restructuring were blocked by powerful vested interests, leading to moves to open up the Soviet political system in ways that inadvertently generated disintegration and collapse.

The living legacy of the Cultural Revolution, in other words, is a communist party that has survived the transition to an utterly transformed economic system that bears little resemblance to the Soviet model; however, it has done so by holding on tightly to a somewhat modified but fundamentally unreformed version of Soviet-style political dictatorship. This outcome, of course, was not at all what the initiators of the Cultural Revolution intended; in almost every sense, it is the virtual opposite and is impossible to square with any version of Maoist ideology. China today is the very definition of what the Cultural Revolution was intended to forestall. It is a caricature of a Maoist's worst nightmare: the degeneration of the Party into a capitalist oligarchy with unprecedented levels of corruption and inequality. This does not mean simply that the Cultural Revolution failed to achieve its goals; it actually created political circumstances that *facilitated* the turn to market reform and *enhanced* the regime's prospect for survival, making China's trajectory so different from that of the Soviet Union.[1]

There is a sense among observers of China that the Cultural Revolution paved the way for subsequent reform. According to Thomas Bernstein, "When it ended, the elite and the population were exhausted, traumatized, and repelled by years of class struggle … The public longed for stability and a better life … the country was ready for something new."[2] And, as Arne Westad has observed, "one of its key effects was probably to kill off Marxism as a credible framework for China's development."[3] This is certainly part of the story. These observations bear on the motivations of leaders, but there remains the puzzle of how China's leaders were able to pull off complex and potentially destabilizing changes without undermining the survival of the Party itself. China's path of

---

1   This is an argument about the political circumstances that facilitated market reform – it is not about the reforms' relative success compared to other transitional economies. The political disruptions that accompanied regime change in other socialist states, especially the Soviet Union, generated deep recessions that immediately put their post-communist reforms on a different economic trajectory. See Walder, Isaacson and Lu 2015.
2   Bernstein 2013, 43.
3   See Westad 2010, 67, 71–75, for a more detailed analysis of its impact on elite ideological trends.

reform has frequently been placed alongside that of the Soviet Union under Gorbachev, and the comparisons usually focus on differences in the political and economic strategies of the two nations' leaders: the Soviet approach being overly broad, ambitious and uncoordinated, while the Chinese approach has been more gradual, cautious and focused.[4] The Cultural Revolution, however, shaped China's trajectory prior to the era of reform in ways that created circumstances very different to those that prevailed in the USSR, and facilitated both the shift to market reform and the Party's survival.

This impact is clearest when we look at China at the beginning of the Deng Xiaoping 邓小平 era alongside the Soviet Union at the start of the Gorbachev era, and note the strikingly different challenges that each leader faced. Four of these differences loom as especially important in setting the two largest communist states on different historical paths.

The first was the Cultural Revolution's devastating impact on the party-state. In the Soviet Union, the Communist Party, the economic bureaucracy, the security services and armed forces had all enjoyed several decades of post-Stalin stability, and in the mid-1980s they represented an array of powerfully entrenched vested interests that stood directly in the way of economic restructuring. In sharp contrast, the Cultural Revolution at some point attacked and disrupted virtually every one of these institutions and their leaders, and their restoration was hampered by controversy and conflict. These institutions had yet to be rebuilt and consolidated at the end of the 1970s, and they lacked the ability of their Soviet counterparts to block the initiatives of a reform-minded leader.

Second, the latter years of the Cultural Revolution inadvertently elevated a senior leader who became the standard bearer for *both* the revival of party-state institutions and economic restructuring. Deng Xiaoping, at Mao's behest, had a vigorous but abortive role in rebuilding these institutions in 1974 and 1975. This identified him with the revival of Party and state institutions, aligning the interests of Party bureaucrats with those of a senior leader who continued this rebuilding even more vigorously during the 1980s. After Mao's death, Deng accelerated the process of restoring disgraced officials to their former prominence, creating political allegiances that enhanced his authority and his ability to direct the process of change. By contrast, as the youngest member of the Soviet Politburo, Gorbachev's authority was stronger on paper than in reality. He eventually tried to open up the political system to circumvent the vested interests arrayed against reform – a fateful move that led to the spiralling collapse of the Soviet Union.

---

4 See Bernstein 2013 for a compelling comparative analysis along these lines. Central to Bernstein's analysis is the success of China's economic reforms versus the failure of those of Gorbachev, a difference that contributed to the survival of the CCP and to the collapse of the USSR. My argument is different: I contend that the Cultural Revolution created conditions that made market reform politically feasible in ways that were not the case in the Soviet Union, in particular because market reform coincided with the rebuilding and strengthening of a badly weakened party-state.

Third, the Cultural Revolution hampered economic development and eroded the country's scientific and technical capacities. China's relative backwardness bred a widespread sense of urgency about economic restructuring that was lacking in the Soviet Union. The economy recovered from the disastrous Great Leap Forward by the mid-1960s, but growth was hampered once again during the Cultural Revolution, during which even more severe damage was inflicted on China's educational and scientific institutions. China remained backward, falling further behind. Although Soviet growth rates had slowed since the 1950s and consumer living standards lagged far behind those of its Western rivals, the Soviet economy was still the world's second largest well into the 1980s, making it a formidable military superpower. Its scientific and technical infrastructure was substantial and world class in some areas. The argument that the Soviet Union was failing to keep pace with the West lacked the sense of urgency of late 1970s China.

Fourth, China's attacks on Soviet "revisionism" during the early 1960s intensified during the Cultural Revolution and generated mutual animosities that threatened to turn into armed conflict by 1969. This prompted Mao's strategic turn towards the United States in 1971 and the gradual revival of ties with Western nations and Japan in the ensuing years. China's strategic realignment with the United States in opposition to a revisionist and "social imperialist" Soviet Union built foundations for a broader opening to Western market economies by the end of the 1970s. The normalization of diplomatic relations with the United States in 1979 completed this process, turning the world's leading market economies into partners eager to assist China's reform and opening. In contrast, hostilities with the Soviet Union further deepened at the end of the 1970s, especially so with the 1979 invasion of Afghanistan and the subsequent boycott of the 1980 Moscow Olympics. Gorbachev could not create a similar opening to the West until he began to withdraw Soviet troops from that country in 1987.

The Destruction of the Party-State Bureaucracy

The Cultural Revolution devastated China's party-state bureaucracy, and for a period essentially eliminated the Communist Party as a coherent national organization. In the first stage of the campaign in 1966, entire departments of the Central Party apparatus were abolished and combined into small working groups, and the majority of their occupants were set aside for investigation and purge. By the end of 1966, civilian Party organizations throughout the country ceased to operate, as rebel groups composed of students and workers kidnapped officials and occupied Party and government offices. Even worse, lower-ranking Party cadres rebelled against their own superiors in a cascading wave of power seizures that reached far down into the grassroots.[5] Rebels in counties and cities

---

5 Walder 2014; 2016.

across the country overthrew top officials, which set off a new round of power struggles with rival rebel groups that continued in most regions well into 1968. The impact on the structure of the party-state can hardly be understated – the apparatus of civilian rule was effectively destroyed.[6]

The 1968 imposition of military control appeared to mark the restoration of order, and indeed, the large-scale street battles came to an end as the military dismantled independent rebel organizations and punished their most strident leaders. In the place of the former structures of government and Party committees a new form of government was established – a "revolutionary committee" made up of a minority of surviving civilian officials, token rebel leaders, and military officers loyal to the local PLA commander who, in most cases, occupied the top position. In most parts of the country, revolutionary committees were a thinly disguised form of military dictatorship.[7]

The new revolutionary committees initially oversaw the further dismantling and downsizing of what remained of the party-state bureaucracy. The vast majority of civilian officials and support staff in government organs, Party offices, newspapers and other public institutions were shipped off to rural camps, described as "May 7 cadre schools," for indefinite terms of reform through labour. Entire departments were consolidated into working groups that were operated by a skeleton staff left behind in the cities. The numbers of officials "sent down" in this fashion are startling – up to 70 per cent of all officials in some provinces. For a period, it appeared that this massive downsizing of the government apparatus was intended to be permanent. The evacuation of civilian officials and staff only enhanced the dominance of military officers in government administration.[8]

These rural camps were closed after the Lin Biao 林彪 affair in late 1971, and efforts to rebuild the national bureaucracy began. Mao had the ranks of the military commanders purged of those deemed loyal to Lin Biao, and the authority of the remaining military commanders over civilian administration went into decline. Mao gave Zhou Enlai 周恩来 the authority to begin the huge task of reviving China's administrative apparatus and rebuilding the Communist Party. The rebuilding of Party committees and branches got underway in 1972, and officials purged earlier in the Cultural Revolution began to return to their posts.[9]

Yet, for the remaining four years of Mao's life, this rebuilding process remained a source of division and conflict. Zhou soon came under attack for moving too fast and too far to restore the status quo ante. He was sidelined during the 1974 "Criticize Lin Biao and Confucius" campaign as Maoist radicals pushed back against the "tide of restoration." The campaign revived factional conflict and street battles on a scale not seen since 1968 in what people at the

6   These developments are documented in MacFarquhar and Schoenhals 2006, 132–238; Walder 2015, 233–253.
7   See Bu 2008, 235–37; Dong and Walder 2012b; MacFarquhar and Schoenhals 2006, 239–246.
8   Walder 2015, 270–71.
9   MacFarquhar and Schoenhals 2006, 337–347; Teiwes and Sun 2007, 25–85.

time described as a "Second Cultural Revolution," through which former rebels aspired to a "second power seizure." The civil disorders, often focused on large state factories and the railway system, halted the fragile revival of the economy.[10]

Mao then decided to elevate Deng Xiaoping to Zhou's former position in order to restore "stability and unity." Deng launched a rectification campaign to remove disruptive radicals from positions of authority, purge the PLA ranks of officers who refused to accept Party discipline, vet the ranks for disruptive Party members who had joined in recent years, and continue to rebuild the Party as a disciplined organization. However, in early 1976, Deng, too, was purged for going too far, and resurgent rebels resumed their attacks on the restoration of former officials, undoing much of Deng's recent labours. These attacks were halted only after Mao's death and the October arrests of the "Gang of Four."[11]

This brief review of the impact of the Cultural Revolution on the CCP and the civilian bureaucracy illustrates the central point. The entire structure of civilian rule was effectively paralysed from 1966 to 1968; what remained was further dismantled under military rule, and efforts to rebuild it made the national administration a battleground of warring factions. One of the most consequential accomplishments of the Cultural Revolution was that it severely damaged the national bureaucracy, leaving it weak and divided. At the end of the 1970s, it was anything but an entrenched and powerful force capable of defending its privileges and vested interests. Officials at this point in time were grateful to be returned to responsible positions, given real authority over their designated areas of operation, and freed of the constant threat of political accusations for alleged errors. The post-Mao characterization of the Cultural Revolution as a "decade of chaos" applies with particular force to the structures of national government.

The destruction of the national bureaucracy also had an inevitable structural consequence – a drift towards decentralization and local self-reliance. Budgeting and planning had long since devolved to provinces and localities. In the absence of strong central direction, local authorities became increasingly responsible for devising development strategies. A decentralized fiscal structure meant that local officials, especially in townships and villages, had a strong pecuniary interest in locally generated revenues that derived from market-oriented entrepreneurship, whether based on small family enterprises or somewhat larger government-founded firms. This turned local Party and government officials – as opposed to central bureaucrats – into active proponents of market-oriented reform. The rapid spread of household farming, small family businesses, and, somewhat later, the explosive growth of township and village enterprises, was a product of this prior decentralization, which turned the local state into a powerful constituency for reform.[12]

---

10 Dong and Walder 2012a; Forster 1990, 139–176; Teiwes and Sun 2007, 146–185.
11 MacFarquhar and Schoenhals 2006, 378–395; Teiwes and Sun 2007, 245–282, 305–381; Vogel 2011, 91–153.
12 On the decentralization of state structures and economic activity in Mao-era China, see Donnithorne 1972; Oksenberg and Tong 1991; Shue 1988; White 1998. Westad 2010, 66–71 provides a cogent

When Gorbachev set out to restructure the Soviet economy along more modern and market-oriented lines in the late 1980s, he faced a fundamentally different situation. The Soviet Communist Party, its national apparatus of ministries and bureaus, its massive security apparatus and huge military establishment had not experienced extensive purges for almost 40 years. These centralized structures had grown and enhanced their authority, had accumulated bureaucratic privileges, and were well prepared to defend both against reforms that threatened the status quo. Gorbachev quickly found that his attempts to initiate economic reforms met with delay and obstruction.[13] One response in 1988 – quite radical in nature – was to remove Communist Party organs from oversight of state enterprises and free the enterprises to engage in market-oriented activities. This attempt to kickstart economic reform initiated an irreversible deterioration of the Soviet economy.[14] Gorbachev began to devise ways of going around his more conservative colleagues by appointing his own special advisors and encouraging independent think tanks.[15] He eventually concluded that the only way to overcome bureaucratic resistance to reconstruction, or "perestroika," was to reduce the power and influence of the bureaucracy and neutralize the security services and armed forces. This was the origin of "glasnost," a greater transparency and openness about the flaws and inequities of the Soviet system, past and present, which was a prelude to an attempt to restructure the political system through competitive elections to new national assemblies.[16] By the spring of 1989, Party secretaries of regions and cities were made to stand for election to legislative assemblies, and many of them lost. The momentum of democratization within Soviet structures, however, split the Communist Party and turned into nationalist mobilization that tore the Soviet Union apart.[17]

One can find fault with Gorbachev's political strategy – clearly, he lost control of the process of liberalization – but it is beyond dispute that he faced an array of opposing forces infinitely more powerful than those facing Deng Xiaoping in China. Had the Cultural Revolution not occurred, and if the Party apparatus and national bureaucracy had grown undisturbed, China's bureaucrats may not have become the powerfully entrenched force, as represented by those in the Soviet Union, but they would have been much stronger than they were in the wake of the Cultural Revolution. Mao's attacks on China's bureaucrats had cleared the way for Deng Xiaoping, who would move in a direction utterly different to the one Mao had in mind.

---

footnote continued

overview of a range of such informal economic practices in the 1970s. On the consequences for local development, especially in rural regions, see Oi 1992; Walder 1995; 1998; Yang 1996.

13 For examples, see Bernstein 2013, 51–54.
14 Ellman and Kontorovich 1998; Gregory 2004.
15 Brown 1996, 130–154; 2007, 69–101.
16 Brown 1996, 155–211; 2007, 103–153.
17 Beissinger 2002; Brown 1996, 252–305; Gill 1994, 78–173. Bernstein 2013, 57–61 provides a concise overview of these final years.

Elevating Deng Xiaoping's Post-Mao Authority

I have just argued that the array of forces against reform and restructuring faced by Deng Xiaoping were far less formidable than those facing Gorbachev, and that the key reason was the Cultural Revolution. However, we should also consider the other side of the coin – the relative authority of Deng versus Gorbachev. While the Soviet bureaucracy was much more powerfully entrenched than China's, Deng Xiaoping also had much more personal authority than Gorbachev. This, also, was owing, to a considerable extent, to the Cultural Revolution and in particular to the twists and turns of its later stages.

We have already seen that in late 1974 Mao entrusted Deng Xiaoping to continue the task begun by Zhou Enlai, who was by then under attack and seriously ill, to rebuild the Party and government and finally eliminate the role of the PLA in civilian administration. Deng did this with vigour and acted with much greater boldness than Zhou to restore order following the "Second Cultural Revolution" of 1974. He moved decisively to end the disruptions to the railway system and major state enterprises by launching rectification campaigns to restore the authority of Party secretaries and purge rebel rivals and their followers, imprisoning several prominent local rebels in the process. He continued the rehabilitation of disgraced officials and began to lay plans to restore China's educational system – especially the ravaged universities – and to revive research institutes and scientific and technical research.[18] In so doing, he became the standard bearer for the restoration of former officials to their posts and the re-creation of the structures of power that predated the Cultural Revolution. This predictably drew the ire of Maoist radicals on the Politburo and their adherents throughout the country, who convinced Mao that Deng had gone too far. Deng was sidelined in January 1976, disappeared from public view, and was the barely concealed target of a new campaign to criticize an "unrepentant capitalist roader." After the Tiananmen demonstrations of April 1976, he was officially removed from his posts and made the target of a campaign to "criticize Deng."[19] The animus directed at Deng made him the leading villain for Mao's radical loyalists, but it also ensured that Deng would become the acknowledged hero of all those who sought to rebuild the structures of the party-state, purge it of disruptive rebels, and rebuild the Party, economy, and scientific and technical infrastructure. The way in which Deng rose to supplant Hua Guofeng 华国锋 as the Party's pre-eminent leader at the end of 1978 is testament to the widespread political support that he earned for his efforts during Mao's last years.[20]

By contrast, when Gorbachev was appointed general secretary of the Communist Party of the Soviet Union at the age of 54 in 1985, he was the youngest member of both the Politburo and Central Committee Secretariat. He was the youngest member of the Politburo by five years, and 13 years younger than the

18   Dong and Walder 2014; Teiwes and Sun 2007, 306–363; Vogel 2011, 91–140.
19   Vogel 2011, 141–172.
20   Baum 1994, 48–56; MacFarquhar and Schoenhals 2006, 451–53; Vogel 2011, 217–248.

average age of Politburo members at that time. He had secured positions on both the Politburo and Secretariat only five years before, in 1980.[21] He was surrounded by more senior figures, the most conservative of whom had served at the apex of the party-state for more than thirty years. Gorbachev's authority at this point was in many ways comparable to Hua Guofeng's in 1976.[22] They both held the top Party and government posts but were relative newcomers to the top echelons and did not have extensive networks of support in the upper reaches of the Party.

The contrast in the authority held by Gorbachev and that enjoyed by Deng is sharpened by the differences in the political opportunities that were available to them. Gorbachev's progressive ideas threatened the vested interests of an entrenched bureaucracy that had grown undisturbed for decades and which now oversaw an enormous military-industrial complex. Deng Xiaoping was in a fundamentally different position. In 1976, he was 71 years old and a veteran of the top reaches of the Party. He had assumed top national posts in Beijing in 1952 before joining the Politburo and becoming the Communist Party's general secretary in 1956. After Mao's death, he was the recognized leader of those who sought to rebuild the bureaucratic institutions destroyed in previous years and resurrect the Communist Party's unity and strength. After Deng Xiaoping returned to political pre-eminence at the end of 1978, he continued the restoration process that was hampered and delayed for so long during the 1970s.[23] Disgraced and sidelined officials were more rapidly rehabilitated, disruptive rebels were systematically purged, and the Party underwent a series of rectification campaigns to identify and punish those who had collaborated with the "Gang of Four." The rectification and rebuilding continued well into the 1980s.

In short, Deng represented the resurrection of the same forces whose vested interests stood in the way of Gorbachev. Deng was leading the way to their recovery towards a more secure and prosperous future, and as it turned out, an integral part of this package of national revival was the restructuring of China's command economy. The Cultural Revolution eased the politics of economic reform by bundling that programme together with the revitalization of the party-state. This opportunity was not available to Gorbachev.

Deepening China's Relative Backwardness

The case for a fundamental restructuring of a Soviet-style economy is strengthened by incontrovertible evidence that the system is failing. The Cultural Revolution enhanced China's relative backwardness in ways that made decisive action seem urgent. The Soviet economy had long laboured under well-known inefficiencies, leading to a gradual stagnation of growth rates, inefficient

---

21 Brown 2007, 30–32.
22 Vogel 2011, 185–87 describes Hua's position in similar terms.
23 Lee 1983.

allocation of capital, lagging technological innovation, and poor delivery of consumer goods and services. These flaws were widely discussed in the Soviet bloc as early as the 1950s.[24] Yet, the Soviet Union still had the world's second largest economy into the late 1980s. It was highly urbanized in ways typical of a modern industrial society, and its military-industrial complex was a major challenge to its Cold War rivals. China's economy had experienced a self-inflicted crisis; the Soviet Union's problems were far less dramatic.

When reliable data on China's economy became available early in the post-Mao era, its level of backwardness and poverty was startling. Adjusted for price and exchange rate distortions, China's per capita GDP in 1976 was US$852 – much higher than Bangladesh (US$540), Burma (US$687) and Nepal (US$654), slightly below India (US$889), and well below Indonesia (US $1,598), Pakistan (US$1,006) and Malaysia (US$2,910). South Korea's per capita GDP was four times higher than China's (US$3,476), and Taiwan's per capita GDP was more than five times higher (US$4,600). In total size, China's economy (US$793 billion) was only half the size of Japan's economy (US$1.3 trillion).[25]

The 1976 figures did not simply reflect the undeniable fact that the People's Republic of China in 1949 had started at a severe disadvantage: China had actually fallen further behind after the 1950s, and if trends had continued, would have permanently remained so. Although Japan's economy was twice the size of China's in 1976, China's economy in 1950 was 50 per cent larger than Japan's, and it would remain considerably larger until the aftermath of the Great Leap Forward.[26] In 1950, South Korea's GDP per capita was 1.7 times China's figure; by 1976, the ratio had grown to 4.4. In 1950, Japan's GDP per capita was 4.4 times that of China; by 1976, the ratio had grown to 13.7. By these same measures, China had clearly outperformed only the worst cases of underdevelopment in the region such as Bangladesh, Burma and Nepal. China's one accomplishment by 1976 was to have closed the gap with India.[27] Figure 1, which displays trends in GDP per capita, provides a visual sense of these trends. China fell further behind not only nearby East Asian economies but also the "revisionist" economies of the Soviet Union and Eastern Europe. Figure 1 makes clear that the gap expanded rapidly after 1966. While much of East Asia was beginning to take off, China was mired in self-inflicted stagnation.

---

24   Kornai 1959; Liberman 1971; Šik 1967. These discussions influenced Chinese economists at the time as well: Fung 1982; Lin 1981.
25   Maddison 2006, 298, 304–05. These figures are adjusted for purchasing power parity, which corrects for distortions owing to exchange rates and differences in domestic prices. The conventional measures at the time, which did not make these adjustments, make China's economy look much worse in relative terms, and they are likely to be the figures that China's leaders worked with in the early post-Mao era. Compare with the standard Gross National Income measures of the World Bank: data.worldbank.org/indicator.
26   Maddison 2006, 298.
27   Ibid., 304–05.

Figure 1: **Growth Trends, China and Selected Countries, 1950–1976**

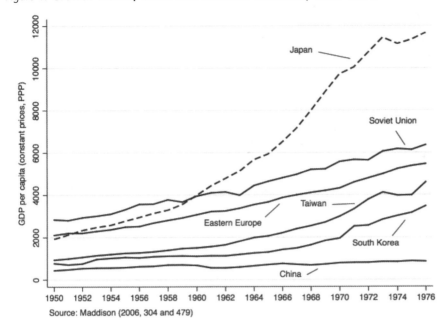

Source: Maddison (2006, 304 and 479)

China's growth trajectory made it more directly comparable to Asian nations still mired in poverty. Figure 2 charts China's growth relative to India, Bangladesh, and Pakistan, and it shows more clearly than Figure 1 the fluctuations in China's development. China began with a lower level of development than any of these countries in 1950, and caught up with or surpassed them rapidly during the 1950s. The Great Leap Forward threw China sharply backward when compared to India and Pakistan – in fact, back to the same level as Bangladesh. There followed a strong recovery in the early 1960s, leading China once again to almost catch Pakistan and India by 1966. However, China was thrown backward once again by the Cultural Revolution. Inconsistent growth resumed after 1968, and by 1976, China had once again almost caught up with India, thanks primarily to India's stagnating economy. This record was nothing for China's political elite to celebrate, especially in light of the comparisons in Figure 1.

The Cultural Revolution was less damaging to China's economy than the Great Leap Forward, which saw GDP per capita shrink by 17 per cent in 1961 alone, but it did greatly slow China's development. China's GDP per capita shrank by 5.5 per cent in 1967 and another 4.7 per cent in 1968, before recovering in 1969 and 1970. After that point, average annual growth by this measure was only 1.5 per cent – there was virtually no growth in 1972 and the economy shrank in 1974 and 1976.[28] The sluggish growth was not solely owing to political

28 Ibid., 304.

Figure 2: **Growth Trends, China and Poor Asian Nations, 1950–1976**

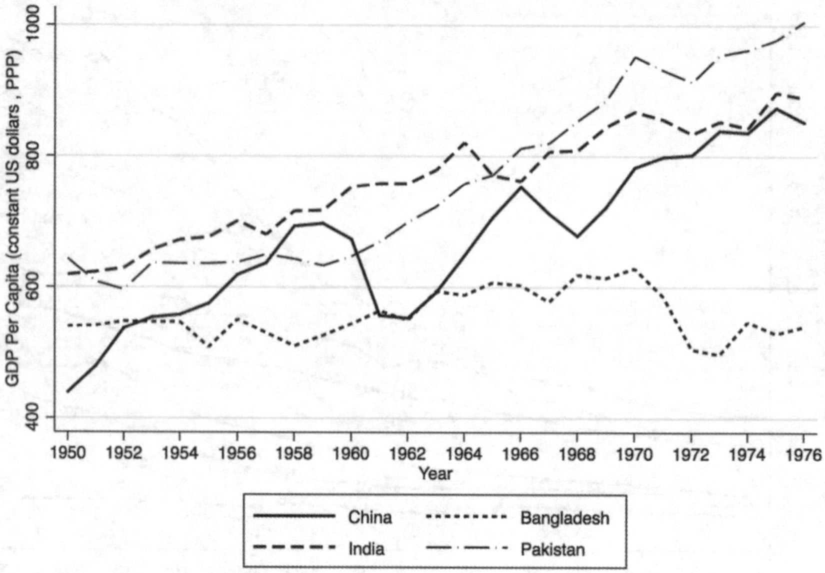

Source: Maddison (2006, 304-305)

upheavals; it was also due to a system of agriculture that was barely able to increase output enough to keep pace with a rapidly growing population, and to
an inefficient heavy industrial sector that absorbed an unusually high percentage
of national investment at the expense of consumer goods, services and housing.
The heavy industrial sector alone absorbed 52 per cent of national investment
in 1953, and it took more than 80 per cent almost every year after the
mid-1960s.[29] Industry deployed its abundant resources very inefficiently. There
were negative returns to investment in industry in 1967 and 1968, and, after a
brief recovery, returns to investment declined steadily after 1971. By the end of
the Mao era, industry was barely producing positive returns.[30]

These figures indicate a development model that was in serious trouble, and by
the end of the Cultural Revolution, the symptoms of backwardness and hardship
were impossible to ignore. Effectively frozen during the Cultural Revolution,
average industrial wages fell close to 15 per cent from 1964 to 1976. Staple
foods and a range of consumer goods were allocated through ration coupons,
and consumer goods were frequently of poor quality and in notoriously short
supply. Housing supply was inadequate and older buildings were deteriorating
badly. Overinvestment in heavy industry came at the expense of urban housing,
which fluctuated between 2.5 and 6.5 per cent of capital investment after 1966 –
compared to the 1953 figure of 12.5 per cent. The result was average urban

29   State Statistical Bureau 1983, 339.
30   Kuan et al. 1988, 583.

housing space of 3.6 square metres per person in 1976 – significantly worse than in 1956, when the figure was 4.3 metres in cities that were already overcrowded.[31] Rural living standards were much worse than those in cities. At the end of the 1970s, one-fifth of the rural population existed on a diet that was below the subsistence level of daily calorie consumption defined by the Chinese government – a figure that was lower than that stated by international agencies. Average daily calorie consumption in rural China was slightly higher than in India but lower than in Indonesia and Pakistan. Early post-Mao surveys of rural living standards generated official estimates that 30 per cent of the rural population, some 237 million people, lived on incomes that were below the poverty level.[32]

The symptoms of deepening backwardness were impossible to ignore. China was no longer catching up and was in danger of falling even further behind. It was easy to make the case for drastic measures, and there was precedent for this in the history of the regime. In the aftermath of the Great Leap Forward, Liu Shaoqi 刘少奇 had taken the lead in defining the economy as a disaster area that required emergency measures, including a reversion to household agriculture on a scale that appalled Mao Zedong.[33] With Mao dead and his followers in prison, Deng Xiaoping was free to revert to the post-Great Leap playbook and make up for years of lost time. The Cultural Revolution made the case for the fundamental restructuring of the economic system much more convincing. There was no plausible case for staying the course; it would be impossible to argue that China risked much by moving in a new direction.

In the Soviet Union, by contrast, the problem was slowing growth and a system that failed to deliver consumer prosperity and industrial innovation. The lack of productivity and innovation in the Soviet economy prevented it from catching up with Western market economies. In 1950, Soviet GDP per capita was only 30 per cent of that of the United States; in 1980, after 30 years, this had only grown to 35 per cent. The comparison with Japan was even less favourable. Soviet GDP per capita was 50 per cent larger than Japan's in 1950, but it was only half of Japan's in 1980.[34] The shortcomings of the economic model were well known and were widely discussed as early as in the 1950s. Changes to the system remained ideologically controversial, and the proposed reforms did not make much headway except in Yugoslavia and, to a more limited extent, Hungary. From the 1950s through to the mid-1980s in the Soviet Union, efforts to implement relatively modest reforms were consistently sidetracked. The system had, after all, turned the Soviet Union into a major industrial economy and a military superpower, and its economy remained the world's second largest until it was overtaken by Japan in 1988.[35] Moreover, the USSR was locked in a Cold War confrontation that

31 Walder 2015, 326–29.
32 Ibid., 333.
33 MacFarquhar 1997, 209–233; Yang 2012, 506–07.
34 Maddison 2006, 279, 304, 479.
35 Ibid., 298, 477.

intensified in the late 1970s. The Soviet Union, unlike China, potentially had a great deal to lose.

Strategic Alignment with the West

The final way in which the Cultural Revolution bent the arc of Chinese history is perhaps the most paradoxical of all: the strategic turn towards the United States as a counterweight to the Soviet Union. What made sense as geopolitical strategy made virtually no sense in ideological terms.

Maoist polemics against the Soviet Union on the eve of the Cultural Revolution led to the mutually antagonistic Sino-Soviet split, over both domestic and foreign policy issues. Domestically, Maoist ideologues denounced the Soviet Union for declaring that class struggle against domestic class enemies was dead, and that the primary task of socialism was to build the economy and improve people's livelihoods. Maoists charged that this gave educated bourgeois experts authority over the working class, that the Soviet wage scales gave excessive salaries and privilege to the highly placed, and that material incentives like piece rates and bonuses were exploitative and did not give play to moral and political incentives that were the hallmark of revolutionary socialism. The relaxation of domestic class struggle and the reliance on experts and material incentives, in this view, showed that the Soviet Union was revisionist and well on the road to restoring capitalism. The polemics against the USSR in 1963 and 1964 laid out what became the ideological justification for the Cultural Revolution, and in particular for the charge that Liu Shaoqi, who allegedly favoured Soviet-like policies, was "China's Khrushchev."

The denunciation of the Soviet Union also had a foreign policy dimension. Mao was adamantly opposed to a relaxation of the confrontation with imperialism, and especially with the United States, and reacted very negatively to Khrushchev's efforts to reduce superpower tensions. The Maoist view was that global confrontation with imperialism was inevitable and necessary, and that support for armed national liberation struggles throughout the world was the only truly revolutionary position. To relax tensions with the West was to abandon revolution, yet another sign that the Soviet Union was a revisionist nation that had betrayed the ideals of world revolution. The final break with the Soviet Union occurred shortly after the USSR signed a nuclear test ban treaty with the United States in 1964. From that time forward, the polemics against the Soviet Union intensified and Mao prepared his Cultural Revolution to ensure that China would never take the Soviet road.[36]

By 1969, the mutual animosities with the Soviet Union had reached the point of armed border clashes. Worried about the military threat of a hostile superpower on China's northern border, Mao began to rethink his geopolitical

36 Lüthi 2008, 273–285; MacFarquhar 1997, 349–366.

strategy. Secret negotiations with the United States in 1971 led eventually to a visit by Nixon in 1973 – a startling rapprochement with the United States.[37] This was a triumph of geopolitical pragmatism over ideology.[38] The denunciation of the Soviet Union had originated in a protest against accommodation with the West, but now China far surpassed the USSR in accommodation – despite the United States' ongoing war in Vietnam. The break with the Soviet Union for relying on scientists and providing bonuses for workers now stood in stark contradiction with China's reconciliation with the world's leading capitalist and imperialist power. China declared its militant opposition to Soviet "hegemonism" and would soon castigate the USSR as "social imperialist," an incoherent inversion of the polemics of a decade before. This turn towards the West was an entirely unanticipated consequence of the Cultural Revolution's harsh polemics against Soviet "revisionism."[39]

Ties with the West remained controversial in the last years of the Mao era, and Zhou Enlai was attacked and sidelined in part for his role in the negotiations with the United States.[40] However, an opening was created that was expanded much further into formal diplomatic and economic ties with leading West European nations and Japan, and eventually with the United States in 1979.[41] The heightened confrontation with the Soviet Union after the invasion of Afghanistan that year intensified the United States' interest in strengthening ties with China and promoting its economic modernization. This occurred at precisely the time when Deng Xiaoping returned to power and created an opportunity for expanding trade, technology transfer, foreign aid and bank finance, and educational exchanges with a range of Western powers and Japan that became a central prop for the reform and opening initiated under Deng Xiaoping. Denunciation of Soviet revisionism, the hallmark of the Cultural Revolution, was to have consequences that were entirely unforeseen by its instigators.

Conclusion

There is a final legacy of the Cultural Revolution that is an enduring consequence of the four paths of influence outlined above. This is the identification of state strengthening with the national revival that accompanied Deng Xiaoping's agenda of the 1980s. Analysts of market reform, especially during its early years, frequently viewed the expansion of market allocation as necessarily

---

37 MacFarquhar and Schoenhals 2006, 308–323.
38 And, according to Westad, also a deeply flawed understanding of world trends. Mao's turn towards a virtual alliance with the United States "originated in one of the great geopolitical misunderstandings of the twentieth century: that the Soviet Union was the ascending superpower and the United States was a power in decline. For Mao Zedong it had become almost an article of faith by the late 1960s that at some point during the coming decade Soviet power would dominate the world, and at that moment, or soon after, the Soviet Union would attack China" (Westad 2010, 76).
39 According to Westad 2010, 79, "Mao's opening to the West was almost an act of panic as confrontation with the Soviet Union seemed to draw nearer."
40 Teiwes and Sun 2007, 85–93.
41 Vogel 2011, 294–348.

implying a relative decline in state power.[42] This is persuasive when the issue is viewed narrowly from the perspective of political economy – but it ignores historical differences in the trajectories of these states.

China's market reforms have proceeded alongside the rebuilding and strengthening of a party-state that was badly damaged during the Cultural Revolution. This has created among the post-Mao Chinese elite an enduring attachment to Soviet-era institutions of dictatorship as an indispensable foundation for national greatness. Chinese elites' identification of Soviet institutions of governance with stability and economic success was reinforced by the traumatic (for them) domestic and international events of 1989 to 1991. To the present day, when reflecting on the end of the Soviet Union, China's leaders view Gorbachev's attempts to democratize as the primary cause of national collapse and dismemberment. The relative openness of China's leaders to ideas about political reform in the 1980s has given way to a resurrected hostility to any type of political reform, indeed to any open discussion of such ideas. As a result, there has been little change in the structures of power copied from the Soviet Union in the 1950s.

One clear implication of the analysis presented in this essay is that this view misinterprets the reasons for the Soviet collapse and overestimates the contribution of consolidated dictatorship to China's own national revival. Gorbachev's experience showed that entrenched bureaucratic opposition to reform made the implementation of economic restructuring much more difficult than was the case in China. From a position of relative weakness, he felt compelled to push for rapid political opening and democratization. The strategy failed and led to the collapse of the Soviet state. Had Gorbachev not faced such entrenched bureaucratic opposition, he would not have felt compelled to push the agenda of democratization so aggressively, and it might have been possible to implement market reforms with a more gradual and careful opening of the political system. This opportunity was not available to Gorbachev but has been available to China's leaders for quite some time. Yet, they remain unable to contemplate any significant redesign of their imported Soviet-era political institutions. The story of Soviet collapse could therefore be told as a cautionary tale about the consequences of an entrenched elite that has the power to block reform until it is too late, rather than a story about the inherent dangers of any approach to expanding openness and significant political reform.

China's leaders now preside over a deeply entrenched bureaucracy with enormous vested interests in the private and public wealth generated by economic growth. China's post-Mao experience has convinced them that consolidating a Soviet-style single-party dictatorship is the formula for permanent success. As the Party faces continuing challenges in the struggle to fight corruption and rein in abuses of power – the primary threats to the regime's stability and its popular legitimacy – the CCP would be well advised to think about the last

42 Examples of this kind of reasoning can be found in Walder 1994, which implicitly holds state strength across socialist states as constant, an assumption undermined by the comparative argument in this essay.

years of the Soviet Union, and the alleged virtues of China's Soviet-style political institutions, in a different light. The Cultural Revolution indeed bent the arc of Chinese history – but with a pronounced twist.

Acknowledgement
Participants in *The China Quarterly* conference on the "Cultural Revolution's living legacies," and particularly Patricia M. Thornton and Chris Berry, provided comments that helped the author shape this final draft.

Biographical note
Andrew G. Walder is the Denise O'Leary and Kent Thiry Professor in the School of Humanities and Sciences at Stanford University, where he is a faculty member in the department of sociology and a senior fellow in the Freeman-Spogli Institute of International Studies. He is the author of *Fractured Rebellion: The Beijing Red Guard Movement* (Harvard, 2009) and *China under Mao: A Revolution Derailed* (Harvard, 2015).

摘要: 跟文革发起者的意图相反, 这场运动为市场导向型经济奠定了政治基础, 同时也创造了一个使得苏维埃式党国体制得以在中国保持凝聚并存续下去的环境。文革削弱了共产党及其政体的结构, 使之变动不居, 并显著削弱了根深蒂固的官僚利益, 减轻了市场化改革可能受到的阻碍。中央政府结构的弱化创造了一个去中心化的计划经济体, 区域和地方领导人乐于迎接初期的市场化机遇。经济与科技因文革而极度落后, 已经无人愿意维持现状。1970 年代中期, 毛泽东在第二次打倒邓小平之前, 曾短暂命其负责政党和经济的重建工作, 无意中使他成为后毛泽东时代重建和恢复工作的领头人。1970 年代初期, 因政治论争所引发的对苏联的共同敌意带来了一个意外转折, 使得中国在战略上倒向美国和其他西方国家, 由此而催生的经济和政治纽带随后推进了中国的改革开放进程。因此, 后毛泽东时代的第一个十年, 是在一名卓越的领导人带领之下克服阻力、走上新轨的重建与复兴的十年。与上世纪 80 年代的苏联相比, 这一遗产的影响尤为显著。80 年代苏联的政治环境截然不同, 戈尔巴乔夫在根深蒂固的官僚利益面前, 试图实施类似的改革, 却最终导致苏联崩溃解体。

关键词: 文化大革命; 后毛时代改革; 邓小平; 戈尔巴乔夫

References
Baum, Richard. 1994. *Burying Mao: Chinese Politics in the Age of Deng Xiaoping*. Princeton: Princeton University Press.

Beissinger, Mark R. 2002. *Nationalist Mobilization and the Collapse of the Soviet State*. New York: Cambridge University Press.

Bernstein, Thomas P. 2013. "Resilience and collapse in China and the Soviet Union." In Martin K. Dimitrov (ed.), *Why Communism Did Not Collapse: Understanding Authoritarian Regime Resilience in Asia and Europe*. New York: Cambridge University Press, 40–63.

Brown, Archie. 1996. *The Gorbachev Factor*. Oxford: Oxford University Press.

Brown, Archie. 2007. *Seven Years that Changed the World: Perestroika in Perspective*. Oxford: Oxford University Press.

Bu, Weihua. 2008. *"Zalan jiu shijie": wenhua da geming de dongluan yu haojie, 1966–1968* (*"Smashing the Old World": The Catastrophic Turmoil of the Cultural Revolution, 1966–1968*). Hong Kong: Zhongwen daxue chubanshe.

Dong, Guoqiang, and Andrew G. Walder. 2012a. "Nanjing's 'Second Cultural Revolution' of 1974." *The China Quarterly* 212, 893–918.

Dong, Guoqiang, and Andrew G. Walder. 2012b. "From truce to dictatorship: creating a revolutionary committee in Nanjing." *The China Journal* 68, 1–31.

Dong, Guoqiang, and Andrew G. Walder. 2014. "Foreshocks: local origins of Nanjing's Qingming demonstrations of 1976." *The China Quarterly* 220, 1092–1110.

Donnithorne, Audrey. 1972. "China's cellular economy: some economic trends since the Cultural Revolution." *The China Quarterly* 52, 605–619.

Ellman, Michael, and Vladimir Kontorovich (eds.). 1998. *The Destruction of the Soviet Economic System: An Insider's History*. Armonk, NY: M.E. Sharpe.

Forster, Keith. 1990. *Rebellion and Factionalism in a Chinese Province: Zhejiang, 1966–1976*. Armonk, NY: M.E. Sharpe.

Fung, K.K. (ed.). 1982. *Social Needs Versus Economic Efficiency in China: Sun Yefang's Critique of Socialist Economics*. Armonk, NY: M.E. Sharpe.

Gill, Graeme. 1994. *The Collapse of a Single-party System: The Disintegration of the Communist Party of the Soviet Union*. Cambridge: Cambridge University Press.

Gregory, Paul R. 2004. *The Political Economy of Stalinism*. Cambridge: Cambridge University Press.

Kornai, János. 1959. *Overcentralization in Economic Administration* (John Knapp (trans.)). Oxford: Oxford University Press.

Kuan, Chen, Hongchang Wang, Yuxin Zheng, Gary H. Jefferson and Thomas G. Rawski. 1988. "Productivity change in Chinese industry: 1953–1985." *Journal of Comparative Economics* 12, 570–591.

Lee, Hong Yung. 1983. "China's 12th Central Committee: rehabilitated cadres and technocrats." *Asian Survey* 23(6), 673–691.

Liberman, E.G. 1971. *Economic Methods and the Effectiveness of Production*. White Plains, NY: International Arts and Sciences Press.

Lin, Cyril Chihren. 1981. "The reinstatement of economics in China today." *The China Quarterly* 85, 1–48.

Lüthi, Lorenz M. 2008. *The Sino-Soviet Split: Cold War in the Communist World*. Princeton, NJ: Princeton University Press.

MacFarquhar, Roderick. 1997. *The Origins of the Cultural Revolution 3: The Coming of the Cataclysm, 1961–1966*. New York: Columbia University Press.

MacFarquhar, Roderick, and Michael Schoenhals. 2006. *Mao's Last Revolution*. Cambridge, MA: Harvard University Press.

Maddison, Angus. 2006. *The World Economy, Volume 1: A Millennial Perspective; Volume 2: Historical Statistics*. Paris: OECD.

Oi, Jean C. 1992. "Fiscal reform and the economic foundations of local state corporatism in China." *World Politics* 45(1), 99–126.

Oksenberg, Michel, and James Tong. 1991. "The evolution of central–provincial fiscal relations in China, 1971–1984: the formal system." *The China Quarterly* 125, 1–32.

Shue, Vivienne. 1988. *The Reach of the State: Sketches of the Chinese Body Politic*. Stanford, CA: Stanford University Press.

Šik, Ota. 1967. *Plan and Market under Socialism*. White Plains, NY: International Arts and Sciences Press.

State Statistical Bureau. 1983. *Zhongguo tongji nianjian 1983* (*China Statistical Yearbook 1983*). Hong Kong: Xianggang jingji daobaoshe.

Teiwes, Frederick C., and Warren Sun. 2007. *The End of the Maoist Era: Chinese Politics during the Twilight of the Cultural Revolution, 1972–1976*. Armonk, NY: M.E. Sharpe.

Vogel, Ezra F. 2011. *Deng Xiaoping and the Transformation of China*. Cambridge, MA: Harvard University Press.

Walder, Andrew G. 1994. "The decline of communist power: elements of a theory of institutional change." *Theory and Society* 23(April), 297–323.

Walder, Andrew G. 1995. "Local governments as industrial firms: an organizational analysis of China's transitional economy." *American Journal of Sociology* 101(2), 263–301.

Walder, Andrew G. (ed.). 1998. *Zouping in Transition: The Process of Reform in Rural North China*. Cambridge, MA: Harvard University Press.

Walder, Andrew G. 2014. "Rebellion and repression in China, 1966–1971." *Social Science History* 38 (3/4), 513–539.

Walder, Andrew G. 2015. *China under Mao: A Revolution Derailed*. Cambridge, MA: Harvard University Press.

Walder, Andrew G. 2016. "Rebellion of the cadres: the 1967 implosion of the Chinese party-state." *The China Journal* 75, 102–120.

Walder, Andrew G., Andrew Isaacson and Qinglian Lu. 2015. "After state socialism: the political origins of transitional recessions." *American Sociological Review* 80(2), 444–468.

Westad, Odd Arne. 2010. "The great transformation: China in the long 1970s." In Niall Ferguson, Charles S. Maier, Erez Manela and Daniel J. Sargent (eds.), *The Shock of the Global: The 1970s in Perspective*. Cambridge, MA: Harvard University Press, 65–79.

White, Lynn T. III. 1998. *Unstately Power: Local Causes of China's Economic Reforms*. Armonk, NY: M.E. Sharpe.

Yang, Dali. 1996. *Calamity and Reform in China: State, Rural Society, and Institutional Change since the Great Leap Famine*. Stanford, CA: Stanford University Press.

Yang, Jisheng. 2012. *Tombstone: The Great Chinese Famine, 1958–1962* (Stacy Mosher and Guo Jian (trans.)). New York: Farrar, Straus and Giroux.

The Cultural Revolution and Its Legacies in International Perspective

Julia Lovell*

Abstract
This article explores the rhetoric and reality of the Cultural Revolution as an international phenomenon, examining (through published and oral histories) the ways in which it was perceived and interpreted beyond China. It focuses in particular on the diverse impact of Maoist ideas and practice on the counterculture movement of Western Europe and North America during the late 1960s and 1970s. Within Europe, Cultural Revolution Maoism galvanized Dadaist student protest, nurtured feminist and gay rights activism, and legitimized urban guerrilla terrorism. In the United States, meanwhile, it bolstered a broad programme of anti-racist civil rights campaigns and narrow Marxist-Leninist party-building. Despite Mao's hopes to launch a global permanent revolution, it appears that, over the long term, enthusiasm for the Cultural Revolution in Western Europe, the United States and parts of South-East Asia helped to splinter the radical left and assisted the right in consolidating its power throughout the 1980s and beyond.

Keywords: Cultural Revolution; Maoism; Western Europe; United States; Singapore

In spring 1966, as the opening struggles of the Cultural Revolution began, Ditu Publishing House issued a new map of the world. The map, in which the People's Republic of China occupied the centre, was headlined by a quotation from Mao: "The socialist system will eventually replace the capitalist system; this is an objective law independent of man's will. However much the reactionaries try to hold back the wheel of history, eventually revolution will take place and will inevitably triumph." To the left and right, the map was framed by two lines from a 1963 poem by Mao: "The four seas are rising, clouds and waters raging/The five continents are rocking, wind and thunder roaring."

The map expressed the international hopes of "Mao's last revolution" in its early, expansively utopian phase. Other print media voiced a similarly global message. Issues of *Peking Review* through 1966 and 1967 reported in several languages on the worldwide multitudes of Mao's admirers – Sri Lankan trade unionists, Malian craftsmen, Argentine opthalmologists, Italian publishers, Guinean

* Birkbeck, University of London. Email: ubra235@mail.bbk.ac.uk.

© The China Quarterly, 2016   doi:10.1017/S0305741016000722

dancers, Syrian journalists, Congolese soldiers, Venezuelan pirates and Mexican schoolgirls. Western diplomats and politicians took this rhetoric about the diffusion of Maoism literally, pointing to "a programme for Maoist world domination" reminiscent "of Hitler's Mein Kampf." Accusing Mao's China of international schemes of subversion and guerrilla warfare, the Australian prime minister in 1966 warned his parliament that, "we face a future in which the security of Australia is in jeopardy."[1]

Peking Review inevitably overstated international adulation of Mao and his Cultural Revolution. Nonetheless, the culture and politics of Cultural Revolution China did permeate global radicalism during the 1960s and 1970s. Mao and his ideas of continuous, peasant revolution appealed to left-wing rebels as well as civil-rights and anti-racism campaigners in the US, Australia and Western Europe. Across the developing world in Asia, South America and Africa, Maoist politics inspired post-colonial nations with idioms such as self-reliance, party rectification and revolutionary spontaneity. This article explores the rhetoric and reality of the Cultural Revolution as an international phenomenon, examining the ways in which these events were perceived and interpreted beyond China. It focuses in particular on the diverse impact of Maoist ideas and practice on the counterculture movement of Western Europe and North America during the late 1960s and 1970s. Within Europe, Cultural Revolution Maoism galvanized Dadaist student protest, nurtured feminist and gay rights activism, and legitimized urban guerrilla terrorism. In the United States, meanwhile, it bolstered a broad programme of anti-racist civil rights campaigns and narrow Marxist-Leninist party-building.

In his article for this volume, Frank Dikötter argues that several of the domestic results of the Cultural Revolution were unintended, or even the reverse of what had been planned. A similar argument can be advanced for the spread of Cultural Revolution Maoism in the territories under consideration here. Mao and his supporters envisioned the Cultural Revolution as launching a global movement against revisionism that would mobilize the grassroots to dismantle imperialism and bureaucratism within governments across the world. Yet, it appears that over the long term, enthusiasm for the Cultural Revolution splintered the radical left and assisted the right in consolidating its power through the 1980s and beyond. One outcome of the instability of the late 1960s in the US and Europe was the gradual shifting of consensus in favour of order and the reinforcement of hierarchies of established power on the right – paving the road to Ronald Reagan and Margaret Thatcher by the early 1980s – a trend that has not significantly reversed itself since.[2]

---

1 Scott 2007, 53–54.
2 See, e.g., Harvey 2005, although Harvey does not contend that the extreme left was the only phenomenon driving the rise of neoliberalism. Instead, he argues that a combination of factors operated, including fiscal crisis, a renewed drive for collective identity and action among Anglo-American business interests, longstanding hostility to the welfare state, and the individualism inherent to the counterculture left of the 1960s and 1970s. Slavoj Žižek also argues for a direct connection between Maoism and the

It would be misleading, however, to argue that the legacy of the global Cultural Revolution was obliterated by, or indeed wholly responsible for, the rallying of right-wing politics. Although the history of Indian Maoism lies beyond the scope of this essay, in central and eastern India the currently resurgent Maoist Naxalite movement (which coheres in part around memory of its earliest, Cultural Revolution-inspired incarnation in 1967) is considered the "single biggest security challenge to the Indian state."[3] In his discussion of the Cultural Revolution, Wang Hui has argued that its significance lies in its facilitation of political debate about party, state, society and economy – a kind of debate that has largely been eliminated in the course of the post-Mao negation of the Cultural Revolution.[4] And, although this article will by no means mute the tragedies, absurdities and misapprehensions of the Cultural Revolution's global travels, it will also consider the possibilities of more positive legacies of far left-wing politics beyond China, such as civil activism. It will explore whether there is a story to be told about the expansion of Maoism that also led to the dissemination of ideas, such as "serving the people," "consciousness-raising" and "cultural revolution" in education, that have had a broad impact on politics outside of China, for instance on feminist, gay rights, racial equality, environmental and academic movements. In West Germany, for example, Maoist-influenced parties became tributaries feeding into the later green movement of the 1980s.

The global travels of Maoism in general, and of the Cultural Revolution in particular, have become the focus of increasing academic attention in recent years. We currently possess accounts of the impact of Cultural Revolution Maoism on some individual national territories, for example on France, Richard Wolin's *The Wind from the East* (2010), and on Italy, Roberto Niccolai's *Cuando la Cina era Vicina* (1998).[5] Within the last year alone, two volumes of essays on global Maoism have been published.[6] But the existing literature for the most part deals with individual countries – Maoism in France, India and so on. Occasionally, two countries are considered alongside each other, for example the US and France in Belden Fields' *Trotskyism and Maoism: Theory and Practice in France and the United States*.[7] However, atomized national studies are more often the norm. The two books that aim at more comprehensive coverage of global Maoism, Robert Alexander's *International Maoism in the*

---

footnote continued

triumph of neoliberalism, although through a very different process. In Žižek's account, the Maoist concept of Cultural Revolution philosophically paves the way for "the reign of today's global capitalism": both represent "Lords of Misrule." See Žižek 2011, 696.

3 Chakrabarty 2014, 118.
4 Wang, Hui 2009, 9–11.
5 Wolin 2010; Niccolai 1998. There is, incidentally, no English-language monograph on the influence of Maoism within the majority of West European states, for example within Italy, West Germany or Norway.
6 Cook 2014; Wang, Ning 2015 and other essays in 2015 *Comparative Literature Studies* 52(1).
7 Belden Fields 1988.

Developing World and his *Maoism in the Developed World*, are reference books of discrete national case studies, each a few pages long, a form which does not lend itself to sustained comparative analysis.[8]

This essay aims to break new ground by exploring and comparing the impact of the Cultural Revolution across Western Europe, the US and Singapore, drawing on published and oral histories in several languages. This transnational approach makes it possible to explore the commonalities and specificities of the reception of the Cultural Revolution in different territories, and the local conditions that account for such particularities. Western enthusiasm for the Cultural Revolution is an exemplary episode in a much longer history of encounters – often marked by selective understanding, reinterpretation and distortion – between China and the rest of the world. For this reason, perceptions of the Cultural Revolution in the US and Western Europe tell us far more about those countries than they do about the Cultural Revolution itself. It is notable, for example, that across Western Europe, Maoist sympathizers in Italy and West Germany – the two countries with the strongest fascist pasts – veered furthest into political violence. Comparative analysis also facilitates the drawing of broader conclusions about the legacy of the Cultural Revolution, namely by tracing a link between the radical upsurge of which Maoist influence was an important part in the 1960s and 1970s, and the fight-back of the political right-wing through the 1980s and beyond.

My argument will be developed through four sequential sections. The essay will begin by accounting for Cultural Revolution fever in the late 1960s, connecting it to the decade's broader counterculture rebellion. The subsequent two sections will chart the radicalization of Maoist politics in countries including West Germany, Italy, France and the US, through party-building and terrorist activity. The fourth part will analyse the long-range impact of Cultural Revolution-infused radicalism on political, cultural and intellectual trends in the US and Western Europe since the 1970s.

The Spiritual Atom Bomb Detonates: Cultural Revolution in Western Europe and the United States

In 1965, the Chinese minister of defence, Lin Biao 林彪, actively encouraged the global export of Maoist revolution in his widely publicized essay, "Long live the victory of people's war":

Comrade Mao Zedong's theory of the establishment of rural revolutionary base areas and the encirclement of the cities from the countryside is of outstanding and universal practical importance for the present revolutionary struggles of all the oppressed nations and peoples ... [I]f North America and Western Europe can be called "the cities of the world," then Asia, Africa and Latin America constitute "the rural areas of the world" ... the contemporary world revolution also presents a picture of the encirclement of cities by the rural areas ... Mao Zedong's thought is a common asset of the revolutionary people of the whole world.

---

8 Alexander 1999; 2001.

This is the great international significance of the thought of Mao Zedong ... All peoples suffering from US imperialist aggression, oppression and plunder, unite! Hold aloft the just banner of people's war ... Victory will certainly go to the people of the world![9]

Upping his rhetoric in 1966, Lin Biao described the book of Mao's quotations, the "little red book" – of which more than a billion copies were printed in dozens of languages between 1966 and 1971 – as a "spiritual atom bomb of infinite power."[10] Across the 1960s, the architects of the Cultural Revolution thus explicitly promoted Mao's theories as the key to launching successful foreign revolutionary wars.

Chinese activists identified a single motivation for global adulation of the Cultural Revolution – admiration for China's struggle against imperialism. This assumption was not groundless. The enthusiasm for Mao Zedong across Western Europe and the United States converged with fierce opposition to American and Soviet foreign policy. During the 1960s, Mao and his Cultural Revolution became a space in which the left wing imagined a "better world," even as this global ideal fractured between local concerns and misreadings.[11]

A sense of solidarity with Third World independence struggles drove sympathy for Cultural Revolution Maoism in the United States and Western Europe. Max Elbaum – participant, observer and later historian of the American "new left" of the late 1960s and early 1970s – spells out the direct connection between condemnation of American foreign policy (as distinctively imperialist) and American radicals' pro-China turn.

[O]nly after 1968 ... did Marxism spread widely among sixties activists. Washington's stubborn continuation of the war in Vietnam was a prime factor in this ideological shift. Despite massive protest at home, international isolation, growing economic difficulties and ... overwhelming evidence that victory was impossible, the US refused to withdraw. Something beyond a single misguided policy simply had to be operating. Young activists ... identified that something as the drive of an imperial system to defend its worldwide sphere of influence.[12]

Horror at the Vietnam War drew millions of protestors onto the streets and Ho Chi Minh was lionized as the leader of Vietnamese resistance to the United States. Yet, Mao's China commanded greater political allegiance because it was seen as having originated the successful formula for "asymmetrical" guerrilla warfare in operation in Vietnam. It was the "high Maoist" strategy summarized by Lin Biao in "Long live the victory of people's war" that seemed to provide a blueprint for Vietnamese and other contemporary independence struggles. Through the Cultural Revolution, the People's Republic portrayed itself as "a new center for the world revolutionary movement (in a way that the Cuban and Vietnamese parties did not) and promoted itself as the shining example and prime champion of liberation movements waged by people of color all over the world."[13]

---

9 Lin 1965.
10 Lin 1966.
11 Gehrig 2011, 191.
12 Elbaum 2006, 42–43.
13 Ibid., 45.

In West Germany, Cultural Revolution China's self-styling as the vanguard of global anti-imperialism also appealed to the 1960s "new left." Rudi Dutschke (later dubbed the "Berlin prophet" of Mao Zedong) rather presumptuously declared in 1964 that "[i]n the judgement of the character of our era, an era of national liberation in Asia, Africa and Latin America, I am Chinese."[14] Gerd Koenen terms the revolutionary Third World the "defining discovery" of the 1960s protest movement in West Germany.[15] Dutschke, Koenen argues, equated violent protest in his country with independence wars in the Third World – both formed part of a global project to overthrow global capitalism – and seemed to believe that the model of guerrilla warfare held for West Germany as it did in Asia, Africa and Latin America.[16] A cell of radical students in 1969 referred admiringly to Lin Biao's theories of "encircling the city from the countryside" in their plan to politicize the Bavarian countryside around Munich by recruiting cadres in rural discotheques.[17] The protest culture of the late 1960s was politically polyglot: a mash-up of Herbert Marcuse, Che Guevara, Ho Chi Minh, Amilcar Cabral and Wilhelm Reich, the Freudian pioneer of free love and orgasms. Yet, amid this smorgasbord of influences, the theory and practice of Cultural Revolution Maoism exercised a particular fascination. Indeed, Maoist language was so ubiquitous throughout Italy in the late 1960s that neo-fascists scrawled on Florentine walls the same Cultural Revolution slogans – "It's right to rebel" and "Bombard the headquarters" – that were being shouted by left-wing students in Milanese piazzas.[18]

In the United States, the struggle against oppression of non-white people had a powerful local relevance in the context of the civil rights movement (which politically awakened many activists before the anti-Vietnam War movement escalated). For dispossessed ethnic groups in the second half of the 1960s who began to identify themselves as "internal colonies" within the US, Mao's anti-imperialist stance resonated. "For blacks, Latins and Asians, and the whites who identified with the Third World, Mao was Marx and Lenin and Stalin but he wasn't white," observed Ethan Young, a middle-class white student activist in the late 1960s.[19] Mao also had a strong message for other sectors of American society agitating against the establishment, declaring in 1968 that "the Afro-American struggle is winning sympathy and support from increasing numbers of white working people and progressives in the United States. The struggle of the Black people in the United States is bound to merge with the American workers' movement, and this will eventually end the criminal rule of the US monopoly capitalist class."[20] Dennis O'Neil, one of many white students

---

14 Gehrig 2011, 204; Slobodian 2012, 173.
15 Koenen 2001, 46–47.
16 Ibid., 49.
17 Slobodian 2012, 194.
18 Niccolai 1998, 70.
19 Interview with Ethan Young, New York, 24 March 2015.
20 Mao 1968.

radicalized by the civil rights movement, spoke of the impact that this statement had on him: "Mao identified the two main elements of the united front, the struggle of the black masses and the working class, and said that they were 'bound to merge' ... This says, if you want to get black freedom, you have to overthrow the system, and the black masses and masses of working people have common interests."[21]

For high-profile activists in the African-American Liberation Movement in the late 1960s, the "little red book" seemed almost made for the turbulence of black militancy. The appeal lay not only in its message of supporting anti-colonial armed struggles, of advocating guerrilla warfare and of building a vanguard party, but also in its style and design. It was easy to understand (and therefore ideal for teaching low-literacy recruits), physically compact and hardily packaged in red vinyl. In early 1967, the founders of the Black Panther Party, Huey Newton and Bobby Seale, sold copies of the little red book to students to make money to buy guns. Once the shotguns had been purchased, remembered Seale, "[we] used the Red Books and spread them throughout the organization ... Where the book said, 'Chinese people of the Communist Party,' Huey would say, 'Change that to the Black Panther Party. Change the Chinese people to black people'."[22] The Revolutionary Action Movement (RAM; arguably the first US organization to try to harness urban unrest among black populations for revolutionary purposes) freely borrowed Cultural Revolution terminology in its public statements: "America is the Blackman's Battleground. Support the Black Cultural Revolution. Join the BLACK GUARD!"[23]

Across Western Europe and the US, Cultural Revolution Maoism stood not just for anti-imperialism but also for youthful rebellion. In each of the countries in which Cultural Revolution fever took hold, youthful protest movements had personal and local, as well as international, reasons for revolt. Students in Western Europe resented their cramped institutions of higher education. In Italy, the student population more than doubled in the 1960s, without any coterminous expansion of university facilities. By 1967, students were frustrated by their overcrowded living and teaching conditions. The privations suffered by southern workers migrating north, meanwhile, turned Italy's industrial heartland into a tinderbox of discontent that would come alight during the "hot autumn" of 1969. Between 1950 and 1968, numbers of students had almost quadrupled in West Germany, where student hostility to the establishment was intensified by suspicions about its Nazi past. Between 1966 and 1968, for example, accusations swirled that Heinrich Lübke, the president of the Federal Republic of Germany (FRG), had been complicit in the building of concentration camps. Cultural Revolution Maoism told the discontented and the young that "it was right to rebel"; that "young people, full of vigour and vitality, are ... like the sun at

21 Interview with Dennis O'Neil, New York, 23 March 2015.
22 Seale 1991, 82–83.
23 Stanford 1986, 216.

eight or nine in the morning ... The world belongs to you."[24] At one anti-Social Democratic Party demonstration in West Berlin in 1969, the students chanted paraphrastically: "You are old, we are young, Mao Tse-Tung!"[25]

It is no coincidence that the Cultural Revolution, in the memories and publications of white American students swept up in the 1968 protest movement, did not attract significant interest until 1968. The Cultural Revolution inspired many US students only when it chimed with their own anti-establishment project: "1968 hit and students looked around for validating events all over the world," remembered Dennis O'Neil. "Before then, we hadn't paid attention to the Cultural Revolution."[26] "The Cultural Revolution," Ethan Young contends, "was seen as the student movement in power. It was a successful, world-changing version of what was going on in Paris, Berkeley, West Berlin."[27] For those with a background of communist sympathies, China's Cultural Revolution offered an alternative to the Soviet Union: revolution within the revolution. "The attraction for young people who didn't have any connection with communism," remembered Dennis O'Neil, "was the idea of putting dunce hats on your high school teachers."[28] American identification with the aims of the Cultural Revolution in 1968, therefore, is far more informative about the preoccupations of these distant observers of Chinese politics than about Chinese politics itself.

In West Germany, rebellious students imitated the political behaviour of the Cultural Revolution as part of a broader project of *Bürgerschreck* (shocking the bourgeoisie). They reproduced translations of Chinese big-character posters and wrote their own, and they recited Cultural Revolution speeches during their occupations of university buildings. In November 1966, student representatives rushed into a meeting with the president of the Freie Universität wearing Mao badges and calling themselves "Red Guards" before presenting a range of very local protests: "We have to cope with poor working conditions, miserable lectures, stupefying seminars, and absurd exam requirements."[29] On a blackboard behind the students gathered at one meeting of the West German Socialist Student Union in 1967, someone had scrawled the Maoist dictum: "To rebel is justified."[30] "To stick on a Mao button," remembered Gerd Koenen, "recite the words of the Great Chairman, or pin his smiling portrait to the wall as the Mona Lisa of the world revolution signified the most radical and striking antithesis to the 'old' bourgeois world."[31] Students gleefully remade the rhetoric and political theatre of the Cultural Revolution into an anarchic Dada-Maoism. Dieter Kunzelmann, one of the most prominent Maoist

---

24 Mao 1957.
25 Koenen 2001, 148.
26 Interview, Dennis O'Neil.
27 Interview, Ethan Young.
28 Interview, Dennis O'Neil.
29 Slobodian 2012, 177–78.
30 Gehrig 2011, 203.
31 Slobodian 2012, 178.

sympathisers, was linked with the French Situationists and the Dutch Provos – two artistic groups of the 1950s and 1960s ambitious to make political rebellion through cultural provocation.[32] Mao's words played a role in many of the publicity stunts carried out by West Germany's first political commune, Kommune 1, founded in 1967 by Kunzelmann and Dieter Langhans. In a text planning the commune, Kunzelmann quoted Mao's irreverent view on intellectual authority: "dogma has less value than cow dung. At least dung can be used as fertilizer."[33]

Against this backdrop of youthful turbulence, specific aspects of Mao's Cultural Revolution's programme (as communicated through *Peking Review*) appealed across Western Europe and the US: its apparent advocacy of the "mass line" and of political participation from the grassroots. Raymond Lotta, an early recruit to the Revolutionary Union (the largest pro-Maoist white American party of the 1970s), recalled:

We were outraged by the brutal oppression of black people and the genocidal war in Vietnam ... and by the workings of capitalism and imperialism. We saw socialism in China and the Cultural Revolution as the model for the liberatory solution. This was a "total revolution" – creating an economy and social institutions to serve the people, and mobilizing people to uproot the oppression of women, revolutionize culture and values, and overcome the great chasm between mental and manual labor. Maoist China was inspiring and supporting revolution throughout the world. And for ten years, the Cultural Revolution prevented the restoration of capitalism and the return of all its horrors, what we see in capitalist China today.[34]

The Cultural Revolution's "anti-bureaucratic content and demands that education serve the people resonated massively," recollected Dennis O'Neil.

I made the same evolution as hundreds of thousands of people in that age cohort ... At first you're against the [Vietnam] war because war's horrible ... And then you're against the war because it's a system: the system of imperialism, which has to have wars. So we need to have a revolution: the civil rights movement had won some battles but not freedom from oppression. What kind of revolution? A socialist revolution. And the Cultural Revolution is the gateway drug to that. Mao says that the masses are the makers of history. This is very important to us because we came out of movements, like civil rights, that were based on that: on ordinary, everyday people facing down horrific terror to register to vote.[35]

From Playful to Party: The Disciplining of Dada-Maoism

After 1968, Cultural Revolution Maoism in West Germany, Italy, France and the US became a more disciplined, authoritarian phenomenon, seemingly offering a way forward for the disintegrating student movement. It provided a blueprint for creating vanguard parties (based on the organizational model of the CCP) that could carry out grassroots revolutionary work in factories and sometimes in rural areas. Almost all such parties pledged unswerving loyalty to the PRC's policies. This shift towards party-building once more highlights the importance of local factors and conditions in determining the ways in which West Europeans and Americans engaged with the Cultural Revolution. It also constituted a

32   Gehrig 2011, 201–02, 220.
33   Slobodian 2012, 176.
34   Interview with Raymond Lotta, New York, 27 March 2015.
35   Interview, Dennis O'Neil.

crucial intermediate stage in the evolution of some of these groups towards violent political extremism, and in the steady fracturing of the left during the 1970s.

In West Germany, the student movement petered out with the passing in 1968 of a new state emergency law (an issue that student activists had hoped to use to build an alliance with the trade unions). Unable to access the trade unions' nationwide organizational base, activists decided to turn to tighter forms of organization: they became interested in an image of Mao not as a provocative jester but instead as a tough party man. Kommune 1 was replaced by a host of Marxist-Leninist cadre parties, the so-called K-Gruppen (the K standing for Kommunistischen, communist, groups), such as the Kommunistischer Bund Westdeutschland (KBW), the re-formed Kommunistische Partei Deutschlands (KPD), and the Kommunistische Partei Deutschlands/Marxisten-Leninisten (KPD/ML).

Andreas Kühn, author of the most comprehensive monograph on the K-Gruppen, emphasizes the ideological rigidity of these parties. They fixated, he writes, on an idea of "correct" revolutionary practice to be instilled through Chinese communist practices and through subscription to the Chinese line on foreign affairs. Life within the K-Gruppen demanded absolute submission to party demands and exhausting self-criticism sessions. The thoughts of Mao seemed to take on a quasi-religious dimension, providing a complete and completely superior worldview, with the answer to everything, including the prevention of natural disasters and the healing of life-threatening injuries. Kühn views the K-Gruppen as "political sects using structures and techniques involving the destruction of individualism, unconditional obedience, isolation, and a vague, confused idea of personal redemption."[36]

Perhaps as many as 3,000 young French Maoists made major lifestyle sacrifices for their beliefs. They abandoned the natural career paths of France's educated elite – a large number came from France's pre-eminent institution of higher education, the École Normale Supérieure (ENS) – for stints "serving the people" (working in factories or in the countryside) as "établis." Others undertook "long marches" through the countryside in order to gain a better understanding of the conditions of the French proletariat. They repeated Mao's terse dictum, "no investigation, no right to speak," as a litany. "I've always kept in mind a quotation from President Mao, which I still like and say a lot," recalled a prominent member of the ENS group, Tiennot Grumbach, in 2008. "'There are those who cross the field without seeing the roses, there are those who stop their horse to look at the roses, and there are those who get off their horse to smell the roses.' That was our idea: to smell the roses. And for us, the roses were the workers."[37] Olivier Rolin, leader of the military wing of the largest post-1968 Maoist party, Gauche Prolétarienne (GP), labelled *établissement* a flight, "exactly like the Exodus … the result of a quite radical reflection on the crisis of the

---

36 Kühn 2005, 58–59.
37 Interview with Tiennot Grumbach conducted by Robert Gildea, Paris, 18 May 2008.

intellectual."[38] There was a self-loathing, self-destructive quality to French Maoism that was highly susceptible to the anti-intellectualism and anarchic politics of the early Cultural Revolution.

In the US, the "new communist" movement – an assortment of mainly Maoist parties that sprang out of the faltering student movement of the late 1960s – aspired to form a basis on which the new left could organize. "Maoism broadly appealed through its emphasis on serving the people, its idea that the correctness of the political line determines everything," recalled Ethan Young. "But at the same time people realized they lived in a country that had a lot of deep-rooted social as well as political conservatism. The harder that we attempted to practise rebellion, the more difficult we found the process of actually changing people was ... So we looked for vehicles, formulae, means to bring about the kind of changes we wanted ... China during the Cultural Revolution represented a particular model for a particular time."[39]

As in West Germany, this quest for a successful revolutionary model often morphed into a slavish adherence to Chinese foreign policy decisions, to techniques of party-building, and to the concept of sending cadres and party members "among the people" to organize local communities and factory workers. The Red Guards in San Francisco and their successor organization, I Wor Kuen (two Asian-American, pro-Mao groups), for example, absorbed Maoist injunctions on party discipline: "We studied the rules of the [CCP]," recounted Alex Hing, a leading member. "If we felt that somebody messed up then we had a criticism-self-criticism ... We did mass work."[40]

The numbers involved in these parties were not enormous. At their peak, the K-Gruppen probably drew in somewhere between 100,000 and 150,000 individuals.[41] Some estimate a maximum of 800–1,000 members of the Revolutionary Union during the 1970s; perhaps 150 remain in its successor organization, the Revolutionary Communist Party, today. During its heyday in the first half of the 1970s, I Wor Kuen could probably call upon around 2,000 cadres. At the peak of the movement in the 1970s, there were around 7,000 French Maoists.[42] Yet, in France, for example, Maoist parties punched above their numerical weight thanks to the cultural influence that they commanded, which owed significantly to their ability to attract talented writers and intellectual celebrities to their cause. The militant French Maoist party, GP, gained much lustre from the support of Jean-Paul Sartre and Simone de Beauvoir.

Extreme sectarianism resulted from the quasi-religious dogmatism with which West German, American and Italian Maoist parties interpreted the Chinese model. Indeed, in almost all of their West-European and North American guises, Maoist parties were about as enthusiastic about consensus-building as the

38   Reid 2004, 86.
39   Interview, Ethan Young.
40   Interview with Alex Hing, New York, 26 March 2015.
41   Gehrig 2011, 210.
42   Bourseiller 1996, 18.

People's Front of Judea in the Monty Python comedy, *The Life of Brian*. In the United States, the 1960s left wing later divided into over 50 groupings that subscribed in some degree to Maoist ideas and outlook.[43] Ethan Young was an eyewitness to the factionalism of US Maoist party-building in the mid-1970s. "The machine shop I was working in on the south side of Chicago was a focal point for many different, mostly Maoist, groups ... I found myself lost in the alphabet soup, and getting used to approaches from all sorts of different groups, and having people say to me, did you hear what these jerks did last week, look at this leaflet they put out."[44] Young's recollection conjures up a paradoxical picture of former students-turned-Maoists clogging the grassroots, all competing fractiously to recruit each other and somehow failing to reach the real proletariat.

The Cultural Revolution Legacy and the Politics of Terror

Some analysts have directly linked the Cultural Revolution-inspired radicalism of the late 1960s to the terrorism of groups such as the Red Army Faction (RAF) in West Germany and the Red Brigades in Italy, both of which posed serious threats to the stability of the states within which they operated. Indeed, the police and security services in countries where pro-Mao groups emerged viewed any form of Maoist politics as a credible menace: the French police kept extensive files on Maoist groups, and in the USA, the FBI and CIA waged war on the Maoist-influenced radical movements of the 1960s and 1970s through the infamous, and often illegal, COINTELPRO and MHCHAOS. In West Germany and Italy, in particular, the state's security apparatus would succeed in strengthening itself in the second half of the 1970s in response to Maoist-infused political violence, as will be discussed in the subsequent section.

The rhetorical militancy of Maoism and the Cultural Revolution was undoubtedly an influence on those members of the West German student movement who chose to cross over to a violent, underground revolution. Sebastian Gehrig argues that the Maoist theory of "permanent revolution" led to parts of the student movement seeking ever more extreme positions from which to continue the revolution after the protests faltered in 1968.[45] While some revelled in the radical-chic *burgerschreck* of the student movement's reading of the Cultural Revolution, for others Maoism validated violent rebellion against the FRG state apparatus – an apparatus that the student movement had denounced as genocidal (through its alliance with US foreign policy) and fascistic (owing to its Nazi connections and brutal clashes with student protestors). Several West Germans who later migrated to terrorism were steeped in the general Maoist mood of the late 1960s protests. Two of the founding members of the RAF, Andreas Baader

43 See: http://freedomroad.org/2000/02/family-tree-introduction/ for a visual guide to these parties. There is a "basic" and a "mega" family tree; visitors to the page are warned that their "browser may have trouble" with the complexity of the latter. See Bourseiller 1996, 331, for a French counterpart.
44 Interview, Ethan Young.
45 Gehrig 2008, 156.

and Gudrun Ensslin, waved little red books in the air at their first trial in Frankfurt. At an early stage in their thinking on urban warfare, they marshalled (sporting Mao buttons on their leather jackets) some 50 young people from a care home into a militant group and gave them lessons on the "little red book."[46]

The RAF's first manifesto, on "The urban guerrilla concept," was larded with quotations from Mao: "We must draw a clear line between ourselves and the enemy"; "without investigation there cannot possibly be any right to speak"; "imperialism and all reactionaries [are] paper tigers"; "whoever is not afraid of being drawn and quartered, can dare to pull the emperor from his horse."[47] A further theoretical document of 1972 argued that all violence committed by the RAF was to "serve the people."[48] Mao's works thus created the initial frame of reference for the RAF, a frame of reference that exercised an assured appeal over parts of the protest movement. Till Meyer, who would later join another terrorist group, the 2 June Movement, and take part in the 1975 kidnapping of Peter Lorenz, a mayoral candidate for West Berlin, which successfully bargained for the release of jailed RAF members, recalls his initial response to "The urban guerrilla concept" when a copy was thrust into his hands at a demonstration: "At the top, I saw the Mao quotation. I greedily drank the whole pamphlet down. I was enthused."[49]

Maoism had a similar influence on the Red Brigades in Italy, which from 1970 declared war on the Italian political, economic and judicial establishment, played out in acts of "people's justice" and "proletarian violence" against "the bosses and their lackeys." Renato Curcio, one of the founders of the Red Brigades, had imbibed the late 1960s enthusiasm for the Cultural Revolution. Alberto Franceschini, later his close comrade in the Red Brigades, describes Curcio standing at the front of his university (Trento) wearing a t-shirt sporting a picture of Mao and handing out copies of the little red book.[50] The earliest leaflets of the Red Brigades claimed that theirs "was a resistance oriented towards President Mao's revolutionary China."[51] Franceschini recalled of the Brigades' first kidnapping that they decided to hang around the neck of their victim, a business executive, a notice on which was written: "Kill and flee. Nothing goes unpunished. Strike one to educate one hundred." "We got," Franceschini remembered, "'Kill and flee' from Mao. He had written that the principle of partisan tactics is to kill and immediately run away."[52] In the militant circles in which the Red Brigadists moved, Roberto Niccolai identified that "phrases, slogans, whole speeches were directly or indirectly dedicated to the Great Helmsman."[53]

---

46 Koenen 2001, 175.
47 Smith and Moncourt 2009, 83–105.
48 Ibid., 122–159.
49 Ibid., 158.
50 Franceschini 1988, 19.
51 Niccolai 1998, 67.
52 Franceschini 1988, 62–63.
53 Niccolai 1998, 68.

Theoretical subscription to the idea of a future, violent revolution was a thread that united many of the Maoist-inspired parties of the 1970s, across France, West Germany, Norway and the United States, even if they did not transform this conviction into homicidal action. In 1977, as the KBW grew convinced that the apocalypse of global capitalism was drawing nigh, the organization broadcast the idea that a decisive "armed uprising was the only way to remove the capitalist system in the FRG before it embarked on a new imperialistic world war." Military drills were carried out in parks so that cadres would be battle-ready. "A housewife used to modern kitchen and cleaning appliances," they hopefully conjectured, "would have no difficulty using a machine gun."[54]

In 1966, RAM distributed "The world black revolution," a manifesto fronted by a picture of Mao and scattered with gobbets of Maoism and advocating all-out urban guerrilla war against the white establishment. In the coming "War of Armageddon ... the 'devil's' forces of evil are destroyed by 'God' (Allah), the forces of righteousness ... Let the cry across the planet be 'burn, baby, burn'."[55] After Robert Williams – the president of RAM who sought political exile in China between 1965 and 1969 – showed the manifesto to him, apparently even Mao thought they "might have taken it a bit far."[56]

The Cultural Revolution Legacy beyond the 1970s

Conservative intellectuals – particularly those who have weighed into the "culture wars" of the past two decades – like to claim that, over the past half-century, young left-wing radicals of the 1960s have successfully undertaken a "long march through the institutions" (Rudi Dutschke's phrase), overrunning the establishment with politically correct values. It is true that the countercultural rebellion of which Maoism was a part decisively eroded social and cultural conservatism in the United States and Western Europe, and that the effects of this liberalization are still easily discernible in public life today.

The Western reception of Maoism had a direct influence on the women's and gay liberation movements, on educational reform and on aspirations to racial equality in public life. *Tout!* (the journal of the more liberal wing of French Maoism, the group Vive la Révolution) was a receptive venue for early explorations of women's and gay rights issues. "The idea of women holding up half the sky was all part of the influence of Mao," considers Dennis O'Neil. "The Cuban revolution was very macho ... The Maoist revolution had a very different feel: of social relations being transformed, not by diktat but from the ground up, by the participants themselves. Women modelled a lot of consciousness-raising groups on [China's] 'speak bitterness' meetings, with people denouncing the old ways,

54 Koenen 2001, 453–54.
55 Ahmad 1966, 17, 26.
56 Private communication.

speaking out about the ways in which they're oppressed."[57] Andrew Ross, a professor of American Studies, argues that criticism-self-criticism, popularized by the Mao vogue, has passed into mainstream culture as "an important confessional ritual within the culture of popular therapy and self-help." The Cultural Revolution-inspired interlude of the 1960s and 1970s, he further contends, has contributed to reforms of secondary and tertiary education: "efforts to make curricula, teaching methods and access to learning ... more comprehensible, practical and accountable to socially denied communities."[58] It was, for example, associates of RAM who stayed in the educational system, such as John Bracey (at the University of Massachusetts from 1972), who contributed to the struggle for black studies in universities. The Asian-American Red Guards, and later I Wor Kuen, were involved in protests demanding the introduction of "ethnic studies" in American universities. A connection can be drawn between Cultural Revolution-inspired rebellion and the epistemological scepticism of post-structuralism – Michel Foucault went through a Maoist phase in the early 1970s.[59] Sanjay Seth links Indian Maoism with the emergence of postcolonial and subaltern studies: Naxalite Maoism, he writes, made Indian intellectuals "engage with and in peasant struggles in a manner that left them more receptive to peasant consciousness."[60]

Richard Wolin writes that former French Maoists have subsequently become "luminaries of French cultural and political life: philosophers, architects, scholars, and advisers to the Socialist Party."[61] Alain Geismar, former leader of the militant Gauche Prolétarienne, served through the 1990s in a succession of Socialist Party governments. Between 1973 and 2006, Serge July – another former GP leader – founded and edited Libération, a newspaper that originated from the organized Maoist left but evolved into an influential mainstream broadsheet. Andreas Kühn, in his monograph on the German K-Gruppen, argues that numerous West German ex-Maoists have (alongside other members of the FRG's radical left wing) enjoyed vigorous afterlives in mainstream politics, for the most part in the green movement.[62]

Much work remains to be done in tracing out the long-term impact of Maoist political ideas and practice on the political biographies of such individuals. It would be impossible, remembered Mario Capanna (who later served in the Italian Chamber of Deputies), "to deny the fascination that the Great Helmsman exercised over me ... [One] element of the fascination sprang from his great dialectical ability and the simplicity of his language. All the success

---

57 Interview, Dennis O'Neil. See Houten 2015 for further discussion of this point.
58 Ross 2005, 12, 15.
59 Wang, Ning 2015, 2–3.
60 Seth 2006, 602.
61 Wolin 2010, 15.
62 Kühn 2005, 288. For details on the overlap between Maoist and environmental movements in Western Europe, see Tompkins 2013.

that I achieved in the assemblies or, later, on the electoral platform, I owe to him."[63]

But the success stories of Western Maoism perhaps feature disproportionately in public perception, obscuring the far more numerous casualties of this engagement. The tragic story of Robert Linhart is a case in point. In the mid-1960s, as leader of the breakaway Maoist faction in the French Communist Party, he was acclaimed as the brilliant "Lenin of L'École Normale Supérieure." In the throes of the May 1968 demonstrations, he suffered a nervous breakdown that confined him to hospital for months. In 1981, he attempted suicide with a massive overdose but eventually regained consciousness after weeks in a deep coma. He has barely spoken since.[64]

In certain cases, the Maoist upsurge of the 1970s succeeded in collectively dispiriting the radical left wing after its euphoric successes of the 1960s, and thereby facilitating the rise of right-wing, neoliberal governments during the 1980s. (Some analysts arrestingly argue that neoliberals actually borrowed from the language and techniques of the earlier Marxist-Leninist fever. David Priestland, after Ivan Molloy, asserts that Reagan's "low intensity conflict" was modelled on Maoist guerrilla warfare, and that the belligerence of his speeches against communism was inflected with the apocalyptic rhetoric of Marxism-Leninism.[65]) Max Elbaum blames Cultural Revolution fever for the marginalization of the contemporary American left, writing that "the most damage was done by Maoism" – by a dogmatic loyalty to the theory of the Cultural Revolution and to the twists and turns of Chinese domestic and foreign policy. "Maoism's problems were crystallized in Mao's Cultural Revolution slogan that 'the correctness or incorrectness of the ideological and political line decides everything.' This dictum was cited endlessly by the main Maoist groups, despite the fact that it completely ignored material conditions and the balance of political forces … it not only fostered ultra-left analyses and tactics, but a theoretical purism that led directly to bitter confrontations over even minor points of doctrine and constant interorganizational competition."[66] After years of sectarian struggles, according to Elbaum, America's left wing was too exhausted to resist the conservative resurgence of the Reagan years witnessed in its assault on the trade unions and its tough line against socialist and communist governments in the Third World. Similar observations have been made about Italian Maoism. Italian Maoist groups of the 1970s, observed one insider, "were the product of an explosion of communism that fractured into a thousand splinters … it was a crisis … or only the fragment of a crisis … It was the end."[67]

Ethan Young recalls the psychology prevailing among those who emerged from the American Maoist parties of the 1970s: "The sectarianism leaves the

---

63 Niccolai 1998, 146.
64 Linhart 2008.
65 Priestland 2010, 528–29; Molloy 2001.
66 Elbaum 2006, 321–23.
67 Niccolai 1998, 236.

scar. People who've lived through the sectarian wars react violently against sug-
gestions of forming new parties … They have memories of being lost in intermin-
able debates and struggles that led nowhere. Some people's lives were torn apart;
they were cast out of their groups. There were some suicides. And definitely a
deep, deep demoralization, disillusionment and despair."[68]

Singapore's left-wing opposition party, Barisan Socialis, also ran a Cultural
Revolution fever between the late 1960s and early 1970s that proved highly damaging to its long-term political health. After 1966, Barisan adopted a pro-Maoist
framework for its political rhetoric, education and media, endorsing the Cultural
Revolution's contempt for electoral politics and the Soviet Union's strategy of
"peaceful evolution." This radical turn led all 13 Barisan MPs to resign from parliament, fatally weakening Barisan's political presence in Singapore. This "costly
mistake," Lee Kuan Yew observed appreciatively in 2000, "gave the PAP
[People's Action Party] unchallenged dominance of the Parliament for the next
30 years."[69] Party debates replicated Cultural Revolution-type factional struggles:
Lee Siew Choh, chairman of Barisan from 1962, responded to internal dissent
with Cultural Revolution-style denunciations. With political intolerance enshrined
as a party principle, achieving a broader coalition of the left to oppose PAP became impossible. Yinghong Cheng concludes that "internal fights and schisms
with Cultural Revolution characteristics," combined with Barisan's quest for ideological purity based on dogmatic interpretations of Mao's utterances, caused
Singapore's left to implode.[70] When Barisan returned to electoral politics in
1972, 1976 and 1980, it did not secure a single seat from PAP. According to
this line of argument, PAP did not need to ban the party that in the early
1960s had been its main rival for power; Barisan in part extinguished itself
through adherence to the Cultural Revolution.[71] Naturally, factors other than
Cultural Revolution influence also reduced the efficacy of the Singaporean left
wing, in particular the pressure exerted on leftists during and after Operation
Coldstore in 1963, an operation authored by PAP and British interests.

In her analysis of the post-1945 West German state, Karrin Hanshew argues
that the climax of left-wing terrorism in 1977 ultimately increased the legitimacy
of the FRG and empowered it to strengthen state security with a decisiveness that
it had previously avoided for fear of comparisons with the Third Reich.[72]
Terrorism reoriented the West German left wing away from endorsement of violence and towards forms of peaceful protest often centred around environmental
issues.

The first nine months of 1977 witnessed eight RAF murders and one kidnapping (of the industrialist Hanns Martin Schleyer). West Germany's emergency

---

68 Interview, Ethan Young.
69 Cheng 2011, 225.
70 Ibid., 238.
71 Luofu Ye advances a similar argument concerning the impact of Cultural Revolution politics on Hong
    Kong's left wing after the late 1960s. See Ye 2015, 81–82.
72 Hanshew 2012.

became international when, on 13 October, four members of the Popular Front for the Liberation of Palestine hijacked a Lufthansa plane carrying 86 passengers, and included in their ransom demands the release of ten RAF members held in the Stammheim prison in Stuttgart. The FRG brought the hostage crisis to an end through a surgical strike on the plane at Mogadishu airport carried out by its new anti-terrorism squad; on learning of the failure of the hijacking on 18 October, three imprisoned RAF leaders (including Baader and Ensslin) committed suicide. That same day, the RAF members holding Schleyer executed him and abandoned his body in the back of a car.

These events – the crescendo of terrorist violence, together with the resolve of the West German state to mobilize security forces that had previously been shunned by a government nervous of raising the ghost of Nazi authoritarianism – caused the German left to abandon its widely held view of the West German state as a totalitarian enemy to which guerrilla violence was an acceptable response. According to Hanshew's analysis:

The political impotence and disillusionment [the extra-parliamentary left] felt ... prompted many to actively reengage the political mainstream and, correspondingly, to express an explicit and unprecedented appreciation for nonviolent politics ... By making German patriotism palatable and traditional values commonsensical, Mogadishu ... helped mainstream conservatives pursue a course of moral and national rejuvenation.[73]

For Cultural Revolution enthusiasts in organizations identified as genuine threats to the state, their commitment cost them dear. A former RAM activist pursued for years by the US security services reflected on the toll that political activism had taken on private life: "Half of my family is crazy, totally estranged. My oldest son is in penitentiary ... My children feel they grew up in a situation where I could not provide in the way that other fathers could." Nonetheless, he feels that Mao still has lessons for the African-American struggle today. "As we grew older, we really understood the nature of protracted struggles. It's been going on all our lives. Your strategy and tactics differ when you understand it's a protracted struggle. You learn retreat. All of that is in the philosophical principles of Mao."[74]

Conclusion

The Cultural Revolution's rhetoric of anti-authoritarian rebellion inspired revolts outside China that took aim at a broad range of political, cultural and social customs: at domestic and foreign policy; colonial rule; electoral representation; relations between the sexes; education, film and literature. The impact of the Cultural Revolution (upper-case) is part of a much more diffuse (and often liberalizing) process of cultural revolution (lower-case) that has transformed society, culture and politics since the 1960s, especially in the developed West. In countries riven by deep historical, ethnic or socio-economic fault lines (post-fascist

73 Ibid., 237. See Lumley 1990, 337–38 for similar remarks about the response of the Italian judiciary to left-wing terrorism.
74 Private communication.

Germany and Italy; post-segregation America; post-independence India), the Cultural Revolution's legitimization of political violence served as the spark that lit a prairie fire – a fire that in some instances is still burning today. The United States is regularly jolted by revelations of racist police brutality; for veterans of the 1960s and 1970s African-American liberation struggle inspired by Cultural Revolution Maoism, some of the political ideas suggested by their readings of Maoist theory and practice remain relevant. More often, however, the rhetorical and actual violence of Cultural Revolution politics, in combination with the often dogmatic, sectarian way in which they were interpreted by radicals outside China, generated setbacks, both for the individuals who devoted so much time and energy to these ideas and for the left-wing causes in which they militated.

Acknowledgement

The author would like to thank Thelma Lovell for invaluable assistance with Italian and German language sources. She is also grateful for the helpful comments from the editors of this special issue, Robert Macfarlane and two anonymous reviewers. Especial gratitude is due to the Philip Leverhulme Prize, which made possible travel and research assistance.

Biographical note

Julia Lovell is reader in modern Chinese history at Birkbeck College, University of London. She is currently writing a global history of Maoism.

摘要: 文章考察了文化大革命作为一种国际现象的修辞和现实状况, 并 (通过已出版和口述历史文献) 对文革在海外被理解和诠释的方式进行了研究。文章特别就 1960 年末和 1970 年代期间, 毛泽东思想及其实践对西欧和北美的反文化运动的不同影响, 进行了集中的论述。在欧洲, 关于文化大革命的毛泽东思想, 给达达主义 (Dadaist) 学生反抗运动提供了支持, 培育了女权主义者和同志争取权利的激进主义, 并为城市游击战恐怖主义提供了合法依据。而在同时期的美国, 毛泽东思想又为广泛的反种族主义民权运动, 以及狭义马克思列宁主义的政党建设, 推波助澜。尽管毛泽东的愿望是发动一场全球范围的持久革命, 但从长远来看, 在欧洲、美国和东南亚部分地区, 对文化大革命的热情, 加速了激进左翼的分裂, 而在 1980 年代和之后, 巩固和强化了右派的势力。

关键词: 文化大革命; 毛泽东思想; 西欧; 美国; 新加坡

References

Ahmad, Akbar. 1966. "The world black revolution," https://antiimperialism.files.wordpress.com/2012/10/ahmad-s.pdf. Accessed 12 May 2015.

Alexander, Robert J. 1999. *International Maoism in the Developing World*. London: Praeger.

Alexander, Robert J. 2001. *Maoism in the Developed World*. London: Praeger.

Belden Fields, A. 1988. *Trotskyism and Maoism: Theory and Practice in France and the United States*. London: Praeger.

Bourseiller, Christophe. 1996. *Les Maoistes: La Folle Histoire des Gardes Rouges Français*. Paris: Plon.

Chakrabarty, Bidyut. 2014. *Communism in India: Events, Processes and Ideologies*. Oxford: Oxford University Press.

Cheng, Yinghong. 2011. "The Chinese Cultural Revolution and the decline of the left in Singapore." *Journal of Chinese Overseas* 7, 211–246.

Cook, Alexander (ed.). 2014. *Mao's Little Red Book: A Global History*. Cambridge: Cambridge University Press.

Elbaum, Max. 2006. *Revolution in the Air: Sixties Radicals Turn to Lenin, Mao and Che*. London: Verso.

Franceschini, Alberto. 1988. *Mara Renato e Io: Storia des Fondatori delle BR*. Milan: Arnoldo Mondadori.

Gehrig, Sebastian. 2008. "'Zwischen uns und dem Feind einen klaren Trennungsstrich ziehen': Linksterroristische Gruppe und maoistische Ideologie in der Bundesrepublik der 1960er und 1970er Jahre." In Sebastian Gehrig, Barbara Mittler and Felix Wemheuer (eds.), *Kulturrevolution als Vorbild? Maoismen im deutschsprachigen Raum*. Frankfurt: Peter Lang, 153–177.

Gehrig, Sebastian. 2011. "(Re-)configuring Mao: trajectories of a culturo-political trend in West Germany." *Transcultural Studies* 2, 189–231, http://journals.ub.uni-heidelberg.de/index.php/transcultural/article/view/9072. Accessed 10 May 2015.

Hanshew, Karrin. 2012. *Terror and Democracy in West Germany*. Cambridge: Cambridge University Press.

Harvey, David. 2005. *A Brief History of Neoliberalism*. Oxford: Oxford University Press.

Houten, Christina van. 2015. "Simone de Beauvoir abroad: historicizing Maoism and the Women's Liberation Movement." *Comparative Literature Studies* 52(1), 112–129.

Koenen, Gerd. 2001. *Das Rote Jahrzehnt: Unsere kleine Deutsche Kulturrevolution 1967–1977*. Köln: Kiepenheuer & Witsch.

Kühn, Andreas. 2005. *Stalins Enkel, Maos Söhne: Die Lebenswelt der K-Gruppen in der Bundesrepublik der 70er Jahre*. Frankfurt: Campus Verlag.

Lin, Biao. 1965. "Long live the victory of people's war!" https://www.marxists.org/reference/archive/lin-biao/1965/09/peoples_war/index.htm. Accessed 13 May 2015.

Lin, Biao. 1966. "Foreword to the second edition of quotations of Chairman Mao Tse-tung," https://www.marxists.org/reference/archive/lin-biao/1966/12/16.htm. Accessed 13 May 2015.

Linhart, Virginie. 2008. *Le jour où mon père s'est tu*. Paris: Editions du Seuil.

Lumley, Robert. 1990. *States of Emergency*. London: Verso.

Mao Zedong. 1957. "Youth," https://www.marxists.org/reference/archieve/mao/works/red-book/ch30.htm. Accessed 27 June 2016.

Mao, Zedong. 1968. "A new storm against imperialism," https://marxistleninist.wordpress.com/2008/12/26/two-articles-by-mao-zedong-on-the-african-american-national-question/. Accessed 10 May 2015.

Molloy, Ivan. 2001. *Rolling Back Revolution: The Emergence of Low Intensity Conflict*. London: Pluto Press.

Niccolai, Roberto. 1998. *Quando la Cina era vicina: La Rivoluzione Culturale e la sinistra extraparlamentare Italiana negli anni '60 e '70*. Pisa: Associazione centro de documentazione de Pistoia.

Priestland, David. 2010. *The Red Flag: Communism and the Making of the Modern World*. London: Penguin.

Reid, Donald. 2004. "Etablissement: working in the factory to make revolution in France." *Radical History Review* 88, 83–111.

Ross, Andrew. 2005. "Mao Zedong's impact on cultural politics in the West." *Cultural Politics* 1(1), 5–22.

Scott, David. 2007. *China Stands Up: The PRC and the International System*. Abingdon: Routledge.

Seale, Bobby. 1991. *Seize the Time: Story of the Black Panther Party and Huey P. Newton*. Baltimore: Black Classic Press.

Seth, Sanjay. 2006. "From Maoism to postcolonialism? The Indian 'sixties,' and beyond." *Inter-Asia Cultural Studies* 7(4), 589–605.

Slobodian, Quinn. 2012. *Foreign Front: Third World Politics in Sixties West Germany*. Durham, NC: Duke University Press.

Smith, J., and André Moncourt. 2009. *The Red Army Faction, A Documentary History: Volume 1, Projectiles for the People*. Oakland, CA: PM.

Stanford, Maxwell. 1986. "Revolutionary Action Movement (RAM): A Case Study of an Urban Revolutionary Movement in Western Capitalist Society." MA diss., University of Atlanta.

Tompkins, Andrew S. 2013. "'BETTER ACTIVE TODAY THAN RADIOACTIVE TOMORROW!' Transnational Opposition to Nuclear Energy in France and West Germany, 1968–1981." PhD diss., University of Oxford.

Wang, Hui. 2009. *The End of the Revolution: China and the Limits of Modernity*. London: Verso.

Wang, Ning. 2015. "Introduction: global Maoism and cultural revolutions in the global context." *Comparative Literature Studies* 52(1), 1–11.

Wolin, Richard. 2010. *The Wind from the East: French Intellectuals, the Cultural Revolution, and the Legacy of the 1960s*. Princeton, NJ: Princeton University Press.

Ye, Luofu. 2015. "Propaganda as leftist culture: Hong Kong's involvement in the Cultural Revolution." *Comparative Literature Studies* 52(1), 80–96.

Žižek, Slavoj. 2011. "Revolutionary terror from Robespierre to Mao." *Positions* 19(3), 671–706.

Mummifying the Working Class: The Cultural Revolution and the Fates of the Political Parties of the 20th Century

Alessandro Russo[*]

Abstract
A number of prolonged political experiments in Chinese factories during the Cultural Revolution proved that, despite any alleged "historical" connection between the Communist Party and the "working class," the role of the workers, lacking a deep political reinvention, was framed by a regime of subordination that was ultimately not dissimilar from that under capitalist command. This paper argues that one key point of Deng Xiaoping's reforms derived from taking these experimental results into account accurately but redirecting them towards the opposite aim, an even more stringent disciplining of wage labour. The outcome so far is a governmental discourse which plays an important role in upholding the term "working class" among the emblems of power, while at the same time nailing the workers to an unconditional obedience. The paper discusses the assumption that, while this stratagem is one factor behind the stabilization of the Chinese Communist Party, it has nonetheless affected the decline of the party systems inherited from the 20th century.

Keywords: Cultural Revolution; working class; depoliticization; political parties

---

Rethinking the living legacies of the Chinese Cultural Revolution means to advance in a groping fashion in a heavy mist. Shrouded in the anathema of the official campaign to "thoroughly negate" (*chedi fouding* 彻底否定) the Cultural Revolution,[1] for four decades it has been the object of unanimous execration, both in governmental and scholarly discourses, albeit with several exceptions at the grassroots.[2] It is almost as if the Cultural Revolution had never happened.

---

* University of Bologna. Email: alessandro.russo@unibo.it.
1 The term appears in "Guanyu jianguo yilai dang de ruogan lishi wenti de jueyi" (On some questions concerning the history of the Party since the founding of the PRC), *Renmin ribao*, 1 July 1981, 1–7. The official campaign to "totally negate" the Cultural Revolution took place in earnest between 1984 and 1986, with dozens of editorials appearing in official newspapers calling for the total eradication of so-called "leftist" elements formerly associated with the Cultural Revolution.
2 For an accurate discussion of such exceptions, especially in China, see Gao 2008. For a recent reassessment of one key passage of the events, the Shanghai Commune, see Jiang 2014.

Nonetheless, I would risk the hypothesis that a proper assessment of the 1960s in China not only is vital for finding new political paths but is also necessary for investigating the present day changes in forms of government around the world.

In re-examining the Cultural Revolution as a fount of possible intellectual resources, I will focus on two interwoven layers of legacies: the apparent stalemate in the visions and practices of modern egalitarian politics, and a profound change in the governmental circumstances of the contemporary social world. While the two plans have discrete logics and different temporalities, they manifest themselves in a web of entangled relations.

The first point is the most directly political. It concerns the possibility of rethinking egalitarian politics under the conditions of today's worldwide anti-egalitarian governmental policies. How to discontinue the deadly repetition of the present rule of the world, which is based on the deletion of any political value of labour, the unlimited extension of social inequalities and the general trend towards a rampant militarization of contemporary societies? Without a thorough reassessment of the 1960s, I argue, the intellectual horizon of egalitarian politics will remain weak and inconclusive. Such a reassessment, moreover, certainly requires a deep rethinking of the most critical issues of modern politics, since the Cultural Revolution marked an impasse that reverberates retroactively on all egalitarian inventions, from the French Revolution onwards.

A second series of "legacies," although delayed and less obvious, lies in the substantial changes in contemporary governmental forms, namely the decline of party systems in the last decades of the 20th century. We must examine at least two paradoxes. Although the Cultural Revolution was the point of no return in a crisis faced by communist parties that started at least ten years before and is nowadays definitive for almost all of them, the largest communist party that has ever existed is in power in China today. Furthermore, far from marking the over-hastily proclaimed triumph of their competitors, the parliamentary parties, this crisis has indeed induced their inexorable decline also. My point is that re-examining the political stakes of the Cultural Revolution and their impasses is a prerequisite for investigating the vicissitudes of contemporary party systems, including the enigmatic persistence of a communist party in China.

A Mass Experimental Political Laboratory

To start with, a definition necessarily schematic is in order, given the magnitude of the topic. The Cultural Revolution was, in the last analysis, a mass political laboratory that tested the political value of the communist party. Its reach extended beyond China and indeed it was at the epicentre of the global political configuration of the "long sixties."

My working hypothesis is that the period initiated by the Sino-Soviet dispute of the late 1950s and brought to an end with the suppression of the Solidarity movement in Poland in the early 1980s, was a political configuration in the sense of a prolonged political process that was both unitary and manifold.[3] The Cultural Revolution played a decisive role, not as a "revolutionary centre" that replaced the USSR, although somebody could have fantasized about that scenario at that time, but as the site that concentrated the most controversial political issues shared by the configuration as a whole.

The 1960s were a worldwide multifarious configuration that comprised countless political experimentations of any sort, whose core issue was an anxious rethinking about a possible political existence of workers. Worker politics was vital, for being the most problematic and obscure in modern politics. How is it possible to invent egalitarian relationships in industrial workplaces which are structurally the most despotic sites in the world? Can workers exist politically, since their social existence is confined to the sale of their labour-power as a commodity that is interchangeable like any other in the global market? The novelty of the 1960s lay in the fact that not only were these key political issues radicalized in the capitalist regimes, but they were also deeply questioned within the communist parties and the socialist states which had promised to completely overcome the conditions of wage slavery. Could the organizational conditions of the communist parties create a political role for workers, or were they only disciplinary rituals for obtaining obedience from subordinates? Were the socialist states an alternative to capitalism, or even the "historical" antecedent of communism, or were they just peculiar forms of domination?

Since such "impossible" questions were at the core of the 1960s, the horizon of the configuration was vast and encompassed an unprecedented wealth of political topics. Virtually everything that has to do with "the government of others" was the object of a series of inventive probes: the school, the university, men and women, the conflicts between generations, even the army, the asylums and the prisons. How to conceive of egalitarian relationships in such disparate fields? One key feature of the 1960s was the simultaneous appearance of a multiplicity of egalitarian experiments in all arenas of collective life and of one political nub – the questioning of the political existence of the workers, even under the conditions of socialism.

This was the sign that no egalitarian agenda can elude the issue of the political destinies of modern wage slavery and, vice versa, that in order to invent egalitarian relationships in the workplace all other forms and modes of "governmentality" must be questioned, or, as Mao wrote, "it is only when the proletariat has liberated the entire human race that it can eventually liberate itself."[4] Even apart from the historical-political framework of a class-based vision of politics,

---

3 Russo 2016.
4 In response to the 1966 letter written by the first group of Red Guards founded at the Tsinghua University Middle School, Mao wrote: "Marx said: the proletariat must emancipate not only itself but all mankind. If it cannot emancipate all mankind, then the proletariat itself will not be able to achieve final emancipation. Will comrades please pay attention to this truth too." Taken from Schram 1974, 260–61.

this issue is still vital and was even more urgent in the 1960s when it put into question the entire tradition of modern worker politics.

There is another essential reason that made worker politics the central issue of the 1960s. From the beginning of the mass phase, 1965–1966, the lowest common denominator of the political configuration of the 1960s was the existence of myriad organizations independent from the parties of the 20th century. In fact, the workers did not enter immediately on to the political scene of the 1960s. In many cases, as is known, the students organized politically first. However, the extra-party nature of that unprecedented mass political activism not only entailed, in different situations, a radical questioning of the value of the political parties of the 20th century as a whole, but also necessarily opened up the issue of the political subjectivity of the workers with respect to the party systems.[5]

Since the recognition of a degree of workers' political existence, although subjected to all sorts of restrictions, had been the prerequisite of the mass parties of the 20th century, the radical questioning of their political value in the 1960s aroused the workers' mobilization and inevitably raised the issue of the relationship between the "working class" and the communist parties. Below, I discuss how the aftermath of this process still has a decisive influence on the current crisis faced by political parties.

The popular narratives of the 1960s often portray a somewhat turbulent, colourful youth movement which brought about a change of manners all over the world, including China, but which was undermined by the "terrorist utopian" movement to establish an "ideal society." Alternatively, it could even be said that what the Cultural Revolution set out to achieve at all costs was communism but what it eventually achieved was capitalism. The sarcasm, albeit malevolent, is not ungrounded, but as such, it remains fatalist or revanchist. An alternative path is to investigate the 1960s and the Cultural Revolution as an experimental mass laboratory, which, I suggest, provides not only a way to examine any possible political legacy but also to formulate some conjectures on the relationship between the Cultural Revolution and contemporary capitalism.

Surely, after the exhaustion of previous intellectual frameworks, it is imperative to rethink a term that has become so obscure nowadays: "politics." In the common acceptation, "politics" usually refers to what we could better call "governmental subjectivities," that is, the actions, statements and intentions of those who strive to satisfy their desire to rule others. Such "enjoyment of power" corresponds to the well-known Weberian definition of politics.[6] "Politics as vocation" is, ultimately, driven by the wish to occupy superordinate positions at the various levels of collective life.

We assume instead that besides politics as a response to an alleged transcendent "calling" to exercise power over subordinates, other immanent forms of

---

5 The issue concerned both the global movements of the 1960s and the PRC specifically. See Russo 2016.
6 Weber 2015[1919], 136.

politics can exist. In rare and discontinuous moments of the collective life, unexpected egalitarian inventions do appear, grounded on experimentation with new relationships among people in the most different fields. It is understood that "politics as calling" and politics as egalitarian inventions are, respectively, the rule and the exception. The former comprises few variations on the same theme, which is the satisfaction in deciding the life of others. The latter, instead, cannot but be a set of singular experiments, since nobody knows *a priori* what equality in the human world could be.

From this perspective, the political legacies of the 1960s that are worth examining are collective egalitarian experiments, the results of which are still to be explored, with the additional difficulty that these experiments were pushed by the urgency of rethinking the entire ideological and organizational tradition of modern egalitarian politics. They were political experiments that challenged the established visions of equality. Previous paradigms, such as the class-based vision of politics, underwent such a thorough critical enquiry that we are unable to adopt them as conceptual tools either for examining that political period or for investigating political phenomena in general.

The main testing ground – not the only one, but the subjective crux of the events – was the scrutiny of the organizations that, at that moment, were the undisputed "representatives of the working class." The communist parties proclaimed to embody a historical paradigm that guaranteed the political existence of the workers and of all possible egalitarian politics that had the "working class" as central. The experimental results of the 1960s proved, instead, that despite any alleged "historical connection" between the communist parties and the "working class," the political role assigned to the workers was fictitious and mostly reduced to the pathetic and tragic "man of marble" protagonist of Andrzej Wajda's film of the same name.[7]

As apparatuses, the communist parties were deeply integrated in the state forms of the 20th century. Since the late 19th century, the legalization of worker parties has played a critical role in the constitution of modern forms of government and in the generalization of the parliamentary system. Moreover, for several decades, from the 1920s to the 1970s, the existence of the socialist states was a decisive factor in curbing the inequalities inherent in the capitalist rule of the modern world.

Yet, the "long sixties" proved that the communist parties had much more in common with their "bourgeois" counterparts than what appeared to be the case during the ideological disputes and geopolitical contrasts of the Cold War. The socialist state "was not so different" from the capitalist one, "except for the ownership of the means of production," and without fresh political inventions it would have been much easier to pass from socialism to capitalism than to

---

7 Wajda's 1977 film, *Man of Marble*, was a profound questioning of the role of workers in Polish socialism, and anticipated the Solidarity movement.

communism. These were Mao Zedong's 毛泽东 conclusive theses at the final stage of the Cultural Revolution.[8]

The issue of the relationship between the communist parties and the "working class" was decisive during the whole course of the political configuration. Key moments, such as the Shanghai "January storm" of 1967, the "hot autumn" of 1969 in Italy, or the Solidarity movement in Poland in 1980, each of which led to the creation, albeit in embryonic form and gropingly, of workers' organizations independent from the communist parties and often in sharp contrast with them, disproved that there existed an alleged "proletarian social basis" of the socialist states. It was in their relationship with the "working class" that the communist parties failed the test.

Here, we meet the first analytical difficulty. After the closure of that mass political laboratory, its experimental results were apparently suppressed and dispersed. In China, namely, they were in reality transformed and redirected towards completely different targets, targets that were indeed the very opposite of the original ones, through a process that needs careful consideration. It could be said that the experimental energies of the egalitarian political configuration, which had revealed the inconsistency of previous forms and modes of government, were then subsumed under new forms of government that were even more strictly hierarchized. It is not surprising that China has been at the epicentre of this process, since the thorniest issues of the worldwide configuration were concentrated in the Cultural Revolution.

This transformation, however, cannot be examined in terms of either "class restoration" or the "triumph of parliamentary democracy" over "totalitarianism." We lack solid categories for analysing the change from the egalitarian political configuration of the 1960s to the current dominant governmental policies, so patently neo-oligarchical. Obviously, the latter, characterized by fundamentalist anti-egalitarianism, an obsession with hierarchies and the general contempt of rulers for ordinary people, are the reverse of the 1960s. However, on closer inspection, the transition is marked not by a radical discontinuity but rather by a redirecting, and surely a distortion, of the experimental results of those egalitarian political energies towards the new governmental circumstances.

The current supremacy of policies that extend inequalities, I argue, is indeed the reverse of the political subjectivities of the 1960s, but in the sense that it constitutes a "hollow imprint" of them. In other words, these changes are not only the result of the new ruling elites' ability to react to the political stakes of the 1960s but they are also the new forms of domination that have been shaped through a unique "hollowing out" of the main issues of that political configuration. The changes in the contemporary party systems, I argue, are unreadable without considering this process.

Viewing the discontinuities in the Chinese Communist Party (CCP) after the Cultural Revolution through this lens, I argue that the subjective energies that

---

8 Mao, Zedong 1998[1974].

allowed the Chinese elites to create a new governmental order capable of putting an end to the egalitarian experiments come essentially from those very experiments. The "new order" incorporated the results of the political test of the "previous disorders," and integrated them into a totally opposed subjective intention.

The mixed picture that this presents requires some explanation. The CCP, the first communist party to undergo the explosion of the party–class relationship crisis, has so far enjoyed unprecedented success and growth: nearly all other communist parties are virtually extinct. On the other hand, the system of parliamentary parties, which appeared to dominate following the crisis faced by the communist parties has, since the 1980s, suffered an irremediable decline. We can surmise then that this unequal development pertains to the same process of change experienced by the 20th-century political parties.

The Ban of a Political Assessment

The assumption that China's "new order" is the result of an "emptying out" of the previous experimental period must be examined from the beginning of the process. The final phase of the Cultural Revolution deserves special attention, both for having a momentous impact on the closure of the 1960s as a whole – the "Chinese Thermidor" of 1976 – and for the protracted effect it has had on today that goes well beyond the Chinese boundaries. The strategy that allowed Deng Xiaoping 邓小平 to direct China's transition to reform and opening up is clearly at the root of the CCP's current stability. The global impact of Deng's strategy, however, is less discernible without first examining some crucial stages.

The first step in Deng's strategy, which I have examined elsewhere,[9] can be traced back to a specific episode in 1975, a crucial year in China's political transition. China's "long sixties" was not brought to a close with a defeat exactly, but rather with the banning of political and intellectual assessment. One major prerequisite of the well-known governmental decree of "thorough negation," which effectively sealed the revolutionary decade in China, has been the pre-emptive prohibition of any self-reflection on the right and the wrong of the political events that took place in the preceding years.

In the autumn of 1975, at the height of an intense dispute with Mao, Deng lost the leading positions that he had acquired earlier that year. Although he was not formally dismissed until April 1976, restrictions had already been imposed on Deng's reform initiatives six months earlier. In the summer of 1975, the diverging views of Mao and Deng had become increasingly apparent, especially following the programmes developed by Deng with the support of his think tank, the State Council Political Research Office (*Guowuyuan zhengzhi yanjiushi* 国务院政治研究室).[10]

---

9 Russo 2013.
10 The activities and the documents issued by this Research Office are described in Cheng and Xia 2004.

The real breaking point, though, did not just spring from those programmes. It came also from Deng's categorical refusal to accept Mao's proposal in early October that Deng lead a national campaign focusing on what "had not worked" in the Cultural Revolution, literally *yousuo buzu* 有所不足. The episode, which has not attracted much scholarly attention, is not so clear-cut. Although Mao had in the previous weeks openly argued against Deng's "creative" and in fact misleading interpretations of his last political positions, he also repeatedly extended the invitation to Deng to direct the *yousuo buzu* campaign.[11] Deng's refusal caused a temporary but serious weakening of his own position but, in the long term, proved crucial to his overall strategy.

The strong opposition posed by Deng was decisive, but its effectiveness was inversely proportional to an internal weakness of the Maoists themselves. Mao sought to overcome the failure among revolutionaries, himself included, to assess their own experience and their own limitations in the preceding events accurately. And, given that Mao had reopened, in new terms, a mass theoretical reflection on the socialist state form (the "dictatorship of the proletariat") in the previous months, as I discuss below, it would be reasonable to assume that Mao would have been able to push forward his proposals for the *yousuo buzu* campaign at that time. However, for his part, Deng, who had been totally refractory and hostile to the issues of that campaign, acted in a consistent manner, preventing the assessment proposed by Mao.

Mao's verdict on the Cultural Revolution was definitely positive, though with a critical reserve. He was convinced that the Cultural Revolution had opened up new possibilities for egalitarian mass activism, but he was also aware that it had led to destructive and self-destructive behaviour and that serious injustices were committed. There were different opinions, he maintained. Some complained about being unfairly abused, others just wanted to "settle scores" (*suanzhang* 算账). Only an open debate and research that extended across the entire country, he argued, could clarify the issues.[12]

We can speculate that a mass campaign at the end of 1975 on "what had not worked" in the Cultural Revolution would have likely been a large-scale movement, even dramatic and turbulent, involving high subjective tension. It was time to criticize politically several unjust treatments and to recognize the reasons why those unfairly accused had suffered. Yet, to distinguish between those who complained about unfair treatment and those who just wanted to "settle scores" would not have been an easy task.

A mass debate of that kind would have reopened innumerable personal cases, often very painful, and should have re-examined difficult and uncomfortable truths, involving the culpability of many people from all factions, the "rebels," the "loyalists," cadres at all levels, the army, and so on. Lastly, such a debate would have, inevitably, entailed even a re-examination of a number of Mao's

---

11 Cheng and Xia 2004; Mao, Mao [Deng] 2000.
12 See Cheng and Xia 2004 and Russo 2013.

political decisions during the decade. A reassessment would demand a deep capacity for collective criticism and self-criticism in order to discern the right from wrong, which new roads the mass activism had paved and which grave mistakes should not be repeated.

The proposal for a re-examination of the Cultural Revolution, starting with its "inadequacies," was in many respects the continuation of a major theoretical-political movement, the campaign for the "study of the theory of the dictatorship of the proletariat," initiated by the Maoist group in the spring of 1975. The prerequisite for a reassessment of the decade was necessarily a thorough theoretical rethinking of this concept, which guided the relationship between the Party and the "working class." The Cultural Revolution had undermined the conceptual framework that supported the keystone of the communist organization and its governmental functions.

Late in 1974, Mao openly questioned the "dictatorship of the proletariat," a concept that still needed to be clarified he maintained, and launched an appeal to the "whole country" for a mass campaign of theoretical study. Without theoretical clarification, Mao considered the failure of the revolutionary endeavour to be almost inevitable. In short, an internal assessment of the Cultural Revolution required a broad theoretical horizon and the widest intellectual involvement possible of ordinary people in order to re-examine the key conceptual issues of revolutionary politics.

Despite his sharp opposition in October 1975 to the mass debate proposed by Mao, or rather consistently with his refusal to participate, Deng's strategic choices rested on a careful assessment of the Cultural Revolution. Clearly, here were two completely divergent perspectives: for Mao, the priority was to promote a mass rethinking of egalitarian politics; for Deng, the priority was to restore a governmental order, and any mass initiative would bring more disorder. Mao's aim was to promote a political self-assessment carried out by an indefinitely multiple set of egalitarian subjectivities, which he considered capable of "educat[ing] themselves by themselves" and "liberat[ing] themselves," we can infer, through their own mistakes. In contrast, Deng, for his part, aimed at reconstructing well-defined hierarchies that would be able to free themselves from any egalitarian initiatives of the masses, which he considered to be inherently anarchic.

Deng turned down Mao's proposal in autumn 1975 on the grounds that he was not the right person to lead the campaign as he had not participated in the Cultural Revolution. Clearly, this was not his primary reason, since not only was he well aware of the details of the Cultural Revolution but he also had clear thoughts on it. As the leader of such a campaign, he could have exerted a strong influence. Deng, though, was surely one of those who just wanted to "settle scores." In the previous months, he had openly laid down his strategy of "putting in order" (*zhengdun* 整顿), or as he said, "putting everything in order in all fields," which meant a drastic closure of all sorts of experiments that had been launched during the Cultural Revolution. A new assessment campaign, albeit in a self-critical mode, would have pre-emptively discredited the stance he would take in the near future for a "thorough negation."

Still, we should not take Deng's prescription for a "thorough negation" too literally. Although Deng's stance had been "thorough" when he refused to lead the assessment campaign in autumn 1975, when it came to the Cultural Revolution as a whole, the "negation" was anything but "thorough." Deng Xiaoping's position of strength lay in the fact that he was able to assess carefully the political results of the decade and use them "positively," albeit in an inverse sense, in the formation of a new hierarchical order.

The Cultural Revolution proved the inconsistency of revolutionary class politics as a method of government. Especially in the Maoist version, it required the constant testing, and in the last analysis, the reinvention of the political role of the workers. For Deng, instead, such constant testing was incompatible with the stability of the party-state. Yet, although Deng had "negated" the experimental results of the decade, he reworked and incorporated them in his own strategy.

Depoliticizing the "Working Class"

While the crux of the ideological differences lay in defining the relationship between the workers and the Party, the key organizational issues during the Cultural Revolution concerned the destiny of the socialist factory. In the first half of the 1970s, the Maoists launched a number of original and controversial initiatives in several industrial units, or *danwei* 单位. They maintained that the discipline and labour regimes in the socialist factory, lacking new political experiments, or, in their language, "newborn things" (*xinsheng shiwu* 新生事物), were not so dissimilar to those of the capitalist command.

Various experiments, like the workers' universities, the workers' theoretical groups, the participation of cadres in manual work and, conversely, the participation of workers in decision-making, were all aimed at deconstructing the "technical" hierarchies of the socialist factory and were critical of their presumed neutrality or objectivity. Such hierarchies, the Maoists argued, were not so different from those that made workers "dispossessed of mental powers of production" and enslaved for a lifetime to machine systems in the "big capitalist industry," as analysed by Marx.

One fundamental difference between socialism and capitalism is that under socialism, labour-power is not a commodity to be sold on the "free market." However, this point made the command within the industrial *danwei* even more complicated and equivocal, as often participation in an egalitarian collective project was enmeshed with relations of patronage. Moreover, the Maoists argued that the non-commodification of labour relations was only a temporary exception produced by socialism, one which it was quite possible to suppress, for re-establishing the ordinary rule of the capitalist government of the industrial work. A precise forecast indeed.

All of these issues, which had emerged under the pressure of the unexpected appearance of independent workers' organizations in late 1966, created a serious political quandary that jeopardized the political and technical structure of the socialist factory. The initiatives promoted by the Maoists in the years that followed to deal with the crisis faced by the industrial *danwei* affected the overall organization of industrial work, namely the entanglement between the "technical division of labour" and the factory system of command. More essentially, they affected the conceptual relationship between the "working class" and the Party.[13]

Most of the technical and governmental cadres from the industrial *danwei* reacted spontaneously in defence of the status quo but were unable to restore the previous order, which the events of the decade had strongly called into question. There were tensions and conflicts between cadres and worker activists in some places but, overall, the situation in the factories in 1975 was not as chaotic and anarchic as Deng portrayed. Indeed, according to government sources subsequent to the reforms, there was considerable "productivity" at this time.[14] The issues at stake involved radical political differences.

For the Maoists, it was vital "to clarify" fundamental theoretical issues and, at the same time, explore new forms of organization in the workplace that were open to the possibility of liberation from the established hierarchies. The most radical experiments even declared their urgent commitment to the long-term project of abolishing the divisions of labour. For Deng, on the other hand, the most urgent issue was how to rebuild stable hierarchies in the industrial workplace. This was the main objective behind his reiterated appeals in 1975 for "order."

Deng was aware that he could not simply restore the previous system of command but instead would have to create a new one. He also had to be able to map out a protracted strategy for effectively establishing "order," that is, to reestablish authority over workers in the factories. By considering the whole process of reform, it is possible to identify at least three basic consistent moves: the suppression of the Maoist experiments in the factories; the full commodification of labour-power; and the maintenance in the government discourse of the ideological reference to the "working class" and its "historical" connection with its "class vanguard," the Communist Party.

---

13 The most celebrated in those years were the "worker universities," the "workers' theoretical groups" and the regular participation of cadres in manual labour. To date, these experiments still lack detailed research. From the late 1950s, there was also the perspective of a thorough revision of the Soviet model of industrial management.

14 Although it is often taken for granted that the Chinese economy was a disaster during the ten years of Cultural Revolution, the available data from official sources reveal a very different picture. Cheng and Xia (2004, 590) cite a growth of GDP between 1974 and 1975 of 11.9 per cent and 15.1 per cent in industry. The figures for economic growth in 1975 given in Mao's official biography published by the Party school are different but equally positive: GDP 8.7 per cent; industry 15.1 per cent; agriculture 3.1 per cent (see Feng and Jin 2003, 1,752). While the Chinese economic statistics of the revolutionary era are generally considered as problematic, the Chinese economists estimate that GDP growth for 1967–1976 was 7.1 per cent. I am grateful to Cui Zhiyuan, professor of public policy and management at Tsinghua University, for discussing these data with me.

The first obstacle to overcome was the set of experiments that had called into question the technical and political order of the industrial *danwei* and the related re-discussion of key theoretical issues. This prerequisite was achieved very early on. The Chinese "Thermidor" of October 1976 quickly shut down these experiments, declaring them to be just "conspiracies" of a small "gang" of usurpers. As for the moves to set up a "movement for the study of theory," the new government immediately proclaimed that these were a "nonsense" that was aimed at "defaming the dictatorship of the proletariat" and ultimately "overthrowing" it.

The next step, the commodification of labour-power, was inevitably more gradual but a crucial element for any "re-order." Once the "historical-political" command structure of the industrial *danwei* had been discredited, only the full commodification of labour-power could make effective the conjoint authority of the "technical division of labour" and "factory despotism." The process started in the late 1970s. It began first with the generalization of the piecework wage, praised as the highest achievement of the Marxist principle "to each according to his work" (*an lao fenpei* 按劳分配).[15] In the 1990s, following the bloody suppression of the Tiananmen Square movement, the commodification of labour-power was fully established, with millions of internal migrant workers moving to form a massive precarious labour force.[16]

The celebrated transformation from the *danwei*, proclaimed obsolete and constrained by "old ideological dogmas," to the "enterprise" (*qiye* 企业), regulated by indisputable "technical" relationships, fully established the three basic conditions that Marx described as the foundations of the "big capitalist industry," namely, the rigid division between "manual and intellectual work," the despotism of the factory-barrack, and the "free market" of labour-power. The organization of the work at Foxconn, a "model factory" in contemporary China, which Pun Ngai's research describes in the most terrifying detail,[17] essentially amounts to that of the capitalist factory analysed by Marx, but with an even greater despotism.

Such a definitive "putting in order" could not have been achieved without a further key element which was ultimately vital to the policy of reform. Mao had predicted that, "in China it would be easy to establish capitalism."[18] Except that, in order to establish capitalism in China, where the political role of workers had been so intensely disputed (actually even before the Cultural

---

15 In the meantime, the Chinese media were engaged in a widespread campaign of defamation against the workers, whom they portrayed as being dependent on the "iron rice bowl" (*tiefanwan*), that is, they were models of "laziness" and parasites feeding on public resources.

16 The suppression of the Tiananmen movement was one prerequisite for imparting an even more strictly "neoliberal" drive to the "reforms" in the months that followed. On this key passage of economic policies in the 1990s, see Wang 2003.

17 Pun and Chan 2012. See also the new extensive study by Pun, Chan and Selden 2015.

18 "Zai Zhongguo gao zibenzhuyi hen rongyi:" Mao 1998[1974], 415.

Revolution), it was also essential to prevent any counter-effects, namely to impede the possibility that the workers might organize themselves politically.[19]

After all, it did happen in late 1966. The new rulers clearly perceived the danger, and all of them had in mind Marx's dictum: "The bourgeoisie creates its own gravediggers." Repressive measures would have been ineffective and hazardous, although when necessary the Chinese government has given ample proof of its readiness in this area, especially against workers.[20] Pre-emptive measures based on a governmental discourse that leaves no doubt as to the state's intention to wield an iron fist against those who violate the rules have hitherto been more successful. These measures form part of an apparently contradictory but actually consistent strategy in which the upholding of the icon of the "working class" among the insignia of power paralleled and definitely supported its depoliticization.

A clarification on the concept of depoliticization can help my argument here. The de-politicization of the working class in China has been a lengthy and ongoing process. Its starting point, and its continuing raison d'être, is the closure of political experiments concerning the relationships between the workers, the workplace and the Party. "Depoliticization" in this case is not meant as the waning of the *amicus-hostis* (friend-enemy) distinction in the Schmittian sense, but as the effect of a series of government policies aimed at voiding, politically, certain areas and sites where egalitarian experiments have taken place.

Here, it is necessary to make a distinction between a *depoliticization1* (a weakening of the friend-enemy distinction) and a *depoliticization2* (the closure of a set of egalitarian experiments). The homonymy partially matches the double acceptation of "politics" mentioned above, as the scope of governmental subjectivities or as mass inventions. Nonetheless, the relationship between them, as I will show, is not specular, but is in fact quite tortuous.

In the first case, de-politicization, meant as the absence of the regular operative principle of the "political" (the structural distinction between friend and enemy), concerns essentially the typical dynamics in the field of the governmental subjectivities of a given socio-historical world, especially at the level of the ruling elites. Rulers and would-be rulers of all ages are perpetually engaged in conflict with one another and also in weaving friendships according to the circumstances most conducive to their pursuit of "the conquest and the distribution of

---

19 As is well known, forms of resistance by workers, such as strikes, demonstrations and riots, are prevalent throughout China today. In his study on the protests of laid-off workers from SOEs, William Hurst documents that local authorities have a range of responses for dealing with such protests, from the most stringent to the most compromising, depending on the circumstances (Hurst 2009, 108–131). However, whilst grievances and claims concerning wages and welfare are, to varying degrees, tolerated, it is strictly unacceptable for any form of worker organization to claim a political role that positions itself against the "class vanguard" of the CCP. For updated documentation on workers' struggles, see the website of SACOM (Students and Scholars against Corporate Misbehaviour), http://sacom.hk.

20 The spur for the order for military intervention at Tiananmen Square in 1989, which came after the disbandment of the student movement, was the nascent formation of workers' autonomous organizations. For elements of analysis of the tragic episode, see Pozzana and Russo 2006.

power." The Weberian definition of the essence of "politics as vocation" fits well with the Schmittian "categories of the political." In the case of *depoliticization1*, the mutual hostilities between competitors among the ruling elites are in a sense "deregulated" since they do not form clear-cut, opposing fronts.

Depoliticization2, on the other hand, involves different dynamics and stakes. It is the result of successful governmental policies that hinder and prohibit egalitarian inventions. Depoliticizing policies obviously take advantage of their internal weaknesses, which are intrinsic to their experimental nature. The very idea of political equality cannot but be the result of an endless series of precarious inventions, to be repeatedly tested, of new forms of collective life beyond the ordinary hierarchical regime. Egalitarian politics is therefore not reducible either to the *a priori* friend-enemy conflict or to the acts that "strive for the conquest and the distribution of power."

Equality can only exist as a set of inventive exceptions that alters the ordinary rituals of social hierarchies. Such exceptionality is thus also at the root of the rarity, fragility and discontinuity of the egalitarian inventions. They are always on the point of being "depoliticized" and any possible revitalization requires innovation. The "depoliticization of the working class" in China is therefore a *depoliticization2*, in that it has evolved from the series of measures that the coalition, guided by Deng, adopted to halt mass experimental politics and to restore a hierarchical discipline.

However, the new modes of disciplining labour in China are not just a restoration of the previous "socialist" ones. The conditions of wage labour in China are a paradigm of despotic capitalist command in the workplace, and the labour market is among the most "flexible" in the world. In the factories, a strictly Taylorist organizational form prevails: a fast turnover of staff is an organizational strongpoint at Foxconn. The Chinese "working class" of today has nothing in common with that of the industrial *danwei*.

Nonetheless, the new ruling elites in China have felt that it is necessary to maintain certain key terms from the previous hierarchical rituals, namely the affirmation of a special relationship between the "Communist Party" and the "working class" in the Chinese governmental discourse. In the most recent CCP Constitution, for instance, the first sentence proclaims, as in all the previous versions, that the Party is "the vanguard of the working class" (*gongren jieji de xianfengdui* 工人阶级的先锋队).[21] Is it a flashy anachronism? Reform policies have received so much praise for their "pragmatism" and for having rejected what Deng called "ideological chit-chat" that it is hard to believe that the formula is merely a residue of a past that still performs the function of an obsolete liturgy.

The Chinese government is so eager to affirm technocratic values in labour relationships that one may wonder why it has not adopted a more "post-socialist" and more "modern" language. After all, the CCP must have acquired more

21 Zhongguo gongchandang 2012, 1.

up-to-date expertise in political propaganda. The reason why the CCP claims to be the "vanguard of the working class" cannot merely be because of the long pedigree of the formula or the fact that in socialist states it was often an effective way of maintaining authority over the workers. China's rulers know very well that they can no longer rely on outdated clichés; the Cultural Revolution demonstrated that the workers themselves disbelieved the disciplinary rituals of the "working class."

So, being neither nostalgia nor liturgy, the assertion that the CCP is "the vanguard of the working class" must therefore satisfy a critical need, which ultimately must be the prohibition of all forms of independent workers' organizations. It is true that all the above-mentioned steps in the process of depoliticization were conceived with this purpose in mind. Yet, a major concern of the new Chinese elites seems to be that without a clear-cut and definitive declaration, a *depoliticization2* could be ineffective, or misunderstood. The insistence on pairing the "Chinese Communist Party" with the "working class" by the concept of political "avant-garde," which is the equivalent of political "organization," loudly proclaims to every single worker, and to anybody in China, that "I am the Chinese Communist Party, and thou shalt have no other political organizations before me."

If, for example, a *dagongmei* 打工妹 (a young female worker) at Foxconn, or one of her *dagongzai* 打工仔 (fellow males) would object that, after all, such a "vanguard" is nothing more than a peculiar organization of the capitalist command, she or he would be informed with plenty of doctrinal details that the "laws of historical development" today require capitalism. In the Chinese governmental discourse, capitalism is a condition of a "historical progress" that will lead to progressively advanced stages of socialism until the day the very "development of the productive forces" will also bring communism. The first paragraph of the CCP Constitution ends with the assertion that the "highest ideal" and the "ultimate goal" of the Party is to "realize Communism" (*shixian gongchanzhuyi* 实现共产主义).

In China, it is understood perfectly by all – both by those who write and those who must read these formulas – that they mean only one thing: independent political organizations are unacceptable, especially for the workers, who are under special surveillance in contemporary China. Anyone violating this principle knows full well what the consequences of doing so are. Far from being an ideological remnant, such formulas continue to have a very real and powerful impact today. They establish *depoliticization2* as the basic principle of government in China, although there is no knowing how long it may continue to be effective.

The Resilience of the CCP and the Decline of the Parties of the 20th Century

Lastly, a working track on the assumption, mentioned above, about *depoliticization2* in China as a process that has affected an overall change in contemporary party systems. The results have been clearly divergent. In the span of a few decades, with the exception of the CCP, almost all other communist parties have collapsed, including the founding father, the Soviet Union. However, parliamentary systems have been too hasty in claiming victory. Political sociologists have analysed their transformation into "catch-all parties," "parties without partisans," or even "postmodern parties." Richard Katz and Peter Mair have diagnosed the "cartelization" of the parliamentary parties, i.e. their transformation into organizations similar to the most opportunistic alliances among economic and financial oligarchies, and have concluded that the "mass party is over," or in other words, the party system of the 20th century is obsolete.[22]

Moreover, Katz and Mair argue that intertwined with this "cartelization" is the depoliticization of the parliamentary parties, which has led to the loss of any real opposition from programmes, policies and organizational forms, and in some cases has even led to mutual "collusion." In a different theoretical framework, Wang Hui also considers depoliticization as key to analysing the exhaustion of ideological and political conflicts in the CCP in the era of reform.[23] The concomitance between disparate and even opposite phenomena could explain the resilience of the CCP and the decline of the party system as a whole. However, the distinction between the two types of depoliticization may be helpful for clarifying the possible connections in the changes of the various party systems, as well as for hypothesizing the reasons behind their different states of health. I will limit myself to a few examples from Europe.

First, how to explain the different fates of the CCP and the Communist Party of the Soviet Union (CPSU)? I suggest that the parties of the Soviet bloc lacked the capacity of the CCP to make *depoliticization2* the main source of their stabilization. They firmly suppressed all political innovations, from the Prague Spring to the Solidarity movement, but were unable to subsume the experimental results from these innovations into new forms of domination. The Polish events were the final evidence of the radical crisis that was occurring in the relationship between the communist parties and the "working class," a crisis that would undermine the overall stability of the Soviet-type states. Yet, the response of the Soviet-bloc governments only went so far as military repression; they failed to gain any "reactive" strength comparable to that which animated Deng's policies. Gorbachev's "perestroika" came too late and at a time when the system of government in the Soviet Union was so fragile and discredited that just a tiny coup would lead to its disintegration.

The Italian case is also emblematic. A similar decline, although more prolonged and with continuing consequences, hit the Italian Communist Party (PCI), which was once the largest communist party in a parliamentary regime. The PCI was at the fore of the movement to suppress the independent worker organizations that arose in the 1960s, proclaiming them to be homogeneous with "terrorism." It even made it a point of honour to sponsor the judicial

22 Katz and Mair 1995; 2009.
23 Wang 2006.

harassment of Antonio Negri and other leaders of "Autonomia operaia";[24] however, it failed to draw any "positive" lessons from these events. It congratulated itself on having achieved an apparent stability, but the very next day after the collapse of the Berlin Wall it hastily changed its name, removing the term "communist," and thus began a decline that has continued for more than two decades. A few months later, the Christian Democrats, which had been the main ruling party since the Second World War, also collapsed, and so followed the whole system of Italian parties of the so-called "First Republic."

The phenomena of "collusion" among the successors to those parties and the vanishing of differences between them, I suggest, are rooted in that passage. Despite the obvious disparities, we can conjecture that upstream of the *depoliticization1* of Italian political parties there was a process analogous to that which determined the collapse of the Soviet-type ruling parties in the 1980s, that is to say, they failed to make *depoliticization2* the starting point for the reorganization of forms of control. The downfall of the USSR certainly played a major role in the disappearance of opposing politics between the PCI and the Christian Democrats and eventually in their shared ruin, since the very structure of the Italian parliamentary system after the Second World War was shaped by the geopolitics of the Cold War. Yet, the decline of the PCI, which was the first significant step in the undoing of the Italian party system, had begun much earlier and was primarily a consequence of the key issues at stake in the 1960s.

While taking account of the individual processes, I will now make some clarifications on the hypothesis about the global effect of *depoliticization2* in China. The issue of worker politics has been crucial.

The end of the 1960s was marked in different national contexts by a strong anti-worker drive. Given the strong political nature of the configuration, its closure would require a strong re-disciplining of the workers. As noted above, one major episode that brought about that closure was the clampdown on the Solidarity movement in Poland in 1980; however, the first episode that marked the beginning of the end was the coup in China in 1976. It was not a coincidence that three of the members of the so-called "gang of four," the Maoist group arrested at that time, were among the most active leaders in the Shanghai "January storm": one had even initiated the first rebel workers' organization. In brief, from the second half of the 1970s, over the span of a few years, a series of counter-attacks was able to suppress the experiments that were aimed at rethinking the political status of workers.

While the main factor behind the defeat of those experiments was their inability to overcome their internal weaknesses – and political novelties are intrinsically fragile – it is significant that in key situations such as those in China, Poland and Italy, the communist parties acted with the same resolute intent to exact revenge on an insubordinate "social base." The different means of suppression, however,

---

24 These vicissitudes are discussed in Murphy 2005.

produced different outcomes. The singular force of Deng's leadership came from knowing the gravity of the crisis. His appeals in 1975 to the Party cadres to be "daring" in the task of "putting everything in order" bore the weight of a life-and-death issue. He was then able to develop a prolonged strategy of "thorough depoliticization" which culminated, as discussed above, with the stratagem of mummifying the concept of the "working class" and keeping that concept at the forefront of governmental insignia, while at the same time nailing the workers to the most stringent capitalist regime.

The way in which the CCP achieved a new governmental order demonstrated to the world a means of bringing the worker politicization of the 1960s to a close. Despite the preservation of elements of a "class" discourse, it soon became clear that the very concept of a "working class" had become a mere fiction in China. That this had occurred in a socialist country, notably one where there had been prolonged attempts to revitalize the political figure of the worker, could not but have profound consequences for all other contemporary governmental circumstances.

The announcement that China's rulers had found a way to obliterate the workers politically and to reduce their role in negotiations to mere sellers of their labour-power signalled a sea change to governments around the world. The modern ruling elites' old dream of a capital that does not need to negotiate anything political with the waged labour seemed to be coming true. The end of the worker as a political figure proclaimed the beginning of an era of non-negotiable capital.

Of course, this is just a perverse dream, but not without real consequences for government forms in general. Clearly, by "capital" we mean the control of wage labour, which is at the core of the governmental circumstances of the contemporary socio-historical world.[25] The largest electronic manufacturing firm in China is at the epicentre of a general pattern of non-negotiable capital, which, while determined by its relationship with Apple, is actually a triarchy pivoting on the role of the CCP via the changes it triggered after the decade of the Cultural Revolution, and definitely as a reaction to it.

Such changes, I suggest, far from being mere technical adjustments of the industrial management, have deeply affected systems of government in the contemporary world, namely the role of the party systems. The turning point in China has determined the rapid decline of the parties of the 20th century because it has shattered their foundations. From the late 19th century onwards, the key point in the transition from "parties of notables" to "mass parties" was the recognition, to a certain degree and with all sorts of limitations, of the political existence of the workers. Any form of government, even Fascism and Nazism in specific ways, had to negotiate in some way or another its very existence with the workers. Particularly in parliamentary systems, the parties, besides the

---

25 The sadistic desire to obtain the unconditional obedience of the workforce extends in fact to everybody in the human world. For example, Terry Gou, the founder and CEO of Foxconn, compared workers to animals: "as human beings are also animals, to manage one million animals gives me a headache." He also proudly declared that he had hired experts from Taibei zoo to improve the training of Foxconn managers. See http://www.businessinsider.com/foxconn-animals-2012-1?IR=T. Accessed 31 July 2016.

trade unions, were ultimately the main hub of negotiations between capital and labour. Since the 1980s, in contrast, workers have been erased politically and the ideal of a non-negotiable capital has been proclaimed, and thus the parties have lost their raison d'être. In other terms, "the mass party is over" since the previous forms of the political existence of workers are over.

The "negation" of the value of the political tests of the 1960s, in fact, did not restore the "labour movement" to the state it enjoyed, for example, in the 1950s. On the contrary, since the nub of the 1960s was the mass scrutiny of the organizational tradition of labour politics, to reject that experimental political passage has implied resetting to zero the value of everything that, for over a century, had made a series of extensive alterations to the structural circumstances of the capitalist rule of labour. It was because the 1960s were a prolonged political test of the historical horizon of the negotiations between capital and labour that the "negation" of the political 1960s resulted in the suppression of the possibility of even giving thought to that series of exceptions to capitalism that existed throughout the 20th century.

To summarize my arguments and draft some tentative conclusions, the depoliticization of the working class in China after the Cultural Revolution has had two orders of consequences.

One concerns a serious impasse in the horizon of egalitarian politics. Having banned any self-assessment of the decade and at the same time having distorted the experimental results, the "thorough negation" has left a radical uncertainty about the destiny of key concepts such as "working class" and even "communism" as resources for new egalitarian experiments. Can a class-based vision of politics be a reference for revitalizing worker politics, and how to conceive of the very idea of "communism" when both terms are icons of a governmental order that is hitherto one pillar of contemporary capitalism? The urgent need to rethink the intellectual and organizational conditions of politics is the most important legacy of the Cultural Revolution.

Equally urgent is the need to develop fresh ideas about contemporary governmental circumstances. Capitalism, on the one hand, no longer has any systemic alternative, a role socialist state planning appeared once to play. On the other hand, it does not correspond to one specific form of government but is compatible with any of them, whether they are parliamentary, communist, hereditary monarchies, or warlords. The current ideal of a non-negotiable capital involves the specific phenomenology of a multi-dimensional capital. No longer is there just "capital-parliamentarianism;" there is also "capital-communism," in which the name "communism" carries such weight and such a peculiar meaning!

Acknowledgement

I would like to thank Claudia Pozzana for having discussed at length the issues contained in this article, Patricia M. Thornton, Peidong Sun and Chris Berry for the tenacity of the project, and two anonymous referees for their helpful remarks.

Biographical note

Alessandro Russo teaches sociology at Bologna University. He has recently completed a manuscript on *Cultural Revolution and Revolutionary Culture*.

摘要: 文化大革命期间, 在许多中国工厂里, 一系列持续的政治实验表明: 即便共产党与 "工人阶级" 之间存在所谓的 "历史性" 连接, 但是由于缺乏深层次的政治再造, 在社会主义, 工人的角色被框定成惟上是从, 跟资本主义对工人的掌控甚少差别。文章认为, 邓小平的改革的一个关键点是精准考量上述实验结果, 纵然将其推向相反方向, 即更加严格地规训雇佣工人。到目前为止, 这种做法的结果是缔造出一种国家话语, 在以 "工人阶级" 的名义的权杖维续中, 它起到了重要作用, 同时将工人 "钉" 于无条件服从的境地。本文讨论的假设是, 虽然这个策略是中国共产党保持稳定的因素之一, 但它也影响 20 世纪政党制度的衰落。

关键词: 文化大革命; 工人阶级; 去政治化; 政党

References

Cheng, Zhongyuan, and Xia Xingzhen. 2004. *Lishi zhuanzhe de qianzou. Deng Xiaoping zai yijiuqiwu* (*The Prelude to the Historical Turning Point: Deng Xiaoping in 1975*). Beijing: Zhongguo qingnian chubanshe.

Feng, Xianzhi, and Jin Chongji. 2003. *Mao Zedong zhuan, 1949–1976* (*Biography of Mao Zedong, 1949–1976*). Beijing: Zhongyang wenxian chubanshe.

Gao, Mobo. 2008. *The Battle for China's Past*. London: Pluto Press.

Hurst, William. 2009. *The Chinese Worker after Socialism*. New York: Cambridge University Press.

Jiang, Hongsheng. 2014. *La Commune de Shanghai et la Commune de Paris*. Paris: La Fabrique.

Katz, Richard S., and Peter Mair. 1995. "Changing models of party organization and party democracy: the emergence of the cartel party." *Party Politics* 1(1), 5–28.

Katz, Richard S., and Peter Mair. 2009. "The cartel party thesis: a restatement." *Perspectives on Politics* 7(4), 753–766.

Mao, Mao [Deng Rong]. 2000. *Wo de fuqin Deng Xiaoping: "wenge" suiye* (*Deng Xiaoping, My Father: The "Cultural Revolution" Years*). Beijing: Zhongyang wenxian chubanshe.

Mao, Zedong. 1998[1974]. "Guanyu lilun wenti de tanhua yaodian, 1974 nian, 12 yue" (Main points of the talk on the theoretical problems, December 1974). In Zhonggong zhongyang wenxian yanjiushi (eds.), *Jianguo yilai Mao Zedong wengao* (*Manuscripts of Mao Zedong after 1949*), Vol. 13. Beijing: Zhongyang wenxian chubanshe, 413–15.

Murphy, Timothy S. 2005. "Introduction." In Antonio Negri, *Books for Burning: Between Civil War and Democracy in 1970s Italy*. London: Verso Books.

Pozzana, Claudia, and Alessandro Russo. 2006. "China's new order and past disorders. a dialogue starting from Wang Hui's analyses." *Critical Asian Studies* 3, 329–351.

Pun, Ngai, and Jenny Chan. 2012. "Global capital, the state, and Chinese workers: the Foxconn experience." *Modern China* 38, 383–410.

Pun, Ngai, Jenny Chan and Mark Selden. 2015. *Morire per un i-Phone.* (Ferruccio Gambino and Devi Sacchetto (eds.)). Milan: Jaca Books.

Russo, Alessandro. 2013. "How did the Cultural Revolution end? The last dispute between Mao Zedong and Deng Xiaoping, 1975." *Modern China* 39(3), 239–279.

Russo, Alessandro. 2016. "The sixties and us." In Alex Taek-Gwang Lee and Slavoj Žižek (eds.), *The Idea of Communism 3: The Seoul Conference*. London: Verso, 137–178.

Schram, Stuart (ed.). 1974. *Mao Tse-Tung Unrehearsed. Talks to the People: Talks and Letters: 1956–71*. Harmondsworth: Penguin.

Wang, Hui. 2003. *China's New Order*. Cambridge, MA: Harvard University Press.

Wang, Hui. 2006. "Depoliticized politics, multiple components of hegemony, and the eclipse of the sixties." *Inter-Asia Cultural Studies* 7(4), 683–700.

Weber, Max. 2015[1919]. "Politics as vocation." In Tony Waters and Dagmar Waters (ed., trans.), *Weber's Rationalism and Modern Society*. New York: Palgrave Macmillan.

Zhongguo gongchandang. 2012. *Gongchandang zhangcheng* (*Constitution of the Chinese Communist Party*). Beijing: Renmin chubanshe.

Debates on Constitutionalism and the Legacies of the Cultural Revolution

Wu Changchang[*]

Abstract
This article focuses on the debate surrounding constitutionalism that has been driven by a constitutionalist alliance of media reporters, intellectuals and lawyers since 2010, and follows its historical trajectory. It argues that this debate forms a discourse with a structuring absence, the roots of which can be traced back to the taboos surrounding the Cultural Revolution, the 1975 Constitution, and everything associated with them. The absence manifests itself in the silence on workers' right to strike, a right which was deleted from the 1982 Constitution in an attempt to correct the ultra-leftist anarchy of the Cultural Revolution. Previous and in contrast to that, there was a Maoist constitutional movement in the Cultural Revolution, represented by the 1975 Constitution, that aimed to protect the constituent power of the workers by legalizing their right to strike. Today, we are witnessing the rise of migrant workers as they struggle for trade union reform and collective bargaining with little support from the party-state or local trade unions. In this context, a third constitutional transformation should be considered that is not a return to the 1975 Constitution but which instead adds some elements which protect labour's right to strike to the 1982 Constitution.

Keywords: China; constituent power; the constitutionalist alliance; the constitutionalist revolution; the constitutional transformation; right to strike

In the middle of 2010, a debate on constitutionalism erupted among intellectuals and netizens at a time of heightened political uncertainty in China.[1] Over the course of the following three years, this debate evolved into a long-running cyber campaign denouncing the Cultural Revolution and the 1975 Constitution.[2] The campaign, which was given a great deal of publicity by the commercial mass media and liberal academic magazines, was driven by a constitutionalist alliance composed of media reporters, intellectuals and lawyers.[3] This

* School of Communication, East China Normal University. Email: wuchangchangpkk@163.com.
1 Constitutionalism, as proposed by the reformists and the constitutionalist alliance in China, refers to the reform of the 1982 Constitution in an attempt to limit the power of the Party and recover the primacy of the state constitution over the Party constitution, not vice versa.
2 For the 1975 Constitution, see People's Republic of China 1975; for discussion of the 1975 Constitution, please see Gardner 1976; Cohen 1978; Hua, Shiping 2014.
3 In my article on online activism in China, I call the constitutionalist alliance the transnational discursive alliance. See Wu 2014.

© The China Quarterly, 2016   doi:10.1017/S0305741016000710   First published online 30 June 2016

alliance often gained the upper hand in separate strands of the debate,[4] such as in the crusade against the "Chongqing anti-mafia" campaign, the "Defending constitutionalism movement," which was in favour of the constitutionalist revolution launched by the magazine *Spring and Autumn Annals* (*Yanhuang chunqiu* 炎黄春秋), and the "Red Guard apology" episode. Finally, the campaign ended in an intra-alliance wrangle that descended into a flame war after May 2013.

In the first four sections of this article, I present an examination of this debate from 2010 onwards and follow its historical trajectory based on analysis of online texts collected from the "Chinese Twitter," Sina Weibo, between July 2010 and August 2013. In an effort to break completely from the traumatic Cultural Revolution and effect a correction to the anarchic leftism of that period, the constitutionalist alliance advocates constituted power instead of constituent power, and insists that the Party should be subject to the constitution and the law. In the constitutional law field, modern constitutional states are considered to be "the assemblage of two different but ultimately antagonistic components."[5] Constituent power, the political activity of producing a constitution, preceding constituted power both chronologically and conceptually, can be exerted once-and-for-all at the founding of a new state, and through its action, "a constitution in a positive sense arises."[6] In contrast, constituted power aims to transform the newly created constitution into a self-sustaining and self-serving legal system that grounds the validity of the constitution and constitutes the core of constitutionalism and the limited government theory.

Building upon the distinction between constituent power and constituted power, I argue that from 1949 until now there have been two opposing constitutional movements in socialist China. One has been driven by constituent power and its constitutional routinization – which includes legalizing workers' right to strike – and is aimed at preventing the creation of a new bureaucratic class within the Party and at strengthening the power of the Chinese Communist Party (CCP) as the sole governing party.[7] The other has been a liberal-inspired constitutional movement or constitutionalist alliance that, since the late 1970s, has sought to use Western-derived legal language to affirm the fundamental role of the 1982 Constitution to subject the Party to the rule of law. The latter movement culminated in the 2011 debates surrounding constitutionalism.[8]

---

4 This observation is different to Yuen 2013, which describes liberals as victims of the party-state.
5 Lindahl 2007, 9.
6 Ibid., 21. For the distinction between constituent power and constituted power in the West, see ibid.; Negri 1999. Here, the detailed distinction between the two powers, especially the trans-lingual practice of those two concepts from the West to China, actually becomes an authentic entry point from which to analyse the debates on constitutionalism in China. Constituent power derives from Bodin, then Rousseau, and culminates in the German jurist Carl Schmitt's priority of constituent power over constituted power, and accordingly, democracy over norm, politics over law. Constituted power is generally acknowledged to have been established by Hans Kelsen, whose book was translated into Chinese in as early as 1996, and has been embraced by the constitutionalist alliance. In contemporary China, the two different positions lead to two schools within the Chinese constitutional law field: constitutional law (or the constitutionalist alliance here) and political law. See Chen, Duanhong 2010.
7 For a new class in the communist society, see Djilas 1962.
8 For these debates on constitutionalism in China, please see Creemers 2015; Yuen 2013.

In the conclusion, I contend that this constitutionalist discourse, dominated by the constitutionalists, has a structuring absence as the alliance is unwilling to consider constituent power and a constitution that protects labour rights. The structuring absence can be traced back to the 1982 Constitution and its deliberate disassociation from the Cultural Revolution, the 1975 Constitution, and everything connected to them. I then reopen the discussion of a constitutional transformation that, rather than restore the Maoist constitutional movement, would nevertheless protect labour rights and the constituent power of the workers by legalizing their right to strike within the existing constitution. I discuss this in the context of the increasing number of workers' strikes in recent years despite the fact that the right to strike was removed from the 1982 Constitution.[9]

The 1982 Constitution and the Rise of Reformist Demands for Constitutionalism

Since the end of the Cultural Revolution, there has been a growing consensus within the CCP that its own ideological emancipation should encompass rule of law. The Party's espousal of the rule of law paved the way for debates on constitutionalism, democracy and human rights amongst the reformists and the intellectuals in the 1990s. This shift was first evident in the official report of the fourth session of the eighth National People's Congress in 1996, and that of the 17th Party Congress in 1997. However, the principle that "developing socialist democracy presupposes a legal system" and the precept of "allowing no organization or individual to operate beyond the law" had already been proclaimed at the third plenum of the 11th Party Congress in 1978.[10]

In response to the emphasis on rule of law, the reformists rose as a radical force within the Party to launch the alternative constitutional movement to promote democratic constitutionalism from within. Most of these reformists were intellectuals, including Li Rui 李锐, Hu Jiwei 胡绩伟 and Liu Zaifu 刘再复,[11] some of whom had played a key role in the Democracy Wall movement and had garnered substantial support from top Party leaders Zhao Ziyang 赵紫阳 and Hu Yaobang 胡耀邦.[12] Leading reformist Liao Gailong 廖盖隆 proposed in his report, referred to as "The 1980 reform" (*gengshenbianfa* 庚申变法), three critical processes that were necessary in order for a new evolutionary constitutionalism to take off: bicameralism in the National People's Congress (NPC); judicial independence; and the separation of powers into a tripartite Party structure of central

9 On the number of workers' strikes, especially by migrant workers during the reform era, see Lee, Ching Kwan 2003, 77–87; and Li 2011.

10 CCCPC Party Literature Research Office 1982, 10. Here, legal system is the earliest version of rule of law, countering rule by law in the Cultural Revolution. See Pan 2003.

11 Hu 1992, 176; Chen, Xiaoping 2010.

12 On the reformists inside the Party, see "Renmin wansui" (Long live the people), *Renmin ribao*, 21 December 1978, 1; and Zhu Huaxin, head of opinion monitoring on the *Renmin ribao* official website, and his revealing serial blogs (Zhu 2010, Ch. 16); also see Qian 2012, 199–200; Chen, Xiaoping 2010.

commissions for Discipline Inspection, Vigilance and Administration.[13] The logical incarnation of the recent online constitutionalist slogans and initiatives can be dated back to these three critical processes.

The rise of these reformists from within the Party and their radical demands for Westernized political reform – and in particular, constitutionalism – often resonated with the aspirations of college students and liberal intellectuals. Inspired by the direct election of NPC delegates at the county and township level in accordance with the 1979 revision of the Electoral Law, and as an immediate response to Liao's "1980 reform," students from Peking University demarcated a district-based constituency in October 1980, and 18 students put themselves forward as candidates for the NPC.[14] This election marked a watershed in the history of constitutionalism in the PRC because the people, for the first time, were conferred voting rights by the constitution rather than by the Party. On 15 November 1980, an appeal to extend the "1980 reform" was delivered by Xu Wenli 徐文立, an influential activist in the social democratic movements launched by college students and radically liberal intellectuals at the time.[15] He argued for all-embracing political reforms, including the separation of the four powers (the Party's power to supervise, legislative power, state administrative power and judicial power) and the introduction of the three freedoms (freedom of thought, of the press, and of association). This appeal was no less vociferous than, and not as circumspect as, the Charter 08 signed by Liu Xiaobo 刘晓波 and other intellectuals in 2008, or even the Jasmine Revolution a few years later.[16]

In addition, an ideological emancipation movement inside the Party after the Cultural Revolution resulted in the promulgation of the "Resolution on certain questions in the history of our Party since the founding of the People's Republic of China" at the sixth plenary session of the 11th Central Committee of the CCP on 27 June 1981.[17] This document re-evaluated the Cultural Revolution as being the result of ultra-leftism. The revised 1982 Constitution was a consequence of this anti-Cultural Revolution mentality and an unprecedentedly assertive attempt to establish the supremacy of the constitution and the ensuing laws in the event of any possible perverse tyranny. A few years after the 1982 Constitution was approved, a circular entitled "All Party members should firmly uphold the socialist legal system" was issued by the Party Central Committee on 10 July 1986. It demanded that the Party, as the sole ruling party, function within a proper legal framework instead of on an extra-legal level.[18]

---

13 Qian 2012, 200–01.
14 See Zhang, Lühao 2010 on electoral law reform. On college students running for the NPC, see Hu and Wang 1990, 250–59; Qian 2008; 2012, 181–82.
15 See Qian 2012, 201–02.
16 For Charter 08, see http://www.2008xianzhang.info/chinese.htm. Accessed 25 May 2016. For an analysis of the Jasmine Revolution in China, see Wu 2014.
17 See CCCPC Party History Research Office 2010.
18 CCCPC Party Literature Research Office 1986, 17–19.

In response to the 1989 Tiananmen incident, the constitutional movement first launched by the reformists in the 1980s inspired a new generation of middle-aged and middle-class intellectuals in the 1990s, who, since the turn of the 21st century, have been joined by media reporters, lawyers and students in the struggle for a constitutionalist revolution. This diffusion represents the passing of the constitutionalist torch from the democratic group in the 1980s to a hopeful alliance that is mostly educated, computer-savvy and technologically literate, and which resents the incompetency, abuses of power and misrepresentations of the government.[19] In turn, this new generation has largely convinced the reformists to adopt democratic constitutionalism as the panacea for all political challenges.

Since the Deng era, the 1982 Constitution has gone through four amendments, including the notable 2004 constitutional amendment that states, "The lawful private properties of citizens shall not be encroached upon."[20] The Party's equivocal attitude towards constitutionalism allows a great deal of wiggle room for the Chinese constitutionalist alliance to trade on the titillation of scandals inside the Party, such as the Gang of Four during the Cultural Revolution and the Bo Xilai 薄熙来 case in 2012, to advocate online for constituted power and democratic constitutionalism. The Charter 08's criticisms and the arrests of human rights activists and lawyers around 2009 have further fuelled the debates on constitutionalism. The debates that have emerged since 2010 are divided about the Cultural Revolution and whether constitutionalism belongs to capitalism or socialism. In other words, the Cultural Revolution is the litmus test that displays China's intellectual political spectrum.

Conventional Intellectual Appeals for Constituted Power: The Bo Xilai Drama and the Crusade against the Chongqing Anti-Mafia Campaign

For the alliance, constitutionalism is no longer a potpourri of abstract ideas but a fixed collection of canonical texts. One example of its dynamic manoeuvres in sync with the political situation is its crusade against the Party's monopoly in Chongqing after 2010. When Bo Xilai came to power in Chongqing and carried out large-scale anti-mafia campaigns from 2009 to 2012, the counterbalancing crusade commenced. It was led first by a group of liberal lawyers, including Li Zhuang 李庄, who volunteered to defend the suspected gang leaders, Gong Gangmo 龚刚模 and Li Qiang 黎强, in 2009.[21] Then, jurists including Zhang Qianfan 张千帆 and the once politically exiled He Weifang 贺卫方 joined the crusade. By early 2010, they had spun the Chongqing anti-mafia activities into an open, intellectual debate

---

19 Wu 2014.
20 The 1982 Constitution was amended four times, in 1988, 1993, 1999 and 2004. For details, see Zhonghua renmin gongheguo xianfa 2014. For the debates surrounding property rights being written into the constitution in 2004, see Wilhelm 2004; Upham 2009.
21 Li Zhuang, a disqualified lawyer, defended gang leader Gong Gangmo, who reported to the prosecutor that Li had induced him to provide false testimony in November 2009. Li was consequently sentenced to 18 months in prison on 9 February 2010 after two court trials.

on constitutionalism. Subsequently, through the power of the internet and social media, intellectuals and their allies were able to capitalize on the unfolding of the Bo Xilai drama in 2012 and the collapse of his Chongqing powerbase and its leftist law and order regime by seizing onto the Li Zhuang case and the anti-mafia campaign to further their argument.

The constitutionalists' tireless advocacy of constitutionalism from the late 1990s onwards[22] implied that only constituted power, which is situated at the core of constitutional democracy, "falls within the sphere of juristic competence."[23] The key to constituted power lies in the constitutionally limited power of the Party and its supervised government exercised in conformity with, instead of outside of, the existing constitution. They cited the *Marbury versus Madison* ruling of 1803, which established judicial review of the actions of the United States government, to argue that China should follow a similar path in order to guarantee the Party's adherence to constitutional limits and restore sanity to political life.[24] Sanity here signifies a state constitution that upholds constitutionalism and constituted power, and which practically seeks to contain, regulate and institutionalize the expansive, and therefore hazardous, leviathan of Party power and the Party constitution. The authority of the state constitution over the Party constitution, and the constituted power's denial of constituent power are what constitutionalism, or rather the constitutionalist revolution, is built upon. This is my point of entry for analysis of the notion shared throughout Weibo, namely, that the Bo Xilai case *is* and *ought to* be the critical step for China to usher in a new era of constitutional democracy walled off from intra-party power struggles.

A research report on the Chongqing anti-mafia campaign was independently completed in 2011 by Tong Zhiwei 童之伟, a law professor, known for his constitutionalist views, at East China University of Political Science and Law.[25] This report was widely circulated in the first half of 2012 and forwarded thousands of times around the Weibo-sphere. Shortly afterwards, the jurist-lawyer alliance demanded that Li Zhuang, Gong Gangmo and other cases be re-tried, claiming that the party-state's power had operated through an arbitrary legal system, which was manifested in the integration of police, prosecutors and courts and in the use of interrogation by torture, with scant regard for procedural justice and human rights. The alliance declared that this inevitably had resulted in miscarriages of justice, and finally had turned the anti-mafia (*da hei* 打黑) campaign into an illegal crackdown (*hei da* 黑打).[26] In brief, the political campaign was compared by netizens to Mussolini's totalitarianism or Stalin's purge in that it was in direct contravention of constitutionalism.[27]

22 For a typical view, see Zhang, Qianfan 2003; Ji 2002.
23 Loughlin 2003, 99.
24 See Zhang, Qianfan 2010; He 2010; 2011. For judicial review in China, see Ip 2012.
25 Tong 2011.
26 He 2010; He, Weifang. 2012. http://weibo.com/weifanghe. Accessed 7 July 2012, now deleted; also Tong 2011.
27 Guo, Yanbin. 2012. 16 March, http://weibo.com/hbu888. Accessed 22 March 2012, now deleted; Diaoyu. 2012. 24 March, http://weibo.com/2186483177/yblDby3vS. Accessed 2 April 2012.

Bo Xilai is a high-profile "princeling" from a Party elite family background. Once a member of the Conservative Red Guards during the Cultural Revolution, he became a chief representative of Party elites who opposed liberal constitutionalism, and rose to sudden prominence for his promotion of pro-people redistribution policies and his overtly Maoist governing style.[28] Therefore, following the exposure of the Bo Xilai scandal, constitutionalist intellectuals maintained that if Bo and his wife were not tried by rule of law, it would mean that China had fallen into an abyss of human rights' abuses.[29] As for the cyber-leftists, they asserted that the constitutionalist alliance's call to resolve the Bo Xilai and other related cases within a legal and constitutional framework was tantamount to depoliticization, an effort to cover up intra-party power struggles.[30] Eventually, the constitutionalist intellectuals and their allies' obsession with a conventional conception of constitutionalism, in addition to their aversion to mass democracy and dictatorship, led them to promote the constitutionalist revolution through their own mouthpiece, *Spring and Autumn Annals*.

Implosion within the Party: *Spring and Autumn Annals* and its Endeavours to Promote Constitutionalism, the 1982 Constitution and the Red Guard Apology Incident

Since 1978, critiques of the Cultural Revolution have chiefly benefited Party reformists, who have access to – or even own – the mass media and thus take the initiative in shaping public opinion and social mobilization. They support further marketization, privatization and global integration. Through declassified CCP files and other yet unopened materials, they also re-narrate and deconstruct the history of the CCP and PRC. To exorcize the spectre of the Cultural Revolution, the reformists inside the Party, who are allied with the intellectuals and other media forces, prefer constituted power to the potentially anarchic constituent power. Introducing American and Western constitutions and constitutionalism, they stress that for post-Cultural Revolution China, constitutionalism means a move towards separating Party from state power, and towards reversing the political positioning of the Party over the law, which, although deleted from the 1982 Constitution in words, is how it goes in practice. This goal is exactly what *Spring and Autumn Annals* set its sights on. *Spring and Autumn Annals* is a monthly reformist academic journal.[31] Its reformist and academic credentials give it leverage within the Party and have enabled it to survive several censorship crises.[32]

---

28 For an analysis of Red Song Singing and the "mafia strike" campaign in Chongqing, see Zhao, Yuezhi 2012; and for an analysis of the Bo Xilai affair, see Lin 2012; Wang, Hui 2012.
29 For a typical view, see He 2011; also He 2007.
30 For a typical view, see Cui 2011.
31 On the magazine, see Mazur 1999.
32 Former editor-in-chief, Wu Si, has stated in several interviews with the VOA, the BBC, Radio Free Asia and *Mingpao Daily* that the *Spring and Autumn Annals* has been criticized, punished or had its independent editorial work interfered with by the Ministry of Culture, Ministry of Publicity and Press and Publication Administration more than ten times since its launch in 1991. See http://history.dwnews.com/news/2013-01-05/59061334-2.html. Accessed 24 May 2016.

Over time, it has gained a reputation among subscribers and within Chinese academia for its combination of reformist perspective and historical critiques.

Since as early as 2008, *Spring and Autumn Annals* has been a high-profile and fearless champion of such values as freedom of speech, human rights and constitutionalism, and has demonstrated its willingness to adopt a daring stance that runs counter to the Party line.[33] For example, an open letter to the NPC was posted on the internet to overseas media, just before the fifth plenary session of the 17th CCP Central Committee, openly expressing dissatisfaction with Xi Jinping's 习近平 21 July 2010 lecture, "Resolutely oppose any erroneous distortion or vilification of CCP history."[34] Led by Mao's former secretary Li Rui 李锐, 23 Party elders, who were either editors, advisors or contributors to *Spring and Autumn Annals*, urged an end to press censorship in China.[35] They claimed that there should be no taboo subjects in Party literature and that citizens should enjoy freedom of speech. In October 2010, the *Spring and Autumn Annals* published a posthumous article by former president of Renmin University, Xie Tao 谢韬, which echoed the intellectual criticisms of Bo's Chongqing model and advocated for constitutionalism. In this article, Xie encouraged readers to believe that only individualism and liberalism can save China and called for vigilance against any backlash from domestic leftists who agitate for the Cultural Revolution and for the seizure of power from bourgeois reformists.[36]

Up until this point, the editorial staff were only testing the margins of what the highest leadership would tolerate. As soon as the Bo Xilai scandal broke and before Xi took power in 2012, they tried to table a constitutionalist agenda for the top leadership, and often used foreign media and social media to boost their standpoint.

On 16 November 2012, *Spring and Autumn Annals* and the Research Centre for Constitutional and Administrative Law in Peking University held the "Reform consensus forum," with hundreds of prominent intellectuals attending. In December, a special issue ran a cover story under the title "Governing by rule of law, rule of constitution." In response to Hu Jintao's 胡锦涛 report to the 18th CCP Conference, as the preface to this special issue stated, the attendees concentrated on relations between the power of the Party and the constitution and its derivative laws. Two requirements for governing by rule of law are highlighted: the Party should function under the constitution and the law, and the relationship between the Party and the state should be clarified. The 1982 Constitution was thus extolled for its excision of the clause, "NPC under the leadership of CCP."[37]

33 See the January and August 2008 and January 2009 editions. In September 2008, a biography of Zhao Ziyang, written by Sun Zhen, the former chief of Xinhua's Sichuan bureau, was published nine months before the 20th anniversary of the Tiananmen Square incident. It is not surprising that the *Spring and Autumn Annals* website was shut down several times and its editor-in-chief forced to quit in 2014. However, the journal has survived.
34 Xi 2010.
35 Bandurski 2010.
36 Xie 2010, 1–2.
37 Hong 2012, 1–2.

Even so, many intellectuals present at the forum remained pessimistic, as the normative relationship between the Party and NPC, although regulated at the 16th CCP Conference in 2002, had not yet been realized.[38] Here, indeed, appears a modern Chinese constitutional paradox within the current framework of Western constitutionalism: the first-in-command of the local Party committee is usually also first-in-command of the local NPC.[39] This political arrangement amounts to a constitutionally and jurisprudentially unacceptable and illogical anomaly, namely that power supervises itself. Moreover, power cannot be overturned and therefore the ideal constitutional review process cannot be guaranteed. Soon after, on 25 December 2012, Zhang Qianfan drafted and posted on the internet a document entitled "Reform consensus petition," which was signed by many of the participants at the recently concluded forum.[40] The petition called for the entrenchment of the market economy and the enforcement of the constitution, in expectation of "a constitutionally governed China."[41] Inevitably, these calls were criticized from inside the Party for being a slanderous attack on and an attempt to subvert the Party. However, it is also the case that in the name of constitutionalism, the emphasis on the separation of the party in charge of political leadership from the state which operates through the NPC to serve the people, when combined with the deepening of marketization, promotes an ever more capitalized and commercialized China.

At the beginning of 2013, an online protest erupted against censorship, along with an offline "flower" campaign in which activists dedicated bouquets in passionate support of *Southern Weekend* (*Nanfang zhoumo* 南方周末 – allegedly the most libertarian newspaper in China) after it had been forced to withdraw its New Year's editorial entitled "Dreams of China, dreams of constitutionalism."[42] In response to the situation, an editorial with the eye-catching headline, "The constitution as the consensus of the political reforms," loomed large on the cover of the first issue of the *Spring and Autumn Annals* in 2013. The editorial urged a united movement to defend the constitution, based on the suspension of differences between rightists and leftists.[43] The editorial was referring to the 1982 Constitution and not the 1975 Constitution. Some of the provisions of the 1982 Constitution were cited in the article as evidence of the supreme status of the NPC and to reaffirm the fundamental principle of the Party being under the constitution. However, although these constitutional provisions have only

---

38 Most jurists hold that the key existing constitutional problem is failure to implement the 1982 constitutional clarification of relations between the CCP and NPC. See Zhang, Qianfan 2010; and Yuen 2013.

39 Hong 2012, 2. Although in the 1975 Constitution, the NPC is led by the CCP (a clause which was deleted from the 1982 Constitution), the political arrangement that the local Party committee secretary, through legal process, is to serve concurrently as the local NPC director has been carried out since the 1990s.

40 Zhang, Qianfan. 2012. "Reform consensus petition," *21comm*, now deleted; see also Gao, Yu. 2013. http://www.l99.com/EditText_view.action?textId=630589. Accessed in July 2013.

41 Oikawa 2013.

42 See Wu 2014.

43 Editorial Staff 2013, 1.

existed in word and not in deed, by publishing them the magazine also revealed its constitutionalist position. Article 13 on the protection of citizens' private property by the state and Article 37 on freedom of the individual were highlighted in particular in a veiled reference to the abuses of the Chongqing anti-mafia campaign and other vicious cases of violations of citizens' property rights.[44] But, significantly, the excised 1975 right to strike for workers was not touched upon by the constitutionalist alliance and remained a taboo subject, despite their arguments against such prohibitions.

In contrast to the 2013 campaign to defend the 1982 Constitution, which was a media event primarily led by the constitutionalist alliance of reformists and jurists, the earlier constitution protection movement that had begun online in 2002 was dominated by leftist intellectuals who proclaimed a desire to hold on to the socialist essence of the existing constitution. Kuang Xinnian 旷新年, a leftist professor in the department of Chinese literature at Tsinghua University, and Lao Tian 老田, an independent scholar and former salesman in a state-owned enterprise, both supported the abandonment of a constitution that emphasized the property rights of citizens in strong favour of a constitution that prioritized the rights of labour. What they really wanted to protect was socialism, and they argued that the constitution should function as a structural bulwark against both the loss of state-owned assets and common wealth and the formation of a bureaucratic bourgeoisie inside the Party.[45] This latter issue was also a concern of Mao's when he was in power. In their view, by guaranteeing the property rights of citizens, the 1982 Constitution constitutes a regression to a thoroughly "capitalist oligarchic constitution." Thus, what is at stake for China is not an amendment to the 1982 Constitution but rather the defence of the socialist constitution based on labour rights. In other words, the issue should be one of protecting workers rather than capital.[46] It is unsurprising that this online movement was short-lived and was almost entirely brushed aside by the jurists and lawyers.

Soon after, whilst covertly establishing its own political line yet overtly adhering to the Party discourse on the Cultural Revolution, *Spring and Autumn Annals* pushed its luck further by orchestrating apologies from former Red Guards. In June 2013, it published a short apology written by a former Red Guard.[47] This garnered an inordinate amount of attention online and galvanized domestic media outlets such as *Southern Weekend, Xiaoxiang Morning News* and *China Youth News* to publish similar apologies or confessions, including one by Chen Xiaolu 陈小鲁, the son of Marshal Chen Yi 陈毅.[48]

---

44 Ibid.
45 Lao 2002.
46 Kuang 2002.
47 Liu, Boqin 2013.
48 See Song 2013; Wen 2013; and Chen, Xiaolu 2013. Early in October 2010, a Red Guard apology appeared in *Nanfang zhoumo* for the purpose of denouncing the Cultural Revolution. See Wang, Youqin 2010a.

However, the media event confused the two different groups of former Red Guards: the children of senior leaders (the Conservatives) and the ordinary students (the Rebels).[49] It was some members of the former group who now made public apologies in the commercial mass media. In the early stage of the Cultural Revolution, the Conservatives had preached the "bloodline theory"[50] and had participated in chaotic and ritual denunciations, as well as the terrorization and humiliation of the "seven black categories" in August 1966, known to history as "Red August."[51] Ironically, since the 1980s, some of this group have become members of the "red second generation," which refers to the children of privileged, top leaders and China's nouveau riche. More significantly, they joined together with members of the aforementioned "seven black categories," whom they had traumatized and physically tortured, to denounce the Red Guard movement and the Cultural Revolution.[52]

When considering the results of an online survey conducted in May 2013 that asked the question, "Do you miss the Cultural Revolution?" it is not hard to see why the constitutionalist alliance and media outlets such as *Spring and Autumn Annals* and *Southern Weekend* engineered Red Guard apologies. This survey, carried out by Tencent, one of the biggest private IT companies in China, originally aimed to shape public opinion in order to contain the "contagion" of commemorating the Cultural Revolution. However, controversially, 78 per cent of respondents voted "yes," and the result was hastily deleted.[53] Nominally, the alliance and media's objective behind the apology movement and social survey was to face up to "our" history; in fact, the media events were motivated by a fear of a return to the Cultural Revolution and the 1975 Constitution.

Different evaluations of the 1975 Constitution determine whether China is seen as being on the road to serfdom or freedom, absolutism or constitutionalism.

---

49 (Mis)understanding the Cultural Revolution as an "anti-rightist" campaign, middle school students with "red" family backgrounds became very active as soon as the Cultural Revolution broke out. This Conservative group classified people according to "class background" (the bloodline theory) and attacked the "seven black categories" (landlords, rich peasants, reactionaries, bad elements, rightists, bourgeoisie, gangs). However, at the beginning of October 1966, the Rebels (with bad family backgrounds) challenged the supremacy of the Conservatives in Beijing by attacking the bloodline theory and highlighting their position as a struggle for equality. See Lee, Hong Yung 1975; Walder 2012.

50 The "bloodline theory" was first criticized by Yu Luoke, who was sentenced to death in 1970. Yu was well known during the early stage of the Cultural Revolution for his fierce opposition to the governing Party policy of judging a person only by their family background and his advocacy of human rights and democracy. See Thurston 1984–1985; Unger 2007, 109–120.

51 During "Red August," the famous Peking Red Guard Pickets group was founded, which evolved into the Joint Action Committee in October. Through these organizations, the Conservatives began to commit acts of violence, first against teachers in middle school and then against the "seven black categories." See Walder 2012. Since 2008, *Spring and Autumn Annals* has published victim or witness accounts of Red Guard activities in 1966. For "Red August," see Wang, Youqin 2010b; also MacFarquhar and Schoenhals (2006, 117–131) provide an authoritative description of the Red Guards' activities in Ch. 7 of their book. See also Weigelin-Schwiedrzik and Cui in this volume.

52 Xianzhi. 2013. "Nanfangxi zaichao 'hongweibing daoqian' juxin hezai?" (Why has the "Red Guards' apology" incident emerged again?), 19 June, http://www.szhgh.com/html/02/n-26302.html. Accessed 20 June 2014.

53 The Tencent 2013 survey result has been deleted. However, it is worth noting – and thought-provoking – that the majority of Tencent users were born in the 1980s and 1990s.

Formulated during the Cultural Revolution, the 1975 Constitution has been la-belled as the outcome of ultra-leftism, both officially and also by the reformists and the constitutionalist alliance. It included some articles that were directly at odds with the 1982 Constitution and the political aims of the reformists and the alliance – for example, Article 8, in which socialist public property is seen as sacrosanct, and Article 13, which defines, as the new forms of socialist revolu-tion created by the people, the "four great freedoms," namely, to speak out freely, air views freely, hold debates freely and to write big-character posters. Those two articles, now long gone, are both literally and practically closest to what constitu-ent power implies: the social liberation of the people, or to be concise, the work-er–peasant alliance. On the other hand, Article 28 of the 1975 Constitution grants citizens the rights to freedom of speech, communication, the press, assembly, as-sociation, and participation in parades, demonstrations and, above all, strikes. It implies that workers, as legal citizens of the PRC, have the constitutional right to strike. The people who own their constituent power and the citizens who have their right to strike constituted the radical and expansive Maoist "constitutional movement."[54] In contrast, the constitutionalist alliance takes a different ap-proach that walks away from a positive understanding of "great democracy" or the "four great freedoms," as manifested in its appropriation of constituted power and rule of law, to construct a stable constitutionalist norm not just for the legal containment of the Party, but also in its eagerness for China to take its place in contemporary capitalist globalization.[55]

Conflicts within the Constitutionalist Alliance: Socialist versus Universal Constitutionalism, and the Father of the New China Incident

On 13 May 2013, a message appeared on Weibo and Chinese news sites describ-ing a classified directive, the so-called Document No. 9, "Concerning the situ-ation in the ideological sphere," which had allegedly come from the Central Committee General Office of the Party leadership. The directive called for all officials to be on the alert for seven potentially damaging values and ideas (ques-tioning reform and opening; criticizing past errors by the Party; Western-style media independence; economic neo-liberalism; civil society; universal human rights; and constitutional democracy).[56] The message triggered an avalanche of mixed reactions throughout the online community, especially in the Weibo-sphere. The secret directive indicated that, instead of going along in order to get along, the brand-new Xi administration was ruling with an iron

54 Marx also mentioned the constitutional movement. See Marx 1975[1871]. Kuang and Lao Tian's online "constitution protection" movement and Feng's call for a constitutional transformative moment to le-galize workers' right to strike in 2013 can be seen as an extension of this constitutional movement from the Cultural Revolution to the present.
55 The constitutionalist alliance, along with its appeal for the constitutional dream, illustrates Backer's analysis of constitutionalism as a meta-ideology. See Backer 2009.
56 Oikawa 2013.

fist. The denunciation of constitutionalism prompted a salvo of attacks by liberals. Most netizens derided the commentaries, stating, for instance, that "the CCP is delivering the Northern Korean blow."[57]

However, the focus of debates turned quickly to the rifts within the constitutionalist alliance that centred on the question of socialist constitutionalism versus universal constitutionalism.[58] The socialist constitutionalists see no contradiction between socialism and constitutionalism and believe that the constitution can impose restrictions on the Party via judicial review.[59] The universalists, on the other hand, believe in American-style constitutionalism and, ultimately, a transition to multi-party democracy. In late May and early June, debates about socialist constitutionalism became an internet sensation. Using his Weibo account as a platform, the famed historian Zhang Lifan 章立凡 encouraged everyone to engage in a free debate on the hot topic of constitutionalism, and especially the question of whether constitutionalism is necessary for contemporary China.[60] Shortly afterwards, an article entitled "Constitutionalism is key to the country under rule of law," published more than four years previously by Xu Chongde 许崇德, the honorary president of the Chinese Constitution Studies Association, was wheeled out to counter the argument that vilified constitutionalism as capitalist or as a plot to subvert China. In his article, Xu refuted both the liberal and the revolutionary arguments against China's constitution. He concluded that constitutionalism must be an integral and imperative part of socialism.[61] As a result, Xu rose to prominence as the core figure in the socialist constitutional force.

Other key figures in the socialist constitutional school of thought include Zhang Qianfan, Hua Bingxiao 华炳啸, director of the Institute of Political Communications at Northwestern University in China, and Tong Zhiwei. Starting on 27 May 2013, Tong delivered a series of essays via his blog and microblog on what socialist constitutionalism means to China and explaining his understanding of the concept. According to this school of thought, the constitution's primary role is to legitimize the CCP as the ruling Party; however, it should also lay down the foundations that guarantee the basic rights of citizens.[62]

Predictably, the more hawkish members of the original constitutionalist alliance rose up against the socialist constitutional ideas by invoking the rhetoric of constitutionalism voiced by Mao and other top CCP leaders from before

---

57 See Wenweneryage. 2013. 24 May. http://helanonline.cn/article/4256. Accessed 22 June 2013.
58 The socialist constitutionalists are mainly composed of liberal progressive intellectuals and lawyers, while the universal constitutionalists are mostly journalists and columnists.
59 The socialist constitutionalists believe that affirming the CCP as the sole governing Party is a prerequisite for China to take the constitutionalist direction. They map out a constitutionalism with Chinese characteristics, in which the Party establishes its constitution and then, rather than restoring Maoist permanent revolution and rule by law with the Party in control, operates under the law, thus transforming the dictatorship of the proletariat into a constitutional rule. See Zhang, Qianfan 2010; Tong 2011; 2013.
60 Zhang, Qianfan 2013; however, Zhang's Sina Weibo account has since been cancelled.
61 Xu 2013[2008].
62 Tong 2013; Hua, Bingxiao 2013.

1949, rhetoric which is rarely seen in official publications. They also quoted speeches given by Hu Jintao on several public occasions, in which he acknowledged the positive values of universal ideas.[63] Prominent magazine editor Xiao Shu 笑蜀 insisted that under no circumstances "could any qualifiers, even just an adjective, be put in front of constitutionalism," for constitutionalism must be "supreme," "unconditional" and "the first principle."[64] Zhao Chu 赵楚, an irascible military expert and columnist, held that the advocates of socialist constitutionalism had committed three deadly sins, one of which was their attempt at the theoretical endorsement of the current party-state and its legitimacy by making use of European leftist democratic socialism, which was actually precisely the negation of the party-state's ideological orthodoxy.[65] The universal constitutionalists proclaimed an inevitable ontological shift from rule by a single-party dictatorship to constitutionalism – another version of a Fukuyama-style "end of history."[66] This stance led to an ugly and open divorce with their previous allies, the socialist constitutionalists.

In no time, the debates risked degenerating into a bitter argument centred on socialism versus capitalism. Henceforth, the conclusion that constitutionalism, just like the market, is the common cause of all mankind took hold. Furthermore, casting the party-state and its legitimacy as anti-constitutional, or dichotomizing the most democratic and libertarian societies and the most authoritarian states, obscures and inverts the political history of constituent power and its socialist essence. For the constitutionalists, constitutionalism is reified as "a substantive force," separating itself from human relations. This is a "terminological fetishism" that turns constitutionalism into a fixed object "whose effectiveness in the world appears to stand apart from specific social relations."[67]

When a lecture delivered by the renowned conservative scholar, Liu Xiaofeng 刘小枫, was posted online in mid-May 2013 prior to being published in the September 2013 issue of *Open Times*, the debate became more complex. Liu, who in past decades had gained liberal intellectuals' respect for his critiques of the Cultural Revolution,[68] now appeared to turn to the left by openly discussing the problem of who the father of the nation was. The online transcripts of Liu's lecture that were posted on *iFeng* and *21ccom.net* were taken out of context, leading to a misinterpretation of Liu's evaluation of Mao Zedong.[69] Liu's positioning of Mao as the "father" of China and his confirmation of the positive values of the

63 Mao's "On new democratic constitutionalism," originally published in 1940, and Hu Jintao's lecture on universalistic values were forwarded by jurist Xu Xin and He Weifang through their Weibo accounts. See Xu Xin. 2013. http://weibo.com/1701401324/zxQqLs7CN. Accessed 12 September 2013; and He Weifang. 2013. http://weibo.com/weifanghe/1437151321678. Accessed 12 September 2013.
64 Xiao 2013.
65 Zhao, Chu 2013. Along with Zhao, He Weifang and Liu Junning, who even denounces socialist constitutionalism as constitutionalist Nazism, can be seen as the hard core of universalists. For more, see http://www.hybsl.cn/zonghe/zuixinshiliao/2014-09-23/48390.html. Accessed 24 May 2016.
66 Fukuyama 1992.
67 Rofel 1999, 109.
68 See, e.g., Liu, Xiaofeng 1988.
69 See Liu, Xiaofeng 2013a for the online transcripts.

Cultural Revolution were intolerable to Chinese liberal intellectuals. In fact, Liu's edited version, published in *Open Times*, justifies the CCP as the ruling party in light of its past, and therefore argues that the highly polarized question of how Mao Zedong is evaluated is the kernel of the debate on constitutionalism.[70]

Spring and Autumn Annals responded with a cover story by Zhang Qianfan in June 2013. Pinpointing the difference between the preamble to China's four constitutions and the preamble to the American constitution, Zhang wrote that although "jurists inside and outside China debate whether constitutional preambles are legally binding in the same way as the main body of the constitution," the preamble "should embody its essence." It should therefore include the constituent subject and the basic principles, rather than merely provide a eulogistic description of historical achievements in order to establish the legitimacy of the ruling party as the ideological founder, or highlight the names of the ruling party and top leaders, as is the case for the constitutions of both China and North Korea.[71] Zhang's views indirectly echoed those of Zhang Xuezhong 张雪忠, a professor at East China University of Political Science and Law, who wrote an open letter to the minister of education to request the removal of Marxism, Mao Zedong Thought and Deng Xiaoping Theory as compulsory courses in college.[72]

In the latest debates on constitutionalism, the alliance, although split internally, has focused on discredited single-party rule. For them, rather than an essential power base of the nation, constituent power has so far been a definitive aspect of mass democracy, the Maoist constitutional movement, and the people's dictatorship during the Cultural Revolution in particular. Therefore, constituted power's role is to locate the workers, represented nominally by the Party, under the rule of law, as well as to limit the Party's power.

Returning to a Constitution that Protects Labour Rights: the Right to Strike, Constitutional Transformation and Legacies of the Cultural Revolution

Liu's speech on the Cultural Revolution and its constitutional significance deepened the intellectual divide and caused the re-alignment of academic politics. His published article was the precursor to Tsinghua University professor of law Feng Xiang's 冯象 constitutional theory. Feng's discussion circulated around cyberspace in June 2013. In his article, Feng debated the following questions: should the right to strike be written into the constitution, as was the case in 1975, or be put under rule of law, as in the 1982 Constitution? How can workers

---

70 Liu, Xiaofeng 2013b.
71 Zhang Qianfan (2013) points out approvingly that the CCP appears in the 1975 Constitution 12 times but not at all in the body of the 1982 Constitution.
72 Zhang Xuezhong's Sina Weibo account was cancelled soon after, and then the Ministry of Education replied. See Hai 2011 and van Sant 2013 for VOA reports. For the open letter, see Zhang, Xuezhong 2011.

regain their constituent power and thus reclaim their socialist state by launching strikes which are now illegal within the existing constitution? And, finally, how can we evaluate the legacies of the Cultural Revolution and the 1975 Constitution?

These questions have become a structuring absence in the current debates on constitutionalism and in the ongoing constitutionalist revolution. This absence reveals that the alliance is actually driven by a deep-seated fear of the Maoist Cultural Revolution and a determination to wipe out the legacies of its lawless terror. For neither the Party organs and the top leadership nor the constitutionalists talk about the workers' right to strike, which had been institutionalized within the 1975 Constitution as the supreme principle of the socialist legal system.

As far as the workers' right to strike is concerned, Mao insisted that only by writing it into the 1975 Constitution could the contradiction between the state, factory managers and workers be resolved.[73] This is clearly confirmed by the file entitled "Instructions on coping with strikes," issued by the Central Committee in 1957, in which the expressed purpose of supporting the right to strike was, above all, to overcome officialdom and expand the reach of socialist democracy.[74] This move strengthened routinized constituent power in the form of workers' strikes, which not only confirmed workers as the leading class but also legitimated the CCP by instituting a bottom-up mode of supervision of its governance. Mao's 1967 call on the workers to prioritize production was confirmation that he had transferred his faith to them and away from the Red Guards.[75]

However, in 1982, the right to strike was excised from the constitution with the aim of casting off the ill effects of the Cultural Revolution. According to Zhang Youyu 张友渔, "the right to strike is the product of China's ultra-leftist thought," and "the resulting halt in production damages all the people including the workers."[76] In the new century, workers' strikes of all kinds have posed a challenge to the increasingly neo-liberalized economic restructuring. To a certain extent, it can be said that the party-state's shift towards "economic construction" paved the way for the constitutionalist revolution discussed by Zhang Qianfan in his article, "The Copernicus revolution."[77] This constitutionalist revolution demands that judicial review and constitutional review should bring China's constitution close to the people (or, to be exact, the citizens).

It follows, then, that a question arises concerning the essential orientation of the constitutionalist revolution. On the one hand, despite maintaining deep resentment of the Cultural Revolution, the constitutionalist alliance has shared

---

73 Mao 1977[1956].
74 See CCCPC Party Literature Research Office 1994, 153–54.
75 After witnessing the factional scuffles created by the Red Guards in Peking University and Tsinghua University in 1967, Mao decided to stress the leading role of the working class in the Cultural Revolution. See Harding 1991; also see "Gongren jieji bixu lingdao yiqie" (The working class must lead everything), *Hongqi* 1968, 2, 3.
76 Zhang, Youyu 1982, 14. For a typical view, see Bao 1982, whose article was published in *Workers Daily*, supposedly a mouthpiece for ordinary workers.
77 Zhang, Qianfan 2005; also see Zhang, Qianfan 2011.

the dividends of the "four great freedoms" in the cyber-era as part of an anti-corruption campaign from below, conducted inside and outside the Party. The revived practices of supervision by the people beyond the NPC system during the Cultural Revolution[78] are entirely in line with the way the alliance launched the constitutionalist revolution, sparked the debates on constitutionalism and acted as whistle-blowers to reveal the abuses of power and corruption of senior officials.[79]

On the other hand, regardless of the Cultural Revolution-style of their online activities and media mobilization, the alliance's protection of the 1982 Constitution is tantamount to the Maoist constitutional movement during the Cultural Revolution being superseded by the constitutionalist revolution. The Maoist constitutional movement is represented by the 1975 Constitution, a revolutionary constitution[80] (albeit with many arbitrary flaws and ultra-leftist language), and finds its legitimacy in a "continuous revolution"[81] approach under the constituent power conferred on workers, which is different to the constituted power in the Anglo-American legal system. Furthermore, the 1975 Constitution stresses dynamic revolution to protect its socialist core and therefore the centrality, agency and cultural leadership of the ordinary workers in public and political life.

In contrast to the Mao-dominated constitutional system, designed to allow for transformation should a bureaucratic privileged class appear, the modern constitutionalist revolution aims both to absorb the constituent power enjoyed by the working class during the Cultural Revolution into juristic categories, and to prioritize the Party's constituted power. To a certain degree, the alliance's advocacy of rule of law and rejection of the rule of man of the Maoist era[82] is legitimized by their politically radical role in controlling corruption inside the Party. However, they also de-radicalize and de-politicize workers as a whole by stressing equality before the law, turning all individuals – including workers – into citizens, and agreeing that local governments should deal with workers' strikes based on labour contracts and private property in an effort to integrate them into the increasingly neo-liberalized economic structure.

---

78 Mao 1977[1956]; "great democracy" is also at the root of the alliance's fear of the tyranny of the majority, based on what they suffered during the Cultural Revolution. See also Thornton in this volume.
79 Guobin Yang traces such online activities back to media during the Cultural Revolution such as big-character posters. See Yang 2011.
80 Xia Yong (2003) points out that there are three kinds of constitutions around the world: revolutionary constitutions, reform constitutions and constitutionalist constitutions. A revolutionary constitution aims to strengthen the revolutionary outcome, and its legitimacy is rooted not in the past but in the revolution itself.
81 Mao first put forward the theory of permanent revolution in 1958, calling for the technological revolution to guarantee the unity of politics and technology. See CCCPC Party Literature Research Office 1992, 25; also see Schram 1971.
82 In 1958, during the "anti-rightist" campaign, Mao pointed out that, "we cannot rule the majority by law … on the contrary, we count on resolutions and meetings four times a year, and criminal law and civil law are not to be used to maintain the social order." This is what liberal jurists call legal nihilism. See CCCPC Party Literature Research Office 1992, 25.

Therefore, during this time of political and economic transformation in contemporary China, the right to strike and the constituent subject within the 1975 Constitution demonstrate historical foresight. In the context of rising worker demands that have had little support from the party-state or local trade unions in the past, which has paradoxically rendered "the peasant–worker alliance" in the 1982 Constitution little more than a delusion, regardless of whether strikers are state-owned enterprise staff, employees in private or foreign companies, or "new labour" composed of migrant workers,[83] the confirmation of the right to strike indicates a potential constitutional transformative moment.

Here, I propose that this constitutional transformation should evolve not from a return to the 1975 Constitution and the horrifying and redundant revolutionization of politics and everyday life during the Cultural Revolution, but rather be realized by adding the positive elements of the 1975 Constitution that protected workers' right to strike to the 1982 Constitution, and thus relocate workers as the original masters of the country to grasp and defend the socialist core of the existing constitution. From this perspective, the workers' strikes, in spite of divergent views among workers' groups, should be viewed as the inevitable re-radicalization and expansion of normal politics. With the loss of public property, the pauperization of workers and fast-growing social inequality, strikes can be regarded as workers' practical, concrete and continual exercise of their constituent power to fill the otherwise unbridgeable gap between the constitutionally constrained government and the governed, or the workers. This would be an orientation towards the socialist constitution not in a populist way but rather constitutionally, and would be antagonistic to the constitutionalist project of the elite.

Accordingly, during the ongoing political reform and economic renewal in contemporary China, constitutional transformation should not only be part of a struggle to build a new world but also the revelation of an organic unity, and evolve to create a constitution that protects labour rights. This redeployed concept of constitutional transformation helps to recover social space not as a political space of representation but as "a place of the mass exercise of power," that is, the re-politicization of social space as "the direct terrain of its operativity" in the current political economy.[84] Also, it helps to liberate, not dominate, labour in its radicality, expansivity and constancy. This must be a refinement of the legacies of the Cultural Revolution and inscription of them into the 1982 Constitution, a true constitutional transformation. That is exactly what Negri's "constitutive disutopia" refers to,[85] or what Feng describes as a starting point of the constitutional transformative moment.[86] It is the last thing that the constitutionalist alliance and its media outlets want.

---

83 On "new" or migrant labour, see Wang, Hui 2014; also see Lin 2015.
84 Negri 1999, 197, 205.
85 Negri invented this concept to demonstrate the way insurgencies of constituent power help to break the schema of modernity or go beyond the project of rationalization. See Negri 1999, 312–323.
86 Feng 2014.

Acknowledgment

I wish to thank Jisoo Lee for her role in patiently strengthening this manuscript.

Biographical note

Wu Changchang is associate professor in the School of Communication, East China Normal University. His particular interests include new media and online activism, and the political economy of communication in China

摘要: 文章聚焦于 2010 年以来在中国网络上爆发的宪政争论及其历史轨迹, 这场争论由媒体记者、知识分子与律师所组成的宪政话语联盟所推动。文章指出, 这场关于宪政的话语存在一种结构性的不在场, 这种不在场可以追溯到文化大革命、 1975 年宪法以及与此有关的禁忌话题; 它体现在对工人的罢工权的不讨论与沉默, 而工人的罢工权已经从 1982 年宪法中删除。作为对文化大革命期间 "极左无政府主义" 行为的一种 "纠正", 1982 年宪法删除工人罢工权不仅服务于当时以经济建设为中心的国家政策, 更成为一场宪政革命的开端。与之相反, 当然也在这场宪政革命之前, 文化大革命期间涌动着一场毛主义的宪法运动; 这集中体现在 1975 年宪法上, 它以保护工人的制宪权为己任, 例如在宪法的范围内保障了工人的罢工权。当前, 农民工罢工浪潮此起彼伏, 他们主张进行工会改革, 并展开薪酬的集体协商, 却并非总是得到当地工会与当地政府的支持。在这一情境下, 文章认为应当发起一场宪法转型运动, 作为第 3 条道路, 它既不同于 1975 年宪法, 又主张在既定的 1982 年宪法中加入保护工人罢工权的条款。

关键词: 制宪权; 宪政联盟; 宪政革命; 宪法转型; 罢工权

References

Backer, Larry C. 2009. "From constitution to constitutionalism: a global framework for legitimate public power systems." *Penn State Law Review* 3, 671–732.

Bandurski, David. 2010. "Du Daozheng on Hu and Wen, and reform," *China Media Project*, 14 October, http://cmp.hku.hk/2010/10/14/8085/. Accessed 15 April 2014.

Bao, Yin. 1982. "Quxiao bagong de biyaoxing" (On the necessity of deleting the right to strike). *Qianxian* 7, 18–20.

CCCPC Party History Research Office. 2010. "Guanyu jianguo yilai dang de ruogan lishi wenti de jueyi" (Resolution on certain questions in the history of our Party since the founding of the People's Republic of China). Beijing: CCP Party History Press.

CCCPC Party Literature Research Office. 1982. *Sanzhong quanhui yilai zhuyao wenxian xuanbian* (*Documents since the Third Plenary Session*). Beijing: Renmin chubanshe.

CCCPC Party Literature Research Office. 1986. *Shierda yilai zhongyao wenxian huibian* (*Important Documents since the 12th Central Committee of CCP*). Beijing: Renmin chubanshe.

CCCPC Party Literature Research Office. 1992. *Jianguo yilai Mao Zedong wengao* (*Mao Zedong's Manuscripts since 1949*). Vol. 7. Beijing: Zhongyang wenxian chubanshe.

CCCPC Party Literature Research Office. 1994. *Jianguo yilai zhongyao wenxian xuanbian* (*Important Documents since the Founding of the PRC*). Vol. 10. Beijing: Zhongyang wenxian chubanshe.

Chen, Duanhong. 2010. *Zhixianquan yu genbenfa* (*Constituent Power and the Fundamental Law*). Beijing: China Legal Publishing House.

Chen, Xiaolu. 2013. "Daoqianji" (An apology), *Zhongguo qingnian bao*, 16 October.

Chen, Xiaoping. 2010. "Dangdai Zhongguo de xianzheng daolu" (The constitutional way in contemporary China), *21ccom*, 20 January, http://www.21ccom.net/articles/zgyj/xzmj/article_201001202399.html. Accessed 2 January 2011.

Cohen, Jerome A. 1978. "China's changing constitution." *The China Quarterly* 76, 794–841.

Creemers, Rogier. 2015. "China's constitutionalism debate: content, context and implications." *The China Journal* 74, 91–109.

Cui, Zhiyuan. 2011. "Dui lizhuang'an de chubu kanfa," *Renwen yu shehui*, 9 September, http://wen.org.cn/modules/article/view.article.php/2758. Accessed 2 April 2012.

Djilas, Milovan. 1962. *The New Class: An Analysis of the Communist System*. New York: Praeger.

Editorial Staff. 2013. "Xianfa shi zhengzhi tizhi gaige de gongshi" (The constitution as the consensus of the political reform). *Spring and Autumn Annals* 1.

Feng, Xiang. 2014. "Guoge fuyu ziyou" (National anthem confers freedom). *Beida falü pinglun* 15(1), 234–45.

Fukuyama, Francis. 1992. *The End of History and the Last Man*. New York: The Free Press.

Gardner, John. 1976. "The Chinese constitution of 1975." *Government and Opposition* 11(2), 212–223.

Hai, Tao. 2011. "Zhang Xuezhong huyuqu malie, huadong zhengfa yu jiepin" (Zhang Xuezhong will possibly be fired for his appeals for the removal of Marxism-Leninism), *VOA*, 24 May, http://www.voachinese.com/content/article-20110524-uncut-news-122509689/782163.html. Accessed 2 February 2012.

Harding, Harry. 1991. "The Chinese state in crisis." In Roderick MacFarquhar and John K. Fairbank (eds.), *The Cambridge History of China, Vol. 15, The People's Republic, Part 2: Revolutions within the Chinese Revolution (1966–1982)*. Cambridge: Cambridge University Press, 107–217.

He, Weifang. 2007. "The police and the rule of law: commentary on 'Principals and secret agents'." *The China Quarterly* 191, 671–674.

He, Weifang. 2010. "He Bin, He Weifang deng Beijing faxue mingjia yantao Li Zhuang'an" (Discussion on Li Zhuang case by He Weifang, He Bin and other Beijing famous jurists), http://news.mylegist.com/1605/2010-01-05/18658_2.html. Accessed 22 June 2012.

He, Weifang. 2011. "Weile fazhi, weile women xinzhong de nayifen lixiang: zhi Chongqing falüjie de yifengxin" (For rule of law and for our ideal: a letter to the Chongqing legal field), *21comm*, http://www.21ccom.net/plus/view.php?aid=33396. Accessed 22 June 2012.

Hong, Zhenkuai. 2012. "Yifa zhiguo, yixian zhizheng" (Governing by rule of law, rule of constitutionalism). *Spring and Autumn Annals* 12, 1–5.

Hu, Ping. 1992. *Zhongguo minyun fansi* (*Reflections on the Civil Rights Movements in China*). Hong Kong: Oxford University Press.

Hu, Ping, and Wang Juntao. 1990. *Kaituo Beida xueyun wenxian* (*Opening Up: Documents of Students Movements in Beijing University*). Hong Kong: Fengyun shidai chubangongsi.

Hua, Bingxiao. 2013. "Meiyou xianzheng jiu meiyou shehuizhuyi de guangming weilai" (No constitutionalism, no bright future for socialism), *21ccom*, 30 May, http://www.21ccom.net/articles/zgyj/xzmj/article_2013053084526.html. Accessed 20 June 2013.

Hua, Shiping. 2014. "Zhang Chunqiao and the politics of the 1975 People's Republic of China Constitution." *East Asia* 31, 289–303.

Ip, Eric C. 2012. "Judicial review in China: a positive political economy analysis." *Review Law & Economics* 8(2), 331–366.

Ji, Weidong. 2002. *Xianzheng xinlun* (*New Theory on Constitutionalism*). Beijing: Beijing University Press.

Kuang, Xinnian. 2002. "Weishenme women xuyao yige hufa yundong?" (Why do we need a constitution defence movement?), *Kdnet*, 28 December, http://club.kdnet.net/dispbbs.asp?id=646000&boardid=2. Accessed 20 February 2012.

Lao, Tian. 2002. "Jiyoupai jieli weijiao xianfazhong canliude laoyibei gemingjia de geming xinnian" (Ultra-rightists go to great lengths to smooth away the revolutionary faith remnant in the old revolutionaries), *Tianya*, 14 December, http://bbs.tianya.cn/post-no01-32880-1.shtml. Accessed 20 February 2012.

Lee, Ching Kwan. 2003. "Pathways of labour insurgency." In Elizabeth Perry and Mark Selden (eds.), *Chinese Society, Change, Conflict and Resistance*. London: Routledge Curzon, 73–93.

Lee, Hong Yung. 1975. "The radical students in Kwangtung during the Cultural Revolution." *The China Quarterly* 64, 645–683.

Li, Mingqi. 2011. "The rise of the working class and the future of Chinese revolution." *Monthly Review* 63(2), 38–51.

Lin, Chun. 2012. "China's leaders are cracking down on Bo Xilai and his Chongqing model," *The Guardian*, http://www.guardian.co.uk/commentisfree/2012/apr/22/china-leaders-cracking-down-chongqing-xilai. Accessed 22 April 2012.

Lin, Chun. 2015. "The language of class in China." *Socialist Register* 1, 24–53.

Lindahl, Hans. 2007. "Constituent power and reflexive identity: towards an ontology of collective selfhood." In Martin Loughlin and Neil Walker (eds.), *The Paradox of Constitutionalism: Constituent Power and Constitutional Form*. London: Oxford University Press, 9–26.

Liu, Boqin. 2013. "Zhengzhong daoqian" (A formal apology). *Spring and Autumn Annals* 6, 83.

Liu, Xiaofeng. 1988. *Zhengjiu yu xiaoyao* (*Delivering and Dallying*). Shanghai: Shanghai People's Press.

Liu, Xiaofeng. 2013a. "Jintian xianzheng de zuida nanti shi ruhe pingjia Mao Zedong" (The biggest difficulty of constitutionalism in China is how to evaluate Mao Zedong), *21comm*, 17 May, http://www.21ccom.net/articles/sxwh/shsc/article_2013051783576.html. Accessed 22 June 2013.

Liu, Xiaofeng. 2013b. "Ruhe renshi bainian gonghe de lishi yiyi?" (How to evaluate the significance of republican history." *Kaifang shidai* 5, 183–193.

Loughlin, Martin. 2003. *The Idea of Public Law*. London: Oxford University Press.

MacFarquhar, Roderick, and Michael Schoenhals. 2006. *Mao's Last Revolution*. Cambridge: Belknap Press.

Mao, Zedong. 1977[1956]. "Zai Zhongguo gongchandang dibajie zhongyang weiyuanhui dierci quanti huiyishang de jianghua" (Speech at the second plenary session of the eighth Central Committee of the CCP). In Renmin chubanshe (eds.), *Mao Zedong xuanji 5* (*Selected Works of Mao Zedong. Vol. 5*). Beijing: Renmin chubanshe, 313–329.

Marx, Karl. 1975[1871]. "Letter to Friedrich Bolte, 23 November 1871." In Karl Marx and Friedrich Engels, *Selected Correspondence*. Moscow: Progress Publishers, 295.

Mazur, Mary G. 1999. "Public space for memory in contemporary civil society: freedom to learn from the mirror of the past?" *The China Quarterly* 160, 1019–35.

Negri, Antonio. 1999. *Insurgencies: Constituent Power and the Modern State*. Minneapolis, MN: University of Minnesota Press.

Oikawa, J. 2013. "Growing backlash in China to suppression of free speech," *Asahi shimbun*, 7 July, http://ajw.asahi.com/article/forum/politics_and_economy/east_asia/AJ201302210087. Accessed 2 December 2013.

Pan, Wei. 2003. "Toward a consultative rule of law regime in China." *Journal of Contemporary China* 12(34), 3–43.

People's Republic of China. 1975. *The Constitution of the People's Republic of China*. Beijing: Foreign Language Press.

Qian, Liqun. 2008. "Buneng yiwangde sixiang: 1980 Zhongguo xiaoyuan minzhu yundong shuping" (Unforgettable thoughts: review of the Chinese college students movement in 1980). *Modern China Studies* 1, 4–10.

Qian, Liqun. 2012. *Mao Zedong shidaiyu hou Mao Zedong shidai* (*The Maoist Era and the Post-Maoist Era*). Taipei: Lianjing chubanshe.

Rofel, Lisa. 1999. *Other Modernities: Gendered Yearnings in China after Socialism*. Berkeley, CA: University of California Press.

Schram, Stuart R. 1971. "Mao Tse-tung and the theory of the permanent revolution." *The China Quarterly* 46, 221–244.

Song, Jichao. 2013. "Wo ye laidao geqian" (I come to apologize), *Nanfang zhoumo*, 20 June.

Thurston, Anne, 1984–1985. "Victims of China's Cultural Revolution: the invisible wounds: part I." *Pacific Affairs* 57(4), 599–620.

Tong, Zhiwei. 2011. "Chongqing da heixing shehui guanli fangshi yanjiu baogao" (Research report on the Chongqing anti-mafia movement), *21comm*, http://www.21ccom.net/articles/zgyj/ggzhc/article_2012021353482.html. Accessed 2 February 2012.

Tong, Zhiwei. 2013. "Shexianpai, fanxianpaiyu fanxianpai de 2008" (The socialist constitutionalists, the anti-constitutionalists and the universal constitutionalists in 2008), *Tong Zhiwei's Blog*, 14 June, http://tongzhiwei.blog.21ccom.net/?p=64. Accessed 22 June 2013.

Unger, Jonathan. 2007. "The Cultural Revolution at the grass roots." *The China Journal* 57, 109–137.

Upham, Frank. 2009. "Chinese property rights and property theory." *Hong Kong Law Journal* 39(3), 613–627.

Van Sant, Shannon. 2013. "US–China college partnership strained by treatment of outspoken," *VOA*, 30 September, http://www.voanews.com/content/us-china-college-partnership-strained-by-treatment-of-outspoken/1759695.html. Accessed 10 October 2013.

Walder, Andrew G. 2012. *Fractured Rebellion: The Beijing Red Guard Movement*. Cambridge, MA: Harvard University Press.

Wang, Hui. 2012. "The rumour machine." *London Review of Books* 34(90), 13–14.

Wang, Hui. 2014. "Liang zhong xin qiongren jiqi weilai" (Two kinds of new poor men and their future). *Kaifang shidai* 6, 49–70.

Wang, Youqin. 2010a. "Daile ge haotou: hongweibing daoqian" (A head start: the Red Guard's apology), *Nanfang zhoumo*, 22 October, http://www.infzm.com/content/51494. Accessed 4 May 2011.

Wang, Youqin. 2010b. "Kongbu de hong bayue" (Terrorist Red August). *Spring and Autumn Annals* 10, 55–57.

Wen, Qingfu. 2013. "Tangguo 45 nian de xinling jiushu" (Mind journey through the past 45 years), *Xiaoxiang Morning News*, 27 July.

Wilhelm, Katherine. 2004. "Rethinking property rights in urban China." *UCLA Journal of International Law and Foreign Affairs* 2(Fall/Winter), 227–300.

Wu, Changchang. 2014. "Inside-out and outside-in: the making of a transnational discursive alliance in the struggle for the future of China." *International Journal of Communication* 8, 1–30.

Xi, Jinping. 2010. "Jianjue fandui renhe waiqu chouhua Zhonggong lishi de cuowu qingxiang" (Resolutely oppose any erroneous distortion or vilification of CCP history), *iFeng*, 21 July, http://news.ifeng.com/mainland/detail_2010_07/21/1811502_0.shtml?_from_related. Accessed 22 December 2010.

Xia, Yong. 2003. "Zhongguo xianfa gaige de jige jiben lilun wenti" (Some basic theoretical problems on the constitutional reform in China). *Zhongguo shehui kexue* 2, 4–17.

Xiao, Shu. 2013. "Shehuizhuyi xianzheng, haishi xianzheng shehuizhuyi?" (Socialist constitutionalism or constitutionalist socialism?), 1 June, http://blog.sina.com.cn/s/blog_496df5fb0101o0y7.html. Accessed 20 June 2013.

Xie, Tao. 2010. "Women cong nalilai dao naliqu" (Where are we from, where are we going). *Spring and Autumn Annals* 10, 1–7.

Xu, Chongde. 2013[2008]. "Xianzhengshi fazhiguojia yingyouzhiyi" (Constitutionalism is key to the country under rule of law), *21ccom*, 22 May, http://www.21ccom.net/articles/zgyj/xzmj/article_2013052283948.html. Accessed 22 June 2013.

Yang, Guobin. 2011. *The Power of the Internet in China: Citizen Activism Online*. New York: Columbia University Press.

Yuen, Samson. 2013. "Debating constitutionalism in China." *China Perspectives* 4, 67–72.

Zhang, Lühao. 2010. "Xuanjufa lici xiugai huigu" (Introduction to the amendments to the Electoral Law), China.com.cn, 8 March, http://www.china.com.cn/news/txt/2010-03/08/content_19552915.htm. Accessed 2 February 2012.

Zhang, Qianfan. 2003. "The People's Court in transition." *Journal of Contemporary China* 12(34), 69–101.

Zhang, Qianfan. 2005. "Cong renmin zhuquan dao zhuquan: Zhongguo xianfaxue yanjiu moshi de bianqian" (From popular sovereignty to sovereignty: shifts in approach to the constitution studies in China). *Zhengfa luntan* 23(2), 3–9.

Zhang, Qianfan. 2010. "A constitution without constitutionalism? The path of constitutional development in China." *International Journal of Constitutional Law* 8, 950–976.

Zhang, Qianfan. 2011. "Zhongguo xianzheng de lujingyu juxian" (The approach and limits of the Chinese constitutionalism). *Faxue* 1, 72–80.

Zhang, Qianfan. 2013. "Xianfa xuyanjiqi xiaoli zhengyi" (Preface to the Constitution and its effect). *Spring and Autumn Annals* 6, 1–7.

Zhang, Xuezhong. 2011. "Zhi jiaoyubu buzhang de yifeng gongkaixin" (An open letter to the Ministry of Education), *China Digital Times*, 22 September, http://chinadigitaltimes.net/chinese/2011/09/%E5%BC%A0%E9%9B%AA%E5%BF%A0%EF%BC%9A%E3%80%8A%E8%87%B4%E6%95%99%E8%82%B2%E9%83%A8%E9%83%A8%E9%95%BF%E7%9A%84%E4%B8%80%E5%B0%81%E5%85%AC%E5%BC%80%E4%BF%A1%E3%80%8B/. Accessed 22 January 2012.

Zhang, Youyu. 1982. "Guanyu xiugai xianfade jige wenti" (Some problems on the revision of the constitution). *Faxue yanjiu* 3, 1–9.

Zhao, Chu. 2013. "Shexianlun de dashenhua" (Socialist constitutionalism as a myth), *21ccom*, 6 June, http://www.21ccom.net/articles/zgyj/xzmj/article_2013060685005.html. Accessed 22 June 2013.

Zhao, Yuezhi. 2012. "The struggle for socialism in China: the Bo Xilai saga and beyond." *Monthly Review* 64(5), 1–17.

Zhonghua renmin gongheguo xianfa (Constitution of the People's Republic of China). 2014. http://www.gov.cn/guoqing/2014-03/06/content_2630691.htm. Accessed 11 May 2014.

Zhu, Huaxin. 2010. "*Renmin ribao*, jiaoyisheng tongzhi taichenzhong" (*People's Daily*, it is too heavy to call you comrade), 4 April, http://vdisk.weibo.com/s/uh8RJMrrM-qiw. Accessed 12 July 2011.

The Cultural Revolution as a Crisis of Representation

Patricia M. Thornton[*]

Abstract
The May 16 Notification, which set the agenda for the Cultural Revolution, named the movement's key targets as those "representatives of the bourgeoisie who have sneaked into the Party, the government, the army, and all spheres of culture." The ensuing uprising of students and workers, many of whom claimed to be the loyal "representatives" of revolutionary and radical forces at the grassroots of society, exposed the fulminating crisis of political representation under CCP rule. This article considers the Cultural Revolution as a manifestation of a continuing crisis of representation within revolutionary socialism that remains unresolved to the present day, as demonstrated by the tepid popular response to Jiang Zemin's "three represents" and widespread contemporary concerns about the Party's "representativeness" (*daibiaoxing* 代表性) in the wake of market reform. Although the Cultural Revolution enabled both public debate of and political experimentation with new forms of representative politics, the movement failed to resolve the crisis. The Party's lingering disquiet regarding issues of representation thus remains one legacy of the Cultural Revolution.

Keywords: political representation; Cultural Revolution; China; revolutionary committees; Red Guard congress

Although the Cultural Revolution is frequently portrayed as originating in an elite power struggle within the Chinese Communist Party (CCP), its earliest salvos were replete with references to the brewing crisis of mass political representation. The ninth polemic response to the Soviet Open Letter released in 1964 lambasted the members of the "revisionist Khrushchev clique" as "the political *representatives* of the bourgeoisie" who "stand diametrically opposed to the Soviet people … and to the great majority of the Soviet cadres and Communists."[1] Just over a year later, the May 16 Notification, hailed as a "blueprint" for the Cultural

---

* Department of politics and international relations, and Merton College, University of Oxford. Email: patricia.thornton@politics.ox.ac.uk.
1 "Guanyu Heluxiaofude jia gongchanzhuyi jiqi zai shijie lishishangde jiaoxun" (On Khrushchev's phony communism and its historical lessons for the world), *Renmin ribao*, 14 July 1964, 1.

© The China Quarterly, 2016   doi:10.1017/S030574101600076X

Revolution,[2] specifically targeted those "*representatives* of the bourgeoisie who have sneaked into the Party, the government, the army, and all spheres of culture."[3] The editorial note published alongside Nie Yuanzi's 聂元梓 "big character poster" (*dazibao* 大字报) in the *People's Daily* took aim against *representatives* of a fake "and "revisionist" Communist Party that would be swept aside "by the raging tide of the Great Cultural Revolution surging forward."[4]

Such incendiary charges raise questions about the nature of political representation during Mao's time as well as today. Wang Shaoguang recently proposed that contemporary China aims to be a "representational democracy" (*daibiaoxing minzhu* 代表型民主), differing in form and substance from the Western model of "representative democracy" (*daiyixing minzhu* 代议型民主).[5] However, as Xu Jilin has pointed out, in the absence of clear and reliable mechanisms of authorization and accountability, such claims are difficult to assess.[6] As Larry Backer acknowledges, in forwarding the "three represents," the Party claims to represent "advanced productive forces," "advanced culture," and the interests of "the people as a whole" over those of any particular class or group, rendering representation under the CCP even more indirect and abstract.[7] Some have gone so far as to charge that this shift has all but rendered the CCP a diluted "catch all party" (*jianrongxing zhengdang* 兼容性政党) like the German Christian Democratic Union, which aims "to represent everyone."[8]

Yet, such charges are hardly new: similar concerns about the changing nature of the Soviet Communist Party under Khrushchev propelled Mao and his supporters into action five decades ago in an effort to prevent the CCP from degenerating into an "all people's party" (*quanmin dang* 全民党) that effectively represents no one. Official discourse in the years leading up to the Cultural Revolution was replete with worrying references about the relationship between representation and mass political participation, suggesting the existence of a brewing crisis within revolutionary socialism that could not be resolved within the Party itself. Indeed, one of the chief goals of the Cultural Revolution, according to the 11th plenary session of the eighth Party Congress in August 1966, was to have "the masses, under the leadership of the Party, educate themselves as to the best new organizational forms" (*xin zuzhi xingshi* 新组织形式) for the nation, which, "like the Paris Commune, must implement a comprehensive electoral system" (*quanmiande xuanjuzhi* 全面的选举制) with universal suffrage and the right to recall those elected.[9] This wave of political experimentation began with an

---

2   MacFarquhar and Schoenhals 2006, 92.
3   "Tongzhi" (Notification), *Renmin ribao*, 17 May 1967, 1.
4   Renmin jiefangjun guofang daxue dangshi dangjian zhenggong jiaoyanshi 1988, 36–37. Emphasis added.
5   Wang, Shaoguang 2014, 4–12; 2012, 152–174.
6   Xu 2011.
7   Backer 2006, 32.
8   Gao 2010, 9.
9   "Xuexi shiliu tiao, shuxi shiliu tiao, yunyong shiliu tiao" (Study the 16 points, learn well the 16 points, utilize the 16 points), *Renmin ribao*, 13 August 1966, 1.

initial stage of mass criticism and an attack on the representative nature of existing organizational structures, was followed by enjoinders from the centre that grassroots groups "link" or "join" up and form "grand alliances," and ended with the fostering of new representative mass organizations (congresses and alliances) that were ultimately co-opted and remoulded by the central party-state. Three interlinked political experiments shed particular light on the crisis of representation during the Cultural Revolution: the rise of Red Guard and rebel factions among Beijing high school and university students, many of which later participated in the Red Guard Congress (*hongdaihui* 红代会); the mobilization of the workers in Shanghai and, later, across the country, which led to the establishment of the Workers' Congress (*gongdaihui* 工代会); and, finally, the founding of the Shanghai Commune, and its subsequent replacement by the Revolutionary Committee, a new political form that was theoretically designed to bring together representatives of the revolutionary masses, the army and reliable cadres in a single governing body.

None of these new political forms succeeded in resolving the crisis of representation, in part because they lacked clear means of either authorization or accountability. In the absence of institutionalized mechanisms for representing the plurality of interests below, claims for legitimacy could only come from above in the form of official recognition. Thus, potential new vehicles for representation at the social grassroots vied for recognition from the centre, which lacked the capacity to manage the roiling competition below. Both the Red Guard and workers' congresses quickly became sites of contestation for warring factions, and the Revolutionary Committees, most agree, focused on the restoration of order rather than on developing stable mechanisms of mass representation.

The strenuous re-imposition of Party discipline in the early post-Mao era, policed by various mopping-up campaigns such as those carried out against "three kinds of people," likewise weakened the Party's radical activist wings on both the left and the right without redressing the gap between the Party and those it claims to represent. Contemporary debate regarding the Party's declining "representativeness" (*daibiaoxing* 代表性) and, perhaps most notably, Jiang Zemin's 江泽民 "important thought" on the "three represents," reflects the persistent irresolution of this essential dilemma. The Party's continuing crisis of representation therefore remains one of the chief legacies of the Cultural Revolution in contemporary China.

Parliamentary Representation in Revolutionary Socialism

In Hannah Pitkin's seminal account, formal representation involves an act of *authorization* – defined as the means by which a representative obtains his or her standing, status, position or office – and a mechanism of *accountability* through which constituents recall representatives who are unresponsive to their preferences. Legitimate forms of political representation involve a "substantive acting for others" in the sense that a representative "[promotes] the interest of the

represented." In stable democracies, the representative is also "a professional politician in a framework of political institutions, a member of a political party who
wants to get reelected, and a member of a legislature along with other representatives." Political representation thus involves a balancing of interests on the part
of the representative, and the ability of constituents to assess and hold delegates
accountable over time.[10]

However, substantive representation also takes place beyond the sphere of institutionalized democratic practices. Although traditional views of democratic representation presume stable constituencies with interests that are endogenous to
the political process, as Lisa Disch recently argued, it is also a dynamic and mobilizational process that facilitates the formation of political groups and identities.[11]
Delegates, in both democracies and non-democracies, do not merely respond to
pre-existing interests and preferences; they also play an active role "in searching
out and creating them."[12] Would-be representatives "need to be creative actors,
offering portrayals and enticements to constituents and audiences," and in so
doing, can recruit supporters and even call new constituencies into being.[13]

In Marxist-Leninist thought and Maoist practice, political representation is potentially dynamic and mobilizational but imperfectly realized by the revolutionary party which serves, on the one hand, as a vehicle for mobilization by activists,
and on the other, as a facilitator of "the self-emancipation of the working class."
The vanguard role assumed by the Leninist party rests upon two assumptions:
first, that a single party is capable of representing the interests of the working
class as a whole without a critical opposition to help remedy omissions, inaccur-
acies and mistakes; and, second, that the vanguard is capable of speaking in a
single, united voice for those it claims to represent, in the absence of competition.[14] Marx anticipated that universal suffrage would allow the majoritarian
working class authentic and full representation; Lenin envisioned that a revolutionary party could provoke direct action.[15] Yet, both acknowledged that although the Paris Commune conjoined universal suffrage with self-rule, the
communards did not and could not represent Parisian society as a whole. The
tensions between direct participation and political representation in a society
composed of plural class interests, and ruled by a revolutionary party, were left
unresolved.

Originally concurring with Lenin's assessment that the way out of bourgeois
parliamentarianism lay "in the conversion of the representative institutions
from mere 'talking shops' into working bodies,"[16] Mao supported the creation
of the National People's Congress (NPC) and People's Consultative Congress.

---

10 Pitkin 1967, 141, 155.
11 Disch 2011.
12 Mansbridge 2003, 518.
13 Saward 2008, 274.
14 Geras 1981.
15 Bensaïd 2002.
16 Lenin 1933, 35.

However, this was supplanted by the concept of "people's democratic dictatorship," which restricted the democratic right of representation to the ranks of "the people."[17] Beginning in 1956, Mao began to contrast "great" and "small democracy," proposing that the former – characterized by direct participation and mass mobilization "under the leadership of the proletariat" – would be opposed both by the democratic political parties of the United Front and those CCP cadre-bureaucrats who feared popular wrath.[18]

Remaining CCP support for parliamentarianism eroded during the Hundred Flowers movement, when a loose coalition of NPC deputies openly proposed that China's "mass organizations be given a degree of control over the Party and the state."[19] The group attacked the voting system as "undemocratic," and as a "formalistic" (*xingshizhuyi* 形式主义) and thinly "disguised [system of] appointment" (*bianxiang de renming* 变相的任命) by the Party.[20] Finally, in June 1957, the minister of communications, Zhang Bojun 章伯钧, argued that, "The Party must be removed from its position of superiority to the NPC and the government ... and the NPC must be made an organ of genuine power."[21] In the backlash that followed, 54 NPC deputies were accused of being rightists, and the parliamentary model of representation was abandoned. Mao later remarked that:

> In China, the people's congresses included those participating as representatives of the bourgeoisie, representatives who had split off from the Nationalist Party, and representatives who were prominent democratic figures. All of them accepted the leadership of the Chinese Communist Party. One group among these tried to stir up trouble, but failed.[22]

As Kevin O'Brien notes, no new legislation was passed between 1957 and 1965, and NPC resolutions were increasingly seen as "secondary technical bills ... mechanically confirming reports or edits originating in some other organ." The "crippled" body of the NPC "limped on until 1965," and then did not convene again for another nine years, during which time its "existence became a mere formality."[23]

The Model of the Paris Commune

With the NPC discredited in the aftermath of the "anti-rightist" campaign, interest was revived in the Paris Commune as an alternative model combining mass representation and direct political action. In 1958, radical theorist Zhang Chunqiao 张春桥 praised it for ensuring that "special privileges and the official allowances" would disappear "along with the high dignitaries themselves."[24] Two years later, on its 90th anniversary in 1961, another prominent editorial

17 Defined as "the working class, the peasantry, the urban petty bourgeoisie and the national bourgeoisie."
     Mao 1949.
18 Mao 1956.
19 Harding 1981, 122.
20 Li, Youyi 1957, 7.
21 O'Brien 1990, 38–42.
22 Mao 1961–62.
23 O'Brien 1990, 45–55.
24 Zhang 1958, 7.

lauded the Paris Commune's "great innovation" (*weida chuangju* 伟大创举), not as a "bourgeois capitalist-style parliament" but as a representative body combining "both legislative and administrative functions."[25]

In 1966, on the Commune's 95th anniversary and on the eve of the Cultural Revolution, *Red Flag* published a substantive editorial revisiting the model of the Paris Commune. Zheng Zhisi 郑之思, the author of the editorial, proposed that the key lesson to be drawn from the historical experience of the Commune was that it was not sufficient for revolutionaries simply to seize power from below. The significance of direct election and recall to the system of political representation in the Paris Commune, while commendable in Zheng's view, had been overemphasized by "revisionist" Soviet historians who sought to negate the importance of both direct participation and armed insurrection. Zheng took particular aim at "Khrushchev revisionists, [who] under the pretext that times have changed, publicize the deceitful myth that the proletariat can seize state power without smashing the state machine of the bourgeoisie and that socialism can be built without the dictatorship of the proletariat." The Commune was not merely "a product of a ballot by the whole people and of 'pure democracy'": the new political form was chiefly the product of revolutionary violence carried out by the masses. Although the Paris Commune and October Revolution had been "inherited and further developed" by the CCP, Zhang descried the fact that the Party was "struggling resolutely against all renegades who have turned their backs on the principle" of the Paris Commune. "The masses were the real masters in the Paris Commune," and it was the "revolutionary enthusiasm and initiative of the masses [that] was the source of the Commune's strength." Twenty thousand communard activists attended daily meetings, Zheng claimed, and "the masses also carefully checked up on the work of the Commune and its members."[26]

Months later, Mao hailed Nie Yuanzi's "big character poster" as the "declaration of a Chinese Paris Commune for the sixth decade of the 20th century, the Beijing Commune."[27] The historical analogy appeared again in the "16 points," which hailed the organizational forms for the movement as "new and of great historical importance." According to the outline, in order to transform fledgling revolutionary grassroots organizations into permanent institutions, a system of direct election and recall, would prove key:

It is necessary to institute a system of general elections, like that of the Paris Commune, for electing members to the Cultural Revolution groups and committees and delegates to the cultural revolutionary congresses ... The masses are entitled at any time to criticize members of the Cultural Revolution groups and committees and delegates elected to the cultural revolutionary congresses. If these members or delegates prove incompetent, they can be replaced through election or recalled by the masses through discussion.[28]

---

25 "Bali gongshe de weida chuangju" (The great undertaking of the Paris Commune), *Renmin ribao*, 18 March 1961, 1.
26 Zheng 1966.
27 Chen, Boda 1966, 116.
28 *Renmin ribao*, 9 August 1966, 1; "Bali gongshe shixing de quanmian de xuanju zhi" (The Paris Commune's implementation of a system of universal suffrage), *Renmin ribao*, 15 August 1966, 2.

Within days, a *People's Daily* editorial on 15 August, running under the title "Implementing the comprehensive electoral system of the Paris Commune," recounted the details of the Paris Commune's system of universal suffrage and election. Once elected under a scheme of proportional representation, officers were subject to supervision and recall by the voters. Quoting Marx's observation that since the majority of the officers were naturally either themselves members of the proletariat, or widely recognized as representing the working class, the author concluded that the experience of the Paris Commune, which included "its comprehensive electoral system, constitutes an extremely precious legacy for the worldwide working class movement."[29]

In early November, Marshall Lin Biao 林彪 linked the model of representation employed by the Paris Commune to Mao's notion of mass participation in the form of "great democracy," exclaiming to a national audience of revolutionary teachers and students that, "in accordance with the principles of the Paris Commune, [we must] fully implement people's democratic rights. Without this type of great democracy (*da minzhu* 大民主), it is not possible to launch a genuine proletariat cultural revolution."[30] The popular right of recall and replacement for members of political organizations leading the Cultural Revolution was repeatedly stressed in the *People's Daily*: Cultural Revolution committees in factories, mining and other productive enterprises must not be:

appointed from above or controlled from behind [the scenes], but must, in accordance with the principles of the Paris Commune, implement a comprehensive electoral system and pass through the masses' complete inspections (*chongfen yunniang* 充分酝酿), repeated discussions, genuine [competitive] elections, and moreover be subject to re-election, dismissal and recall at any time.[31]

Yet, notwithstanding such admonitions, the organizational experiments launched during the Cultural Revolution bore little resemblance to the Paris Commune. Mechanisms linking delegation, mass supervision and recall were never established, and practices of authorization and accountability were never institutionalized. Instead, a generation of self-authorizing activists sprang into the breach claiming to represent constituencies and political viewpoints, with tenuous, if any, mechanisms of accountability. The early failure to resolve the brewing crisis of representation arguably generated more contention as various self-declared representatives vied to mobilize constituencies to support their claims.

The Attack on Representatives of Enemy Classes: Red Guards

When the capital's student population began mobilizing in earnest in June 1966, the slow and uncertain response of existing Party and mass organizations

29 *Renmin ribao*, 15 August 1966, 2.
30 "Zai jiejian quanguo gedi lai Beijing geming shisheng dahui shang Lin Biao tongzhi de jianghua" (Comrade Lin Biao's speech at the reception of revolutionary teachers and students coming to the capital from all corners of the country), *Renmin ribao*, 4 November 1966.
31 "Yingjie gongkuang chiye wenhua dageming de gaochao" (Welcome the high tide of the Great Proletarian Cultural Revolution in factories and mining enterprises), *Renmin ribao*, 26 December 1966.

triggered a growing sense of a representation gap at the grassroots. As Andrew Walder has shown, work teams ostensibly "representing" the Party centre were initially welcomed by some, but their presence complicated the situation considerably, and contributed to the rapid escalation of the conflict.[32] From the second half of June to the middle of July, the work teams counter-attacked, launching a drive to "oppose disruption," singling out students and staff members when they could and labelling them as "rightists," "fake leftists [who are] true rightists," and "counterrevolutionaries."[33] During what came to be known as the crackdown "against interference" (*fan'ganrao* 反感饶), the more aggressive stance taken by the teams alienated even some who had initially welcomed their arrival. The question of whose interests the work teams represented quickly emerged as a sticking point on some Beijing campuses. Third-year chemical engineering student Kuai Dafu 蒯大富 at Tsinghua University argued that the work team was as repressive of the revolutionary left as the old Party committee had been.[34]

At the heart of Kuai's complaint was the tension between direct participation and political representation. On 21 June, he scrawled the following on a wall poster:

The primary task of revolution is to seize power. Previously, power was in the hands of the school Party committee, and we struggled and overthrew them; now power is in the hands of the work team, and every one of us revolutionary leftists must now ask ourselves: does this power *represent* (*daibiao* 代表) us? If it represents us, then we'll support it, if it doesn't represent us, then we'll seize power again.[35]

A backlash that became known as the "white terror" crystallized around the issue of political representation.[36] School authorities and work teams accused student radicals of being "representatives of the anti-Party anti-socialism capitalists [who are] waving the red flag to oppose the red flag," while activists asked campus communities "to consider whether the power held and exerted by the work team" in fact "does or does not represent the Party centre, Chairman Mao, [and] the proletariat."[37]

At the 27 June public debate organized by the work team at Tsinghua University, radical students seized upon the work team's claim that, "we represent the proletariat masses, we represent the new municipal Party committee, and we represent Mao Zedong Thought." Not even Party vice-secretary Bo Yibo 薄一波 could assuage the rebels: while reviewing the thousands of wall posters displayed at the Tsinghua University campus, Bo's vigorous assertion that "the work team is representing the Party's leadership" following the original university Party committee's dismissal was mocked and derided.[38]

---

32   Walder 2009.
33   Liu 1987, 18.
34   Qinghua daxue jinggangshan hongweibing xuanchuandui bian (n.d.), 8.
35   Ibid.
36   Ibid., 90.
37   Ibid., 13, 27.
38   Ibid., 15, 32.

These claims were linked to Mao's increasingly acerbic critique of Party organizations over the course of the 1960s. The Party no longer reflected proletarian consciousness or a revolutionary class position; instead, Mao accused the Party and the Communist Youth League (CYL) of harbouring undesirable social elements that were steering those organizations in a new and worrying direction. Official statements and the state-controlled press were awash with speculation about the activities of "representatives" (*daibiao renwu* 代表人物) of counterrevolutionary classes in the Party and state bureaucracies. By contrast, the student rebels portrayed themselves as representatives of the true revolutionary left, struggling against indwelling enemies: aside from Mao himself, no one was above suspicion. Unable to rely upon the usual stable referents of Party and CYL for ideological assurance, the original Red Guards swore to "be forever loyal to the proletariat line *as represented by Chairman Mao*,"[39] as opposed to the "general line" of the newly suspect Party.[40]

Confusion and contestation over representation were common even on campuses where the work teams sided with radical activists. Although the work team at Tsinghua High School, the birthplace of the Red Guards, supported the rebellious students at the outset, the relationship soured when the work team insisted that the school's new Cultural Revolution committee should have "broad representation" outside the Red Guard organization. The Red Guards rebelled, later reporting their unhappiness with the work team to the campus's new revolutionary committee.[41]

Radical Students and Self-Representation

Following the withdrawal of the work teams at the end of July 1966, the student discourse on representation shifted. The so-called "16 points" released on 9 August declared that the new Cultural Revolution committees formed in the schools to be "long-term, permanent new mass organizations" of "great historical significance," and elected "according to the principles of the Paris Commune." "Nomination lists must be thoroughly discussed by the masses before the elections," and committee members, once elected, could "be criticized at any time, and if they turn out not to be suitable for the post, after discussion among the masses, new elections can be held and they can be replaced."[42]

Yet, the Paris Commune model conveyed different lessons for various student activists: those who had cooperated with the work teams and held positions on their school's Cultural Revolution committees were reassured that these were "permanent" new organs of power, whereas those who fared less

---

39 Qinghua daxue fushu zhongxue hongweibing 1966, emphasis added.
40 Bu 2008, 158–163.
41 Ibid., 169–170.
42 "Zhongguo gongchandang zhongyang weiyuanhui guanyu wuchan jieji wenhua dageming de jueding" (Central Committee of the Chinese Communist Party's decision regarding the Great Proletarian Cultural Revolution), *Renmin ribao*, 9 August 1966, 1.

well focused on the document's criticisms of the work teams as the representatives of "anti-Party, anti-socialist elements who infiltrated the Party." Rather than alleviating the polarization of the social grassroots in most schools across Beijing, the "16 points" instead contributed to a growing competition among activist groups and students for control over the new Cultural Revolution committees.[43]

The first battleground was the "preparatory committees," which were hastily established by the work teams on most campuses just prior to their withdrawal. Unsurprisingly, these were largely composed of students, teachers and employees who had cooperated with the work teams. At Tsinghua, the preparatory committee issued a call for students to unite under its leadership to carry the movement forward. The following day, students in favour of intensifying criticism of the work team organized the "August 8 alliance" – which included those who were attacked alongside Kuai Dafu – to push their agenda. The next day, the preparatory committee established an "August 9 alliance" to redirect the movement against the school's "revisionists." Two weeks later, on 22 August, the "August 8 alliance" established a new political organization, the Maoism Red Guards. Enjoined to "link up" and form "grand alliances," the "August 9" group invited representatives of similar groups from 12 other schools to a meeting to agree a coordinated strategy: Paris Commune-style elections should be held in short order. Groups without representatives on the preparatory committees sought to delay the elections, arguing that, without levelling the playing field, the planned elections would lack legitimacy.[44]

In September, 24 "minority faction" Red Guard groups not favoured either with seats on preparatory or school Cultural Revolution committees banded together in the city-wide Capital Third Headquarters. When Zhou Enlai 周恩来 addressed them on 26 September, he said: "You really bring together – and your views represent – the people who have been suppressed. That's why in your case 'to rebel *is* justified'."[45] Yet, in the absence of either a clear process of delegation, the claims of these grassroots organizations to give voice to or act on behalf of mass constituencies grew more tenuous over time. In most schools across the capital, preparatory committees either selected student representatives from pre-movement class leaders who found favour with the work teams, or, on campuses on which the work teams had been discredited, selected rebel student leaders who had opposed them.[46] Electoral participation was restricted to students with unimpeachable revolutionary credentials, and candidates were chosen and screened by the preparatory committee. All or most of the delegates owed their participation to superordinate levels rather than to expressions of grassroots support.[47] Unsurprisingly, instead of serving the

---

43 Walder 2009, 95–97.
44 Ibid., 102–110.
45 MacFarquhar and Schoenhals 2006, 134.
46 Interview with informant C, Beijing, 3 March 2015.
47 Interview with informant B, Beijing, 3 March 2015; interview with informant D, Beijing, 5 March 2015.

interests of or giving voice to the concerns of broader mass constituencies, the new representatives competed to become the tools of the centre, and, in particular, served as "gullible … gofers" for the central Cultural Revolution group.[48]

By the end of 1966, substantive political representation appeared more elusive than ever. Continuing violence had fractured the potential constituencies student activists might have otherwise represented: self-authorizing Red Guards on both "conservative" and "rebel" sides had eroded the institutionalized mechanisms under which representation could have conceivably taken place, and were locked in a contest for recognition from the centre. If the legitimacy of one's status as a representative was to be judged by the numbers of supporters one could mobilize into action, as 1966 drew to a close, the student activists set their sights on other venues: the working class was their next port of call.

Self-Representation and Radical Workers in Shanghai

The first major delegation of 170 Red Guard representatives from Beijing arrived in Shanghai on 24 August 1966, seeking to "light a fire" (*dianhuo* 点火) and spread the Cultural Revolution to the "Paris of the East." A second wave, consisting of tens of thousands organized into divisions and battalions and calling themselves the "Southern touring regiment of capital universities and institutes," arrived on 10 September and immediately fanned out to various Shanghai schools and factories. A third group, dispatched by Jiang Qing 江青 and Zhang Chunqiao, arrived a month later charged with overturning the Shanghai Municipal Party Committee, and quickly established links with rebel workers in nearby factories.[49]

The influx of Beijing Red Guards brought the debates about representation to a head by the end of August in Shanghai, a city in which the old power structure had remained more or less intact. Despite an official welcome staged at the Cultural Square, the first wave of visiting Red Guards complained that their reception had been "hastily organized" (*congcong zuzhi* 匆匆组织) and was "fundamentally not genuine" (*genben bushi zhenxin* 根本不是真心). The self-authorized Beijing Red Guard representatives complained that several Shanghai schools refused them entrance because they lacked official letters of introduction; that they had to purchase tickets when boarding public transportation; and that it had been difficult to meet with local Party leaders. The Municipal Party Committee apologized, but the delegates were adamant. On the morning of 31 August, more than a dozen Beijing Red Guards marched to Yan'an Road 延安路, demanding to see the municipal Party leadership. Before a crowd of more than a thousand onlookers, they rushed the building to find Mayor Cao Diqiu 曹荻秋 meeting with two self-proclaimed Beijing Red Guard representatives who had likewise demanded an official audience. In the fracas that ensued,

---

48 MacFarquhar and Schoenhals 2006, 145.
49 Perry and Li 1997, 10–11.

the deputy mayor, Song Liwen 宋季文, was struck on the head by a Red Guard representative, and the glass door to the building was shattered.[50]

Defying the Central Committee's September 1966 ban, Beijing Red Guard representatives entered factories and workplaces around Shanghai in the name of establishing the "worker–student united movement" (*gongren xuesheng lianhe yundong* 工人学生联合运动).[51] In early November, the Capital Red Guards' Liaison Station organized a meeting that attracted at least 30 workers from 17 different factories, and the Shanghai Workers' Revolutionary Rebels' General Headquarters (*Shanghai gongren geming zaofan zongsilingbu* 上海工人革命造反总司令部) was founded, with Number 17 Cotton Mill security officer Wang Hongwen 王洪文 as its chair. When Mayor Cao refused to attend the inaugural ceremony on 9 November, over a thousand angry workers surrounded the municipal Party committee building and staged a sit-in before deciding to take their protest to Beijing. Well over a thousand workers headed to Shanghai North Station the next morning and boarded three trains bound for the capital. A State Council directive from Premier Zhou Enlai halted the trains, snarling national rail lines for hours. The train that happened to be carrying Wang Hongwen was stopped outside of Anting 安亭 station, leading to a stand-off between the workers and local authorities. The Central Cultural Revolution Small Group dispatched Zhang Chunqiao to mediate the conflict and he formally recognized the new workers' organization.

But, official recognition of the rebels quickly triggered a backlash: "conservative" workers demanded a voice and a seat at the table as well. The leader of what would later become the Scarlet Guards later recalled how he approached the mayor in November 1966:

Since the rebels had established an all-city organization, I asked whether we might not also establish an all-city organization to counter them … At our factory, the work team composed one faction, the rebel "warriors to defend Mao Zedong Thought" were another faction, and the factory CR committee was yet a third faction. I said to the work team captain Wang Ming, "We also want to participate." Wang retorted, "We represent organizations; what do you represent?" I said, "Then I'll establish an organization, too!"[52]

The counter-mobilization had a recursive effect across the city: "The more militant the rebels at a particular factory, the more active the conservatives became as well."[53] Although relatively short-lived, the Scarlet Guards confronted the rebel forces in two high-profile incidents in December before popular support for the Conservatives dwindled amidst widespread strikes, work stoppages and slowdowns that paralysed the city.

Institutionalizing Mass Representation

Trumpeting the early success of the Cultural Revolution in October 1966, Chen Boda 陈伯达 proclaimed that in its first two months it had already proved "even

---

50   Li, Xun 2015, Vol. 1, 122–28.
51   Shanghai "wenge" shiliao zhengli bianzhu xiaozu (n.d.), 152–53.
52   Perry and Li 1997, 78.
53   Ibid., 82.

more tempestuous than either the Paris Commune or the October Revolution, with an even more profound impact on the international proletarian revolutionary movement" than either of its illustrious predecessors. Nonetheless, he acknowledged that there were persons who "oppose Mao Zedong Thought ... and oppose the Paris Commune principle of election," and who were using the tactic of stalling until the ideal composition of a unit's "preparatory" or "revolutionary committee" might be secured.[54] Three months later, he appeared to do a U-turn, counselling caution in Beijing in January 1967:

The seizure of power on a city-wide basis ought to be in the style of the Paris Commune, using a representative body of workers, peasants, soldiers, students and merchants ... This requires some preparation, however. Don't you think you should first consult the workers, peasants, students and merchants, as well as the cadres and urban residents concerned, and on that basis form a preparatory committee with representation from the entire Beijing municipality? Granted this will be a temporary organ of power, but it is certainly better than a bunch of small groups seizing power from one another. What do you think?[55]

Chen's shift reflected the fact that by 1967, the Cultural Revolution had entered a new phase in which the modus operandi was the seizure of political power by revolutionary and rebellious social forces. The *People's Daily* and Red Guard publications began declaring that instead of appearing as a blueprint for mass election, delegation, accountability and recall, the new lesson to be drawn from the Paris Commune was the importance of destroying pre-existing power structures. On 31 January 1967, a front-page editorial in the *People's Daily* reminded readers of Mao's earlier declaration that the Beijing Commune would be a Paris Commune "for the sixth decade of the 20th century":

At that time, Chairman Mao ingeniously foresaw that a new form would appear in our state machinery and mobilized from bottom to top hundreds of millions of people to seize power from the handful of persons within the Party who are in authority and are taking the capitalist road, smash the old things, create a new situation and ... enrich and develop the experience of the Paris Commune, the Soviets and Marxism-Leninism.[56]

The rebels' power seizure and founding of the Shanghai People's Commune in January 1967 – depicted as a heroic measure carried out by workers and residents to keep production going – began as a series of largely uncoordinated mass actions that were subsequently "ideologically transformed into a national political model."[57] The efforts by a core group of seven Workers' General Headquarters' members to restore the city's basic transportation and communication systems were heralded by Zhang Chunqiao only a week later as a "newborn thing, a new form of political power," and an "'economic soviet' replacing the Shanghai people's government."[58]

---

54   Chen, Boda 1966.
55   Zhou, Jiang and Chen 1967.
56   "Lun wuchan jieji gemingpai de duoquan douzheng" (On the proletarian revolutionaries' struggle to
      seize power), *Renmin ribao*, 31 January 1967, 1.
57   Wu 2014 , 96–97.
58   Perry and Li 1997, 146–47.

Yet, the rebel groups that united to "seize power" in early January were quickly overwhelmed by the complexity of the task at hand. By 15 January, Zhou Enlai and Chen Boda were warning rebel delegations to "guard against the seize management wind" (*fangzhi jieguan feng* 防止接管风) that swept Shanghai.[59] Ominous diatribes against "anarchism," "departmentalism," and "ultra-democracy" followed over the next few days, culminating in the 23 January decision to order the People's Liberation Army (PLA) to intervene in the Cultural Revolution by supporting the rebels.[60] On 31 January, the Shanghai Commune model was jettisoned in favour of the "three-in-one" power seizure model implemented in Heilongjiang, where rebels had joined forces with former provincial Party committee cadres and senior officers of provincial PLA units to take power. Whereas provincial administrations had previously been divided into separate bureaucratic systems, the new "three-in-one" model created a single bureaucracy overseen by a revolutionary committee that included military officers, rebel leaders and veteran cadres, and admitted no division between Party and state.

The Paris Commune model of universal suffrage and the rights of election and recall quickly fell by the wayside. Instead, Zhang Chunqiao asserted that, "if [it can be said that] there is a new idea in the 'three-in-one' revolutionary committee, that would be because it has mass representation. Cadre representation and military representation were part of the original [structure]. Its goodness rests in it having mass representation."[61] However, the percentage of mass representatives serving on provincial-level revolutionary committees varied, from a high of 63.8 per cent of the committee's membership in Xinjiang to a low of 13.3 per cent in Sichuan.[62] Furthermore, these mass representatives were generally unelected and were instead chosen by a provincial committee composed of senior Party members, PLA officers and rebel leaders.[63] The chief reason for abandoning election in favour of appointment was the need of the central leadership to guarantee the inclusion of radical rebel forces on the new revolutionary committees, a position consistent with the "16 points" specific instruction that the Party's leadership become more adept at identifying, developing, and expanding leftist forces.[64] In a public discussion in April 1967, Zhou Enlai pointed to the "reversal" of the revolutionary process then underway in Tianjin, where, in the wake of unjustified and excessive violence purportedly carried out by rebel Red Guards and workers, not a single member of the rebel forces had managed to win a seat on the preparatory small group (*choubei xiaozu* 筹备小组) entrusted with setting up Tianjin's new revolutionary committee. Kang Sheng 康生 interrupted the premier to warn against putting blind faith in elections: "under specific

59   Zhou and Chen 1967.
60   Bridgham 1968, 11.
61   Shanghai 'Wenge' shiliao zhengli bianzhu xiaozu (n.d.), 572.
62   Dangdai Zhongguo yanjiusuo shu 2012, 70.
63   Chen, Fenglou 2012, 190–92.
64   *Renmin ribao*, 9 August 1966, 1.

circumstances, elections are not as good as consultative democracy." Zhou quick-ly clarified for his audience: "Why must we not hold elections? Because the revo-lutionary committee is a provisional mechanism of authority, [we] still haven't united up to 95 per cent. We must take the rebel factions as the nucleus, and carry out consultation."[65] By March 1968, the very notion of ballots being cast for seats on revolutionary committees was derided as "election superstition" (*mixin xuanju* 迷信选举), and as a manifestation of "conservative thought" (*baoshou sixiang* 保守思想). Revolutionary committee members were to "not be produced by elections, but instead by relying directly on the revolutionary ac-tion of the broad masses." This process involved the careful selection of mass representatives following "repeated arguments, deliberations, consultations, and examinations":

> Democracy has a class character. The revolutionary organ of power … conforms better to pro-letarian democracy and democratic centralism, and reflects the interests of the proletariat and working people in a much more deep-going way than those organs of power produced in the past only by means of elections.[66]

During the Beijing wave of power seizures in early 1967, attempts were made to institutionalize representative assemblies for Red Guards and rebel workers, and to place them under the control of the new Beijing Revolutionary Committee, but internecine squabbling between the participants prevented the plan from being realized.[67] On 22 February 1967, the University Red Guard Congress (*hongdaihui* 红代会) was established in Beijing at the behest of the central leadership; middle school Red Guards established a separate assembly just over a month later. Similar assemblies were formed across the country at county, city, regional and provincial levels in quick succession, the goal of which was not to guarantee mass political representation but instead ensure coordination and control over the Red Guard movement.

Although central leaders asserted that the Red Guard Congress was not merely a "consultative body" but a genuinely "revolutionary organization and a repre-sentative assembly," the organization reflected the needs and interests of its foun-ders instead of its grassroots participants. Crippled from the outset by factional strife, "chaotic name-calling" (*luan koumaozi* 乱扣帽子) broke out frequently among the representatives, and it was never seen as a bona fide organization with political influence.[68] Instead, by April 1967, Capital Red Guard Congress representatives were waging pitched battles against each other in fierce competi-tion for recognition from above.[69] A national representative assembly of Red Guards was never formed.

The new Workers' Representative Assembly suffered a similar fate. Although Zhang Chunqiao announced that, unlike the All-China Federation of Trade

---

65 Zhou, Chen and Zhang 1967; Wang, Hui 2013, 167–174.
66 Hongqi bianji bu 1968.
67 Qi 1967.
68 Xie and Qi 1967.
69 Walder 2009, 217–222.

Unions organization, the Workers' Representative Assembly had been established by "rebel worker forces to ensure their engagement in class struggle," it quickly became the site of competition between rivals seeking official recognition. In March 1967, the Beijing Workers' Representative Assembly was formed (*Beijing gongdaihui* 北京工代会) under the control of the new Beijing Revolutionary Committee. Its first high-profile action, in April 1967, was to organize a march of over 200,000 workers calling for Liu Shaoqi's 刘少奇 downfall.[70] Within weeks, at the behest of Chairman Mao, rebel worker factions within the former official union branches at every district, county and department level were instructed to link up to form preparatory committees with the intention of establishing worker representative assemblies to replace the former labour unions. Once again, Zhang Chunqiao warned the rebels not to bother with "trivial philosophy or superstitious bourgeois class democracy … carrying out elections by ballot and choosing representatives, making such a mess." Zhang enjoined the rebels to use "livelier" methods to produce "better" representatives than those that prevailed in bourgeois democracies. However, clear procedures and mechanisms for doing so were never agreed upon by the Central Cultural Revolution Small Group, and as such, haphazard methods of selection prevailed.[71]

Conclusion: the Problem of Delegation

When the "Paris Commune principle of election" collapsed amidst the storm of power seizures, complex questions concerning the mechanisms of authorization and accountability were overridden in the interest of securing centralized control and social order. Having rejected the nascent Shanghai Commune in favour of the revolutionary committees, Mao's terse 1967 order calling for the "implementation of the revolutionary 'three-in-one combination' principle" aimed to "establish a provisional mechanism of power that is revolutionary, representative, and has proletarian authority."[72] Yet, the precise composition of these new bodies varied widely, and the means of delegation remained opaque.[73] Within the year, it was clear that the revolutionary committees' power was chiefly exercised by the military, and by the end of the decade, the revolutionary committees served to reconstitute the Party's battered structure. Lacking clear mechanisms of delegation and accountability, the representatives of the revolutionary masses were indistinguishable from either the self-authorizing representatives of indeterminate origin or the appointed tools of more highly placed political actors.

Why did the Paris Commune model of mass representation fail to take root after the initial stage of the Cultural Revolution? In their recent discussion of

70 Zhong 1998, 1257–61.
71 Li, Xun 2015, 1025–27.
72 Mao 1967.
73 Bridgham 1968.

socialist political representation, Michael Hardt and Antonio Negri observe that, in failing to develop fundamentally different conceptions of representation and democracy, 20th-century socialist and communist movements ended up reproducing bourgeois models of sovereignty because they were trapped by the need for the unity of the state, the failure of which facilitated the collapse of East European socialist regimes in the 1980s.[74] In Alain Badiou's view, the institutionalization and then elimination of grassroots Red Guard and rebel groups under the reconstituted remnants of the centre is evidence of the Cultural Revolution's failure to liberate "politics from the framework of the party-state that imprisons it." Although the model of the Paris Commune was invoked as an early declaration that "the dictatorship of the proletariat cannot be a simple statist formula," it was not clear whether the "new" revolutionary committees "reduplicate[d], or purely and simply replace[d], the old and dreaded 'party committees'." In the end, "the Cultural Revolution is the Commune of the age of Communist Parties and Socialist States: a terrible failure that teaches us some essential lessons" about the difficulty of securing both mass representation and mass participation under revolutionary socialism.[75]

These contradictory impulses – between the Party's attempt to absorb fully the rebellious radical left and its attempt to retain control over the process of representing the masses – was already evident in the August 1966 "16 points," which directed Party cadres to institute a Paris Commune-type system of regular elections to guarantee delegation, representation and recall, and to recognize, develop, expand and rely firmly upon the ranks of the *true* revolutionary left. Given the inherent antagonism of these two goals, it is hardly surprising that the Cultural Revolution's radical political experiments could neither resolve nor eliminate the contradiction between the plural nature of mass representation in a heterogeneous socialist state, and the disciplined unity imposed by an elite revolutionary party. The Great Helmsman's 1967 decision to support the revolutionary committees and to protect the role of the Party plotted a future course for the Party's control over mass political representation that has remained firmly in place down to the present day.

In the rush to "thoroughly negate" the Cultural Revolution, the post-Mao leadership shelved discussion of the critical unresolved issues the movement raised about the nature of mass representation under Party rule. These were put on hold again during the process of opening China to international market forces, and deferred yet again under Hu Jintao 胡锦涛, who cited the "tribulations" of the recent past. Xi Jinping 习近平 reformulated the problem early on by recognizing that the Party's rule was authorized by the power of the people – "power conferred by the people, and power exercised on their behalf" (*quan weimin suo fu, quan weimin suo yong* 权为民所赋, 权为民所用).[76] However, as Yu Keping

---

74 Hardt and Negri 2004, 252.
75 Badiou 2010, 107, 190, 137, 278.
76 Li, Weidong, and Cheng 2011, 10.

俞可平 observed, in the absence of mechanisms ensuring mass authorization and accountability, Xi's reformulation remains little more than a mere abstraction: "The fundamental premise underlying 'power conferred by the people' remains in grasping that the governmental power of Party and state officials should represent the popular will of its citizens,"[77] and, of course, in securing the institutional means by which mass authorization and official accountability can be realized.

Biographical note

Patricia M. Thornton is an associate professor in the department of politics and international relations, and a tutor in the politics of China at Merton College, University of Oxford.

摘要: 《五一六通知》为十年文化大革命重要的纲领性文件之一, 并以 "混进党里、政府里、军队里和各种文化界的资产阶级代表人物", 视为文化大革命清洗、斗争的主要目标。此时许多学生与工人认为他们是代表底层的革命者与先进力量, 进而开始抗争, 就此揭露共产党 "代表性" 的概念存在, 及深刻的矛盾。社会主义的代表性, 我认为此概念从文化大革命到现在一直有着同样的矛盾, 而此矛盾到目前为止还是悬而未至, 例如江泽民 "三个代表" 概念并没有受到人民热烈的爱戴, 并从改革开放时代到现在, 人民对共产党的 "代表性"一直保持著怀疑。虽然文化大革命对代表性的概念促进了公共辩论, 并体现了代表性的新方式, 但未能解决代表性本身的矛盾。因此, 文化大革命遗产之一就是共产党对 "代表性" 问题一贯性的沉默以对。

关键词: 代表性; 文革; 革委会; 红代会; 工代会

References

Backer, Larry Catá. 2006. "The rule of law, the Chinese Communist Party, and ideological campaigns: *sange daibiao* (the 'three represents'), socialist rule of law, and modern Chinese constitutionalism." *Journal of Transnational Law and Contemporary Problems* 16(1), 29–102.
Badiou, Alain. 2010. *The Communist Hypothesis*. London: Verso.
Bensaïd, Daniel. 2002. "'Leaps, leaps, leaps': Lenin and politics." *International Socialism* 2(July), 95, http://pubs.socialistreviewindex.org.uk/isj95/bensaid.htm.
Bridgham, Philip. 1968. "Mao's Cultural Revolution in 1967: the struggle to seize power." *The China Quarterly* 34, 6–37.
Bu, Weihua, 2008. *Zalan jiu shijie* (*Destroy the Old World*). Hong Kong: Chinese University of Hong Kong Press.
Chen, Boda. 1966. "Chen Boda dui liangge yue yundong de zongjie" (Chen Boda's summary of the February adverse current) (Oct. 24). In Song Yongyi (ed.). 2010. *Zhongguo wenhua da geming wenku* (*Chinese Cultural Revolution Database*) (3rd ed.). Hong Kong: Chinese University of Hong Kong.

---

77   Yu 2011, E31.

Chen, Fenglou (ed.). 2012. *Zhongguo gongchandang ganbu gongzuo shigang (1921–2002)* (*Survey of the Work of Chinese Communist Party Cadres (1921–2002)*). Beijing: Dangjian duwu chubanshe.

Dangdai Zhongguo yanjiusuo shu (ed.). 2012. *Zhonghua renmin gongheguo shigao 1966–1976* (*Draft History of the People's Republic of China 1966–1976*), Vol. 3. Beijing: Dangdai Zhongguo chubanshe.

Disch, Lisa. 2011. "Toward a mobilization conception of democratic representation." *American Political Science Review* 105(1), 100–114.

Gao, Qiqi. 2010. "Xin Zhongguo zhengdang yu gongmin shehui guanxi bianqian yanjiu" (Research on the vicissitudes of the relationship between China's new ruling party and civil society). *Shanghai xingzhengyuan xuebao* 11(6), 4–12.

Geras, Norman. 1981. "Classical Marxism and proletarian representation." *New Left Review* 125 (Jan–Feb), 75–89.

Harding, Harry. 1981. *Organizing China*. Stanford, CA: Stanford University Press.

Hardt, Michael, and Antonio Negri. 2004. *Multitude: War and Democracy in the Age of Empire*. New York: The Penguin Press.

Hongqi bianjibu. 1968. "Xishou wuchanjieji de xinxian xue ye – zhengdang gongzuo zhongde yige zhongyao wenti" (Absorb the fresh blood of the proletariat: an important problem in Party rectification work), 14 October. In Song Yongyi (ed.). 2010. *Zhongguo wenhua da geming wenku* (*Chinese Cultural Revolution Database*) (3rd ed.). Hong Kong: Chinese University of Hong Kong.

Lenin, Vladimir. 1933. *The State and Revolution*. London: Martin Lawrence.

Li, Weidong, and Cheng Min. 2011. "Jinian 'Guanyu jianguo yilai dang de ruogan lishi wenti de jueyi' fabiao sanshi nian zuotanhui zongshu" (Summary of symposium to commemorate the 30th anniversary of the publication of "Resolution on certain questions in the history of our Party"). *Yanhuang chunqiu* 10–16.

Li, Xun. 2015. *Geming zaofan niandai: Shanghai wenge yundong shigao* (*The Age of Revolutionary Rebellion: A Draft History of Shanghai's Cultural Revolution Movement*). Hong Kong: Oxford University Press.

Li, Youyi. 1957. "Lun woguo de xuanju zhidu" (Theorizing the Chinese electoral system), *Renmin ribao*, 29 November, 7.

Liu, Guokai. 1987. *A Brief Analysis of the Cultural Revolution*. (Anita, Chan (ed.)). Armonk, NY: M.E. Sharpe.

MacFarquhar, Roderick, and Michael Schoenhals. 2006. *Mao's Last Revolution*. Cambridge, MA: Harvard University Press.

Mansbridge, Jane. 2003. "Rethinking representation." *American Political Science Review* 97(4), 515–528.

Mao, Zedong. 1949. "On the people's democratic dictatorship," 30 June, https://www.marxists.org/reference/archive/mao/selected-works/volume-4/mswv4_65.htm.

Mao, Zedong. 1956. "Speech at the second plenary session of the eighth Central Committee of the Communist Party of China" (15 November). In *Mao Zedong xuanji* (*Selected Works of Mao Zedong*). 1999. Vol. 5. Beijing: Renmin chubanshe, 313–329.

Mao, Zedong. 1961–62. "Reading notes on the Soviet text 'Political Economy'." In Moss Roberts (trans.). 1977. *Mao Zedong, A Critique of Soviet Economics*. New York: Monthly Press, 60–75.

Mao, Zedong. 1967. "Bixu shixing gemingde 'san jiehe,' jianli geming weiyuanhui" (The necessity of implementing the revolutionary 'three-in-one,' and establishing revolutionary committees). In Song Yongyi (ed.). 2010. *Zhongguo wenhua da geming wenku* (*Chinese Cultural Revolution Database*) (3rd ed.). Hong Kong: Chinese University of Hong Kong.

O'Brien, Kevin J. 1990. *Reform without Liberalization: China's National People's Congress and the Politics of Institutional Change*. Cambridge: Cambridge University Press.

Perry, Elizabeth, and Li Xun. 1997. *Proletarian Power: Shanghai in the Cultural Revolution*. Boulder, CO: Westview Press.

Pitkin, Hannah F. 1967. *On the Concept of Representation*. Berkeley, CA: University of California Press.

Qi, Benyu. 1967. "Qi Benyu jiejian Beijing hongdaihui choubei renyuan shi de jianghua" (Qi Benyu's talk at the reception of the Beijing Red Guard Congress preparatory personnel) (13 February). In Song Yongyi (ed.). 2010. *Zhongguo wenhua da geming wenku* (*Chinese Cultural Revolution Database*) (3rd ed.). Hong Kong: Chinese University of Hong Kong.

Qinghua daxue fushu zhongxue hongweibing. 1966. "Hongweibing shici" (Red Guard oath) (June). In Song Yongyi (ed.). 2010. *Zhongguo wenhua da geming wenku* (*Chinese Cultural Revolution Database*) (3rd ed.). Hong Kong: Chinese University of Hong Kong.

Qinghua daxue jinggangshan hongweibing xuanchuandui bian (ed.). N.d. *Qinghua daxue dazibao xuan (Kuai Dafu tongzhide dazibao)* (Selected big character posters by Tsinghua University student Kuai Dafu). Tianjin: Tianjinshi diyi mianfenchang hanwei Mao Zedong sixiang zaofandui fanyin.

Renmin jiefangjun guofang daxue dangshi dangjian zhenggong jiaoyanshi (ed.). 1988. "*Wenhua da geming" yanjiu ziliao (shang ce)* (*Research Materials on the "Great Cultural Revolution" (vol. 1)*. Beijing: Renmin jiefangjun guofang daxue chubanshe.

Saward, Michael. 2008. "Making representations: modes and strategies of political parties." *European Review* 16(3), 271–286.

Shanghai 'wenge' shiliao zhengli bianzhu xiaozu (eds.). N.d. *Shanghai "Wenge da geming" shihua* (*Narrative History of Shanghai's Great Proletarian Cultural Revolution*). Internal publication.

Walder, Andrew G. 2009. *Fractured Rebellion: The Beijing Red Guard Movement.* Cambridge, MA: Harvard University Press.

Wang, Hui. 2013. *Tianjin wenge: qinli jingshi* (*The Cultural Revolution in Tianjin: A Personal Chronicle*). Taiwan: Lantai chubanshe.

Wang, Shaoguang. 2012. "Daibiaoxing minzhu yu daiyi minzhu" (Representational and representative democracy). *Kaifang shidai* 2, 152–174.

Wang, Shaoguang. 2014. "Zhongguode 'daiyixing minzhu'" (China's representational democracy). *Zhonggong Hangzhouwei dangxiao xuebao* 1, 4–12.

Wu, Yiching. 2014. *The Cultural Revolution at the Margins.* Cambridge, MA: Harvard University Press.

Xie, Fuzhi, and Qi Benyu. 1967. "Xie Fuzhi Qi Benyu zai jiejian hongdaihui hexin zuchengyuan ji bufen gongzuo renyuan shide jianghua" (Xie Fuzhi and Qi Benyu's talk at the reception of Red Guard Congress core group members and divisional working personnel), 4 March. In Song Yongyi (ed.). 2010. *Zhongguo wenhua da geming wenku* (*Chinese Cultural Revolution Database*) (3rd ed.). Hong Kong: Chinese University of Hong Kong.

Xu, Jilin. 2011. "Jin shinian lai Zhongguo guojia zhuyi sichao zhi pipan" (Critique of the rising tide of nationalist thinking over the past decade), 5 July, http://www.aisixiang.com/data/41945-2.html. Accessed 9 June 2016.

Yu, Keping. 2011. "Jingwei minyi" (Esteeming the will of the people), *Nanfang zhoumo*, 20 January.

Zhang, Chunqiao. 1958. "Pochu zichan ieji de faquan sixiang" (Eliminating the legal rights thinking of the capitalist class), *Renmin ribao*, 13 October, 7.

Zheng, Zhisi. 1966. "Bali gongshe de weida qishi" (The great inspiration of the Paris Commune), *Hongqi* 4, 4–7.

Zhong, Ming (ed.). 1998. *Zhongguo gongyun dadian, 1840–1997 (xia juan)* (*Dictionary of the Chinese Labour Movement, 1840–1997 (2nd vol.*). Beijing: Zhongguo wuzhi chubanshe.

Zhou, Enlai, and Chen Boda. 1967. "Zai shoudu he waidi zaijing geming zaofan tuanti 'zhua geming, cu shengchan' dahui shangde jianghua" (Speeches at a "Grasp revolution, promote production" meeting before rebel groups from in- and outside the capital) (15 January). In Song Yongyi (ed.). 2010. *Zhongguo wenhua da geming wenku* (*Chinese Cultural Revolution Database*) (3rd ed.). Hong Kong: Chinese University of Hong Kong.

Zhou, Enlai, Chen Boda and Zhang Chunqiao. 1967. "Zhongyang shouchang jiejian Tianjin zhujun ji ganbu qunzhong daibiao de jianghua" (Central leaders' speeches at the reception of representatives from the Tianjin garrison, cadres and masses) (10 April). In Song Yongyi (ed.). 2010. *Zhongguo wenhua da geming wenku* (*Chinese Cultural Revolution Database*) (3rd ed.). Hong Kong: Chinese University of Hong Kong.

Zhou, Enlai, Jiang Qing and Chen Boda. 1967. "Zhongyang shouchang zai shoudu dou bufen yuan-xiao shisheng zuotan huishang de jianghua" (Central leaders' speeches at the forum of students and teachers in the capital) (23 January). In Song Yongyi (ed.). 2010. *Zhongguo wenhua da geming wenku* (*Chinese Cultural Revolution Database*) (3rd ed.). Hong Kong: Chinese University of Hong Kong.

Cultural Revolution as Method

Michael Dutton[*]

Abstract
This paper treats the Chinese Cultural Revolution as a means by which to open on to a more affective approach to the question of the political. It examines one piece of art-technology of that period and shows the way it intuitively worked within the fluidity of power to produce political intensity. This one technology is a microcosm of the Cultural Revolution notion of the political that was built around an attempt to channel and harness affective power towards revolutionary ends. Both because it attempts to direct the political through the affective dimension and because its methods of doing so resembled contemporary art practices, this paper opens on to the possibilities of a method based on an art rather than a science of the political.

Keywords: Cultural Revolution; methodology; Maoism; political; art; intensity

A movement that would "touch people to their very souls" (*chuji renmen de linghun* 触及人们的灵魂) was how the Party mouthpiece, *Renmin ribao* 人民日报 (*People's Daily*), described the Cultural Revolution in 1966.[1] The idea stuck. A revolution that could touch people to their very souls could just as easily have been described as an "affective revolution." Affect is, after all, the experiential state that involves an active discharge of emotion leading to an augmentation or diminution of one's bodily capacity to act.[2] When the "soul" is touched, bodily capacities are augmented to such a degree that affect has the potential to be transformed into a revolutionary weapon. Such a weapon is, in the language of Carl Schmitt, a form of political intensity.[3]

Maoism undertook a series of experiments in synaesthetic homologization to bring "idea" and "affect" into correspondence and, through that process, to "weaponize" their union.[4] If Maoist "machines" brought affective energy flows

* Goldsmiths, University of London. Email: M.Dutton@gold.ac.uk.

1 "*Renmin ribao* shelun: wenge shi chuji renmen de linghun de weida geming" (*People's Daily* editorial: the Cultural Revolution is a great revolution that will touch people to their very souls), *Renmin ribao*, 2 June 1966.

2 This understanding of affect is drawn largely from the work of Gilles Deleuze and Felix Guattari (2004, 441) who refer to it as a discharge of emotion and as a weapon that alters a bodily capacity to act.

3 Carl Schmitt (1996, 26) refers to the nature of the political in the following terms: "The specific political distinction to which political actions and motives can be reduced is that between friend and enemy." He then goes on to point out that this "distinction of friend and enemy denotes the utmost degree of intensity of a union or separation, of an association or disassociation."

4 Benedict de Spinoza makes the distinction between idea and affect in Axiom 3, Section 2, of *Ethics*, when he notes that while modes of thinking about, say, love cannot exist without an idea of the

to the surface as a clustering of intensely *felt* political ideas, it did so by channelling them through the ever narrowing vector of the friend/enemy dyadic structure of the political.[5] This was to enable the velocity and intensity of the affective flow to be constantly and rapidly increased.

The Cultural Revolution, as the apogee of this experiment in deploying affective revolutionary technology, has come to be regarded as a disaster for China, but if the various attempts to harness affective energy flows and channel them towards a productive intensity were understood as being the basis of a particular and unique mode of being political, then this disaster opens onto a new way of understanding the dynamics propelling the Maoist political on the ground, and offers an entirely different focus to the ongoing theoretical debate about the Schmittian political.[6]

It suggests that rather than focusing on questions of representation – which was the locus of Schmitt's work – the concept of the political demands that attention needs to be re-directed towards the more ethereal question of politico-affective flows and the technologies that "guide" them.[7] This re-alignment fundamentally alters the way we might begin to look at Maoist politics. It suggests that each mass-line Maoist political campaign, far from being a smokescreen disguising the "real" politics taking place behind the scenes was, in fact, the key to understanding the dynamics propelling this mode of politics. This is because it operated as a key technology for the channelling and harnessing of the affective flow into an overtly political form. It also suggests that work in the cultural and aesthetic realm, far from being merely epiphenomenal propaganda, was actually central to the construction of the political, for Maoist China was the site of an experiment designed to calibrate an approach to political transformation through the channelling of the affective flow. Moreover, it also suggests that, collectively, these technologies, perhaps even more than the battles taking place between individual

---

footnote continued

    thing loved, the idea of love can itself exist separately from the state of being loved. See Spinoza 2015. Drawing on this, Gilles Deleuze (1978) notes that ideas are representational whereas affects are not. The Maoist "trick" was to weave them into one form.

5 The friend/enemy distinction is, of course, what Carl Schmitt calls the unique criteria "to which all action with a specifically political meaning can be traced" (Schmitt 1996, 26). As I have shown elsewhere, this duality can be traced all the way to China where it would sit at the heart of the Maoist political. On the centrality of this to the Maoist political, see Dutton 2005.

6 For Schmitt, this friend/enemy distinction was always concrete, rather than metaphoric or symbolic (Schmitt 1996, 27), leading Jacques Derrida to claim that "the political is only available as practical identification" (Derrida 1997, 117). In other words, the political in Schmitt always takes a representational form. By focusing on the transformation of affective energy flows into a political intensity, the political comes to centre upon the non-representational "fluid" aspects.

7 For Schmitt, the jurist, it was the manifestation of intensity as "solids," structures or "things" – be they institutional forms, like state organs, concepts, like friend and enemy, or juridical concepts such as sovereignty – that became the focus of the concept of the political. The centrality of the concept of representation to Schmitt's thinking can be gleaned from one of his early works written (in 1923) before he developed the concept of the political. Simona Draghici (1988, 23) in the introduction to that work (Schmitt 1988) suggests that the concept of representation was so important to Schmitt that he not only wrote about it but also took on a PhD student to research the question further.

"leading figures" within the conventional political realm or the factional struggles taking place within institutional sites, hold the key to understanding the dynamic propelling the Maoist political. If that holds true, then this has ramifications not just for our understanding of the dynamics of Maoist politics but also more generally for the very definition of the political. To unearth this aspect of the political, however, requires an altogether different approach to the question. In short, it requires an approach that could be termed an art of the political.

An art of the political is neither a political science nor simply a mentality of government (governmentality).[8] Rather, it turns on understanding a set of culturally and site-specific process-driven practices and machines that intuitively work within the fluidity of power to produce political outcomes. Directional rather than intentional, an art of the political focuses on those social technologies that attempt to channel, harness and make concrete the fluidity of the affective realm.[9] An art of the political focuses on the channelling mechanisms that encounter the heterological, intangible and affective flows, and either turns them into political intensities or dissipates them by other means. An art of the political is, then, concerned with those technologies that work either to intensify or to de-intensify the power of an affective energy flow. If commodity markets are the central means by which such flows are de-intensified and dissipated in our world, the Cultural Revolution opens on to the technologies and machinery of class struggle designed to produce and expand the production of political intensity in theirs.

Collectively, these technologies of the Cultural Revolution worked to turn the rational cognitive processes that produced a strong intellectual belief in revolution into goosebumps on the surface of the skin, lumps in the back of the throat, tears in the eyes of the believer, and anger in the heart of the revolutionary.[10] The novelty and invention of this Maoist political apparatus lies precisely in its experimentation with technologies of fusion that brought together and intensified idea and affect. It would lead to thought being pushed into excess, action into "chaos" and reason into "madness," all through the singular focus being placed on fighting the (class) "enemy."[11] If that class-based focus on tapping into and channelling this affective flow led to people being touched to their very souls, the binary

---

8 This is not to reject the notion of governmentality but merely to note a limit on thinking of this flow as being restricted to matters of government. Rather than a mentality, this form of thinking in some ways resembles the broader frame that Edward Said has called a "style of thought," which, he notes, informs all writing, thinking and acting on "the Orient." Having said this, it should also be acknowledged that the rendition of the political given here draws heavily on the Foucauldian insistence that power is fluid, mobile and relational rather than "a thing." On governmentality, see Foucault 1991. On the Said notion of a style of thought, see his description of Orientalism in Said 1978, 12. On Foucault's rendition of power as fluid, see Foucault 1978, 94–95.

9 It could, perhaps, in the language of Delueze and Guattari, be called a (political) "becoming." For details of how this might be the case, see Massumi 1992, 94–95.

10 How these are "measured," and thereby become unfelt in our world, is described in Massumi 1995, 83–109.

11 Massumi (1995, 85) notes the way intensity is always organized around an either/or.

logic being deployed produced the occasional violent intensity that left some very deep scars.

With varying degrees of moral indignation and intensity, China area studies scholarship has been picking away at these scars ever since. Picking at scars led to stories of abuse that resulted in widespread disenchantment and revulsion. As the critiques mounted, they buried any claims to the Cultural Revolution being a socio-political experiment. All it seemed to have done, it appeared to suggest, was scar a generation. Whether that generation is scarred or genuinely touched, is, however, in terms of political theory at least, less significant than the fact that it "affected" them. That is to say, in marking the soul, it moved the question of class struggle beyond the rational, homogenous realm and into the realm of affect. It was here, in this realm of the heterological, that the socio-political affective revolutionary experiments of the Cultural Revolution took place. These experiments were, in a sense, being carried out "underground" for they were buried within a concept of the political that was itself embedded within a discourse of Maoist revolutionary experiment.

Maoism would never speak of this "affective" revolutionary experiment directly for it was regarded as little other than a set of techniques or means to an end, and that end was the manifest revolutionary experiment extending around the category of class struggle. Yet, under this other language game centring on the words "class struggle," a "style of thought" could be discerned that revealed affective dimensions within a series of symptomatically linked practices, ideas and techniques Maoism either devised or developed.

What was the nationwide, rhythmic, mass campaign if not an expression of a guiding process being imposed upon a pulsating energy force designed to build into a political intensity? How could one understand the Maoist notion of continuous revolution without an intuitive grasp of the fluidity of power and the political? How could one understand micro-level techniques such as typification and the formation of "models" without an appreciation of how political anthropomorphism led to a condensation and intensification of the figure of the (typified) enemy? Together, these and other techniques that aimed to touch the soul worked within what has been referred to as the "one big concept" of Maoism.

This term, "one big concept," comes neither from Mao or Maoism but from the conceptual artist Cai Guoqiang 蔡国强 as he reflected upon the power of one Maoist "model" artwork that he re-worked for the Venice Biennale of 1999. That original artwork was called the *Rent Collection Courtyard* and, when unveiled during the Cultural Revolution, it was said to "reflect a true picture of the soul-stirring (*jingxin dongpo* 惊心动魄) struggle of the old society in the countryside."[12] It was a monumental work – being 118 metres long and featuring 114 life-sized mud statues – and profoundly political in nature: it was

---

12 "Shouzuyuan, chuanbu nisu zhongxin fanzhi zai Beizhanchu" (Reproductions of all the clay statues of the *Rent Collection Courtyard* go on exhibition in Beijing), *Renmin ribao*, 3 December 1966.

proclaimed a "model" for the plastic arts at the beginning of the Cultural Revolution in 1966.[13]

Housed in the central courtyard of the Manor House Museum of a former Sichuan landlord, Liu Wencai 刘文彩, in the township of Anren 安仁, the *Rent Collection Courtyard* was of interest to Cai less for its manifest politics than for its material form. The unstable nature of the un-kiln dried mud statues enabled Cai to interrogate processes of creation and destruction as the mud cracked and fell away from the surfaces of his remade *Rent Collection* statues in Venice. Where the original had been a "finished" set of figurative and realist art-objects designed to tug on the emotions and channel political intensity through a narrative description of the ongoing class struggle in the countryside, Cai's *Venice Rent Collection Courtyard* re-focused the work on the more abstract, contemplative question of flow. Cai's partially completed, completed and slowly deteriorating mud statues were inspired by a Taoist notion of cyclical birth, life and death flows.[14] His focus on the power of flow was anchored to the impermanency of the statues' material form. Mud would dry and crack and, as it did, the cyclical flow of the Taoist notion of birth, life and death came to the fore. By bringing the question of flow to the surface, Cai's work helps us to understand its function within the original work, but it is his memory of what inspired his interest in this original Maoist work that brings us back to the question of the affective element in any life flow:

When I was a schoolboy and first saw the *Rent Collection Courtyard*, I was moved by the adult next to me who looked at it and cried because he had really suffered at the hands of his landlord. I felt his pain. The exhibition guides who explained the story of the *Rent Collection Courtyard* to [our class] also cried as they spoke … and when they cried, the whole class began to cry. They gave us some really inedible food that tasted like straw, and they explained that this was a peasant staple in the old society. We forced down the food and, with tears in our eyes, looked at the statues as the severe hardships of the old society were explained to us. Now that I look back on this from an artistic point of view, this whole thing is really interesting. It was a work not just about statues, but about the tears of the guide who explained things, and the horror of the disgusting food we were being forced to eat … These things were all part of the same big concept.[15]

The statues, the tears, the food and the horror were existentially felt effects tied together and intensified by the same big concept. It was this one, big, politico-affective concept that Cai's conceptual art replaced with its own particular focus on flow. Yet, despite the evisceration of the "narrative string" that had held in place the affective, cathartic and political dimensions of the original work, Cai's re-working still functioned like a palimpsest revealing the shadowy traces of the original focus of the work in the faces of his slowly deteriorating mud

---

13 See Erickson 2010, 123. For an excellent English language account that contextualizes the *Rent Collection Courtyard* within the Manor House series of exhibits, see Lee 2014, 197–242.
14 As Anne Wedell-Wedellsborg says, it involved "questions of authenticity/originality/copying in art works as well as formal copyright, of socialist realism versus postmodernism, of the process of creation and destruction, individual and collective, of timelines, context and site specificity, of local and global, of the concept of aura, and of course again of different expectations, China versus the West." See Wedell-Wedellsborg 2010.
15 Interview with Cai Guoqiang, New York, 24 March 2010.

statues.[16] By removing the narrative thread, Cai's reconstruction enabled the focus to shift to the process of production rather than to the finished product or content. In de-centring the original work's (political) content and replacing it with a focus on the act of making, Cai Guoqiang's process-based work could well be accused of being an aestheticization of the political. Oddly, however, it was precisely because Cai shifted the focus of his work out of the space of an overt Maoist political aesthetic and into the more abstract space of contemporary art that he was able to reveal some of the key techniques of the original work. By shining the spotlight on process – here meaning not just the technical process of sculpting but the panoply of process-based techniques employed by the original Maoist sculptors to create the work – the mechanisms devised to channel the affective flow of the political towards a cathartic intensity begins to come into focus. Developed in unison with other techniques designed to channel and intensify the flow, the original *Rent Collection Courtyard* statues reveal a certain machine-like quality in the way they produced this effect.

This is not the machine art of Vladimir Tatlin designed to cognitively estrange, but the art-machine of Maoism designed to draw in and emotionally inspire and direct.[17] Where Tatlin's work was produced in the age of steel and made to make iron "stand on its hind legs" and seek an artistic formula,[18] these statues were made of mud and drew upon the telluric techniques of the peasant artisan wed to the didacticism of a theatrically based political narrative. It was artisanship rather than artistry, mud rather than steel, and it was the art of emotional identification rather than an art of estrangement or contemplation. A cognitive understanding of the *Rent Collection Courtyard* story line was insufficient for the goal was to produce a work that would be intensely felt as well as understood.

Working within another machine – the Manor House Museum – the *Rent Collection Courtyard* exhibition was designed to lead to one single political effect: the raising of revolutionary consciousness. These were technologies of political intensification, not estrangement, and they were attempting to weave together multiple and parallel strands and flows into one big concept. The original sculptors worked to intensify the emotional effect of the *Rent Collection Courtyard* by

16 Faces were important to the sculptors of the *Rent Collection Courtyard*. Long Taicheng, who worked on the original statues and was then chosen to go to Beijing and work on the reproductions being made there, explains: "When I went to Beijing to reproduce the statues, I had to observe numerous faces. Every day as we took the bus from Hepingli to the Art Museum, we observed many northern boys' faces. In my work, I tried to mix the faces of northern boys with those from the south. I also studied their expressions of anger and resistance. They looked very different from the anger and resistance being displayed on the faces of adults." Interview with Long Taicheng, Chongqing, 21 August 2011.

17 It was Victor Shklovsky who spoke of Tatlin's Tower as being an "architecture of estrangement." According to Svetlana Boym, this notion of *ostranenie*, or estrangement, suggested both a distancing (dislocating, *depaysement*) and making strange. For an elaboration on this, see Boym 2008, 18–19.

18 Once again, these are the words of Shklovsky (2005, 69–70). The association of Tatlin and machine art, however, comes from the Dadaists. It was at the Berlin Dadaist Fair of May 1920 that two of the founders of the Dadaist movement, George Grosz and John Heartfield (Helmut Herzfeld), held up a large placard taken down from the gallery wall with the slogan, "Art is Dead – Long Live Tatlin's Machine Art" written across it. They were then famously photographed holding up the placard. For them, *Machinenkunst* flagged the death of art. For details, see Lynton 2009, 30–67. See also Tafuri 1990, 136.

collecting, editing and weaving together into a single tale the numerous stories of exploitation peasants suffered at the hands of their landlords.[19] Intensification was not a depiction of real events but of real affects. This would involve re-modelling peasant gestures not on the gestures of "real life" peasants but on "typifications" of such gestures modelled by actors of a Sichuan Opera troupe. Their gestures and comportment signified a stylized and intensified bodily form used for dramatic effect[20] and purposively designed to produce crying, anger and enthusiasm (*jin* 劲) as a response.[21]

This Maoist artwork did more than just convey a message in mud: it attempted to inscribe this message emotionally in the audience's mind. More than that, it also wanted to mould politically the artists sculpting the mud statues. Through a very different process-driven practice to that which informs conceptual art, the original sculptors became imbricated in the transformation process. As Li Shaoyan 李少言 pointed out: "The process of creation was also a process of thought reform for the artists concerned."[22] In other words, the making of this work involved a much broader set of transformative processes than the sculpting of mud. The ethnographic fieldwork necessary to produce a plot-line that would touch the peasants "to their souls" demanded that the sculptors themselves be touched. To be touched, the sculptors would have to bury themselves in the peas-ant life they were depicting. They had to live with the peasants to understand ex-istentially the life they lived, and it was this experience that would then have ontological effects upon them and transform their work own styles.

From the peasants, the sculptors not only learned the indigenous techniques of mud statue making, they also learned a pedagogy of frugality and self-reliance. These techniques would be used to alter the practices of these classically trained "academic" sculptors. Moreover, the demand that this be a collective rather than individual enterprise forced these sculptors not just to reflect upon their craft but also upon their own work practices within art.

As an artwork machine created specifically to channel the flow of the political, the *Rent Collection Courtyard* was, therefore, to have cognitive effects upon those who worked on the design and production of these statues as well as upon the viewing public. The work required intense thought being given to the emotional effects these material objects would have upon the masses. "Wax statues in the

---

19 Wang, Zhi'an 2001, 159, 163.
20 Interview with Zhao Shutong, one of the original lead sculptors on the project, Chengdu, 19 August 2011. See also Wang, Zhi'an 2001, 165.
21 These are the "emotions" that the sculptors of the original *Rent Collection Courtyard* decided to focus on and "produce" through the artwork they were creating. For further details on the way they attempted to tap into these emotions, see Wang, Zhi'an 2001, 202.
22 Li Shaoyan, who was head of the Sichuan "arts council" (*meixie*) at the time, made these remarks in relation to the weight being placed on the collective nature of the enterprise, which, he claimed, helped combat the individualism of the artist (Li 1965, 6). But he was not the only one. Ma Li, who was the Wenjiang area committee propaganda ministry chief at the time, addressed the sculptors saying that, "in going through the process of creating this work, you also go through your own type of ideological reform, and towards your world view, and view of humanity, you undergo your own huge revolution" (Wang, Zhi'an 2001, 191).

exhibition offer gloomy, frightful figures that evoke real fear" one sculptor would say … "ahh yes, but the reality of the old society was about a hundred times gloomier and more frightful" came the reply, and so the debate on appearance and its ability to carry a strong political message continued.[23] It required experimenting with various indigenous materials and knowledge forms to "place" the work, not just in a site-specific location, but within a style of thought that was readily intelligible to ordinary rural people.

Using everyday materials and motifs that local people were familiar with meant learning from the masses. "From April 1965 onwards, I understood our role as being to offer support, which meant 'learn at work and work in learning' (*gongzuo zhong xuexi, xuexi zhong gongzuo* 工作中学习，学习中工作)," the Western-trained lead sculptor of the project, Zhao Shudong 赵树同, would say.[24] It meant living and working with peasants, developing a sense of self-reliance, and adopting a collectivist and self-critical attitude towards oneself and one's work. Lastly, it required an attitudinal change such that challenges and hardships encountered in the process of making the work were treated as part of the work. It was an honour bestowed rather than a burden carried. "In those days it was really hard … things were really hard but no one had any demands because, from our perspective, we felt really honoured" junior sculptor on the project, Long Taicheng 隆太成, said.[25] The process was profoundly experiential and utterly Maoist. Indeed, it was another example of "greater, faster, better, [and] more economical" production (*duokuaihaosheng* 多快好省) being operationalized, but this time in mud rather than in the economy.

The sheer scale of the project made it "greater" (*duo* 多). The honour felt by young sculptors such as Long Taicheng was harnessed by a Stakhanovite-like work drive that led them to produce this massive work in just four and a half months (faster – *kuai* 快). The use of simple, cheap and indigenous-based artisan technologies brought a new economy to the usually expensive art of figurative sculpture, reducing the cost of each statue to just three yuan per statue (economical – *sheng* 省).[26] Moreover, through the fusion of modern political energy with figurative art practices merged with demotic indigenous telluric technologies, the plastic arts themselves would be transformed (better – *hao* 好).

"It is a revolution in sculpting," crowed the official Party organ, the *Renmin ribao*. Declared a "model work" by Mao's wife, Jiang Qing 江青, the original *Rent Collection Courtyard* would be hailed as the harbinger and prototype of a

---

23 Wang, Zhi'an 2001, 140.
24 According to Paul Clark (2008, 206), the statues were made by teachers and students of the Sichuan Academy of the Arts, but that is not entirely true as peasant artisans were involved. Indeed, according to Zhao Shutong, the indigenous element, not the academy, played the primary role. The role of the Academy in the construction of this suite of statues, he asserted, has been overstated by others such as the other leading sculptor on the project, Wang Guanyi. Interview, Zhao Shutong.
25 Interview, Long Taicheng.
26 Three yuan is the figure given in *Renmin ribao*, 6 November 1965. On today's exchange rates, that is less than US 50 cents per statue.

new revolutionary practice in the plastic arts.[27] What it shared with the other "model," or *yangban* 样板, artworks was that, like them, it was designed to channel and heighten political intensity in a manner that would, simultaneously, stretch the boundaries of the art form it worked within by fusing modern and indigenous telluric technology and knowledge.[28]

Such fusion practices – that brought the telluric into the modern – stretched well beyond the arts to include all those things that were labelled "socialist new things." The "new medical methods" of Maoism, for example, demonstrated a similar re-alignment and fusion of modern Western medical techniques with traditional Chinese medicinal practices to produce a new model for medical science.[29] Model art, model science, model theatre – this concept of the model, as Børge Bakken demonstrates, is deeply embedded in traditional Chinese cultural practices and spreads into educational and even social-control discourses.[30] What turned model-making from a tradition into a revolutionary practice, however, was not just the ability to set a norm but also its capacity to turn that norm into a device to incite class-based feelings of love and hatred.

Typification was used both to produce positive love and also to generate hatred. Negative models, such as the landlord Liu Wencai in the *Rent Collection Courtyard*, were created by building upon the "proper name" such that it came to embody all the negative traits of the particular class they represented. The narrative string holding such a biography together would be based on the revealed tales of exploitation and excess. Endless stories tipped into the single figure of Liu Wencai erupted into a single political torrent. The unity of the proper name and the typified life intensified the effect: "When the labouring masses viewed this work, they remembered suffering so much pain that they lost their voices (*tongku shusheng* 痛苦失声) but simultaneously developed a heightened sense of class hatred," said the *Renmin ribao*.[31] Even before completion, this artwork seemed to touch raw nerves: "Because we left the courtyard gate open when we were working, a lot of the peasants got a sneak preview and when they were

---

27 In February 1966, Jiang Qing identified the *Rent Collection Courtyard* as a model for other artists to emulate in a speech entitled "Summary of the forum on literature and art in the armed forces with which comrade Lin Piao entrusted Chiang Ch'ing." Chung and Miller 1968, 208. For further commentary on this work as a model, see Zhang 2005, 46.

28 Paul Clark claims that the model operas made just these sorts of claims and that was what made them "models." While not untrue, the key thing that made models exemplary was that each constituted a machine component within what one might call, to steal a line from the Dadaist about Taitlin, a machine-art form. This made Maoist art-forms technologies for the channelling and intensification of the flow into a single political cathartic end. For a more prosaic account of the characteristics that led to them being technologies of the flow, see Clark 2008, 57–58, 73–75.

29 On Maoist innovations in medicine, see Beijing City Hygiene Bureau Small Leadership Group of the Revolutionary Committee of the Beijing Number Two Hospital 1969.

30 Børge Bakken traces this penchant for the model, the typification and the exemplary back to traditional times, noting that Chinese pedagogy contains a "fundamental assumption ... that people are capable of learning from models." Bakken 2000, 8. Ouyang Zongshu on Chinese genealogical records illustrates this with reference to the exemplary ancestors being used as models for future generations in the late dynastic period (Ouyang 1992). For further details on how this late dynastic tradition fed into the Maoist pedagogy, see Dutton 2004.

31 "Shouzuyuan" (*The Rent Collection Courtyard*), *Renmin ribao*, 6 November 1965.

invited in they were intensely aroused (*qunqing jifen* 群情激奋) and choked back their tears (*qibuchengsheng* 泣不成声). Some even fainting (*hundao zaidi* 昏倒在地)," said one of the leading sculptors, Wang Guanyi 王官乙.[32]

To produce this effect, the *Rent Collection Courtyard* could only work within a very specific cultural milieu in which the one big concept propelled all affective energy streams towards an intense political conclusion. Indeed, the art-ful-ness of the original *Rent Collection Courtyard* project lay not in the realm of aesthetic appreciation or estrangement but in the channelling function it performed within a particular overarching political culture. Its artfulness in this particular politico-cultural milieu led to it operating as a catalyst for the harnessing of emotions such that they would intertwine and be channelled into a single and powerful political intensity.

Like the "new medical methods," the *Rent Collection Courtyard* project attempted to touch people to their souls by pressing upon key political affective pressure points. This method took it beyond an appreciation of a cognitive-based knowledge regime that offered an account of past oppression and attempted in-stead to reproduce, in facsimile, the taste, tears and pain of past suffering via a mud-based "condensation" of the rural class struggle.[33] Peasants fainting as they saw their own pasts caught in mud; silent pain developing into class hated; teardrops welling in a schoolboy's eye as food was ingested but proved to be hard to swallow because of the crimes of the evil landlord, Liu Wencai. These were just a few of the physical manifestations of a visceral connection being created between cognitive and affective states of being. These affective states were not simply based upon "revelation" but produced through a manipu-lation and channelling of the affective energy flow that surfaced as a series of powerful emotions connected ultimately to a political campaign.

Sipping his tea and talking to the artists while they sculpted the work, the local Party chief and patron of the work, Ma Li 马力, said: "Concerning the creation of the *Rent Collection Courtyard*, I want to raise a small request. The spirit (*qifen* 气氛) of the overall statues needs to be grasped and grasped accurately, for the aim of this work is to lay stress on the overwhelmingly positive aspects and if this healthy trend does not prevail, then a perverse or evil energy flow (*xieqi* 邪气) will."[34] The evil energy flow of the landlord "enemy" would, therefore, not be the central driving force of this political narrative.[35] Rather, the enemy

---

32 Wang, Guanyi 1996, 38.

33 *Renmin ribao* said that: "We have many young people in this country who have seen the reality of man's exploitation of man, and man's oppression of man. And even though many people have obviously seen this, it was quite a while ago and the influence of this upon them has grown ever more faint. So the role of these mass clay statues, in reflecting the leadership of Mao Zedong thought, is to awaken people from their light sleep and to get them to rise up, getting them to recognize and reflect upon the fact that the old society acted against the people's interests, and from this vantage point strengthened their love of the current new society of socialism." See "Shouzuyuan" (*The Rent Collection Courtyard*), *Renmin ribao*, 11 June 1965.

34 Ma Li, quoted in Wang, Zhi'an 2001, 191.

35 This tends to contradict the important point made by Leo Strauss on Schmitt's work, which suggests that the enemy is always philosophically central. See Strauss 1996.

would be used to catapult the peasants into a realization that there was a need for their energy to be directed, guided and organized. Tears would be shed, remembrances of past horrors would flood in, and all the feelings of humiliation and misery would be gathered together pointing, inexorably, to one solution: the need for revolutionary organization. That is, it would point to the need for a friend.[36] To reach that conclusion, the original statues were designed to transcend logical-cognitive connections and tap into the affective flow to release three key emotions – crying, hatred (*chouhen* 仇恨), and strength or drive (*jin* 劲):

[If] we want the masses, when viewing the *Rent Collection Courtyard*, to think about old China … then, in emotional terms, we need to induce three emotional changes within them: crying, enmity, and drive.
Crying – this would deeply arouse the masses, allowing for the production of a mass consciousness by moving them with feelings of tragedy.
Enmity – here we wanted the audience to hate the landlord class, hate reactionaries, and hate the old society.
Drive – after undergoing "speak bitterness" sessions (*yiku sitian* 忆苦思甜), the people would be inspired to a higher class consciousness, transforming their class hatred into a form of powerful resistance.[37]

It was in the penultimate section of the original *Rent Collection Courtyard* work entitled "resistance" (*fankang* 反抗), that crying and hatred would be transformed into strength and drive. Wang Zhi'an 王治安 explains how these energy flows were channelled through these emotional states into a unidirectional torrent:

The final section of the work was themed "resistance" (*fankang*) and the key point here was enmity (*chouhen*) – the enmity of the peasants towards the landlord. Here, there was a self-generating notion of struggle tied to a growing consciousness of that struggle. Hence, [enmity and resistance] were two halves of the same coin: one expressed an abstract "hatred" (*hen* 恨); the other, the peasants' growing self-awareness of where that hatred would lead. Here, the idea of hate is expressed as a form of spontaneity (*zifaxing* 自发性), while the growing peasant self-awareness pointed towards organization.[38]

To understand, concretely, how the channelling of spontaneity and self-awareness could produce revolutionary organization, the artists packed their bags and went and lived in a former partisan basecamp known locally as "little Yan'an."[39] There, they lived a spartan peasant life, sharing the food of the peasants and working alongside them in their labours. "This was all part of the creative process," lead local sculptor, Li Qisheng 李奇生, would insist.[40]

36 Here, then, we witness a very important theoretical shift taking place. "Of the two elements of the friend-enemy mode of viewing things, the 'enemy' element manifestly takes precedence." Strauss tells us about Schmitt (Strauss 1996, 88). For Ma Li and the Maoists, things are different. For Ma Li, the enemy is a "tool" to be used to promote class struggle. Moreover, from Ma Li's warning about not allowing "evil energy" to prevail, right through to the sequencing of the *Rent Collection Courtyard* statues leading to the victory of the "collective friend" (the revolutionary organization), the enemy is rendered as the propellant pushing forward the victory of the friend.
37 Wang, Zhi'an 2001, 202. Author's translation.
38 Ibid., 210.
39 The official name of the place they went to was Three Junction Commune (*Sancha gongshe*). Originally, it was the underground basecamp of the west Sichuan Communist Party branch. See Wang, Zhi'an 2001, 163, for further details.
40 Ibid., 162–63.

This experience of living, working and struggling alongside the peasants was all part of a Maoist pedagogy and, when combined with the use of mud and indigenous technology and knowledge, produced the telluric conditions for a political transformation that was constantly being contexualized in terms of an idealized view of peasant life as intrinsically revolutionary.

The use of "found objects" in the *Rent Collection Courtyard* project such as desks, an abacus and a grain thrasher, the employment of site specificity by using the courtyard of the landlord's manor house as a stage, and the leaning of mud statues on doorways or against structural pillars – all these novel art innovations came not from conceptual art theory but out of a profoundly Maoist sense of "making do." Making mud statues, then, was far more complex and process-based than the final sculpted work might suggest. The entire process, however, was designed to produce a political effect. It was, in fact, part of the "one big concept" of Maoism, to return to Cai's phrase, and that could only be imagined in terms of affective productivity operating within a larger sociopolitical context particular to that time, place and culture. In that sense, this work raises the question of site specificity in two ways.

First, in terms of the broader society, this form of art-incitement could only work when the overall regime of veridiction was political rather than market based. In other words, the *Rent Collection Courtyard* was "site specific" in terms of the revolutionary regime of veridiction that required the production, reproduction and harnessing of poetic-political intensities wedding to both cognitive and affective flows. Within that society, this artwork was designed principally around the gathering and channelling of an affective flow so that it would and could be transformed into a political torrent.

Second, in terms of the local context, the original mud statues must be considered in terms of their role within Liu Wencai's manor house. Here, in its original form, the *Rent Collection Courtyard* art machine was but one (albeit penultimate) technology within a larger machine known as the Landlord Manor House Museum. Once again, site specificity takes on a particularly political hue for it was art technologies like the *Rent Collection Courtyard* project that helped to transform Liu Wencai's manor house into what the Maoists at the time would come to call a classroom of class struggle.[41] Yet, even this classroom had a pedagogy that could only operate in the broader context of the Cultural Revolution as one of many machines that would politicize the entire social landscape.

This is not to suggest that these machines always worked. On the contrary, an economy of flows is constantly and permanently shadowed by leakage. Yet, leakages in this regime were potentially productive. Leakages, read symptomatically, often spelled out the word "enemy," which in turn broadened the field of class struggle. Within Maoism, the more these machines leaked, the more they patterned the nature of the class struggle. In other words, through leakages, these

---

41 Wang Zhi'an describes the manor house as a classroom for class education in his book. Ibid., 19.

machines potentially produced the conditions for their own extended use. The *Rent Collection Courtyard*, therefore, is much more than a Maoist timepiece of the Cultural Revolution. It is an artefact of another mode of being political and a window opening onto an understanding of that other mode.

In disposing of affective energy flows by intensifying them, this mode of the political operated along very different vectors to those forms of the political that employed the phantasmagoric to turn intensity into commodity desire. Technologies such as the *Rent Collection Courtyard*, therefore, required reconditioning when the channelling of affective flows was no longer tied to the intensity of class struggle but was instead dispersed and diffused through market fetishization. It was in the transformation of machinery like the *Rent Collection Courtyard* that the legacy of the Cultural Revolution moment reveals itself.

Just as Cai Guoqiang moved the *Rent Collection Courtyard* out of figurative and into conceptual art by changing the location, so too market reforms would transform the *Rent Collection Courtyard* exhibition from a political into an aesthetic machine by a process of mimetic reconfiguration. In the reform era, Liu Wencai's manor house was re-defined as an important feudal-era historic relic,[42] rather than a classroom of class struggle. This process involved transforming the central courtyard that housed the *Rent Collection Courtyard* into an art space. Behind glass, in a temperature-controlled, softly lit gallery space, the *Rent Collection Courtyard* statues entered the white cube. Here was politics transformed into aesthetics through a process of mimetic reconfiguration of the entire Manor House site. Similar mimetic transformations were visited upon Chinese policing practices,[43] government bureaucracies[44] and the operations of businesses.[45] These transformations reveal more than the mimetic faculty of government; they reveal the continuing concern that government displays with the channelling of the affective flow. In the current era, however, any machinery with a capacity to generate political intensity is to be disabled, dismembered, diffused, transformed or repressed. With market veridiction at the heart of the reform system, attempts to disable and transform the Manor House machinery offer one small example of this new political focus. It is this process of transformation that reveals the lasting legacy of the Cultural Revolution as a mentality of government still essentially concerned with the policing of the flow. This continued preoccupation with the channelling of affective flows has, in recent years,

---

42 "A typical reflection of the nature and architectural form of landlord class estates in Sichuan in the modern era" which "epitomises the rise and fall of feudal class production in the modern era of China" was how Wang Zhi'an, Wang Fei and Wang Shao describe it. See Wang, Zhi'an, Wang and Wang 2003, 103–04.

43 The redeployment of Maoist movement structures into law and order campaigns is dealt with in Dutton 2002, while the role of the contract in transforming the mass line is addressed in Dutton 2005.

44 Traits that have been termed a "guerrilla policy style" by Sebastian Heilmann and Elizabeth Perry are said to persist in the reform era. Heilmann and Perry 2011, 12.

45 The operations of the company Hua Wei are founded on notions of self-criticism and self-reliance, learned by the company's founders through years of experience of the Maoist-inspired ethics of the Chinese army. See Cheng and Liu 2003.

however, moved beyond the mimetic transformation of inherited relics and old practices and come to inform contemporary governmental practices in relation to new areas of concern. The internet offers the clearest example of this ongoing concern.

In a recent series of quantitative studies of internet censorship covering over 11 million social media posts from almost 1,400 websites across China, Gary King, Jennifer Pan and Margaret E. Roberts demonstrate this preoccupation in current Chinese government censorship strategies. Contrary to most Western accounts of Chinese censorship as crude and unsuccessful attempts to ban dissent, their studies show that the Chinese censors are less concerned about dissent than about blogs leading to potential collective street-level action. Blogs and sites that attract large numbers of hits and are deemed to have a potential for collective social action are subject to censorship and this is irrespective of whether such blogs foster or fight with the Communist Party.[46]

Chinese government censors, they note, redact pro-government posts and anti-government posts, for their aim is not to stifle criticism but to halt internet viral bursts that could lead to collective political action.[47] To this end, the pro-government "50 cent army" (*wumaodang* 五毛党) bloggers are dispatched not to bombard viral sites with pro-government propaganda and thereby raise the degree of political intensity by heightening the friend-enemy antagonism, but rather to lure traffic away from such sites towards ones with less collective political action potential.[48] In other words, the Chinese censorship strategy is built around halting the eruption of political intensities and not stamping out all criticism.[49] Achieving this end involves, once again, channelling and harnessing affective flows, but unlike the Cultural Revolution, this time the focus is on de-intensification. Nevertheless, it is still a politics that has, as its key compass point, the friend and enemy grouping. Both in the Maoist era and in the reform era, it is still a policing of the affective flow that sculpts the political imagination. The sensitivity around the question of the Cultural Revolution in contemporary China today is, perhaps, a sign of just how deeply the Chinese imagination has been marked by this question of political intensities. The most evocative legacy of the Cultural Revolution, perhaps, is this haunting presence; captured not in words, records or material forms, but in a continued and quite different mentality of government that is still tied to the harnessing and channelling of affective flows.

Acknowledgement

The author wishes to thank Stacy Lo for her help with research and translation, Deborah Kessler for help with proof reading and comments, and Chris Berry,

---

46 See King, Pan and Roberts 2013, 327.
47 King 2013.
48 King 2013.
49 See King, Pan and Roberts 2013; 2014.

Patricia M. Thornton and Harriet Evans for their comments and their original invitation to present this at the Cultural Revolution Legacy workshop organized by *The China Quarterly* in 2015.

Biographical note

Michel Dutton is professor of politics at Goldsmiths, University of London. Although, perhaps, best known for *Streetlife China* (CUP, 1998), Dutton is the author of numerous books on China including, most recently, *Policing Chinese Politics: A History* (Duke, 2005) and, with Lo and Wu, *Beijing Time* (Harvard, 2008).

摘要: 这篇文章将中国文化大革命当作是一个在探究政治问题这课题中能够开辟有关情感方面渠道的工具。它检视那个年代的一种艺术的技术，并展示它如何在权力的流动性里产生政治强度。这个技术是文革中对政治的这概念浓缩，并也是将情感力量转化做革命目标的企图。因为它企图将政治导向情感面向，而这些方法与当代艺术实践相似，这篇文章开辟一种以艺术为基础来研究政治的方法之可能性，而非科学。

关键词: 文革; 方法论; 毛泽东思想; 政治; 美术; 强度

References

Bakken, Børge. 2000. *The Exemplary Society*. Oxford: Oxford University Press.
Beijing City Hygiene Bureau Small Leadership Group of the Revolutionary Committee of the Beijing Number Two Hospital. 1969. *Mao Zedong sixiang tongshui xinyiliaofa ziliaohuibian* (*A Compilation of Materials on Following the Command of Mao Zedong Thought with New Medical Methods*). Beijing: Beijing Health Bureau leadership small group, Beijing Number Two Hospital Revolutionary Group (internal publication).
Boym, Svetlana. 2008. *Architecture of the Off-Modern*. New York: Princeton Architectural Press.
Cheng, Dongsheng, and Lili Liu. 2003. *Huawei zhengxiang* (*The Truth about Huawei*). Beijing: Xiandai Zhongguo chubanshe.
Chung, Hua-Min, and Arthur C. Miller. 1968. *Madame Mao: A Profile of Chiang Ch'ing*. Hong Kong: Union Research Centre.
Clark, Paul. 2008. *The Chinese Cultural Revolution: A History*. Cambridge: Cambridge University Press.
Delueze, Gilles. 1978. "Lecture transcripts on Spinoza's 'Concept of Affect'" (Emilie and Julien Deleuze (trans.)), http://www.webdeleuze.com/php/sommaire.html. Accessed 1 April 2015.
Delueze, Gilles, and Felix Guattari. 2004. *A Thousand Plateaus: Capitalism and Schizophrenia* (Brian Massumi (trans.)). New York: Continuum.
Derrida, Jacques. 1997. *Politics of Friendship* (George Collins (trans.)). London: Verso.
Draghici, Simona. 1988. "Introduction." In Carl Schmitt (ed.), *The Idea of Representation*. Washington, DC: Plutarch Press, 7–25.
Dutton, Michael. 2002. "Dreaming of better times: repetition with a difference and Chinese community policing." In Tani E. Barlow (ed.), *New Asian Marxism*. Durham, NC: Duke University Press, 21–52.
Dutton, Michael. 2004. "Mango Mao: infections of the sacred." *Public Culture* 16(2), 161–186.
Dutton, Michael. 2005. *Policing Chinese Politics: A History*. Durham, NC: Duke University Press.

Erickson, Britta. 2010. "*The Rent Collection Courtyard*, past and present." In Richard King (ed.), *Art in Turmoil: The Chinese Cultural Revolution 1966–1976*. Vancouver: UBC Press, 121–135.

Foucault, Michel. 1978. *The History of Sexuality Part One* (Robert Hurley (trans.)). New York: Pantheon Books.

Foucault, Michel. 1991. "Governmentality." In Graham Burchell and Colin Gordon (eds.), *The Foucault Effect: Studies in Governmentality*. Chicago: University of Chicago Press, 87–104.

Heilmann, Sebastian, and Elizabeth Perry (eds.). 2011. *Mao's Invisible Hand: The Political Foundations of Adaptive Governance in China*. Boston, MA: Harvard University Press.

King, Gary. 2013. "How censorship in China allows government criticism but silences collective expression," https://www.youtube.com/watch?v=hybtm4Fp1jc. Accessed 23 June 2016.

King, Gary, Jennifer Pan and Margaret E. Roberts. 2013. "How censorship in China allows government criticism but silences collective expression." *American Political Science Review* 107(2), 326–343.

King, Gary, Jennifer Pan and Margaret E. Roberts. 2014. "Reverse-engineering censorship in China: randomized experimentation and participant observation." *Science* 345(6199), 891–901.

Lee, Haiyan. 2014. *The Stranger and the Chinese Moral Imagination*. Stanford, CA: Stanford University Press.

Li, Shaoyan. 1965. "Xiang diaosu gongzuozhe xuexi" (Learning from the sculptural workers). *Meishu* 6 November, 3–5.

Lynton, Norbert. 2009. *Tatlin's Tower: Monument to Revolution*. New Haven, CT: Yale University Press.

Massumi, Brian. 1992. *A User's Guide to Capitalism and Schizophrenia*. Cambridge, MA: MIT Press.

Massumi, Brian. 1995. "The autonomy of affect." *Cultural Critique* 31, 83–109.

Ouyang, Zongshu. 1992. *Zhongguo jiapu* (*Chinese Genealogies*). Beijing: Xinhua chubanshe.

Said, Edward W. 1978. *Orientalism*. New York: Pantheon.

Schmitt, Carl. 1988. *The Idea of Representation*. Washington, DC: Plutarch Press.

Schmitt, Carl. 1996. *The Concept of the Political* (J. Harvey Lomax (trans.)). Chicago: University of Chicago.

Shklovsky, Viktor. 2005. *Knights Move* (Richard Sheldon (trans.)). Champagne, IL: Dalkey Archive Press.

Spinoza, Benedict de. 2015. *The Ethics* (R.H.M. Elwes (trans.)). Gutenberg project e-book, http://www.gutenberg.org/files/3800/3800-h/3800-h.htm. Accessed 30 April 2015.

Strauss, Leo. 1996. "Notes on Carl Schmitt, *The Concept of the Political*." In Carl Schmitt, *The Concept of the Political*. Chicago: University of Chicago, 83–107.

Tafuri, Manfredo. 1990. *The Sphere and the Labyrinth: Avant-gardes and Architecture from Piranesi to the 1970s* (Pellegrino d'Acierno and Robert Connolly (trans.)). Cambridge, MA: MIT Press.

Wang, Guanyi. 1996. "Huishou 'Shouzuyuan'" (Looking back on the *Rent Collection Courtyard*). *Diaosu* 1, 38–39.

Wang, Zhi'an. 2001. *Hongtian juechang* (*The Heavens Thundered at the Peak of Poetic Perfection*). Chengdu: Tiandi chubanshe.

Wang, Zhi'an, Wang Fei and Wang Shao. 2003. *Zhuangyuan miwen* (*The Secrets of the Manner*). Sichuan: Sichuan chuban jituan.

Wedell-Wedellsborg, Anne. 2010. "Contextualizing Cai Guo-Qiang." *Kontur* 20, 9–18, http://kontur.au.dk/fileadmin/www.kontur.au.dk/Kontur_20/Microsoft_Word_-_VAM-WEDELL_MOD2.pdf. Accessed 20 November 2013.

Zhang, Youyun. 2005. "Lun gongqun dui nisu 'Shouzuyuan' xingqu zhuangxiang zhi zhuyao gengyuan" (The roots of the changing appreciation of the *Rent Collection Courtyard* in popular perceptions). *Meishu yanjiu* April, 46–53.

Whodunnit? Memory and Politics before the 50th Anniversary of the Cultural Revolution

Susanne Weigelin-Schwiedrzik[*] and Cui Jinke[†]

Abstract

Song Binbin, the daughter of prominent CCP politician Song Renqiong, has long been accused of having played a role in the death of Bian Zhongyun which took place at the Girls' Middle School in Beijing Normal University on 5 August 1966. In January 2014, she publicly apologized for the violence that occurred at her school during the summer of 1966. However, instead of applauding her act of contrition, rebel participants of the Cultural Revolution used the opportunity to criticize the sons and daughters of high-ranking cadres and to try to overturn the 1981 official evaluation of the Cultural Revolution by promoting a positive view of that period in Chinese history. This paper analyses the background, consequences and implications of Song Binbin's apology from a political science cum memory studies perspective. It argues, against the background of a changing political landscape in the People's Republic of China, that the memory of the Cultural Revolution remains a battlefield of divergent memory groups and multiple narratives. In the memory of today, the struggles of the Cultural Revolution have still not come to an end.

Keywords: Chinese Cultural Revolution; memory; Song Binbin; Chongqing model; Bian Zhongyun

Song Binbin's 宋彬彬 apology (*daoqian* 道歉) for her involvement in the events that took place at the Girls' Middle School of Beijing Normal University (today known as the Experimental Middle School, *Beijing shifan daxue fushu shiyan zhongxue* 北京师范大学附属实验中学) in August 1966 ignited a debate among participants of the Cultural Revolution which was somewhat unexpected. Rather than commending her for having the courage to face up to her own past, many commentators were critical of her apology. This paper examines the background, consequences and implications of Song Binbin's apology from a political

* University of Vienna, Austria. Email: susanne.weigelin-schwiedrzik@univie.ac.at (corresponding author).
† University of Vienna, Austria.

© The China Quarterly, 2016   doi:10.1017/S0305741016000734

science cum memory studies perspective. It analyses both Song Binbin's attempt to put forward her narrative on the death of Bian Zhongyun 卞仲耘, the-then vice-principal of the school, during a symposium held in January 2014 organized together with classmates from 1966 and entitled "Coming to terms with the Cultural Revolution and refusing to forget" (*fansi wenge jujue yiwang* 反思文 革拒绝遗忘), and the debate sparked by her apology in the Chinese media.

Our discourse analysis focuses on comparing recent narratives on the memory of the Cultural Revolution with those from 2006. Additionally, we look at the political landscape in the People's Republic of China (PRC) today and its influence on the development of the official historiography of the Cultural Revolution. Our analysis is based on documentation from the symposium published in the electronic journal, *Jiyi* 记忆 (*Remembrance*), which, since 2010, has provided a platform for the exchange of information and discussion about Bian Zhongyun's death.[1] Reactions to Song's apology were published in a variety of formats, ranging from newspaper articles to blog entries. While both authors of this article have been following the debate on Song Binbin's involvement in the death of Bian Zhongyun for many years, neither has been directly involved in the recent or past developments related to this event. As non-participant observers, we rely solely on written sources for our analysis and have explicitly refrained from interviewing the discourse participants introduced below. This makes our contribution different from the many publications in Chinese and English written by authors involved in the event.[2] In contrast to these publications, we focus on the political implications and see the debate surrounding Song Binbin's apology as an important battleground for the power struggle between at least two groups in the Chinese Communist Party (CCP) and in society: those who rely on social as well as economic capital accumulated prior to the Xi Jinping 习近平 administration, and those who see themselves as left behind by the politics of reform and opening.

In comparison to the debates on the Cultural Revolution held before and during the 20th anniversary in 2006, the so-called Maoist rebel faction has been extremely active in recent times and intent on trying to pose a counter-narrative to the position of "totally negating the Cultural Revolution" (*quanpan fouding wenhua da geming* 全盘否定文化大革命) advanced by the 1981 "Resolution on some questions concerning the history of the CCP since the founding of the People's Republic of China" (*Guanyu jianguo yilai dang de ruogan lishi wenti de jueyi* 关 于建国以来党的若干历史问题的决议). According to the rebel faction, Deng Xiaoping 邓小平 and Liu Shaoqi 刘少奇 are to blame for the excessive violence of 1966 and Mao's overall strategy was correct. Xi Jinping's new interpretation of

---

1 *Jiyi* is an electronic journal which has played an important role in making the memory of the Cultural Revolution "public" and in providing a platform for those who were willing to reconsider what they had done during the Cultural Revolution. The journal published several special issues on the so-called "5 August event" and documented the symposium of January 2014. It is a non-public publication but can be accessed at www.xujuneberlein.com/remembrance.idx.html outside China. See also Wu Di 2014a; 2014b.

2 See Wang, Youqin 2004; Ye 2014.

post-1949 history, offered under the motto of "the two thirty years should not negate each other" (*liang ge sanshi nian bu neng xianghu fouding* 两个三十年不能相互否定), demonstrates that the rebel faction's arguments are not totally out of line with the current orthodoxy.[3]

What Happened on 5 August 1966?

Song Binbin in fact first made a public apology in as early as 2010 for her role in the events in August 1966 that led to the death of Bian Zhongyun. However, her apology at that time largely went unnoticed.[4] In 2014, she declared that she had nothing to add to the version of events she gave in her 2010 statement.[5] In this version, she described how the so-called work team had started mobilizing students to criticize Bian Zhongyun and others for their revisionist standpoints already in late June 1966. It was in this context that Bian was accused of being a "false Party member" (*jia dangyuan* 假党员), which made everybody highly agitated and angry with her.[6] In addition, someone from outside the school who had a history of confrontation with Bian Zhongyun aired her grievances and attacked Bian physically. This is when several people started to beat up members of the school's leadership. In response, two teachers along with Song Binbin and her classmate Liu Jin 刘进 were asked to discuss the issue with Deng Xiaoping, whose daughters were enrolled in the Girls' Middle School of Beijing Normal University and who was to supervise the work team (*gongzuozu* 工作组) at this school. However, soon afterwards, the work team had to leave the school, which is why neither the leadership of the school nor anyone else had the authority to control the situation. In fact, those who had cooperated with the work team, such as Song Binbin, were regarded as "conservative" (*baoshou* 保守) and had lost their authority.[7] According to Song:

On 5 August, those serious events took place as a consequence of violent activities in school, which eventually led to the death of Vice-principal Bian. At first, I did not know that the leadership of the school was going to be paraded through the campus; it was only later that I learned that some schoolmates from the first grade of the upper division had started this. That afternoon, Liu Jin and I sat together with some other classmates in the office occupied by the work team on the second floor of the East Building to discuss what to do next. Suddenly, some students from the lower division ran in to tell us that students were beating up people on the sports ground. Liu Jin, myself and some classmates who had been on the students' representatives committee and in the core group ran to the sports ground and saw how Vice-principal Bian and five others from the school's leadership were forced to present themselves … We tried to convince them [i.e. the fellow students] that they should not beat up people, but they … could

---

3   See Zhu 2013.
4   Song 2012.
5   Song 2014.
6   This expression refers to a Party member who was introduced to the Party by someone who later turned out to be a traitor. During the Cultural Revolution, many people who joined the Party during the Anti-Japanese War were accused of being "false party members."
7   Song 2014. For an in-depth analysis of the situation in Beijing, see Walder 2009; for a recent overall assessment of the Cultural Revolution, see Walder 2015, especially 215–19 for the situation in Beijing's high schools. For an analysis by a PRC author, see Xu, Youyu 1999.

not see any wrong in making them march in the streets ... We made the people leave the scene and went back to the second floor of the East Building. Later on, schoolmates from lower grades came and told us that the beatings were still going on behind the sports ground. Liu Jin and I went to have a look and saw many schoolmates gathering behind the sports ground with members of the school's leadership forced to carry soil in baskets which were so full and heavy that they could not move. They were beaten and scolded for that. Liu Jin and I advised the schoolmates who were supervising the school's leadership that to work means to work and cannot be accompanied by beating up people. With the baskets as big as they were, they could not be blamed for not being able to carry them. As we saw that they did not object, we left the scene ... On the evening of 5 August, I heard the rumour that Vice-principal Bian was lying on the sports ground just about to die. Liu Jin and I ran immediately to the sports ground. Teacher Li Songwen was also there. Liu Jin asked a worker on campus to open the backdoor, and we [took] Principal Bian into the Postal Hospital.[8]

Whose Story Is This?

Bian Zhongyun's death, along with the involvement of the students from the Girls' Middle School of Beijing Normal University, has been a topic of internal review and public discussion since the end of the 1990s. Liu Jin, one of the leading student cadres in the school in 1966, reports that she attended the memorial service for Bian Zhongyun in 1978 and that, in the early 1990s, she went back to her former middle school to look for archival materials. She talked to her former teachers but did not find the time to write things down before she went into retirement.[9] Feng Jinglan 冯敬兰, one of the organizers of the aforementioned symposium, claims that she had begun to work on this issue in 1996, and in 2000 wrote down her recollections of the incident.[10] Ye Weili 叶维丽 reports that she began her research into the death of Bian Zhongyun in 2000/2001.[11] After meeting up with Liu Jin in 2002, they both decided to commit time and energy to the project and began to get in touch with others who may have witnessed Bian's death.

Some people started even earlier, among them another former vice-principal of the school, Hu Zhitao 胡志涛, who wrote about the incident in quite some detail in a text entitled "In remembrance of 5 August," which was published in 1986.[12] Wang Youqin 王友琴, who also happened to have been a student at this particular school, started researching Bian's death in the 1990s and wrote at great length about it in her book, *Victims of the Cultural Revolution*, published in 2004.[13] Carma Hinton and Geremie Barmé made a documentary on Red Guard memories of the Cultural Revolution, with many hours of film footage in which both Ye Weili and Song Binbin appear – without once referring to Bian's death, however.[14]

---

8 Song 2012, 8. All extracts and quotations used in the article have been translated into English by the authors.
9 Liu 2012.
10 Feng 1997; 2014. Feng Jinglan reports that Bian Zhongyun was officially rehabilitated in the spring of 1970.
11 Ye 2014.
12 Hu 1986. For more on Hu Zhitao, see Ye and Ma 2005.
13 Wang, Youqin 2004.
14 For more details on the film, see http://www.pri.org/stories/2014-01-24/chinese-filmmaker-points-his-camera-darkest-moments-communist-party-history. Accessed 22 June 2016. For a Chinese version with optional German subtitles, see Hu, Jie 2009.

In 2006, Hu Jie 胡杰 made a 70-minute documentary on Bian with the title, *Though I Am Gone*, with Bian's husband, Wang Jingyao 王晶垚, as his main informant.[15]

From these publications and documentaries, it can be seen that the former schoolmates, all belonging to the so-called *lao san jie* 老三届 generation, were "comrades in arms" at the time of the Cultural Revolution.[16] They had lost touch after the events of 1966, it seems, and re-established their relationships in the early to mid-1990s. It took them nearly 30 years to recover their friendships and form a "carrier group" of Cultural Revolution memory.[17] Carrier groups are formed from among "insiders" sharing similar, and in this case traumatic, experiences as victims or perpetrators. They exchange memories among themselves and refrain from communicating with "outsiders" while developing their own narrative of the past. Soldiers share their memories of war in carrier groups, and participants of the Cultural Revolution preserve their fragmented memory by communicating with their friends from that time. They claim that only people who experienced the traumatic events with them can understand what happened. Because this form of coming to terms with the past is not public, outside observers gain the impression that the Cultural Revolution is forgotten. Instead, different carrier groups develop their own respective narratives, which often differ sharply from the official version given in the 1981 Party Resolution.[18]

The participants of the 2014 symposium have formed a carrier group of Cultural Revolution memory and have also defined the rules of inclusion and exclusion. In their recent statements, they all give their affiliations with different grades of the upper division of the middle school and explain their family background as belonging to the upper, but not the highest, level of central cadre families in Beijing. This shows that social background and belonging to the same grade in school are two important criteria for membership in this carrier group. That is why Wang Youqin does not belong to the group. She does not fulfil the "objective criteria," as she is younger and of a different family background (she comes from a family of teachers). In addition, the carrier group does not allow for any member to be called perpetrator; instead, they explicitly define themselves as more or less "responsible actors." However, Wang Youqin does not accept this definition and instead has accused Song Binbin of having actively participated in the beating which eventually led to the death of Bian Zhongyun.[19] Since Song Binbin's 2012 apology, many people who used to believe Wang Youqin's story are now convinced by Song Binbin's narrative;[20] however,

15 There are several versions of the film available with English, German and French subtitles. For the Chinese version, see www.youtube.com/watch?v=gXWzAsHE-Pg. Accessed 16 June 2016.
16 The expression *lao san jie* refers to those upper-division middle school students who graduated during the years 1966, 1967 and 1968.
17 Weigelin-Schwiedrzik 2008.
18 See Weigelin-Schwiedrzik 2006; 2008; Gao 2008; Yang 2007.
19 Jin 2014.
20 Xu, Youyu 2014.

Wang Youqin still refuses to accept Song Binbin's version.[21] This shows that Wang is not part of the consensus formed by the carrier group and therefore cannot join them.

Bian Zhongyun's husband, Wang Jingyao, is also not a member of the carrier group. One of the reasons why this event has garnered so much attention is because Wang, as he explains in Hu Jie's film,[22] refused to forget and began to gather as much evidence as he could as soon as he was informed of his wife's death on the evening of 5 August 1966. Although some members of the carrier group have had contact with the now 94-year-old Wang Jingyao, he and his family were not present at the official apology ceremony in front of a statue of Bian Zhongyun erected at the Experimental Middle School in Beijing.[23] How was this possible? Wang has, to the best of our knowledge, never claimed that Song Binbin actively participated in what he terms the murder of his wife. Instead, he tried to take another person to court, someone who he believes mobilized the students against his wife, but his request for a trial was turned down in the 1980s on account of the time elapsed. So, how could it be that the apology was not addressed to him, as one might expect? This is because Wang Jingyao does not comply with the rules of the carrier group, which insist that no member of the carrier group can be accused of being the perpetrator and no one must disclose who the perpetrator was. Wang Jingyao, on the other hand, insists that the perpetrator should reveal herself or else be exposed by others. As this demand cannot be complied with, he cannot, and maybe does not even want to, be included in the group. Moreover, Wang Jingyao insists that Mao Zedong should be squarely condemned for his "mistakes" which made possible the outburst of violence in the second half of 1966. Song Binbin's apology at no point referred to Mao's role in the events, and so Wang refuses to accept her explanation and is unconvinced by the narrative accepted by those who participated in the symposium.[24]

There are quite a number of former schoolmates from 1966 who do not form part of the carrier group. Most prominent among them are the daughters of Liu Shaoqi and Deng Xiaoping. Both attended the school at the time and have on occasion been publicly accused of having taken an active part in the beating of Bian Zhongyun.[25] The sister of Bo Xilai 薄熙来 also belongs to this group.[26] The simplest explanation for this is their family background: they all come from families whose political and social position was even higher than those in the carrier group. However, the reason why they stick to their code of silence is more complicated. It relates to an aspect of the Cultural Revolution which has so far never been publicly addressed in the PRC: the participation of the

---

21 Jin 2014.
22 See Fn. 15.
23 Lundunke 2014.
24 Wang, Jingyao 2014.
25 Lundunke 2014.
26 Wang, Youqin 2014.

sons and daughters of the leadership of the CCP back in 1966, and their relationship to their parents at that time. Although it is clear that the so-called Old Red
Guards (*lao hong weibing* 老红卫兵) were heavily involved, no one has so far
taken responsibility for the outburst of violence during the initial phase of the
Cultural Revolution. Instead, the 1981 Party Resolution refrains from assessing
this period and from condemning the Old Red Guards.[27] Recently published
materials show that in as early as 1979, the involvement of this group was
under investigation when Peng Xiaomeng 彭小蒙, a former leading Red Guard
at the middle school affiliated to Peking University, allegedly wrote a letter to
Hu Yaobang 胡耀邦 concerning this issue.[28] Hu Yaobang responded by saying
that many young people had committed mistakes during their time as a Red
Guard, but most of them lacked experience and were used or misled. That is
why they should not be condemned but instead be helped to overcome their mistakes.[29] The silence of the 1981 Resolution on this question is in line with Hu
Yaobang's response, but failed to calm the fears of the former Old Red
Guards. In 1984, Red Guard activism was again under review, with many Old
Red Guards eager to draw a clear line between themselves and the so-called rebels (*zaofanpai* 造反派). In another letter, this time to Chen Yun 陈云, the group
underlined the necessity to abstain from persecuting Old Red Guards who had
committed mistakes; instead, their positive participation in the early phase of
the Cultural Revolution should be acknowledged and they should be mobilized
to participate in the continuing struggle against the "three kinds of people."[30]

Since the early 2000s, the death of Bian Zhongyun has grown into an issue of
emblematic function for the assessment of Red Guard activism in 1966. That is
why, after more than 20 years of research and discussion, we still do not know
for sure who killed Bian Zhongyun. Song Binbin and all other members of the carrier group see themselves as non-participants in the beating; however, they are also
not prepared to reveal the names of those who did take part, as they are all part of a
larger carrier group consisting of those Old Red Guards who regard themselves as
being "used or misled" during the early phase of the Cultural Revolution. Because
they do not want to run the risk of being expelled from this carrier group, they stick
to the rules – even if this means that they themselves remain under suspicion.

In Search of Truth and Reconciliation

The carrier group from the Girls' Middle School set as its major task the search
for the truth about the death of Bian Zhongyun. Liu Jin admits that she was the

27 Weigelin-Schwiedrzik 2006.
28 Xu, Xinhua 2011, 41.
29 Ibid., 42.
30 Mi 2013, 168–69. The "three kinds of people" refers to those who actively supported Lin Biao and the
    Gang of Four, people who were strongly influenced by their political ideas, and people who had parti-
    cipated in riots. The expression was first used in a speech presented by Chen Yun in 1982. In this speech,
    he clarified that members of the "rebel faction" could not be elected to cadre positions. See zh.wikipedia.
    org/wiki/清理三种人. Accessed 16 June 2016.

first to write a big character poster (*dazibao* 大字报) criticizing the so-called work team. Like many others at the time, she criticized the work team for being too rigorous in exerting its leadership over the movement and demanded instead that students should be encouraged to liberate themselves. This big character poster, as Liu Jin states today, was responsible for creating an uncontrollable situation on campus and one of the reasons for the outburst of violence. She has, in fact, been doing research on the 5 August event for a long time, undergoing several rounds of inspection related to the case and writing up documentation for the school's archives. Her contribution is remarkable because of the rigorous attitude she has taken with regards to herself and her contribution to the events, and her convincing attempt to uncover the reasons for her behaviour back in 1966.[31]

In contrast, Ye Weili presents herself as a researcher: "I am a historian as well as one of the students at the Girls' Middle School back then. This means that I cannot stand above or outside [of the events] while trying to find an answer to the question 'whose responsibility' [has to be taken into account] in the context of Principal Bian's death … but that I have to put myself right into this … and shoulder the most horrible collective shame that the Girls' Middle School has accumulated in its history."[32] While Liu Jin mostly looks at her deep-seated, internal motivations, Ye Weili focuses on external pressures and comes to the overall conclusion that the violence of those days was very much owing to the total loss of control of the authorities at all levels of the political system.

Li Hongyun 李红云 represents yet another approach to the death of Bian Zhongyun. In *Jiyi*, she explains that she only became aware of the controversy when the school was commemorating its 90th anniversary in 2007 and some people suggested erecting a statue for Bian Zhongyun on campus.[33] "I am in law, and clarifying the truth about things is the first step before you can make any assessment in a case. As a graduate of the Girls' Middle School and belonging to the generation which personally experienced the Cultural Revolution, I feel that I have a duty to clarify this event."[34] Li Hongyun explicitly refers to the situation in South Africa, underlining that the ultimate goal of coming to terms with the past is reconciliation: "If countries like South Africa, Sierra Leone and Rwanda can achieve reconciliation and mercy in their attitude towards the past, why should a

---

31 Liu 2014.
32 Ye 2014, 13–14.
33 For more details on the anniversary celebrations, see Jian, Song and Zhou 2015. Song Binbin was one of the "eminent graduates" from this school selected for special mention during the school's 90th anniversary celebrations. The photograph used in the commemoration booklet accompanying the celebration shows her participating in the 18 August 1966 parade on Tian'anmen Square when she attached the Red Guard armband to the jacket of Mao Zedong. This implies that Song Binbin's eminence was owing to her participation in the Cultural Revolution. For more about Wang Jingyao's protest at the selection of Song Binbin as one of the "eminent graduates" from the school, see www.360doc.com/content/07/1226/23/16239_927133.shtml. Accessed 16 June 2016.
34 Li, Hongyun 2014, 19.

country with thousands of years of civilization and tradition like China not do the same?"[35]

Song Binbin presents herself as both a leader of the students at the Girls' Middle school and a victim of the political situation during the Cultural Revolution. She begins her contribution to the 2014 symposium by stating: "Since about 40 years ago there have been two Song Binbins: one Song Binbin who from the very beginning argued against armed struggle, violence and 'the theory of descent,' a Song Binbin who can take responsibility for whatever she did. The other Song Binbin is a creation under the name of 'Song Yaowu' 宋 要武 [Song who wants violence], she was fabricated during the Cultural Revolution and the 1990s."[36] In Carma Hinton's film, Song is more forthcoming as she explains that it was Mao Zedong who took her identity away from her by bestowing a new name on her. This name was then used in order to mobilize young people in Mao's struggle against Deng Xiaoping and Liu Shaoqi, as she contends, without her consent. All of this happened because, as Liu Jin states, Song Binbin was chosen by Liu Jin to represent the Girls' Middle School during the mass meeting on Tian'anmen Square on 18 August 1966.[37] It was during this meeting that Song Binbin was given the opportunity to place a Red Guard armband on Mao's jacket sleeve: "that Chairman Mao wore the armband of the Red Guards, together with the phrase 'how about some violence' (*yao wu ma* 要武嘛), ignited some kind of madness to protect the great leader of the country … Together with everyone and every family I want to denounce all violence which took place because of 'Song Yaowu' and other reasons."[38] But, her role as a victim of the Cultural Revolution has yet another side to it. Later on in her presentation, she talks about her father being labelled as a "capitalist roader" in 1967, her mother and brother being paraded in the streets of Shenyang, and how she herself was kept in isolation.[39] This experience was very typical for Red Guards with her family background. It is why her self-perception as a victim of the Cultural Revolution dominates the narrative of her apology and makes it less convincing.

Looking at the documents published by *Jiyi*, one can gain a good understanding of the enormous efforts the members of the carrier group have made since the 1990s in coming to terms with the death of Bian Zhongyun. Their courage to confront this event publicly is admirable. Alas, while all of them concentrated on defining their own role in the event and unanimously came to the conclusion that none among them was directly involved in the beating, they have not had the courage to present the names of those who were directly involved. This, of course,

---

35 Ibid., 23. The public's interest in the reconciliation process in South Africa is reflected by the recent translations and publication of books on the issue by Albie Sachs and Desmond Tutu. See Sachs 2014 and Tutu 2014.
36 Song 2014, 31.
37 Liu 2012, 17.
38 Song 2014, 32.
39 Ibid., 33–35.

leaves the victims as well as the interested public unsatisfied and doubtful, as it is clear that there is something to this case everybody knows but nobody dares to address.

This is exactly the reason why Bian's husband, Wang Jingyao, condemns what he deems "a false apology": "As long as the full truth about the '5 August event' is not out there, I will definitely not accept the false apology given by Red Guards from the Girls' School of Beijing Normal University."[40] However, the reason why this truth has not fully come out is not because the perpetrator is among them; instead, we would argue that it is precisely because no member of the carrier group was directly involved that they can do the research and go public. Only with the carrier group remaining as active and diligent as they are can the group of direct participants stay silent.

The question arises why Song Binbin and her classmates decided to present their public apology at this particular moment. Some of the reasons seem quite obvious. All of those who were at the centre of events have retired. Both psychologically and from the point of view of practicability, it is easier to confront one's own past in a situation where one is able to choose one's own social contacts. The risk of being met with mistrust, criticism or unfriendly behaviour at work or in one's professional life is no longer there. Other reasons are less obvious and relate to the political climate in the PRC. As economic growth slows down, the initiators of the opening and reform policy are afraid of losing momentum while a counter-narrative is in the making which is critical of the reform and of the role the reformers played during the second half of 1966. The offspring of the reformers, such as Song Binbin, try to be proactive in presenting their version of events during the early phase of the Cultural Revolution.

A Counter-narrative in the Making

Until recently, Old Red Guards were regarded as having committed mistakes, which, however, did not prevent them from going on to forge a political career in China. In contrast, those who were said to have belonged to the so-called "three kinds of people" were expelled from the system during the Cultural Revolution and hardly ever found their way back. These people now recognize that Song Binbin has provided them with the opportunity to use the obvious flaws in her apology to present their own version of the Cultural Revolution.

This seems to be the reason why on 13 January 2014, when the debate on Song Binbin's apology was first ignited, the Internet Information Bureau of the State Council of the PRC (*guowuyuan hulianwang xinxi bangongshi* 国务院互联网信息办公室) issued a directive saying: "Because the mood on the net is complicated, all websites should hold reports on the apology of Song Renqiong's 宋任穷 daughter Song Binbin at a low temperature, [which implies] that reports on

---

40 Wang, Jingyao 2014.

this issue should be erased from the front page and connecting links on this issue should not be presented."[41] While this directive was meant to bring the discussion to a sudden end, *Nanfang zhoumo* 南方周末 (*Southern Weekend*) continued to publish articles on the issue. The editor-in-chief consequently had to write a report and accept that the newspaper was no longer allowed to publish articles on Song Binbin's apology.[42] However, both the Chinese and non-Chinese language press outside of the PRC continued to discuss the issue, and blog entries were posted in the internet.

The verdict on the Old Red Guards can be construed from the absence of any verdict on their activism during the early phase of the Cultural Revolution in the 1981 Party Resolution.[43] In contrast to what one might assume from reading blog entries posted by the Maoist faction, there is also no straightforward verdict on the rebel factions included in the 1981 Resolution. One of the Resolution's main aims was to prevent the continuation of factional struggles and so it omitted to include a verdict on either the Old Red Guards or the rebels.[44] However, we can see from the reactions to Song Binbin's apology that the rebels from among the "three kinds of people" are now attempting to overturn what they perceive as the implicit verdict of the Resolution. In one blog entry by Li Yang 黎阳, a commentator well known for his affiliation with the Maoist faction, Li criticizes Song Binbin's apology for providing everybody who did similar things during the Cultural Revolution with the opportunity to absolve themselves of their responsibility by simply apologizing. This ritual implies the possibility that people not only ask for apologies by other individuals but want, as Xu Youyu 徐友渔 supposedly claims, the state to take on collective responsibility and forward an apology to every victim of the Cultural Revolution. Li Yang contends that under these conditions, it could be argued that the state is "a criminal organization." Song Binbin's apology – according to Li Yang – might help her personally and as an individual, but it threatens the stability of the state and is therefore dangerous.[45]

Another entry in a blog explains:

Even if Bian Zhongyun was really harmed by extreme brutality, this should not be counted as something related to Mao Zedong. This is because Mao launched the Cultural Revolution with the aim of mobilizing bottom-up against bureaucrats and the capitalist roaders inside the Party. Who would have guessed that some people from the upper levels would use this opportunity to

---

41 See http://chinadigitaltimes.net/2014/01/red-guard-apologies-role-teachers-death/. Accessed 4 June 2015. According to its official website, *China Digital Times* (*Zhongguo shuzi shidai*) is based in Berkeley, CA, and is an independent, bilingual media organization that publishes uncensored news and online voices from China. The Chinese version of CDT has a section called the "Truth department directions" (*zhenlibu zhiling*), where one can see the censorship instructions issued by all kinds of censorship departments in China. For the Chinese version, see http://chinadigitaltimes.net/chinese/category/有关部门/真理部指令/. Accessed 15 June 2016.
42 Nanzhou gengzheng 2014.
43 "Guanyu jianguo yilai dang de ruogan lishi wenti de jueyi" (Resolution on some questions concerning the history of the CCP since the founding of the People's Republic of China), *Renmin ribao*, 1 July 1981, 1–8.
44 Weigelin-Schwiedrzik 2006.
45 Li, Yang 2014.

change the mode of struggle into a top-down mobilization under the leadership of the bureaucrats? They changed the object of the struggle from the bureaucrats to the students, the teachers and workers at the first front of production ... and thus destroyed Mao's strategic orientation for the Cultural Revolution.[46]

According to this narrative, what happened to Bian was not part of Mao's strategic plan but rather belongs to an anti-Cultural Revolution strategy invented by those Mao wanted to expel.

In January 2014, another blogger comes to the conclusion that:

It is now time to reverse the verdict on the Cultural Revolution because only a positive assessment of the Cultural Revolution can be the basis of a positive assessment of Mao and the 30 years under his leadership. I see that some of those who offer apologies for the Cultural Revolution have ulterior motives. One of their aims is to stick to the total negation of the Cultural Revolution. Thus, the parent generation of Chen Xiaolu 陈小鲁[47] and Song Binbin who made enormous contributions to the founding of the People's Republic can forever be regarded as victims and the embodiment of the truth, their parents will forever have been correct, and Mao Zedong will forever have been mistaken. The masses of the people will never again have the opportunity to challenge the bureaucratic class which acts against the principles of communism, while those bureaucrats who misuse their power for their own interest or who have degenerated can sit back and relax in peace and happiness.[48]

The negation of the Cultural Revolution, driven by the 1981 Resolution, implies total disempowerment for the masses.

In yet another blog entry, the author argues against the 1981 Party Resolution. According to this author's interpretation, the Red Guards were ordered by their parents to destroy the Cultural Revolution before it ever got started. They acted on behalf of the class of leading families who wanted chaos to break out in the hope that this would prevent the Cultural Revolution from fanning out across the whole country. However, once the Cultural Revolution group brought this to a halt, the offspring of the leading bureaucrats had to break publicly from their parents.[49] From a family point of view, the Old Red Guards see themselves as victims of the Cultural Revolution, yet from an individual point of view, they see themselves as victims of Mao Zedong. The Maoist bloggers, however, argue that they were persecuted by "the bureaucrats." When the movement to clarify the ranks of the "three kinds of people" was launched, those among the rebels who had taken over leading positions at the lower levels of the state were interrogated, degraded and sometimes even sent to prison. After the Cultural Revolution, many of them were never given the chance to take up important political or bureaucratic positions. Both Old Red Guards and rebels, while commonly regarded as perpetrators, insist on being victims.

This new discourse strategy is radically different to the situation in and around 2006. At that time, the debate excluded those victims who were maltreated,

---

46 Shidai Jianbing 2014.
47 Chen Xiaolu is the son of Marshall Chen Yi. He first offered his apologies to his former teachers in Beijing No. 8 Middle School in a blog entry of alumni from his school before he went public during a visit to the school on 7 October 2013. See Huang 2013.
48 Fu Niu Shi 2014.
49 Wenhua Hong Weibing 2014.

murdered or driven to suicide, and victim status was seen as something nega-tive.[50] Now, ten years later, both the Old Red Guards and the Maoist rebels seem to regard their status as victims of the Cultural Revolution as social capital which they can use in their struggle for satisfaction, impact and power. However, in a continuation of the tone of the 1981 Resolution, they do not express any em-pathy for the dead victims.

The Maoist rebels see the Cultural Revolution as the antithesis of all that is happening in China today: workers and peasants were "the masters of the coun-try" (*dang jia zuo zhu* 当家做主) instead of being threatened by unemployment and the loss of their land. This argument is often put forward by members of the Maoist faction who were too young to have actively participated in the Cultural Revolution; they were primary school children at the time and often not aware of the details of what happened back then. In 2005/2006, they criticized the reform and opening up policy by juxtaposing the situation in China today with life during the Cultural Revolution.[51] The Maoist faction among the rebels seems to have aligned with this younger group of Cultural Revolution partici-pants and, as a result, they have formed a much more prominent force in the discourse.[52]

The Changing Orthodoxy of the CCP Historiography

The 1981 Resolution constructed "universal complicity" with the aim of pacify-ing the tension between different factions, the perpetrators and victims, the win-ners and losers, of the Cultural Revolution. However, the notion of "universal complicity" was not accepted by those who had experienced the Cultural Revolution and, as a result, the Resolution was contested as soon as it was passed. Another reason why it failed to establish itself as the dominant text in the discourse on the Cultural Revolution is because for some the Resolution was not pronounced enough in "negating" (*fouding* 否定) the Cultural Revolution; for others it went too far. As a result, the CCP has tried to block public discussion of the Cultural Revolution, albeit with little success.[53]

The new slogan promoted by Xi Jinping about the "two 30 years" is meant to balance the relationship between the "first 30 years" and the last 30 years of re-form and opening.[54] As such, Party historiography can find positive aspects of

50 Weigelin-Schwiedrzik 2008.
51 Gao 2008 analyses the web communications on the Cultural Revolution around the 2006 anniversary and finds that the "younger" generation nostalgically referred to the Cultural Revolution as a time of justice and equity, in contrast to the aggravating social injustice they observed in the China of reform and opening. See also Yang 2007. Both Gao and Yang argue that the internet can serve as a platform to voice alternative views on the Cultural Revolution despite the official ban on publicly discussing the issue.
52 We would like to thank Yin Hongbiao from the School of International Studies, Peking University, for drawing our attention to this aspect of Red Guard memory.
53 Weigelin-Schwiedrzik 2006.
54 The slogan of the "two 30 years" first appeared in 2009 in an article published in the *Renmin ribao* on 17 August. The article explained how the first 30 years following the founding of the PRC could not be

the Cultural Revolution just as it can describe negative aspects of the period since 1978. The overall aim is to come to a positive assessment of 100 years of CCP history in 2021 as well as 100 years of PRC history in 2049. So far, Party historiography has basically underlined Mao's positive role in CCP history; however, as a consequence of Mao's antagonists taking control at the end of the Cultural Revolution, Party historiography also has to criticize Mao in order to make the policy of reform and opening plausible in the context of CCP history. The more arguments began to circulate stressing that the consequence of reform and opening was exactly what Mao had warned against when he talked about "restoration," the more the policy of reform and opening had to be supported by criticism of Mao Zedong.[55] The recent discussions on the Cultural Revolution demonstrate that the Maoist faction among the rebels wants to push Party historiography into a more positive assessment of Mao while reinforcing their fight against social injustice, bureaucracy and corruption.

The question arises why Party historiography needs to respond to the demands of the Maoist faction. As is well documented, Xi Jinping was elected as the leader of the Chinese Communist Party after one of his most important rivals, Bo Xilai, was sentenced to life in prison. Although everybody refers to Bo Xilai's policies in Chongqing as being nostalgic of Maoist times, very little analysis has so far been offered of how these policies were connected to the Cultural Revolution. That there is more to Bo Xilai's relationship with the Cultural Revolution was first pronounced by the-then premier Wen Jiabao 温家宝 at a press conference in 2012 following the meetings of the National People's Congress and the People's Consultative Congress.[56] But, as Xu Youyu points out, already before then there were rumours afloat that the so-called "Chongqing model" (*Chongqing moshi* 重庆模式) owed much to the Cultural Revolution.[57] Indeed, it can be argued that the Chongqing model shared much with the Cultural Revolution in its ability to mobilize people. As the channels of participation have not changed since the end of the Cultural Revolution, Xu Youyu argues, it is perhaps inevitable that people remember the model of the Cultural Revolution as a means of instigating change in instances of mass dissatisfaction.[58] Interestingly, this is true both for national leaders such as Wen Jiabao who were obviously highly agitated by the thought of a reoccurrence of the Cultural

---

footnote continued

    used to negate the last 30 years of the PRC, and vice versa. See Wang, Tinglian 2009. In 2013, Xi Jinping reiterated this idea when he gave a speech to the newly elected and alternate members of the CCPCC. See Mei 2013.

55 Wang Tinglian argues that "the two 30 years" should be interpreted in a balanced way also in order to arrive at a proper assessment of Mao Zedong. Wang, Tinglian 2009.

56 Xu, Youyu 2014, 3.

57 Ibid.

58 Ibid., 4–5.

Revolution, and for the led masses who followed Bo Xilai for a certain period of time. Xu writes:

The Chongqing model awakens our attention to [the fact] that the Cultural Revolution is not a nightmare which we all have forgotten long ago. It is a real danger right in front of our eyes. It is not the catastrophe propagated as set in stone, but an event which quite a number of people regard as a big festival and the political instrument [with which] to achieve equity in social reality ... The reality we have to confront is: the Cultural Revolution was supported by millions of people. They participated in this political movement with sincerity and enthusiasm. If we want to understand why there are so many today who call for a cultural revolution, we have to understand what reason they had back then to throw themselves into the Cultural Revolution.[59]

If Xu Youyu's analysis is right, the present leadership of the CCP has to confront a dilemma: Bo Xilai and the Cultural Revolution enjoyed considerable support in China, but the current leadership expelled Bo Xilai from the elite ranks in order to install Xi Jinping. The leadership cannot allow for any signs of open support for Bo Xilai, which is why they feel compelled to give space to more and more positive memories of the Cultural Revolution instead. It is also why we can now observe that it is more difficult in China to offer apologies for violence in the early stage of the Cultural Revolution than it is to overturn the official opinion of the Cultural Revolution as given by the 1981 Resolution. As for Party historiography, the need to accommodate the arguments from those who demand a positive assessment of the Cultural Revolution is, under these conditions, more urgent than the need to respond to those intellectuals and their families who were murdered or seriously injured during those turbulent times.

Conclusion

According to the analysis presented above, the memory of the Cultural Revolution has again turned into a battlefield of conflicting carrier groups. While members of the Old Red Guards tried to avoid losing momentum by proactively proffering their apologies, the Maoist faction among the rebels identified a window of opportunity through which they could attempt to reverse the CCP verdict on the Cultural Revolution and overcome the negative image they have borne for so many years.

The discourse on Song Binbin's apology shows that perceptions of social justice, of what is politically right and wrong, and of dreams for the future are still shaped by ideas propagated during Maoist times, especially during the Cultural Revolution. The more the present situation is regarded as unsatisfactory, the more the Cultural Revolution emerges from the discourse as a possible and feasible alternative. Paradoxically, this is true despite the fact that all discourse participants claim to be victims. The factional divide responsible for much of the violence during the Cultural Revolution still exists to the degree that the participants are not yet ready for reconciliation. The victims have little empathy for

59 Ibid., 6.

each other and are still competing with each other for recognition and power. In this sense, the Cultural Revolution is still going on.

The attempts of the CCP to ban public discussions of the Cultural Revolution have had a limited effect. Although it is still impossible to dispute the 1981 Resolution openly, internet blogs are used to create a counter-narrative, which is much more pronounced than ten years ago in laying the blame for the violence that occurred in 1966 at the feet of those responsible for the policy of reform and opening after 1978. Against the background of growing criticism of the social injustice in China and the slowing down of economic growth, the Cultural Revolution emerges as an alternative to a market economy. At the same time, those who were targeted as "the objects" of criticism back then are now made responsible for the emerging social dissatisfaction. In order to avoid being downgraded again, Song Binbin and other Red Guards have to erase the stain seeping from rumours that they were actively involved in acts of murder. They either deny direct involvement, as Song Binbin did, or they claim moral superiority by openly admitting their involvement, as Chen Xiaolu did.[60] In both cases, they did not receive the expected response. Song Binbin's apology represents an abortive attempt at preserving the positive image of leading cadres and their families based on their victimhood during the Cultural Revolution.

Biographical notes

Susanne Weigelin-Schwiedrzik is professor of Sinology at the department for East Asian studies at the University of Vienna, Austria.

Cui Jinke is a doctoral student of Sinology at the University of Vienna, Austria.

摘要: 1966 年 8月5日, 北京师范大学附属女子中学的卞仲耘校长被学生打死在校园里。中国共产党的高级领导人宋任穷的女儿宋彬彬, 很长一段时间以来都被指责参与了这一事件。2014 年 1月, 她公开为 1966 年夏天发生在自己学校的暴力事件道歉。但是, 她的道歉并没有获得掌声, 而是受到了一系列批评。部分当时属于造反派的文革参与者们利用这个机会来批判高级干部子女, 并借此来否定中国共产党 1981 年的决议以及传播对于文化革命的积极评价。本文以政治学与记忆研究的视角分析了宋彬彬道歉事件的背景、后果和影响。以中国的政治图景最近所发生了各种变化为背景, 本文认为, 对于文化革命的记忆还是分散性的记忆团体和多样性叙事的战场。今天的记忆是文革派性斗争的延续.

关键词: 文化革命; 记忆; 宋彬彬; 重庆模式; 卞仲耘

---

60 See Fn. 48.

References

Feng, Jinglan. 1997. "Jiyi de chuangba" (The scar of the memory). In Feng Jinglan, *Ni daodi yao shenme* (*What Do You Really Want*). Beijing: Zhongguo guoji guangbo chubanshe, 123–128.

Feng, Jinglan. 2014. "Xiaozhang shi zenme si de? Yuan Beijing shida nü fuzhong wenge chuqi 'ba wu shijian' zongshu" (How did the principal die? A summary of the "5 August event" at the girls' middle school attached to Beijing Normal University). *Jiyi* 106(15 January), 8–11, www.xujuneberlein. com/Rem106.pdf. Accessed 4 June 2015.

Fu Niu Shi. 2014. "Wenge daoqian beihou de yiyun" (The hidden meaning behind the Cultural Revolution apologies), http://www.yzxwk.com/Article/zatan/2014/01/313051.html. Accessed 4 June 2015.

Gao, Mobo. 2008. *The Battle for China's Past: Mao and the Cultural Revolution*. Ann Arbor, MI: Pluto Press.

Hu, Jie. 2009. *…nicht der Rede wert. Die Ermordung der Lehrerin Bian Zhongyun am Beginn der Kulturrevolution*. Neckargemünd, Vienna: Edition Mnemosyne.

Hu, Zhitao. 1986. "'Ba wu' ji" (In remembrance of "5 August"), *21ccom.net*, 4 August, http://www. 21ccom.net/articles/lsjd/lsjj/article_20140804110518.html. Accessed 4 June 2015.

Huang, Cary. 2013. "Chen Xiaolu apologizes for torture of teachers at Beijing alma mater," *South China Morning Post*, 16 October, http://www.scmp.com/news/china/article/1332588/ chen-xiaolu-apologises-torture-teachers-beijing-alma-mater. Accessed 4 June 2015.

Jian, Guo, Yongyi Song and Yuan Zhou. 2015. *Historical Dictionary of the Chinese Cultural Revolution*. Lanham, MD: Rowman & Littlefield.

Jin, Zhong. 2014. "Fangwen wenge yanjiuzhe Wang Youqin" (Interview with Cultural Revolution researcher, Wang Youqin), *open.com.hk*, 3 February, http://www.open.com.hk/content.php?id= 1701#.V04ck5F95b4. Accessed 22 June 2016.

Li, Hongyun. 2014. "Wo dui 'ba wu shijian' de yanjiu" (My research on the "5 August event"). *Jiyi* 106(15 January), 19–23, http://www.xujuneberlein.com/Rem106.pdf. Accessed 4 June 2015.

Li, Yang. 2014. "Song Binbin daoqian shi dahao shi" (How wonderful that Song Binbin has apologized), *Huayue luntan*, 14 January, http://szhgh.com/Article/opinion/xuezhe/2014-01-14/42572. html. Accessed 4 June 2015.

Liu, Jin. 2012. "Miandui lishi de zeren – Liu Jin fangtanlu" (Confronting the responsibility for history – an interview with Liu Jin). *Jiyi* 80(31 January), 16–28, www.xujuneberlein.com/Rem80.pdf. Accessed 4 June 2015.

Liu, Jin. 2014. "Ba wu fansi" (Coming to terms with 5 August). *Jiyi* 106(15 January), 24–30, http:// www.xujuneberlein.com/Rem106.pdf. Accessed 4 June 2015.

Lundunke. 2014. "Shengyuan 93 sui de Wang Jingyao – jianping Song Binbin de xuwei daoqian" (In support of 93-year-old Wang Jingyao – evaluating the false apology of Song Binbin), *blog.wenxuecity. com*, 5 February, http://blog.wenxuecity.com/myblog/61670/201402/3595.html. Accessed 22 June 2016.

Mei, Hong. 2013. "Ruhe zhengque pingjia gaige kaifang qianhou de sanshi nian" (How to correctly assess the 30 years before and since reform and opening), http://dangshi.people.com.cn/n/2013/ 0219/c85037-20530313.html. Accessed 4 June 2015.

Mi, Hedu. 2013. *Kong Dan koushu: nan de bense ren tianran* (*An Oral History of Kong Dan: It's Hard to Be Frank*). Hong Kong: Zhonggang chuanmei chubanshe.

Nanzhou gengzheng. 2014. "Jiyi zhi jia" (Home of remembrance), http://zhenhua.163.com/14/0505/ 17/9RGFVU3P000465TM_all.html. Accessed 4 June 2015.

Sachs, Albie. 2014. *Duanbi shang de huaduo: rensheng yu falü de qihuan lianjinshu* (*The Strange Alchemy of Life and Law*) (Chen Shuji and Chen Ligong (trans.)). Guilin: Guangxi shifan daxue chubanshe.

Shidai Jianbing. 2014. "Wang Jingyao jujue daoqian de mudi shi yingshe Mao Zedong" (Wang Jingyao rejects that the objective behind the apology is to implicate Mao Zedong), http://www. wyzxmk.com/Article/zatan/2014/02/313478.html. Accessed 4 June 2015.

Song, Binbin. 2012. "Sishi duo nian lai wo yizhi xiang shuo de hua" (What I have been wanting to say for 40 years). *Jiyi* 80(31 January), 3–15, http://www.xujuneberlein.com/Rem80.pdf. Accessed 4 June 2015.

Song, Binbin. 2014. "Wo de fansi" (Coming to terms with my past). *Jiyi* 106(15 January), 31–37, http://www.xujuneberlein.com/Rem106.pdf. Accessed 4 June 2015.

Tutu, Desmond. 2014. *Meiyou kuanshu jiu meiyou weilai* (*No Future without Forgiveness*) (Jiang Hong (trans.)). Guilin: Guangxi shifan daxue chubanshe.

Walder, Andrew. 2009. *Fractured Rebellion. The Beijing Red Guard Movement*. Cambridge, MA: Harvard University Press.

Walder, Andrew. 2015. *China under Mao. A Revolution Derailed*. Cambridge, MA: Harvard University Press.

Wang, Jingyao. 2014. "Guanyu Song Binbin, Liu Jin xuwei daoqian de shengming" (Statement about the false apology of Song Binbin and Liu Jin), *21ccom.net*, 31 January, http://www.21ccom.net/articles/lsjd/lsjj/article_2014013099870.html. Accessed 4 June 2015.

Wang, Tinglian. 2009. "'Liang ge sanshi nian,' weihe bu neng xianghu fouding" (Why the "two 30 years" cannot negate each other), http://theory.people.com.cn/GB/40537/9865402.html. Accessed 4 June 2015.

Wang, Youqing. 2004. *Wenge shounanzhe* (*Victims of the Cultural Revolution*), http://www.edubridge.com/erxiantang/l2/victim_ebook_070505.pdf. Accessed 22 June 2016.

Wang, Youqin. 2014. "Huiying Song Binbin deng" (Responding to Song Binbin and others), *21ccom.net*, 26 March, http://www.21ccom.net/articles/lsjd/lsjj/article20140326103090.html. Accessed 4 June 2015.

Weigelin-Schwiedrzik, Susanne. 2006. "In search of a master narrative for 20th-century Chinese history." *The China Quarterly* 188, 1070–91.

Weigelin-Schwiedrzik, Susanne. 2008. "Coping with the Cultural Revolution: contesting interpretations." *Zhongyang yanjiuyuan jindaishi yanjiusuo jikan* 61, 1–52.

Wenhua Hong Weibing. 2014. "Yiwan fuhao gaogan zidi wei shenme lülü shangyan 'wenge daoqian' naoju" (Why are so many off-spring of high-level cadres repeatedly playing out the farce of "Cultural Revolution apologies"?), http://club.china.com/data/thread/1011/2767/33/16/7_1.html. Accessed 4 June 2015.

Wu, Di. 2014a. "Song Binbin daoqian zhi hou" (After Song Binbin apologized), *The New York Times* (Chinese Version), 17 July, http://cn.nytimes.com/china/20140717/cc17sbb/zh-hant/. Accessed 4 June 2015.

Wu, Di. 2014b. "He Wu Di duihua: guanyu wenge de jiyi" (A dialogue with Wu Di: the memory of the Cultural Revolution), *The New York Times* (Chinese Version), 17 July, http://cn.nytimes.com/china/20140717/cc17wudiqa/zh-hant/. Accessed 4 June 2015.

Xu, Xinhua. 2011. *Sanjiji* (*Collection of Three Memories*). Beijing: Kexue chubanshe.

Xu, Youyu. 1999. *Xingxing sese de zaofan. Hongweibing jingshen sushi de xingcheng jiqi yanbian* (*All Kinds of Rebellion. The Emergence of the Red Guard Mentality and its Development*). Hong Kong: Hong Kong Chinese University Press.

Xu, Youyu. 2014. "Chongqing moshi he wenhua da geming – wenge fansi zhi yi" (The Chongqing model and the Cultural Revolution – rethinking the Cultural Revolution). *Zuotian* 32(30 March), http://prchistory.org/wp-content/uploads/2014/08/2014%E5%B9%B43%E6%9C%8830%E6%97%A5%E7%AC%AC32%E6%9C%9F%EF%BC%88%E5%A2%9E%E5%88%8A%EF%BC%89.pdf. Accessed 22 June 2016.

Yang, Guobin. 2007. "'A portrait of martyr Jiang Qing': the Chinese Cultural Revolution on the internet." In Ching Kwan Lee and Guobin Yang (eds.), *Re-envisioning the Chinese Revolution. The Politics and Poetics of Collective Memories in Reform China*. Stanford, CA: Stanford University Press, 287–316.

Ye, Weili. 2014. "Cong 'ba wu' shuoqi" (Talking about "5 August"). *Jiyi* 106(15 January), 13–18, http://www.xujuneberlein.com/Rem106.pdf. Accessed 4 June 2015.

Ye, Weili, and Xiaodong Ma. 2005. *Growing Up in the People's Republic of China*. New York: Palgrave MacMillan.

Zhu, Guimu. 2013. "Waimei: Xi Jinping 'liangge sanshi nian lilun' huo shou Deng Liqun zhinang yingxiang" (Foreign media: Xi Jinping's [theory] on "the two 30 years" probably was influenced by Deng Liqun's think tank), http:// http://news.takungpao.com/mainland/focus/2013-06/1716441.html. Accessed 20 June 2015.

Restricted, Distorted but Alive: The Memory of the "Lost Generation" of Chinese Educated Youth

Michel Bonnin[*]

Abstract

During the 1980s, the immediate memory of the Maoist rustication movement expressed itself almost exclusively through the vector of literature, but since 1990, for reasons worth reflecting upon, a wide range of memorial activities have developed, involving a large number of the former educated youth (*zhiqing*). In the 2000s, this field benefited from the generalization of the internet and is still very much alive today. At each stage, this mainly popular or unofficial (*minjian*) memory had to negotiate a breathing space with a party-state still intent on controlling history and collective memory, especially concerning any topic directly linked with the Cultural Revolution. Thus, if memories of an important event are always varied because of the different personal experiences of the past and different individual situations and aspirations in the present, the spectrum of the *zhiqing* memories has also been complicated by political considerations. This paper does not try to present an exhaustive picture of this large memorial field; instead, through different examples, it attempts to reflect upon the meaning of the strong memorial aspirations of the *zhiqing*. It argues that only a genuine respect for history (as shown in the remarkable endeavours of some former *zhiqing*) will help this generation to transcend the conflict of memories to find meaning in its own fate.

Keywords: *zhiqing*; Cultural Revolution; collective memory; China; rustication movement

The generation of the Cultural Revolution (urban people who came of age at the time of the Cultural Revolution[1]) are in themselves a living legacy of that period. Their collective memory of the period directly influences their conceptions and values, and has an indirect influence on their children. They have been particularly active in all kinds of memorial activities and, given the Chinese Communist Party (CCP) regime's persistent control over historical narrative in

---

* Ecole des hautes études en sciences sociales (EHESS), Paris. Email: bonnin@ehess.fr.
1 For a more detailed definition of this generation, see Bonnin 2006.

© The China Quarterly, 2016   doi:10.1017/S0305741016001053

general, and over that of its own history in particular, these memorial activities unavoidably have a political impact. To understand the breadth of this legacy and its impact, one must rely not only on officially published materials but also on interviews, personal communications and unofficial publications. My 40-year study of the rustication movement incorporates the full range of these sources.[2] Furthermore, the publication of the Chinese versions of my book in 2009 and 2010 has greatly increased my ability to collect additional material from *zhiqing* across the country.[3]

The Red Guard Movement and the Rusticated Youth Movement

If we accept (reluctantly) the official designation of the "ten years of the Cultural Revolution" (1966–1976),[4] we see that two events marked the members of this generation deeply: the Red Guard movement (1966–1968) and the rustication movement (1968–1980)[5]. The rustication movement (*shangshan xiaxiang yundong* 上山下乡运动) of 1968 marked the end of the revolutionary period of the Cultural Revolution by bringing the Red Guard movement to a definitive end, and also extended the Cultural Revolution by putting into practice some of the ideas promoted during the movement. The rustication movement, one of the "newborn things of the Cultural Revolution" (*wenhua dageming de xinsheng shiwu* 文化大革命的新生事物), took different forms during the 1970s, but continued even after the official end of the "ten years" of Cultural Revolution (1977 was the year when the largest number of *zhiqing* was present in the countryside), coming to a halt only in 1980.[6]

I contend that this movement, which disrupted the lives of about 18 million urban youth as well as those of their parents and siblings (including the 1.3 million who went to the countryside before the Cultural Revolution),[7] is a key historical event of the time and central to our understanding of Mao and Maoism. One of its legacies for the participants is a strong sense of belonging to a specific generation, which in turn has triggered a desire to share memories through

---

2 I have been interviewing *zhiqing* (both formally and informally) since the mid-1970s when I met a group who had swam across to Hong Kong illegally. In 1978, I published under a penname, together with this group of *zhiqing* and two other French students of China, a book composed of collective interviews (Michel and Huang 1978). I then completed a PhD thesis on this topic, which was later published as a monograph (Bonnin 2004). My research on the *zhiqing* and the rustication movement thus spans 40 years, and has involved several hundred informants. I have interviewed dozens of former *zhiqing*, visited *zhiqing* associations and held collective and individual discussions with their members in Beijing, Shanghai, Hangzhou, Chongqing, Chengdu and Guangzhou.

3 Pan 2009; 2010. Since 2009, a pirate edition of the Hong Kong version has been circulating widely on the mainland.

4 On the topic of the historical periodization of the Cultural Revolution, see Bonnin 2013, XXI–XXII. A broader debate on this question would certainly bring to the fore the extreme complexity of this multifaceted historical event.

5 I use the term "rustication movement" to express the idea of going to live in the countryside. This movement is sometimes called the "up to the mountains, down to the villages movement" following its use in Thomas Bernstein's seminal book (Bernstein 1977).

6 Bonnin 2013, 176–77.

7 Ibid., 62.

common activities and has led to the development of mutual assistance networks. In *The Lost Generation,* I offered a tentative historical assessment of the rustication movement in the socio-economic, political and ideological realms.[8] A comprehensive assessment of the historical legacy of the Cultural Revolution as a whole would be a more complicated albeit extremely important task.

My objective in the present paper is more modest. It is to analyse the collective memory of the movement's participants which is comprised of very different and often conflicting individual memories. I also aim to show that the evolution of this memory is itself linked to the historical events and circumstances that continue to unfold right to the present day. I argue that the 4 June 1989 massacre was a determinant of the outburst of *zhiqing* memorial activities at the start of the 1990s, and I try to explain why. I also demonstrate that this memory is strongly linked to politics, not only because of the regime's will to control the memory of its own past and the enduring suspicion with which it regards social activities, but also because some of the memorial activities and social events organized by *zhiqing* have led to petitioning, demands for compensation, and the development of mutual assistance networks outside party-state control. Finally, I argue that only a respect for historical truth can overcome the conflict of memories and help those concerned give meaning to their own experience.

This paper builds upon earlier work on the *zhiqing* by Yang Guobin and by myself (see note 17 below) by incorporating new information and new insights concerning the sudden outburst of memorial activities and nostalgia of the *zhiqing* in the early 1990s, the social and political meaning of some of the activities of the *zhiqing* (mutual help but also petitioning), as well as the importance of *minjian* 民间 (popular, unofficial) history in today's China.

The term *zhishi qingnian* 知识青年, abbreviated to *zhiqing* 知青 (educated youth), is not as well-known as the term "Red Guard" (*hongweibing* 红卫兵) outside of China.[9] However, I argue that for this generation, their experience as *zhiqing* has had a deeper and more long-lasting influence than their experience as Red Guards. Not only did their stint as *zhiqing* last longer (about six years on average, but sometimes ten years or more), but their sojourn in the countryside was also a period of reflection and of a more or less common unified fate. This shared experience gave them a strong sense of a common identity, in contrast to the preceding Red Guard movement, which was chaotic, exceptional and full of infighting and which left little time for rational reflection and little opportunity for the development of common feelings. From the point of view of

---

8 Ibid., 401–440.

9 The term "*zhiqing*" (literally meaning "knowledgeable young person") has had different translations in English. "Educated youth" is the closest to the literal meaning and was officially used at the time by the Beijing Foreign Languages Press. I would use it in a paper aimed at a general readership. "Rusticated youth" could be used, too, but is not very common. "Sent-down youth" is less precise, since people sent down (in Chinese: *xiafang*) are not always sent to the countryside (*xiaxiang*): it can also refer to being sent to lower echelons of the administrative system. Since this paper is destined for a scholarly journal on Chinese affairs and since the special flavour of jargon is never fully passed on in translation, I shall use the Chinese term "*zhiqing*."

collective memory, even if Red Guards would acknowledge the importance of this experience for them, they would not have a feeling of belonging to the same generation through this experience, since they were at the time deeply divided. The two main factions (the conservative *baohuangpai* 保皇派 and the rebellious *zaofanpai* 造反派) were themselves divided, sometimes very fiercely, and there was a third group (the unconcerned *xiaoyaopai* 逍遥派).[10] On the contrary, even if the *zhiqing* had different fates according to many factors, such as their socio-political origin, at the time they felt they all were *nanyou* 难友 (fellow sufferers) and showed strong solidarity.

Another important difference regarding the collective memory of these two experiences is that many former Red Guards recall their time as a painful period, either because they were victims or perpetrators (or both alternately), or were at the very least the passive accomplices in acts of violence, which either they regret or do not wish to remember. The *zhiqing* had much less opportunity to do evil things (although some of them did, especially if they arrived in the countryside between 1968 and 1970, when the situation in many rural regions was still violent[11]). This is why they prefer to remember the period of their rustication. Many former *zhiqing* still like to present themselves as "*zhiqing*," even now they are sixty-something and therefore not young any more. By contrast, very few present themselves today as "Red Guards," even if they acknowledge that they once were Red Guards. As we shall see, there are very different memories of the rustication movement. But, both the proponents of a rosy memory of rustication and its fiercest critics agree that the memory of their experience must be kept alive and, if possible, transmitted to future generations.[12] There is no such consensus concerning the Red Guard movement.

Of course, another element must be taken into account when comparing the memory of the two movements: the attitude of the authorities concerning the history of that period. The Red Guard movement is officially considered to be a totally negative phenomenon, even to the extent that it is almost impossible to discuss it publicly. This can explain why there are very few books published on the Red Guard experience inside mainland China (and why they have generally been banned soon after publication).[13] This also explains, at least in part, why the

10   Most works on the Red Guards present the different factions. For a discussion on the diversity of "rebels," see Xu, Youyu 1999a.
11   A description of a commune brigade Party secretary being beaten up by a *zhiqing* is given in Fan et al. 2013.
12   In the introduction of the rather "critical" collection of memories, Deng Peng writes: "The study of the intellectual journey of the pre-CR *zhiqing* will help liquidate the poisonous legacy of the Maoist revolution while stories of their struggle to survive and realize their dreams against great odds may well inspire future generations in China." (Deng 2015, 14). However, in a more "nostalgic" collection, the editors assert: "Each person has only one life to live. We have written faithfully about our youthful experience. We offer this writing to the present time, to the young people of the present, hoping that thanks to that comparison between us and the youth of today, we shall all treasure life even more!" (Kong 1998, 4).
13   Since the 1980s, only a few researchers have been permitted to publish books on the history of the Cultural Revolution, including the Red Guard movement (Bonnin 2007, 54). Outside this official or semi-official realm, some former Red Guards have been able to publish inside the PRC. The most prominent author is Xu Youyu, a researcher in philosophy at the Chinese Academy of Social Sciences (Xu,

small wave of remorse expressed by former Red Guards, which appeared in 2013–2014, was quickly stamped out by the authorities.[14] However, even this fact does not explain why this generation identifies itself more as *zhiqing* than as Red Guards.

Compared to the Red Guard movement, the rustication movement is less politically "sensitive," but it would be incorrect to assume that the memory of the rustication experience was not and is not restricted by the authorities.[15] What is particularly striking is that, in spite of the restrictions, the *zhiqing* are probably the most active group in the realm of collective memory in Chinese society today.

The Memory of a Generation, and its Evolution over More than 30 Years

I call this generation a "lost generation" because they lost their youthful illusions and the pure idealism on which they were raised as children. They also lost the opportunity to study at the age of study, and this has had a lasting impact for most of them.[16] Through literature in the 1980s and then through a host of memorial activities, they have been in search of lost time, not in the sense of a Proustian individual search but rather a collective search (similar in this sense to veterans' memory after a war). It is not easy to give a complete picture of the memorial activities of such a large group during a period of about 35 years since the end of the movement. The past is always remembered in the present and then necessarily tainted by present motivations. Some of these motivations concerning the nostalgia and memorial activities of the *zhiqing* have already been noted: asserting a specific identity and resisting certain trends in society that tend to marginalize them, fighting against the official oblivion of the Cultural Revolution.[17] Thus, the spectrum of memories, which is always varied because of the different personal experiences of the past and different individual situations and aspirations in the present, has also been complicated by political considerations.

---

footnote continued

    Youyu 1998; 1999b). It has recently been more difficult to publish on this topic, but many studies and testimonies have been circulating via electronic magazines such as *Jiyi* (*Remembrance*) and *Zuotian* (*Yesterday*) among a selected list of specialists and interested scholars. Their archives are now fully available on the site of the PRC History Group: prchistory.org.

14 "Cultural Revolution: time to say sorry," *The Economist*, 29 August 2013; Xiao 2014; Pedroletti 2014; as well as the special issue published in *Jiyi* 106, 15 January 2014.

15 Restrictions can fluctuate according to the regime's sense of insecurity and calculations of political risk. For example, the main two-volume work on the history of the movement published by Chinese scholars was subject to alterations. Following its publication in 1998 for the 30th anniversary of the movement, the publisher was not permitted to reprint it until the 40th anniversary (conversation with the authors). See Ding 1998; Liu 1998. My own book was initially accepted for publication by a Chongqing publisher who was not allowed to publish it, whereas my Beijing publisher was given the green light one year later.

16 Bonnin 2013, 433–34.

17 Yang, Guobin 2003; Bonnin 2007; 2011.

As memory is itself subject to historical study, it is interesting to see how these activities have developed. From the end of the 1970s to the end of the 1980s, the memory of this generation expressed itself almost exclusively through literature. As restrictions imposed in this domain are very relaxed, a kind of neo-realist literature surfaced which fulfilled a cathartic role after the terror and sufferings of the Cultural Revolution. *Zhiqing* writers, some of whom wrote secretly for years during their rustication without any hope of being published, began to create a *zhiqing* literature, which formed a large part of the extremely popular literary magazines of the time. Immediately, they spoke for their entire generation, almost never from an individual point of view, but referred to "us" and "our generation."[18] True, as Yang Guobin remarks, at first they exposed the wounds of their generation, but if you look closely at this literature during the whole decade, you can find also many expressions of nostalgia, of pride at belonging to this generation, of praise for its "heroism."[19] In any case, writers seem to have retained the monopoly of preserving this collective memory. They seem to be invested with that task by the rest of the *zhiqing*.[20] In fact, the first works of oral history concerning that generation were also produced by writers, and not by historians or journalists.[21]

I have asked many *zhiqing* why there were no other collective expressions of memory during the 1980s.[22] Their answer is generally that they were "too busy at the time." In fact, the lives of the *zhiqing* were seriously disrupted by their rustication. This is why they are sometimes described as a "delayed generation" (*danwule de yidai* 耽误了的一代).[23] After their return to the cities at the end of the 1970s, they had to make up for lost time and find work, study, marry and have children, all fundamental activities that would normally have happened at an earlier point in their lives had they not been rusticated. Only at the end of the 1980s did they feel more established and were they finally able to care about matters such as reflecting upon their rural experience.

What is striking is the change that occurred in 1990–1991, with the staging of some big *zhiqing* exhibitions and the writing and first publication of historical/memorial books about the rustication movement. Why precisely at that time?

Yang Guobin argues that this surge in *zhiqing* nostalgia was the result of the very specific experience they had had during their adolescence and of an identity crisis triggered by the rapid social changes caused by the economic upheavals.[24] This is certainly true over the long term. But the most destabilizing social changes appeared only later, in the years following Deng's Southern Tour at the

---

18 See, e.g., Bonnin 2013, 432, Fn. 22.
19 Ibid., 439–440. On this literature, see Yang, Jian 2002; Wang, Lijian 2008; Qin 2006.
20 Bonnin 1986.
21 Feng 1991; Zhang, Xinxin, and Ye 1986.
22 In fact, there were some private activities, like trips organized by small groups of former *zhiqing* to the village or farm where they had been sent, but nothing public or large scale.
23 Bonnin 2013, 434.
24 Yang, Guobin 2003, especially 273–76.

beginning of 1992. In fact, after the events of 4 June 1989, reforms had slowed down and there was even a return to more "socialist" policies.[25]

My own hypothesis is that this surge in *zhiqing* memory in 1990–1991 is linked to "4 June" in two different ways: for the *zhiqing* themselves and for urban society as a whole, 4 June in a way blocked the future. The 1980s had been a time of hope, of openness to the outside world and to Western ideas,[26] and of economic and social reforms that were also supposed to bring about political and ideological reforms.[27] As was shown by the debates concerning the film *River Elegy* (*Heshang* 河殇), there was a strong aspiration to develop a new "blue culture" in China (blue being the colour of the ocean, a symbol of openness to the outside) to combat the burden of the traditional "yellow culture" (yellow being the symbol of the yellow earth around the Yellow River, where China had originated).[28] The massacre perpetrated during the night of 3–4 June 1989 in Beijing killed not only people but also this optimism and this openness, especially as the authorities did all they could to reject everything new and Western in the ideological realm and to encourage Chinese people to go back to their own cultural and historical roots.[29] This is the period when traditional practices like martial arts, *qigong* and even the belief in all kinds of fantastic "supernatural powers" (*teyi gongneng* 特异功能) flourished suddenly, especially among very official institutions such as the police and the army.[30] Under these circumstances, the *zhiqing* nostalgia, which had always been latent, became more pressing and, at the same time, the authorities were more willing to allow the *zhiqing* to organize memorial activities (and in fact they encouraged these activities so long as they could control their content). Even if the 1960s and 1970s were a sensitive time, this sensitivity was much less dangerous than the recent past of the spring of 1989. In a way, the tolerance shown by the authorities could be explained as the use of one memory to obfuscate another one. It could also be described as letting some steam out in a tense situation. The first *zhiqing* exhibition, which opened in November 1990 in the Beijing History Museum (bordering Tiananmen Square, where the 1989 events had taken place), had a strong official "flavour." The exhibitions that followed, in Hainan, Chengdu and Nanjing in 1991 and 1993, were also staged

25 Barry Naughton, discussing economic policy, writes that, "The 1990s policy regime emerged with unmistakable clarity only a few years after the Tiananmen crisis, in 1993–1994." He points to "a surprisingly radical retrenchment of reforms" just after Tiananmen. See Naughton 2011, mainly 154–166. See also Lam 1995, mainly 51–75.

26 Wang, Runsheng 1992.

27 In 1986, Deng Xiaoping himself promoted the idea of political reform before changing his mind. The two successive Party general secretaries chosen by him, Hu Yaobang and Zhao Ziyang, were both in favour of some kind of reform. See, e.g., Ruan 1994.

28 On the meaning of the *River Elegy* (*Heshang*), see Chen, Fong-ching, and Jin 1997.

29 In a way, this turn towards the past is still strong today. Even though Deng Xiaoping succeeded in the economic realm to point China again in a forward direction, in the political and ideological realms, the horizon is still blocked by strong prohibitions and by the very historical existence of 4 June 1989. While the Party is unwilling to face this historical black point, it is difficult to imagine how Chinese society will be able to open new political and intellectual horizons.

30 This was the breeding ground for the development of the Falun Gong, which later posed a problem for the authorities. See Palmer 2007 and Ownby 2010.

under the patronage of the municipal authorities and blessed by the calligraphies of top local leaders.[31]

The sudden emergence of unofficial historical books on the rustication movement after 1990 is also intriguing. Before 1989, apart from some "internal" studies not available to the public, the only historical account of the movement had appeared in 1987 as a small chapter in a book written by Party researchers that gave an official presentation of the "ten years of the Cultural Revolution."[32] However, two historical books on the movement, written by former *zhiqing* with no official backgrounds, were published in 1992 and 1993 (one of them having been ready since the end of 1990). Others followed during the 1990s. These books, of course, could not have been published without official approval.[33]

It is also interesting to note that this is precisely when Deng Xiaoping 邓小平 himself began to acknowledge in front of his colleagues the fact that the evaluation of Mao Zedong 毛泽东, made in 1981 under his leadership, was not satisfactory from a historical point of view. In the summer of 1991 and again in January 1993, he said that it had only been a political necessity and would be revised by the next generation in "ten or eight years."[34] Deng, who had taken the ultimate decision for the 4 June crackdown,[35] a decision that demonstrated his paramount power but would probably remain as a stain on his own biography, was ready soon after that to contemplate the revision of Mao's official image, which seemed cast forever by the 1981 Resolution. Although a complete study on this topic has yet to be made, it seems that the trauma of 4 June 1989 has brought China to a new "regime of historicity," which means a new relationship between a society and "time": in this case, a backward-looking tendency to reflect on the more distant past so as to forget the painful present or immediate past, in a situation when previous hopes for the future have been disappointed.[36] The nostalgic mood of Chinese society (which was in total contrast to the idealistic and often impatient expectations concerning the future prevalent in the 1980s) appeared very soon at the beginning of the 1990s. As such, in 1994 a new publishing company, Huaxia publishing house 华夏出版社 (with links to the political department of the army[37]) decided to publish a series of books dedicated to

---

31   Interviews conducted in Beijing in 1991 with a famous *zhiqing* writer who was familiar with the organizers but refused to take part in it because it was too "official," and in Chengdu in 2008 with a group of organizers of the 1991 exhibition. One of them, Qu Bo, gave me some original documents concerning the exhibition. See also Yang, Guobin 2003. On the Beijing exhibition, see Hunxi hei tudi bianweihui 1991.

32   Bonnin 2013, xxxiii.

33   An article that I published in 1989 in an audacious but short-lived magazine in liberal Hainan province appears to have had some influence on the first Chinese unofficial historians of the movement, along with the later publication, in 1993, of a Chinese version of Thomas Bernstein's (1977) book. The publication of Bernstein's book also shows a new tolerance concerning this topic. See Bonnin 2013, xxxiii–xxxv.

34   Xin 2007, vi; Guo 2010.

35   Zhang, Liang, Nathan and Link 2002.

36   See Hartog 2003.

37   Information from a famous *zhiqing* writer who published with this company and who was asked to act also as a literary advisor.

nostalgia under the title *Collection of Nostalgia Literature*. An excerpt from the general preface to the collection and one from the postscript of the fifth volume illustrates this change in the "regime of historicity":

> The sad present has not been able to give us new ideas or new forms which we can acclaim and recall with dignity. So we have no other choice but to look behind us and return to the past.
>
> One of my friends said to me: "Tomorrow is born of yesterday, not of today. I can only concoct my dreams of the future from the traces of the past." These words are an accurate reflection of the mentality of certain urban intellectuals today. Unable to imagine what tomorrow will hold, they try to avoid falling in a state of open anxiety by intoxicating themselves with heady draughts from the past.[38]

Also at that time, another form of memorial activity suddenly emerged in the form of *zhiqing* restaurants, which opened in many large cities and especially in Beijing. In these restaurants, diners could eat the cuisine of the different regions where the local *zhiqing* had been sent, in surroundings and décor reminiscent of the life of the *zhiqing* at that time.[39] They could thus spiritually feed themselves with symbols of their own past. There was, of course, a commercial motive behind these restaurants, but they had a social and cultural function. They became places where former *zhiqing* could get together again, and in one restaurant, diners could pin their name card to a big board, in the hope that a former pal from this period would then be able to get in touch.[40] Sometimes, these restaurants were used as gathering places for groups of former *zhiqing* who not only wanted to eat but also wanted to talk among themselves. The authorities were suspicious of these gatherings and in some cases banned them or punished the restaurant owners by closing their enterprise for a period of time.[41]

During the 1990s, the groups which had organized exhibitions, along with many other groups of *zhiqing*, began publishing collections of remembrances. This broke the monopoly on memory formerly enjoyed by professional writers. Ordinary *zhiqing* were able to retell their stories of their rural experience and share their present feelings about it. Of course, these publications all had to pass through censorship, but with time their number increased. In 1998, for the 30th anniversary of the launch of the movement, the authorities permitted the publication of many of these books. And, during the 2000s, the rapid development of the internet gave more people the opportunity to take part in memorial activities through remembrances and discussions posted on *zhiqing* websites. These websites were created by small groups of *zhiqing* friends and were instrumental to creating more important associations, giving a new visibility to their activities. Hard print magazines were also produced in the major cities.[42]

Some of these activities were certainly stimulated by the mercantile atmosphere of the 1990s, which has prevailed under new forms until now. There is an obvious economic incentive behind the restaurants, the selling of albums of old *zhiqing*

38 Author's translation. More examples and precise references can be found in Bonnin 1996, 38.
39 Ibid.; Hubbert 2005.
40 Hubbert 2005, 40.
41 Ibid., 38.
42 Yang, Guobin 2003.

songs and also the organized trips to the original places of rustication, with the association acting as a travel agency. But, from my interviews with many of the people in charge of these associations, it appears that the commercial motivation for most of these activities is at best secondary. In fact, the costs often outweigh the returns. These activities rely mostly on volunteer work, and when some businessmen play an important role in the association, it is generally because they are the only ones who can afford to provide funding without a return. Their motivation is partly the traditional one for merchants and businessmen in traditional society inside China and in the diaspora, which is to gain prestige by promoting socially useful activities and doing charitable works. It is very often difficult to doubt the sincerity of their desire to do something meaningful for the memory of the rustication movement.[43] It must be remembered that these activities can not only be costly but can also be a source of contention with the authorities. Moreover, the numerous conflicts that arise between different groups or individuals inside the association can easily become a headache for those in charge. From my discussions with some of the group leaders and my observations of the ups and downs of the life of these associations, it seems that only a strong feeling of belonging to a special community (the *zhiqing*, and especially the *zhiqing* of a certain city) and the personal satisfaction they get from doing useful things for this community can fully explain the time and energy these people commit to these projects.

Since the end of the 2000s, museums, big and small, along with permanent exhibitions, have been established across the whole of China to keep the memory of the movement alive. They are the result of individual initiatives by former *zhiqing*, sometimes with the help of official institutions. Some, like the Heihe Zhiqing Museum 黑河知青博物馆 in Heilongjiang, initiated by former Shanghai *zhiqing* under the leadership of the Political Consultative Conference of Heilongjiang province, give a very positive assessment of the rustication experience, while others, such as the Jianchuan Museum 建川博物馆 in Dayi county 大邑县 near Chengdu and the Shanghai *Zhiqing* Museum in Haiwan Park 海湾公园 (in Shanghai's Fengxian district 奉贤区), give a more balanced presentation, including, for example, photos and documents concerning the *zhiqing* campaign to return home at the end of the 1970s.[44]

Different Memories Competing

Different feelings are expressed in all of these memorial activities but, since the 1990s, the most pervasive is certainly nostalgia. I call this nostalgia "paradoxical nostalgia," or "a nostalgia for the bad old days," since at the time of the movement almost all of the rusticated youths had only one goal in mind: to leave the

---

43 I do not want to give names here, but I am thinking specifically of two people, one in Shanghai, one in Chengdu.
44 Personal documentation.

countryside. Virtually no one stayed there when they had the opportunity to return to the cities.

This paradoxical nostalgia can be explained by the fact that their youth has
passed and because they came through an exceptional experience which marked
them deeply. They can express a kind of pride and satisfaction because nobody
will go through the same experience after them. But, even the more nostalgic
and proud have learned something. They do not really want to go back to
Mao's time. They do not respond when other *zhiqing* remind them that they
left the countryside and that they would not like their children to be rusticated
like them.

So, the *zhiqing* nostalgia of the 1990s had a post-modern flavour. It was more
the result of unease about the present and anxiety about the future than a real
desire to go back to the past. It was a time of derision and cynicism, as expressed
in the very popular novels of Wang Shuo 王朔. In one nostalgic *zhiqing* restaurant, I remarked that someone had added small moustaches to the portraits of
Mao and Lin Biao 林彪 on the old newspapers covering the walls and ceiling.
Nobody seemed to care.[45] The 1990s was also a period when Mao and the
Cultural Revolution were widely packaged as merchandise. Indeed, it could be
said that the more that Mao and the Cultural Revolution were marketed, the
more the ideals they incarnated sank into the past.[46]

It is worth noting that those *zhiqing* who gained a degree of success after their
return to their cities tend to have a more positive memory of their experience and
thus are more nostalgic. There are remarkable exceptions to this tendency among
the scholars, writers and artists of that generation, but generally speaking this
seems to be true, especially among officials and businessmen. In both categories,
rustication is often used as a form of political capital, a way of demonstrating that
their success was not obtained easily but only through hardship and perseverance
at the grassroots level, that they had been "tempered" by the rustication movement as Mao had wished.[47] Xi Jinping 习近平 probably provides the best example of this use of the *zhiqing* experience as political capital, as shown by his
high-profile Chinese New Year visit in 2015 to his rustication place in the
North Shaanxi region.[48] In 2002, Xi wrote an account of his sojourn in the countryside called, "I am a son of the yellow earth." In a move reminiscent of Mao's
days, this text was transformed into a song with the same title in 2014.[49]

45 Bonnin 1996, 39.
46 Ibid. On the Mao nostalgia of that time, see Barmé 1996; 2000, 316–344.
47 Of course, they forget that Mao had certainly not intended that this movement should produce such
    people as capitalist entrepreneurs and Party leaders with rich families.
48 See, e.g., "Xi Jinping chonghui Yan'an chadui cunzhuang, yong Shaanbei fangyan jieshao Peng
    Liyuan" (Xi Jinping goes back to the village where he was sent, uses the north Shaanxi dialect to intro-
    duce Peng Liyuan), *Xinhua*, 14 February 2015, http://view.inews.qq.com/w/WXN201502140077890A1?
    refer=nwx. Accessed 28 June 2016. It was not the first time that Xi Jinping went publicly back to this
    place. For the text of Xi's account of his sojourn in the countryside, see Xi 2002.
49 Baidu baike. 2014. "Wo shi huang tudi de erzi" (I am a son of the yellow earth), http://baike.baidu.com/
    link?url=QKDBX0fPNlWOXaJHcARRYovQ8esrdWUYzS0wsJEFhYG5k5lomTbNL0opOMkuya
    ECduLHL7qVFmGwDRrTbnTg2q. Accessed 27 June 2016.

A Wide Spectrum of Memories between Nostalgia and Rejection, Denunciation and Approval

So, we can differentiate between two types of memory, one nostalgic and one critical, but it is not a clear black-and-white picture. Feelings about the *zhiqing* experience are often mixed and not as clear-cut as it would appear. For example, the Chengdu *zhiqing* who organized one of the first exhibitions in June 1991 used a title which became the motto for all nostalgic *zhiqing*: *qingchun wuhui* 青春无悔 (often translated as "we have no regret for our youth").[50] During my discussions with some of the organizers in 2008 and 2009, they told me that while the title was in fact chosen by the municipal authorities (who discussed all the details of the exhibition before authorizing it), they had accepted it because it reflected their feelings. They were later surprised by the fierce criticism of some who accused them of lacking a critical distance from a movement that had brought so much trouble and loss to their generation. They objected that, for them, the meaning of *qingchun wuhui* was in fact *qingchun wufa hui* 青春无法悔 (we have no means to regret our youth). They could not regret this youthful experience because it was a fact of the past that they had not chosen in the first place. It was imposed upon them, but as it had become an important part of their lives which had left indelible traces in their hearts and become part of their collective identity, they just had to face it and, most importantly, to keep its memory alive. The possibility of remembering publicly this period of their lives and organizing an exhibition that would bring them together again allowed them to pay tribute to those *zhiqing* who had lost their lives in Yunnan (part seven of the exhibition). It also revealed to their children an important part of their personal histories, and in their opinion justified the compromises they had had to make in their discussions with the municipality concerning the title and the content of the exhibition. They later published a collection of recorded memories using the same title: *Qingchun wuhui*.[51] But, many years later, some of them also collaborated in the publication of another edited volume that demonstrated that their nostalgic feelings and their sense of belonging to the special community of "*zhiqing*" did not necessarily mean that they lacked a critical distance from their past.[52] Not only did they show in this book the dark aspects of that time and proudly remember the protests that had culminated in their return to the cities, but they also took action to repair one injustice left from that period. Having heard that a *zhiqing* from Chongqing, Jiang Shihua 姜世华, was left crippled and thus unable to work as a result of the ill treatment he had received at the Yunnan farm to which he had been sent aged 17, and that he had not received any help following his return to Chongqing, this group of *zhiqing* used the internet and

---

50 The subtitle was: "Chengdu zhiqing fu dian zhibian huigu zhan" (Retrospective exhibition of the Chengdu educated youth sent to support the border in Yunnan). A special envelope marking the event was issued by the Stamp Company of Chengdu.
51 "Qingchun Wuhui" bianjizu 1991.
52 Qu and Luo 2006.

their "relations" to help Jiang secure a small monthly stipend from the farm, and published the story in their book.[53]

However, "critical memory" is also complex. Painful memories (of physical and moral pain suffered at the time) can easily transform into a critical memory denouncing the system that inflicted those wounds on the *zhiqing* individually and collectively. Fewer people express such memories because remembering pain is itself painful. This is why many *zhiqing* simply "do not dare to look back" (*bu kan huishou* 不堪回首), and even when they are emboldened to do so, they may still be subject to censorship by the authorities. Still, expressions of painful memories do continue in the public domain, especially in literature and cinema.[54]

Even those *zhiqing* who are more critical of the movement evince traces of nostalgia. This is the result not only of the usual nostalgia of youth but also of their personal feelings towards other *zhiqing* or peasants, which emerged naturally from many years spent together in the countryside. The specificity of Maoist society, which imposed the same ideology and the same simplistic culture upon everybody, can also explain why people who may have different conceptions of life today still have a strong sense of a common identity that is triggered by old songs, films or texts that were popular during their time in the countryside. Even dissidents of that generation (including people extremely critical of Mao) participate in singing "red" songs glorifying Mao when they wine-and-dine together in the US, if only because they simply cannot recall other songs from their youth.[55]

Thus, sentiment and reason are not always in line with the memories that the *zhiqing* retain of their experience and the assessment they make of it. A "nostalgic memory" can trigger a totally positive evaluation of the rustication policy but can also coexist with a more balanced evaluation. A "critical memory" can be supported by mainly bad personal remembrances or trigger a refusal to remember the whole period. It can also blend a negative assessment of the movement with personal nostalgic feelings. This variety is still further complicated by the links, inevitable under the Chinese regime, between memory and politics.

Memory and Politics

We have seen that in the case of the Chengdu *zhiqing* who organized one of the first exhibitions, politics (in this case, approval from the municipal authorities)

---

53 Ibid., 471–596.
54 In cinema, the most famous movie expressing the despair felt by female *zhiqing*, who were faced with sexual harassment and rape by local cadres, was directed in the US by Chinese actress Joan Chen (*Xiu Xiu* (*The Sent-down Girl*) 1998). In the realm of literature, which is less strictly controlled than cinema inside China, most of the works by *zhiqing* authors at the time of the "scar literature" and even later express some aspects of their difficulties and pain. This is the case for both mainstream authors like Ye Xin in *Cuotuo suiyue* (Ye 1980) and more marginal authors like Xu Naijian in *Yangbai de wuran* (Xu, Naijian 1981). With the passage of time, the expression of pain has been transformed into irony and black humour, as in Wang Xiaobo's *Huangjin shidai* (Wang, Xiaobo 1997).
55 Meeting with Hu Ping, 31 March 2014.

influenced their memorial activity. From the discussions I had with *zhiqing* in other cities, it appears that many agree that it is worth compromising with the authorities in order to hold large-scale memorial activities. But, there are often disputes, resulting in splits or even boycotts because of differing views on the necessity of such compromises. Quite often, a group of *zhiqing* brand another group or leader as "traitors" for siding with the authorities and trying to please them, while the more accommodating group in turn regards the hold-outs as "troublemakers" with politically motivated agendas that could lead to the banning of their association and activities.[56]

Such conflicts are the inevitable result of the authorities' determination to control both the form and content of *zhiqing* memorial activities. This determination has not abated, even decades later. This is particularly true in the case of high-profile *zhiqing* memorial activities. For example, in December 2013, on the 50th anniversary of their departure, a group of former Shanghai *zhiqing*, who were dispatched to the Xinjiang Production and Construction Corps, organized an evening party in a large venue which could accommodate up to 3,000 former members of those farms and their families. As they are older than the Cultural Revolution *zhiqing*, and as many of their original number are now deceased, this commemoration was particularly poignant. But it was very difficult to get municipal approval for the event, since the Xinjiang *zhiqing* are considered to be particularly restive. They were forced to submit the names of all invitees in advance and to invite a few former "model *zhiqing*" who continue to spread propaganda for the movement (which generates lifelong political capital and economic benefit for them, as they also manage business ventures linked to memorializing the rustication movement). It goes without saying that those who continue to petition for the improvement of the conditions of the *zhiqing* were excluded. As a result of such deliberate staging, the DVD of the event carries no mention of the harsh fate and the discrimination that the Xinjiang *zhiqing* suffered. The texts of the speeches given at the event, as well as the content of all the artistic performances, were pre-screened and a few officials and former "model *zhiqing*" were also put on the programme. The only spontaneous "free expression" was a brief extemporaneous statement uttered by the main organizer, in which he said that history would judge whether their petitioning movement of 1979–1980 had been justified. As the leader of this failed petitioning movement, he had been jailed for four years and had consequently led a very difficult life after his release. It was probably the least that he could do from a moral point of view, but it was also the most he could have said without risking the pre-emptive closure of the event.[57]

---

56 Different interviews with former *zhiqing* from Shanghai, Chongqing and Beijing between 2008 and 2014.
57 Discussion with Ouyang Lian and other participants in the conference, 20 December 2014. The collection of the three DVDs is called *Huihuang de shenghui, 1963–2013: Shanghai zhibian zhishi qingnian fu Xinjiang tunken shubian wushi zhounian jinian dahui* (*A Glorious Meeting, 1963–2013: Memorial Meeting for the 50th Anniversary of the Departure of Shanghai Educated Youth to Help the Border and Reclaim*

Clearly, the official need to control this 2013 event was as pronounced as it had been for the 1991 Chengdu exhibition. But, in both cases, the organizers thought it worthwhile to make the concessions in order to keep the memory alive.

What explains the persistent determination of the authorities to control the memory of the rustication movement down to the present day? The reasons, I think, are twofold. The most important is certainly the desire to maintain a positive image of Mao and the history of the People's Republic of China (PRC) as a source of political legitimacy. Even before Xi Jinping announced that it was not permissible to use the last 30 years of PRC history to critique the 30 years which preceded,[58] I was often asked: "if you consider us a 'lost generation,' how do you explain China's rapid development and extraordinary successes after the rustication movement? It is precisely because rustication was a good policy that China could develop rapidly during the reform period." However, the contrary explanation also receives wide support: it is precisely because such policies were abandoned and radical changes were adopted that China was able to catch up very quickly and leave behind the sad state in which Mao left his country at the end of his life.[59] However, it is more difficult to convince the Party leaders who are striving to create a "globally positive" image of the Maoist period and to label all fundamental criticism of it as "historical nihilism." Xi Jinping's denunciation of "nihilism" is clearly linked to the Chinese Communist Party's ability to hold on to power, since the fall of the Soviet Union is attributed in part to a similar "nihilism" during the last days of the USSR.[60]

The Question of Compensation

Aside from the image of Mao and of the regime in general, the risk of being presented with compensation claims is certainly one reason why the authorities seek to limit the expression of *zhiqing* memory and why they attempt to channel it in the direction of a globally positive appreciation of that experience.

The authorities are indeed confronted with a militant memory. Some groups of *zhiqing* remind them of the pains that they suffered and which are not yet over. For these *zhiqing*, the past is not past and they demand a solution to their present problems. The most important group still making collective claims today is that

---

footnote continued

Land in Xinjiang). On Ouyang Lian (and the Xinjiang *zhiqing* protest movement), see Liu 2004, 445–529, and Bonnin 2010.

58 "Xi Jinping: gaige kaifang qianhou de lishi bu neng huxiang fouding" (Xi Jinping: the historical periods before and after the reforms cannot be opposed to each other), *Xinhua*, 5 January 2013.

59 "Due to Mao's initiatives, China had fallen increasingly behind other nations in its quest for development. Mao left a country that was backward and weak, having fulfilled few of the aspirations of the early 1950s." Walder 2015, 315.

60 Zhonggong zhongyang dangshi yanjiushi. 2013. "Zhongyang dangshi yanjiushi chanshi Xi Jinping liangge bu neng fouding lunshu" (The Central Committee Research Centre on Party History explains Xi Jinping's discourse on the two periods which cannot be negated), *Renmin wang*, 8 November.

of the Shanghai *zhiqing* who were sent to Xinjiang before the Cultural Revolution. Members of this group are making demands for compensation because of the discriminatory treatment they have suffered since the beginning of the 1980s, when they, unlike other *zhiqing*, were not permitted to return to Shanghai.[61] This refusal has triggered a whole host of difficulties for them that continue right up until the present day. In 2000, they tried to organize a delegation of 50 *zhiqing* to go to Beijing to explain their plight to the central authorities. However, before they could depart, they were arrested and three were jailed for a period. Some of them even tried to sue the mayor of Shanghai but, of course, the tribunal did not accept their case.[62] When Xi Jinping became the Shanghai Party secretary in 2007, they wrote an appeal to him and organized a small demonstration with a banner welcoming "the old *zhiqing* Xi Jinping" to Shanghai. But it was to no avail: Xi never replied and left Shanghai after a few months to become a member of the Standing Committee of the Politburo.[63]

Similarly, Ding Huimin 丁惠民, a *zhiqing* who was the former leader of the Xishuangbanna 西双版纳 protest movement of 1978–1979, tried to organize a delegation of former rusticated youths from Chongqing to go to Beijing in 2009 to demand a solution to the many problems that still plague them; however, he was arrested at the station and sent for re-education through labour.[64]

In addition to these petitions for compensation, the notion has often been expressed that the state owes something to the *zhiqing* as a victimized group.[65] This serves to reinforce the determination of the Party to supervise *zhiqing* memorial activities.

The *zhiqing*, however, do not rely only on authorities: one function of their memorial activities is to organize mutual assistance for *zhiqing* in need. Very often, those who have fared better provide funding to those less fortunate than themselves, for example, by purchasing computers or paying the travel expenses of *zhiqing* who are less well off.

Such assistance can have political overtones when *zhiqing* are mobilized, for instance in the aforementioned case of Jiang Shihua. Similarly, the writer Lao Gui 老鬼, who was sent to Inner Mongolia, organized funding to erect a monument to the 29 *zhiqing* who had died fighting a forest fire there, and published a commemorative book of parents' accounts of each of the *zhiqing* martyrs.[66] Former *zhiqing* who have attained a high social status use their influence to urge the authorities to redress injustices and provide comfort to the victims of the rustication movement. This type of *zhiqing* mobilization in self-protection

---

61 Bonnin 2004, 192–202; 2010.
62 Different meetings with the "three scholars" (*san xiucai*) from the group of Xinjiang former *zhiqing* who continue to make regular claims for compensation, and the personal collection of documents produced by this group.
63 Ibid.
64 Communication with a friend of Ding Huimin and postings on Sina Weibo by his lawyer, Liu Xiaoyuan.
65 For a clearly articulated expression of this idea, see Chen, Yixin 1999.
66 Lao 2009.

is a salient and positive legacy of their experience in the countryside, even if its overall effects are limited.

History as a Way to Transcend the Conflict of Memories

Conflicting memories shared among the *zhiqing* can become polarized, particularly on the internet, and deter those seeking more serious reflection about their fate and that of their generation. Memories of the rustication movement (*minjian jiyi* 民间记忆) and unofficial histories (*minjian lishi* 民间历史) were penned during the 1990s by former *zhiqing* who were motivated by a desire to overturn myths, to salvage the history of this period from oblivion and to restore a true image to the movement. Some of the authors were professional historians working on earlier periods (Liu Xiaomeng 刘小萌 and Ding Yizhuang 定宜庄, both researchers studying the Manchu dynasty at the CASS) or scholars in other fields, such as Xu Youyu 徐友渔 or Shi Weimin 史卫民. Other authors included former leaders or cadres who had worked in the administration of the *xiaxiang* movement (for example, Gu Hongzhang 顾洪章, Zhao Fan 赵凡, Xu Fa 许法 and Xie Mingan 谢敏干).[67] Some of these works were published by official publishers, others unofficial: *samizdat* (*ziyinshu* 自印书), independent documentaries or electronic magazines sent to a list of selected people. Only in Shanghai has the work of historians of the rustication movement been recognized as a regular academic activity. Some of these historians work closely with *minjian* associations (for example, Jin Dalu 金大陆 and Jin Guangyao 金光耀).[68] All of these researchers were either *zhiqing* themselves or cadres in charge of *zhiqing*. More recently, a handful of younger scholars have emerged whose work may allow this field of study to outlive the *zhiqing* generation itself. Not surprisingly, they are all children of *zhiqing* and are concentrated in Shanghai. Even people who are not trained as scholars have, in their collections of testimonies, gathered and compared different accounts of the same event, and found valuable information in old newspaper accounts. They, too, have thus contributed to the broader effort to preserve the historical truth and to preserve memory enlightened by historical data.[69]

History is indeed a way to transcend the conflict of memories. It can give the former *zhiqing* a satisfying sense of comprehending their own destiny. To younger generations, it is useful to know something about the history lived by their parents and grandparents. But it remains difficult to overcome the political interests and prejudices of those who are not primarily interested in truth and reflection, particularly when free debate on the Maoist period is still impossible because of

---

67 For a list of the main works of these authors, see the Bibliography in Bonnin 2004, as well as in Bonnin 2007.
68 Bonnin 2007. The Shanghai researchers are doing a very useful job of compiling reference materials and chronicles for further historical research. See Lin and Jin 2014, as well as Jin, Jin and Shanghaishi zhishi qingnian lishi wenhua yanjiuhui 2014.
69 See, e.g., Qu and Luo 2006.

official restrictions. Unfortunately, half a century after the launch of the Cultural Revolution, no one can tell when a balanced historical study of this period will be possible in China itself. Still, in spite of the difficulties, the former rusticated youth have shown a remarkable energy in maintaining the memory of their exceptional experience. Some have already made important contributions to a future detailed and rational history of the Maoist era. To attain this goal, they need to liberate their thinking from the propaganda of the time, which was never officially criticized and is frequently revived for political purposes. This task has a deep meaning for China and for the rest of the world. I suggest that, in China and abroad, dedicated historians of the rustication movement and of the Cultural Revolution meditate this appeal made by the French historian Jacques Le Goff: "Memory [...] endeavours to save the past only to serve the present and the future. Let's see to it that collective memory serves the liberation of men and not their enslavement."[70]

Acknowledgement

Research for this article was funded by the ANR under the ANR–RGC collaborative project, "New approaches to the Mao era (1949–1976): everyday history and unofficial memory" (2013–2016).

Biographical note

Michel Bonnin is professor at the Ecole des Hautes Etudes en Sciences Sociales (EHESS), Paris. During the 1990s, he was the director of the French Research Centre on Contemporary China and of the magazine *China Perspectives*, both of which he founded in Hong Kong. His 2004 book, *Génération perdue. Le mouvement d'envoi des jeunes instruits à la campagne, Chine 1968–1980*, which gives a global presentation of the rustication movement of China's educated youth, has two Chinese editions published in Hong Kong and Beijing, and an English edition entitled, *The Lost Generation: The Rustication of China's Educated Youth (1968–1980)* ("Choice Outstanding Academic Title, 2014"). His main research interests are the social and political questions of the People's Republic of China. He has written mostly on the rustication movement of urban educated youth during the 1960s and the 1970s, on the democratic movement in China, and on popular history and memory, as well as on the question of generations in contemporary China.

摘要: 在 1980 年代, 毛泽东发动的上山下乡运动的记忆基本上只是在文学中才有所表达。但有一件事值得我们反思: 自 1990 年起, 各种记忆活动开始出现, 涉及的前知青数目也相当大。在 2000 年代, 记忆活动因互联网的

---

70 Le Goff 1988, 177. Author's translation.

普及化更有所发展，到现在还是非常活跃。这个记忆主要是民间记忆，在各阶段需要与一直有意控制历史和集体记忆的党国争取一个呼吸空间。有关文革的议题特别难以取得官方的容忍。所以，知青记忆的全景图不但因过去的经历和现在的状况与愿望不同而多元化，还因各种政治顾虑而复杂化。本文没有提供这个广大的记忆领域的全景图的奢望目标，只是通过不同的例子来反思知青保存记忆的强大愿望的意义。文章强调只有在真正尊重历史的情况下，这代人才能超越不同记忆的冲突，而找到自己命运中的意义。在这方面，一些知青已经有不可忽略的贡献。

关键词: 知青; 文化大革命; 集体记忆; 中国; 上山下乡运动

References

Barmé, Geremie. 1996. *Shades of Mao: The Posthumous Cult of the Great Leader*. Armonk, NY: M.E. Sharpe.

Barmé, Geremie. 2000. *In the Red: On Contemporary Chinese Culture*. New York: Columbia University Press.

Bernstein, Thomas P. 1977. *Up to the Mountains and Down to the Villages: The Transfer of Youth from Urban to Rural China*. New Haven, CT: Yale University Press.

Bonnin, Michel. 1986. "The social function of Chinese literature since 1979: the case of the 'lost generation'." In H. Martin (ed.), *Cologne Workshop 1984 on Contemporary Chinese Literature*. Cologne: Deutsche Welle, 233–238.

Bonnin, Michel. 1996. "Peking's theme restaurants: nostalgia for the bad old days." *China Perspectives* 4(March–April), 35–41.

Bonnin, Michel. 2004. *Génération perdue. Le mouvement d'envoi des jeunes instruits à la campagne, Chine 1968–1980*. Paris: Editions de l'Ecole des Hautes Etudes en Sciences Sociales.

Bonnin, Michel. 2006. "The 'lost generation': its definition and its role in today's Chinese elite politics." *Social Research – An International Quarterly of the Social Sciences* 73(1), 245–274.

Bonnin, Michel. 2007. "The threatened history and collective memory of the Cultural Revolution's lost generation." *China Perspectives* 4, http://chinaperspectives.revues.org/2573. Accessed 4 July 2016.

Bonnin, Michel. 2010. "Shanghai et l'héritage douloureux du maoïsme: le destin de la 'génération perdue'." In Nicolas Idier (ed.), *Shanghai: histoire, promenades, anthologie et dictionnaire*. Paris: Robert Laffont, Bouquins, 931–972.

Bonnin, Michel. 2011. "Une génération oubliée? Mémoire, culture et entraide chez les anciens jeunes intruits. *Monde Chinois* 25, 106–112.

Bonnin, Michel. 2013. *The Lost Generation – The Rustication of China's Educated Youth (1968–1980)*. Hong Kong: Chinese University of Hong Kong Press.

Chen, Fong-ching, and Jin Guantao. 1997. *From Youthful Manuscripts to River Elegy: The Chinese Popular Cultural Movement and Political Transformation, 1979–1989*. Hong Kong: The Chinese University of Hong Kong Press.

Chen, Yixin. 1999. "Cong xiafang dao xiagang: Zhongguo de zhiqing yidai, 1968–1998" (From sent-down to laid-off: China's sent-down generation, 1968–1998). *Ershiyi shiji* 8, 219–239.

Deng, Peng (ed.). 2015. *Exiled Pilgrims: Memoirs of Pre-Cultural Revolution Zhiqing*. Leiden: Brill.

Ding, Yizhuang. 1998. *Zhongguo zhiqing shi. Chulan (1953–1968)* (*A History of the Chinese Educated Youth. The First Waves, 1953–1968*). Beijing: Zhongguo shehui kexue chubanshe.

Fan, Chenggang, Su Tongliao, Mei Zhounan and Pan Mengqi. 2013. "'Women shi shaoshu': wenge chanhuizhe de nuli yu kundun" ("We are a minority": the efforts made and difficulties faced by the people who repent for what they did during the Cultural Revolution), *Nanfang zhoumo*, 20 July.

Feng, Jicai. 1991. *Yibaige ren de shi nian* (*How a Hundred People Spent Ten Years*). Nanjing: Jiangsu wenyi chubanshe.

Guo, Daohui. 2010. "Siqian lao ganbu dui dangshi de yici minzhu pingyi" (A democratic evaluation of the Party history by 4,000 old cadres). *Yanhuang chunqiu* 4.

Hartog, François. 2003. *Régimes d'historicité: présentisme et expériences du temps*. Paris: Editions du Seuil.

Hubbert, Jennifer. 2005. "Revolution is a dinner party. Cultural Revolution restaurants in contemporary China." *China Review* 5(2), 125–150.

Hunxi hei tudi bianweihui. 1991. *Hunxi hei tudi* (*Our Soul is Linked to the Black Earth*). Suzhou: Jiangsu renmin chubanshe.

Jin, Guangyao, Jin Dalu and Shanghaishi zhishi qingnian lishi wenhua yanjiuhui (eds.). 2014. *Zhongguo xin fangzhi zhishi qingnian shangshan xiaxiang shiliao jilu, qi juan* (*A Compilation of Historical Materials from the New Annals of China on the Rusticated Youth, 7 vols.*). Shanghai: Shanghai shudian chubanshe and Shanghai renmin chubanshe.

Kong, Huiyun (ed.). 1998. *Zhiqing shenghuo huiyi* (*Remembrances of Zhiqing Life*). Jinan: Shandong huabao chubanshe.

Lam, Willy Wo-lap. 1995. *China after Deng Xiaoping: The Power Struggle in Beijing since Tiananmen*. Hong Kong: PA Professional Consultants.

Lao, Gui. 2009. *Liehuo zhong de qingchun* (*A Youth Spent in the Midst of Fierce Fire*). Beijing: Zhongguo shehui kexue chubanshe.

Le Goff, Jacques. 1988. *Histoire et mémoire*. Paris: Gallimard, Folio Histoire.

Lin, Shengbao, and Jin Dalu. 2014. *Shanghai zhishi qingnian shangshan xiaxiang yundong jishilu, 1968–1981* (*A Chronicle of the Shanghai Rustication Movement, 1968–1981*). Shanghai: Shudian chubanshe.

Liu, Xiaomeng. 1998. *Zhongguo zhiqing shi. Dachao (1968–1980)* (*A History of the Chinese Educated Youth. The Big Upsurge, 1968–1980*). Beijing: Zhongguo shehui kexue chubanshe.

Liu, Xiaomeng. 2004. *Zhongguo zhiqing koushushi* (*Oral History of the Chinese Educated Youth*). Beijing: Zhongguo shehui kexue chubanshe.

Michel, Jean-Jacques, and Huang He. 1978. *Avoir 20 ans en Chine ... à la campagne* (*To Be Twenty in China's Countryside*). Paris: Editions du Seuil.

Naughton, Barry. 2011. "The impact of the Tiananmen crisis on China's economic transition." In Jean-Philippe Béja (ed.), *The Impact of China's 1989 Tiananmen Massacre*. New York: Routledge, 154–178.

Ownby, David. 2010. *Falungong and the Future of China*. New York: Oxford University Press.

Palmer, David. 2007. *Qigong Fever: Body, Science and Utopia in China*. New York: Columbia University Press.

Pan, Mingxiao (Michel Bonnin). 2009 and 2010. *Shiluo de yidai: Zhongguo de shangshan xiaxiang yundong, 1968–1980* (*The Lost Generation: The Chinese Rustication Movement, 1968–1980*). Hong Kong: Chinese University Press. (A slightly different version of this book has been published in 2010 by Zhongguo dabaike quanshu chubanshe, Beijing).

Pedroletti, Brice. 2014. "China's former Red Guards turn their backs on Maoism," *The Guardian Weekly*, 4 May.

Qin, Liyan. 2006. "The sublime and the profane: a comparative analysis of two fictional narratives about sent-down youth." In Joseph Escherick, Paul Pickowicz and Andrew G. Walder (eds.), *The Chinese Cultural Revolution as History*. Stanford, CA: Stanford University Press, 240–266.

"Qingchun Wuhui" bianjizu. 1991. "*Qingchun Wuhui – Yunnan zhibian shenghuo jishi* (*No Regret for our Youth – Chronicles of the Life of Educated Youth Supporting the Border Region in Yunnan*). Chengdu: Sichuan wenyi chubanshe.

Qu, Bo, and Luo Xiaowen (eds.). 2006. *Jufeng guaguo yaredai yulin* (*A Hurricane Passed over the Subtropical Forest*). Beijing: Zhongguo guoji shiyejia.

Ruan, Ming. 1994. *Deng Xiaoping: Chronicle of an Empire*. Boulder, CO: Westview Press.

Walder, Andrew G. 2015. *China under Mao: A Revolution Derailed*. Cambridge, MA: Harvard University Press.

Wang, Lijian. 2008. *Huimou qingchun: Zhongguo zhiqing wenxue (Looking Back on Youth: The Zhiqing Literature)*. Taipei: Airiti Press.

Wang, Runsheng. 1992. "Deuxième vague de 'pénétration du savoir occidental' et métamorphose idéologique en Chine." *Perspectives Chinoises* 7, 37–41.

Wang, Xiaobo. 1997. *Huangjin shidai (The Golden Age)*. Chongqing: Chongqing chubanshe.

Xi, Jinping. 2002. "Wo shi huangtudi de erzi" (I am a son of the yellow earth). *Quanguo xin shumu* 12, http://mall.cnki.net/magazine/Article/QGXS200212029.htm. Accessed 1 August 2016.

Xiao, Han. 2014. "Confessions of the Cultural Revolution," *The New York Times*, 27 January.

Xin, Ziling. 2007. *Hong taiyang de yunluo (The Fall of the Red Sun)*. Hong Kong: Shuzuofang.

Xu, Naijian. 1981. *Yangbai de wuran (The Pollution of Yangbai)*. In Li Guowen, Gao Xiaosheng, *et al., Pan – duanpian xiaoshuoji (Aspirations: A Collection of Short Stories)*. Chengdu: Sichuan renmin chubanshe, 74–85.

Xu, Youyu. 1998. *1966: Women na yidai de huiyi (1966: Memories of Our Generation)*. Beijing: Zhongguo wenlian chuban gongsi.

Xu, Youyu. 1999a. *Xingxing sese de zaofan: hongweibing jingshen suzhi de xingcheng ji yanbian (Rebels of All Stripes: A Study of Red Guard Mentalities)*. Hong Kong: Chinese University Press.

Xu, Youyu. 1999b. *Moran huishou (Turning My Head Back Suddenly)*. Henan: Renmin chubanshe.

Yang, Guobin. 2003. "China's zhiqing generation: nostalgia, identity and cultural resistance in the 1990s." *Modern China* 29(3), 267–296.

Yang, Jian. 2002. *Zhongguo zhiqing wenxue shi (A History of the Literature of the Chinese Educated Youth)*. Beijing: Zhongguo gongren chubanshe.

Ye, Xin. 1980. "Cuotuo suiyue" (The wasted years). *Shouhuo* 5, 4–80; 6, 156–254.

Zhang, Liang, Andrew J. Nathan and Perry Link. 2002. *The Tiananmen Papers*. New York: Public Affairs.

Zhang, Xinxin, and Sang Ye. 1986. *Beijingren (People of Beijing)*. Shanghai: Wenyi chubanshe.

The Collar Revolution: Everyday Clothing in Guangdong as Resistance in the Cultural Revolution*

Peidong Sun[†]

Abstract
Scholars have paid little attention to Maoist forces and legacies, and especially to the influences of Maoism on people's everyday dress habits during the Cultural Revolution. This article proposes that people's everyday clothing during that time – a period that has often been regarded as the climax of homogenization and asceticism – became a means of resistance and expression. This article shows how during the Cultural Revolution people dressed to express resistance, whether intentionally or unintentionally, and to reflect their motivations, social class, gender and region. Drawing on oral histories collected from 65 people who experienced the Cultural Revolution and a large number of photographs taken during that period, the author aims to trace the historical source of fashion from the end of the 1970s to the 1980s in Guangdong province. In so doing, the author responds to theories of socialist state discipline, everyday cultural resistance, individualism and the nature of resistance under Mao's regime.

Keywords: clothing; dress resistance; the Cultural Revolution; Guangdong

After the founding of the People's Republic of China (PRC) in 1949, the Maoist regime intervened deeply in the everyday life of Chinese people, especially during the Cultural Revolution (1966–1976). This paper examines everyday clothing practices in China during the "ten year chaos" – an area that has received little scholarly scrutiny despite the fact that dress is one of the most notable forms of cultural expression. Although it has been argued that the Cultural Revolution "froze fashion by increasing the desire to conform" in many cultural domains,[1] I maintain instead that it increased people's desire to resist, giving expression to diversity, individuality, gender distinction and geographical fusion. An examination of everyday dress habits during the political movement will lead to a better understanding of the legacies of Maoism in China's cultural domain. The diversity and individualism that burst forth in the late 1970s and that has

---

* This paper is translated from Chinese to English by Shan Windscript with Antonia Finnane.
† Department of history, Fudan University. Email: spd@fudan.edu.cn.
1 Obukhova, Zuckerman and Zhang 2014, 559.

grown ever since did not happen overnight, as is commonly assumed; as this examination of apparel shows, its foundation was laid during the Cultural Revolution.

In studies of contemporary China, little attention has been paid to the impact of Maoism[2] on ordinary life, and especially to how Maoist ideologies influenced how people dressed during the Cultural Revolution.[3] By and large, the Cultural Revolution has been interpreted as a history of elite politics and mass movements. Current scholarship on the Cultural Revolution still centres predominantly on power struggles[4] and mass movements[5] – especially those of the workers,[6] sent-down youth[7] and the Red Guards[8] – but says little about ordinary people's everyday life during this major political event.

Mainstream accounts typically portrayed the stereotyped homogeneity of Mao-era clothing during the Cultural Revolution, describing Chinese people as "blue ants," perpetually clad in blue cotton clothing, shuttling back and forth to their workplaces on a daily basis.[9] For example, the everyday clothing in Michelangelo Antonioni's *Chung Kuo* (China, 1972),[10] and Lucy Jarvis' *The Forbidden City* (1973)[11] clearly portrays this stereotype.[12] More recent works have focused on the importance of the "everyday" in our understanding of the Mao era, shedding new light on the crucial role of consumer goods and behaviour in a changing and reproducing social order.[13]

Compared to Shanghai, a place that has drawn much scholarly attention thanks to the many published memoirs of the Cultural Revolution,[14] Guangdong province has remained under-examined despite its unique geographical position. Owing to Guangdong's proximity to Hong Kong, Macau and

---

2 I use Maoism to describe the practices of resistance that arose directly from a set of interrelated features under Maoist rule. The everyday life of people living under authoritarian regimes with centralized economic planning differs greatly from that of people in democratic societies with a market economy. For studies of private life in Stalinist Russia that focus on the impact of Stalinism on individuals' inner worlds and family relations, see Hellbeck 2006; Figes 2007; Fitzpatrick and Lüdtke 2009. See Demick 2009 for research on North Korea that places emphasis on the plight of people under Kim Il-Sung's regime, as evidenced by defectors. New research on the Third Reich has paid attention to the spiritual oppression and exploitation of youth under Hitler (Klemperer 2000; Knopp 2002; Allert 2009.).

3 Pickowicz and Walder 2006 shows how political events changed ordinary people's lives in urban and rural society, and how they acted in turn, and provides a good insight into the Maoist forces and legacies of the 1960s and 1970s.

4 MacFarquhar 1981; Wang, Nianyi 1988; Jin, Chunming 1995; MacFarquhar and Schoenhals 2006; Teiwes and Sun 2007; Liu, Qingfeng 1996; Guo, Wang and Han 2009; Dong and Walder 2011.

5 Wang, Shaoguang 1995a.

6 Perry and Li 1997; Li, Xun 2015.

7 Bonnin 2010.

8 Walder 2009; Chan 1985; Rosen 1981; Lee 1978; Tang 2003; He 2010. The sixth volume of *The History of the People's Republic of China (1949–1981)*, which focuses on the Cultural Revolution, provides no information on the daily lives of ordinary people. See Li, Danhui, and Shi 2008.

9 Guillain 1957, 1–19.

10 Antonioni 1972.

11 Jarvis 1973.

12 Liu, Zhijun 2002, 39.

13 Wang, Shaoguang 1995b; Lei 2000; Xu, Bei 2006.

14 Jin, Dalu 2011.

Taiwan, and because of its links to those places through the Canton Fair, its politics, economy and culture have been influenced by the West to a greater degree than any other place in mainland China. This permeability creates the context and the possibility for other expressions of individualization and difference that I will discuss in the following sections. Elsewhere, I have examined Guangdong people's everyday clothes and fashion during the Cultural Revolution,[15] and "bizarre clothes" with respect to state discipline at that time.[16]

Although mainstream ideologies significantly determined dress codes, the degree of resistance in the way people dressed within their established norms during the Cultural Revolution should not be underestimated: over the course of the revolution, people's understanding of beauty and fashion pluralized and personalized. This paper aims to provide new dimensions to current understandings of the Cultural Revolution by focusing on the neglected topic of everyday dress. Based on a study of Guangdong province, it first examines the influence of Maoism on clothing between the 1960s and 1970s, revealing the historical foundations of the creative burst of Chinese fashion from the end of the 1970s to the 1980s. Second, it responds to theories related to socialist state discipline, everyday cultural resistance, individualism and the nature of resistance under Mao's regime. I argue that a reconsideration of people's everyday clothing practices during the Cultural Revolution reveals that the agency for individual resistance and expressions of diversity at the grassroots was in fact much greater, even during the heyday of the Mao era, than previously believed.

Research Method and Sources

Primary data for this paper were gathered from semi-structured in-depth interviews with 65 registered Guangdong residents. The interviews explored how individuals used clothing as a means of resistance during the Cultural Revolution, the specific social contexts that shaped their behaviour, and their subjective perceptions of their social contexts. My informants had all worked or studied in Guangdong during the Cultural Revolution, and were chosen for this study using "life history case studies"[17] and "birth cohort theory."[18] Most were born between the 1930s and 1950s. There were 33 male and 32 female participants. They were drawn from 15 of Guangdong's 21 prefecture-level cities. In order to maximize the range of cases across age, gender, education, occupation and location, they have been methodically sorted. Between March 2005 and October 2006, I conducted one to two interviews per person, with each interview lasting about one to two hours. Most of the photographs used in this paper were

15 Sun 2012.
16 Sun 2010.
17 Denzin 1978.
18 Ryder 1965.

provided by the interviewees. Some of the photos were provided by the Integrated Education Gallery of the Sun Yat-sen University library.[19]

Dress Resistance

"There is no power without potential refusal or revolt."[20] Everyday dress resistance is often manifested in small actions that are "unorganised, unsystematic and individual, opportunistic and self-indulgent."[21] Such resistance is described by Michel de Certeau as a "tactic" that is "an art of the weak;" in the everyday context, individuals can use "popular tactics" to articulate their acts of resistance.[22]

Whereas both de Certeau and James Scott look at resistance and weapons of the weak in societies marked by inequality and exclusion (either class differences in advanced capitalism or in colonial/post-colonial rural societies), I wish to apply their ideas about resistance to a society filled with both "agents and victims" whose roles were fluid and in constant flux.[23]

On the one hand, dress resistance in the Cultural Revolution is marked by a sense of visibility. People complied with mainstream dress conventions during the Cultural Revolution because acting in line with the dominant political and ideological orders gave them a sense of security, much as they used revolutionary names: "more popular and thus safer."[24] Clothing was also a cultural practice of everyday resistance: personalized, gendered and rationalized clothing practices such as altering the sleeves, collars, waists and trouser leg openings can be seen as major expressions of people's resistance.

On the other hand, people may have been adopting the subtle forms of contestation we see in the "weapons of the weak" but without knowing exactly whose exercise of power they needed to resist and against whom they needed to protect themselves. The Cultural Revolution created a *mutually injurious society* (*huhai shehui* 互害社会), where different forces took turns to wield power and the boundaries between victim and perpetrator were permeable. People who could be persecuted owing to inappropriate clothing behaviour included Red Guards, village headmen, production team leaders, workplace leaders, union presidents, neighbours, colleagues, peers, friends and even spouses and children. Expressions of resistance had to remain not only more subtle but potentially even more "ambiguous" than in the cases named by Scott and de Certeau.[25] Ambiguous expressions of resistance can actually protect those who resist by allowing them to deny that they were in fact engaged in any type of subversion or critique.

19 See the library's website at: http://202.116.65.75/web/EN/home. Accessed 10 May 2016.
20 Foucault 1981, 253.
21 Scott 2008, 50.
22 De Certeau 1984, 26–37.
23 Siu 1989.
24 Obukhova, Zuckerman and Zhang 2014, 576.
25 Thornton 2002.

Dress resistance in the Cultural Revolution was conditioned by a sense of political uncertainty under Maoist rule, which was also a major source of people's feelings of insecurity.[26] Therefore, people's dress resistance was a silent and subtle undertaking rather than an overt form of political action or confrontation. However, as my informants asserted during our interviews, they felt that their choice of clothing silently "spoke" to the public. Everyday dress resistance, like Hakim Bey's "nomadology," provided my informants with a "temporary autonomous zone," that is, a site of individual resistance for "an era in which the State is omnipresent and all-powerful and yet simultaneously riddled with cracks and vacancies."[27] In short, everyday dress resistance under Maoist socialism was a persistent phenomenon. Although its effectiveness was limited, it should not be neglected. Oppressed in a climate of political uncertainty, people's strategically performed acts of resistance could bring them a sense of autonomy and individuality.

Defying Economic Deprivation: the Invention and Use of the Detachable-Collar Shirt, Gunnysack Shirt, and Fertilizer Trousers

Three factors were behind the monotony of everyday clothing during the Cultural Revolution: economic deprivation, political discipline and moral punishment.[28] Economic deprivation led to uniformity of clothing as, without material resources and bound by social and political rules, people were limited in their freedom to choose what to wear and had to rely on their own resourcefulness and imagination. Therefore, dress resistance was, first and foremost, a reaction against material scarcity.

The emergence and popularity of detachable-collar shirts in Chinese cities and towns reflected ordinary people's desire for "face" even at a time when money was short. It was also called the "economic collar" (*jingji ling* 经济领) or "thrifty collar" (*jieyue ling* 节约领). It consisted of a half-collar shirt with two shoulder strap attachments that were there to avoid any possible embarrassment arising from the use of an easily dislodged detachable collar. One of the interviewees, who worked as a bench worker at a car repair factory during the Cultural Revolution, recalled an embarrassing moment when talking about his wedding day:

I got married in August. The weather was hot. After I brought the bride home, I took off my lapel-collar suit coat (*fanling wen zhuang* 翻领文装) because I felt very hot. Then people saw my detachable-collar shirt. They all started laughing at me; my wife started to cry, refusing to enter the "bridal chamber" with me. My mother-in-law was scolding me, saying I'd never worn anything but cheap work clothes when we were dating, too. How embarrassing! I felt like a drowning mouse![29]

26 Sun 2013, 91–118.
27 Bey 1991, 101.
28 Sun 2010.
29 Interview with retired worker, Guangzhou, November 2006.

Detachable collar shirts were popular in the late 1970s and early 1980s. They looked good and were easy to wash. They also saved on fabric. Typical attire for men at that time was a plain coloured, detachable-collar shirt under a hand-knitted sweater; for women, the detachable-collar shirt was often made of floral fabric. In short, detachable-collar shirts are an indication of how individuals used available sartorial resources to construct their individual identities and to shape their self-esteem in specific social contexts.

The gunnysack shirt was invented by rural cadres who exploited limited local resources to their own advantage. The cadres were able to obtain gunnysacks, a rare local source of fabric, from their production teams (*shengchandui* 生产队). They ripped out the seams of the gunnysacks and re-fashioned them into Chinese-style shirts with two big pockets at the waist. A primary school principal in Guangdong witnessed three ranks of cadres (commune cadres, team cadres and village cadres) attending a conference, all wearing gunnysack shirts: "If you saw someone wearing a gunnysack shirt, you would know that he must be a ranking cadre. It was a sign of power and prestige!"[30] Apart from rural cadres, urban blue-collar workers also wore gunnysack shirts. A man who worked as a porter at the Guangzhou Machinery Factory during the Cultural Revolution recalled that, "We porters also used rice gunnysacks to make clothes. This type of material was durable, warm, and saved on the use of cotton. It even saved on material for protective sleeves. You could say that it gave you three things for the price of one."[31]

For rural cadres and urban porters alike, wearing gunnysack shirts was an expedient response to the shortage of fabrics and cloth coupons. The gunnysack shirt is a demonstration of the flexibility and capacity for innovation on the part of ordinary people within the limitations imposed by their material conditions. At the same time, shirts made from hemp sacks came to be an indication of the wearer's position in the political order and their corresponding social identities.

The emergence of fertilizer trousers was related to China's chemical import projects. After the Lin Biao Incident 林彪事件 in 1971, the Central Committee adjusted their policies of ultra-leftism; also in the same year, the PRC took its seat in the United Nations, leading to an increase in international contact. Following US President Nixon's visit, Western countries began to establish connections with China and foreign trade and international economic cooperation proliferated. In the new national and international political economic climate, advanced petrochemical technology was introduced to China in an effort to solve the country's clothing issues. With the support of the vice-premier, Li Xiannian 李先念, four chemical fibre projects and 13 fertilizer projects were launched. The main fertilizer was urea (carbamide) imported from Japan.[32]

---

30   Interview with retired middle school director, Guangzhou, November 2006.
31   Interview with retired worker, Guangzhou, October 2006.
32   Shan 2001, 587.

In rural Guangdong, urea was assigned to local supply and sales cooperatives in bags made of chemical fibre nylons, similar in texture to cotton silk. At the time, a family's annual allocation of cloth coupons was not adequate to clothe the whole family. Commune and team cadres therefore used various means to purchase the fertilizer bags from the supply and sales cooperatives to make clothes. Each bag cost about four cents, and two bags were enough to make a pair of trousers. Many commune cadres wore trousers made of these fertilizer bags, winning admiring and envious looks from the peasants.

Envy was accompanied by humour. The front and back of the fertilizer bags were marked with words such as "urea" and "Japanese xx corporation." When the bags were made into trousers, the words appeared around the waistband of the trousers and were very prominent. The effect is recorded in popular jingles of the time: "Japan is in the front, urea at the back; behold the crotch, nitrogen – 45 per cent!" (*Qianmian shi Riben, houmian shi niaosu; zaiwang dangli kan, han dan liang 45%!* 前面是日本, 后面是尿素; 再往裆里看, 含氮量 45%!). And, again: "Little commune cadres all in nylon trousers/Japan is in the front, urea at the back/ Some dyed black, others dyed blue/ for commune members none at all" (*Gongshe xiaoganbu, chuanzhe ninlong ku. Qianmian Riben chan, houmian shi niaosu. Ranheide, ranlande, jiu shi meiyou sheyuande* 公社小干部, 穿着尼龙裤。前面日本产, 后面是尿素。染黑的, 染蓝的, 就是没有社员的).[33]

Fertilizer trousers, like gunnysack shirts, were invented by rural cadres as markers of social identity to differentiate themselves from ordinary peasants in everyday contexts. It shows that those with special access to items were able to "wear" that access to signal their power in the centrally planned economy. I argue that in the 1970s, the Cultural Revolution had created a great levelling between cadres and the masses, and between managers and workers, across all workplaces. Such clothing strategies, ridiculous as they may sound today, were used by local political elites to construct their identities. In addition, fertilizer trousers provided a window to modernity for rural Chinese people in the 1970s. The fact that a mere fertilizer package was made of soft and comfortable nylon fabric gave rise to speculation about the wealth of Japan and the West, in contrast to mainland China where even material for clothing was extremely scarce.

The above three cases show some of the ways in which clothing became a site of resistance in people's everyday life, and a means by which social actors could build their identities. Constrained by the political system, individuals could be strategically obedient, or they could make a variety of conscious choices, by using their initiative and coming up with inventions. These inventions reflect the cleverness and humour of the people in Guangdong at that time, as well as expressing their preoccupation with the exercise of social power and identity formation.

33 Interview with retired cadre, Guangzhou, November 2006.

Resisting Political Discipline: the "Colour Revolution" and Personalized Dress

For most of the 65 interviewees, the olive-green army uniform was seen to be the desirable outfit during the Cultural Revolution. But, a few of them – even people belonging to the five red categories – explicitly resisted, or showed contempt for, the uniform. One interviewee, who was a shipyard worker in Guangzhou, said that he had never worn an army uniform or army cap, and when his younger brother gave him one as a gift, he sent it to be dyed blue at a dye house.[34]

His dislike of army uniforms arose from something that happened to his co-worker during the Cultural Revolution. At that time, the trousers they were allocated all had wide crotches, which many young workers found ugly. Those with sewing machines at home were able to alter the trousers to ensure a better fit. The interviewee's co-worker altered the bottoms of his trousers to make them skinnier. Red Guards confiscated and destroyed his trousers, and wrote big character posters to criticize his "rotten bourgeois" thinking. After that, the interviewee felt antagonistic towards army uniforms and the people who wore them. In his view, clothes and fashion in the Cultural Revolution originated from the "new fundamentalism" of the extreme Mao cult. During that "dark age," army uniforms conformed to the revolutionary trend but in his view were ridiculous. Having put himself at odds with the current line being propagated, he dreaded the potential consequences if it were discovered that he had dyed his army uniform blue. When a green army uniform was dyed blue-grey, it looked similar to a navy uniform; and at the shipyard where he had worked, from the director down to the workers, many people were navy veterans and wore navy uniforms. The interviewee obtained a certain psychological security from wearing a blue-grey navy uniform.

This case reveals that in a society where individuals' private living spaces are closely monitored by political forces, their forms and means of resistance are different to those in a market economy society. In China during the Cultural Revolution, clothing, as a form of visual text that is directly visible, became a tool by which Chinese individuals struggled for self-expression and representation.[35] By dressing in accordance or discordance with the mainstream norm, ordinary Chinese people expressed their acceptance of or opposition to the existing order. In doing so, they effectively challenged the dominant dress discourse dictated by the larger socio-political force. The deliberate colour manipulation was indeed a way of expressing resistance.

Personalized dress was a reaction to the national suppression of "bizarre clothes." On 7 June 1964, the *Liberation Daily* published an article to spark mass debate about, and mass criticism of, the wearing of strange clothes, declaring that such attire was a manifestation of an "unhealthy lifestyle" and a vulgar

---

34 Ibid.
35 Ai and Bu 2009.

Figure 1: *Cun zai* in Suits

Source:
  Photographed by his relative in Guangzhou 1972, offered by the interviewee.

reflection of "decadent, declining bourgeois ideology."[36] After this nationwide mass debate and criticism, unconventional clothes gradually disappeared from people's daily lives. Under this political pressure, the nation established an aesthetic of "only the political is beautiful" (*zhengzhi wei mei zhuyi* 政治唯美主义), to make people oppose unconventional clothes and legitimate the criticism of people's clothing choices in the name of class struggle.[37]

One interviewee who admitted that he was ahead of his time and bold in his attire, was criticized for being *cun zai* 寸仔(Cantonese for bad person) by his classmates and teacher because he once wore clothes he received as gifts from his Hong Kong relatives. Wearing black straight-legged jeans and a bright blue T-shirt made him the subject of criticism by the school authorities who viewed him as a "negative example." But he admitted that those clothes made him feel good and vigorous. He believed that dress choice should be a personal freedom, and should not be interfered with. He recounted one heroic act with much pride: in 1972, he ventured to a photographic studio, opened by his relative, to have his picture taken wearing a bright red tie given to him by his relatives in Hong Kong, even though he knew that people were not allowed to wear ties at that time.[38]

Some other interviewees recalled how they had racked their brains for ways in which they could alter their work uniforms in order to convey a sense of personality and taste. For a while, the trend among factory workers was to wear blue work clothes. One worker used a piece of wood to give her jeans a scrubbed look. She always found ways to make her clothes more "form-fitting" in order to show off her figure.[39] In a centrally planned economy that produces a limited range of clothing, individualization can itself be a form of resistance to the

36 Sun 2010.
37 Ibid.
38 Interview with retired worker, Guangzhou, October 2006.
39 Zhai 2008, 261.

existing power structure – although this would not necessarily be the case with individualization in a liberal capitalist society.

According to Yunxiang Yan, Maoist China was "the first stage in the Chinese path to individualization," when the Chinese people came "out of the shadow of the ancestors but re-molded as a rust-less screw" in the collectivist programmes of social engineering; the "individuality, independence, and desires of the Chinese individual at the tail end of Maoist China were both weakened and strengthened to certain degrees."[40] Although people's private lives were dominated by Maoism, my interviewees in general sought to carve out a space for self, individualism and personal aesthetic views.

The dissatisfaction expressed by the three interviewees above with the dress order of the Cultural Revolution is indicative of two things. First, none of them fully abided by the highly homogenizing dress conventions that promoted uniformity and denied individuality. Second, the ways in which they sought to personalize their clothes show that individualism and aesthetic instinct still existed in their manner of dress. They paid attention to their private lives, implying the existence of subjectivity. Here, management of private life had become an effective means for resisting public power.

Resisting Moral Punishment: Gendered Clothes and the "Revolution on the Collar"

Ordinary life during the Maoist era, as epitomized by women's clothing in the Cultural Revolution, has been regarded as a climax of masculinization and puritanical asceticism.[41] It is therefore not difficult to understand why some scholars consider Chinese women's interest in beauty and fashion as a new, post-Mao phenomenon.[42] Jean Kunz posits that, since the Cultural Revolution, beauty and fashion have been defined by the dominant political ideologies; beauty and fashion were singularized and people's creativity was suppressed before being reactivated by the economic reforms of the 1980s.[43] Under the new, proletarian morality of the PRC, the CCP denigrated women who did not abide by the conventions of revolutionary dress, labelling them as deviant (*bu zhengjing* 不正经), dishonest (*bu laoshi* 不老实), flirtatious (*fengsao* 风骚), vain (*aimu xurong* 爱慕虚荣), fox spirits (*hulijing* 狐狸精) who worship foreign things, or bourgeois ladies (*zichanjieji xiaojie* 资产阶级小姐).

However, Hung-Yok Ip questions the idea that women's interest in and pursuit of beauty is a newly developed trend of the post-Mao era, and argues that, "an interest in feminine beauty … was always present in the [Chinese] revolutionary process," and the strategic use of appearance was important for revolutionary

40 Yan 2010, 493–94.
41 Honig and Hershatter 1988, 11; Yang 1999, 35–67.
42 Yang 1999; Croll 1995, 151–52; Evans 1997, 82; Honig and Hershatter 1988, 41–51
43 Kunz 1996.

politics.[44] Tina Mai Chen discusses how Mao suits and military uniforms helped to produce a new subjectivity under the new socio-political system from 1949 to 1966.[45] Antonia Finnane examines clothes and fashion in the Cultural Revolution from the perspectives of gender, class and nationalism, revealing that fashion has been an important part of Chinese people's everyday life since the late imperial period.[46] Even in the revolutionary era, Chinese women still managed to find ways to resist what my respondents termed the androgenization of clothing implemented by the party-state.

Fashion is a means of artistic and political expression. The use of tattoos can be understood as an opposition to the commodification of bodies.[47] As such, the collar revolution during the decade of turmoil can be seen as Chinese women's opposition to the homogenizing and oppressive dress order by revealing their unique senses of gender- and self-identity. In Dongguan 东莞, one interviewee recalled that *zhiqing* 知青 (sent-down youth) women especially liked to alter their collars, from V-shaped, square and pointed collars to the more fashionable round-shaped, stand-up, boat and wing collars. For Chinese men, turned-down collars, turtleneck and stand-up collars were fashionable preferences.[48] A 1975 photograph of a group of *zhiqing* women taken in Yuexi 粤西, Guangdong, proves that the wing-collar was very popular among the female *zhiqing* community.[49]

The ways in which women from different social classes manifested resistance to Cultural Revolutionary norms, and the intensity of the resistance, varied. In her memoir, Zhang Hanzhi 章含之, a translator at the Ministry of Foreign Affairs, recalls: "I always wanted to do something different with my clothes. Before attending a UN meeting once, I picked a piece of turquoise-coloured fabric – no one else would have chosen that [at the time] – and had it made into a coat, with a round collar instead of a square one. I also added a grey detachable fur collar."[50] Zhang was criticized on this account and labelled as "unconventional and individualistic" (*biao xin liyi* 标新立异). However, she was not deterred. In the lobby of the Great Hall of the People, there was a mirror next to the cloakroom. After hanging up her coat, she always checked herself in the mirror before entering the conference venue. This made her the target of criticism for engaging in bourgeois activities. In fact, the dress resistance practised by Zhang was something beyond the realm of possibility for ordinary people. Before being appointed as a translator for the Ministry of Foreign Affairs by

---

44 Ip 2003, 330. Fashion (self-adornment as disguise) could be useful for the CCP's underground activities, and dressing up could help revolutionaries carry out their mission and to construct a positive image of the CCP. See Ip 2003.
45 Chen 2001.
46 Finnane 2008.
47 Fisher 2002.
48 Interview with retired local official, Guangzhou, August 2006.
49 See group photo of female *zhiqing* advanced delegation of congress, photographed by Zhou Zeming in Maoming 1975, at the Integrated Education Gallery of the Sun Yat-sen University library.
50 Zhang, Hanzhi 1994, 88–99.

Mao Zedong in 1971, Zhang had been his English teacher for seven years. Ordinary people would have been criticized and denounced or would have lost their lives for donning the sort of "unconventional" clothes she wore.[51]

During the Cultural Revolution, the collar was also used as a symbol of identity for brides. Although women wore dark coloured outfits on their wedding day, they used pink collars to intimate their newlywed status.[52] In addition, women refashioned their sleeves, altering ordinary long sleeves into puff (灯笼袖 *denglong xiu*), bell (喇叭袖 *laba xiu*), ruffle (泡泡袖 *paopao xiu*) and petal sleeves (花瓣袖 *huaban xiu*).

There is a long history of altering collars and sleeves to convey a sense of individual and gender identity within the framework of the CCP's highly politicized "red aesthetics." On Women's Day in Yan'an 延安 in 1940, more than 500 students from the Chinese Women's University performed a dance wearing Lenin suits that they had tailored themselves. This created a great stir in Yan'an at a time when everyone, from Party members to students, wore the Eighth Route Army uniforms.[53] Using the collar as sign of struggle, people reacted to the state's overt moulding of the masses, appropriating and manipulating available symbols into oppositional forces. Collars and sleeves symbolized a personal, private space where people could entertain "an illusion of power and control."[54] They desired a free, easy and even sentimental private life rather than a pan-politicized everyday existence centred on class struggle.

Women also used hair-ribbons and hair clips to express their sense of self. One interviewee recounted that she had devoted much time to thinking about how to make her hair look different. She also designed and made colourful hair strings. A photograph she provided shows her in a short haircut, parted on the side from the left to the right in an attempt to create a sort of asymmetrical style, with a little pigtail fastened on the top-right side of her head. The hair tie she used to fasten the pigtail was made by herself, using threads she had teased from her worn-out floral-patterned clothes – presents she had received from her Hong Kong relatives.[55]

Women with more financial resources could afford colourful hair clips to adorn themselves with. Their short revolutionary haircuts were often cleverly and nicely decorated with hair clips.[56] The hegemonic revolutionary taste had not extinguished people's desire to express themselves and their tastes, and they would find all kinds of ways to do just that by using jacket coverings, zippers, white masks,[57] and even glass fibres.[58]

51 Sun 2010.
52 Deng 2008, 124.
53 Xu, Lan 1999, 253.
54 Kuhn 1999, 285.
55 Interview with retired worker, Guangzhou, October 2006.
56 Deng 2008, 123.
57 Qing 2006, 44.
58 Zhu 2006.

During the Cultural Revolution, dresses and skirts were introduced to the Chinese public via officially sanctioned political gatherings and celebrations. In 1974, China participated for the first time in the Asian Games, held that year in Tehran, Iran. At the opening ceremony, the Chinese women athletes entered the stadium wearing the Jiang Qing 江青 dress. This type of dress retained traces of a uniform, but because it was a frock and generally made of a soft material like imitation silk or satin cotton, it tended to show the curves of the female body shape.[59] Jiang Qing's sufficient political privileges empowered her to "revolutionize" Chinese women's fashion – within certain boundaries. Her venture into design reveals the scarcely perceptible growth of women's gender awareness in the revolutionary age.[60]

Furthermore, the local government of Guangdong permitted women to wear dresses when welcoming foreign guests. One interviewee told me a story about his Indonesian cousin, who was a secondary school student in Guangzhou during the Cultural Revolution. She and her classmates were required by their school to wear skirts when greeting foreign guests. Some of her classmates had to borrow hers in order to comply with this rule.[61]

Clothes often serve as a barometer of a country's political atmosphere, and as such, skirts and dresses were the weather vanes for women's fashion in Mao-era China. The rise of the Soviet-style "Blazy" dress (布拉吉 bulaji) in China was closely related to the state of Sino-Soviet relations in the 1950s. The changing collars, the re-emergence of skirts and dresses, and the colours and patterns of shirts could effectively reflect public perceptions of political, economic and social life in later decades. Guangdong people's everyday dress habits demonstrated that while the larger clothing culture of the time hindered people from freely expressing their identities and individualities, collars, sleeves, waists and trouser-legs provided them with spaces in which their acts of resistance could occur.

Resisting Geographical Barriers: the Inflows of Foreign Dress and Fashion

Individual clothing resistance in Guangdong was possible in large part because of the province's geographical proximity to Hong Kong, and because it was the site of the Canton Fair,[62] which gave sporadic but targeted official permission to the (at least temporary) adoption of Hong Kong/Western/foreign goods for the sake of increasing trade.[63] It also exposed Guangzhou residents to a variety of

---

59 Zhang, Hong 2004.
60 Ibid.
61 Interview with retired university professor, Guangzhou. October 2006.
62 A biannual trade fair founded in Guangzhou in 1957, the Canton Fair continued to attract foreign businessmen to China throughout Cultural Revolution. They brought with them not only trading opportunities but also exotic clothing.
63 By the 1960s and 1970s, the Party had adopted a policy that explicitly advocated "adopting long-term plans and making full use of acquiring foreign currencies for importing equipment sets and gears." See Ma 1979.

Figure 2: **Family Picture**

Source:
Photographed by Ruxiong Liang in Guangzhou 1968, Integrated Education Gallery of the Sun Yat-sen University library.

sartorial possibilities and stylistic innovations[64] that, in a sense, may have provided them with a ready-made toolkit of "repertoires of resistance" from which to draw.[65]

To the people of Guangdong, Hong Kong, Macau and also Taiwan were no doubt windows on to the world of fashion. Figure 2 shows a Guangdong/Hong Kong family photo taken at the Yanfang Photographic Studio in Guangdong before the 1968 Spring Festival. Three generations of 22 family members are shown, variously sitting and standing. One can identify where they are from just by looking at the clothes they are wearing: those with rather conservative hairstyles and stern facial expressions who are wearing Chinese-style tunic suits with Mao badges pinned to their chests are apparently from Guangdong; in contrast, those who are in Western-style suits with scarves tied around their necks are the relatives from Hong Kong.

Figure 3 shows another photograph of daily life in Guangzhou, taken during the later period of the Cultural Revolution, where one can sense the influence of Hong Kong, Macau and Taiwan. The young woman in the photograph is wearing a pullover sweater with bell-bottoms (*laba ku* 喇叭裤), looking quite stylish

---

64 In the 1950s and 1960s, the Guangzhou municipal government and Guangdong provincial government often invited delegations from Hong Kong and Macau to attend the Chinese National Day celebrations. In the 1960s, the total number of Hong Kong visitors to mainland China averaged 347,000; that number slightly decreased to 253,198 in 1967 and 1968, but from 1970 began to grow again. See Zhang, Baojun, and Zhao 1997.

65 Tilly 1991.

Figure 3: **Citizens Visit a Park**

Source:
    Photographed by Minsheng Meng in Guangzhou 1975, Integrated Education Gallery of the Sun Yat-sen University library.

even by today's standard. Other women in the photograph are wearing shirts that feature slightly wider-cut necks. The colours and decorative patterns of their skirts were criticized as "bourgeois patterns" (*zichanjieji huawen* 资产阶级花纹) at the beginning of the Cultural Revolution.

Among the 65 interviewees, 49 of them, that is, 75.38 per cent, said that they or their family members had received clothes as gifts from Hong Kong, Macau, Taiwan, the USA or South-East Asian countries during the Cultural Revolution. According to these data, Guangdong maintained a relatively high level of clothing exchange with the outside world. Clothing from outside of Guangdong, which was more stylish than the local clothing and made of better quality fabric, presented a cultural challenge to China, throwing down the gauntlet to the revolutionary fashion that predominated in the province.

At a time when the street scene in mainland China was dominated by highly politicized revolutionary clothing, Guangdong's encounter with foreign fashion elements made the province a special place in the country, where everyday clothing styles looked quite different to those of inland Chinese cities. Until the end of the 1970s, when family members who lived outside the mainland returned to visit Shanghai, they brought with them clothes as gifts for relatives.[66] On 16 May 1976, as the tenth anniversary of the launch of the Cultural Revolution was being celebrated across the nation, Guangdong's political atmosphere was noticeably different. For example, a photograph taken in Harbin shows hundreds of thousands of people celebrating the anniversary together, conveying a strong

66 Cai 2008, 103.

Figure 4: **Parade in Harbin**

Source:
  Photographed by Zhensheng Li in Harbin 1976, Integrated Education Gallery of the Sun Yat-sen University library.

Figure 5: **Parade in Guangdong**

Source:
  Photographed by Zeming Zhou in Guangzhou/Gaozhou 1976, Integrated Education Gallery of the Sun Yat-sen University library.

political atmosphere (Figure 4). The first two rows of the podium are occupied by officials. Under the podium steps, six soldiers stand with their hands behind their backs, facing the podium with their backs to the masses. Several fully armed soldiers stand guard on the rally ground; behind them is a sea of people, the revolutionary masses. In contrast, a picture taken on the same day at the Army and People's Commemoration Rally (Figure 5), jointly organized by Guangzhou and Gaozhou 高州, shows more than 20 female students walking past a podium wearing red scarves and holding flowers. Some of them are wearing frocks, others skirts, all in different colours and patterns, with more than a dozen decorative designs. In another photograph, taken in Gaozhou on the same day, three girls holding a banner walking in the front are all wearing skirts. Many bystanders among the crowd, however, are barefoot, wearing straw hats or holding umbrellas (also Figure 5). Even when taking the contrast in local climates into account, the difference between Harbin and Guangzhou is profound.

What the overseas relatives of Guangdong residents brought into their lives were more than just some colourful, fancy second-hand clothes. They also brought the possibility of a different lifestyle in a different society, prompting people to think about what freedom, individuality and "self" meant. "Alien" (*tazhe* 他者) clothes also meant an alternative (*linglei* 另类) fashion for Guangdong people. Many interviewees said that their wedding outfits were bought in Hong Kong, or given to them as gifts by their Hong Kong relatives. The colour, style and quality of their imported wedding outfits would attract much attention and admiration from their local communities. People could not help but think that, "[Guangzhou and Hong Kong] are so close. How come things from Hong Kong are so much better than ours? How come we don't have them here?"[67] In short, Guangdong's unique geographical location is one important external factor that has contributed to the contrast between Guangdong's clothes and fashion and those of other, inland Chinese provinces. Having been subjected to more foreign influences than other parts of China, many people in Guangdong had the opportunity to make alternative fashions a point of reference for everyday clothing. In contrast, inland Chinese people had little exposure to foreign cultures during the Cultural Revolution and as a result their overall clothing styles tended to be much less diversified than those of Guangdong.

The four types of dress resistance that I have discussed are interrelated. No authority was left unchallenged; rather, it would always face resistance and struggle from individuals or groups. There are many reasons for, and forms of, dress resistance. What I have discussed here are individual means of resistance to economic deprivation, to political discipline, to moral punishment and to geographical isolation.

Conclusion and Discussion

On the surface, clothing and fashion in the first three years (1966–1969) of the Cultural Revolution appear to have been hegemonic. The mainstream dress preferences of the time were army uniforms, work uniforms, Zhongshan 中山 suits, Red Guard uniforms and Lenin suits.[68] However, this article has demonstrated that while clothes and fashion may have indeed seemed to be unvarying between 1966 and 1976, there were also undercurrents of resistant forces beneath the surface. Such forces of resistance paved the way for the radical fashion explosion in China in the 1980s. Many of the "new fashions" that burst onto the scene at the end of the 1970s were nothing more than the existing unofficially recognized

---

67 Interview with retired female worker, Guangzhou, November 2006.
68 Sun 2012.

everyday clothes practices that ordinary people had been quietly carrying out in the 1960s and 1970s. Everyday dress resistance during the Cultural Revolution showed its profound accumulative consequences later: "Things brewed in the Seventies, blossomed in the Eighties, and bore fruit in the Nineties."[69]

The conclusion of this article is two-fold. First, the unique geographical location of Guangdong province played an important role in softening or weakening the dominant political power over local people's everyday life, prompting a clothing culture that was more diverse than that in other places where people could not express their "hidden desires." Second, Guangdong people's dress revolution was carried out by using everyday clothing as a means of resistance. Dress resistance is an expression of opposition to the existing dress order and a way of expressing diversity, individuality, gender distinction and geographical fusion. By challenging the mainstream ideology and the power of conventional dress culture/political or revolutionary culture, Guangdong people's dress revolution carved out a new space for cultural resistance practices or a new transgressive culture.

How could there be dress resistance under an authoritarian political system and planned economy? First, it had something to do with people's changing identities and their explorations of subjectivity. Personal identity has been an all-consuming concern for the Chinese government. In 1949, the CCP urged Chinese people to decide their own fate and thereby take control of the fate of the nation. In the 1950s, the Party began systematically to institutionalize and standardize social constructions. By the 1960s, the Chinese subjectivity which the Party itself had created had become problematic. The memorable Cultural Revolution slogan, "down with the *Yanwang* 阎王 (King of Hell), liberating the small devils," meant that people from all revolutionary classes could oppose and challenge the institutional structures that had constrained their lives. As a result, "heterodox currents of thought" (*yiduan sichao* 异端思潮) emerged one after another during the Cultural Revolution.[70] Dress was one of the most convenient tools people could use to express their various senses of "self."

Second, compared to the early phase of the Cultural Revolution, the CCP's control over public opinion slightly relaxed in the late 1960s and early 1970s. This paved the way for the fashion liberation and revival that took place in the late 1970s and early 1980s. In the early 1970s, while the CCP on the one hand still advocated that personal consumption should adhere to the "revolutionary" and "collective" principles, on the other hand it stressed that revolutionary and collective principles did not mean over-simplification.[71] Meanwhile, China's international circumstances began to improve. The large-scale import of foreign technologies and equipment led to an improvement in the quality of people's clothing, and ultimately laid a solid foundation for resolving people's food and clothing problems in the 1980s.[72]

---

69 Li, Ling 2008, 248.
70 Wang, Shaoguang, et al. 2013.
71 Shang 1972.
72 Shan 2001, 587.

Third, the emergence and development of fibre technology provided the material conditions for the later diversification of clothing. Dacron (的确良 *diqueliang*) was first developed successfully in Guangdong. Although the production of Dacron was impeded during most of the Cultural Revolution, by 1973 it had become one of Guangdong's top exports.[73] Compared to cotton, Dacron is very strong, highly durable and quick drying, and its local production unquestionably opened the door for the personalization and diversification of dress during the Cultural Revolution.

Finally, the core reason why people used dress as a means of resistance is a natural, human wish to pursue their desires and normal lifestyles. Other social phenomena during the Cultural Revolution have demonstrated the resilience of human nature: the "great criticism" campaign led to the a resurgence of and a fad for writing traditional poetry;[74] manuscript copies of romantic and pornographic fiction rose considerably during the decade;[75] and many Shanghainese privately traded revolutionary propaganda for profit.[76] When cadres, educated youth and workers were sent down to Sunan 苏南 (rural areas of southern Jiangsu province), they took with them technologies and market information that benefited the local communities.[77]

Acknowledgement

The author acknowledges the financial support of the Chinese National Philosophy and Social Science Foundation (Project ID: 15ZDB051). She thanks Ning Wang, Nicolas Herpin, Deborah S. Davis, Guobin Yang and two anonymous reviewers for helpful comments on earlier drafts. She also thanks Shan Windscript and Antonia Finnane for their flawless translation. This paper forms part of a major project by the Chinese National Social Sciences: "Collection and arrangement of data and documentary research on the sent-down campaign during the Cultural Revolution."

Biographical note

Peidong Sun is an associate professor in the department of History at Fudan University. Her main areas of research focus on comparative and historical sociology, the Chinese Cultural Revolution, and social history and institutional change during the 20th century. She has been published in *Open Time* (Guangzhou), *Twenty-first Century* (Hong Kong), *Youth Studies* (Beijing), as well as many other peer-reviewed journals. Her latest books include *Fashion*

73 "Fangzhi gongye zhi" (Textile industry's records), Guangzhou shi difang zhi, http://www.gzsdfz.org.cn/gzsz/06A/fz/frameest.htm. Accessed 6 February 2007.
74 Mei 2007.
75 Liu, Dong 2005.
76 Jin, Dalu 2011, 309.
77 Fei 1992, 24.

and Politics: Fashion in Guangdong Province during the Cultural Revolution (People's Publishing House, 2013) and *Who Will Marry My Daughter? The Parental Matchmaking Corner in the People's Square of Shanghai* (Chinese Social Sciences Press, 2012, 2013).

摘要: 长期以来, 学界对毛主义的力量和遗产, 尤其是毛主义对文革时期民众日常着装的影响及其后果少有研究。本文提出被视为同质化和禁欲主义达到高潮的文革日常着装, 自文革初期起, 就成为多样化、个性化、性别化和地域化的一个抗争之场。文章表明民众如何透过有意无意的日常着装 "越界" 行为表示抗争, 并以此显示动机、阶层、性别和地域层面的差异。以 65 个文革亲历者的口述史和大量被访者提供的照片为基础, 作者揭示了 1970 年代后期至 1980 年代以广东为代表的中国着装时尚井喷式爆发的历史原因; 其次, 通过日常着装反抗的研究, 回应了社会主义国家规训、日常文化抗争以及毛体制下个人主义和个体抗争的性质等相关理论.

关键词: 着装选择; 着装抗争; 文化大革命; 广东

References

Ai, Xiaoming, and Bu Wei. 2009. "Shijue sheyun: Ai Xiaoming, Bu Wei duitan" (Visual-social movement: a conversation between Ai Xiaoming and Bu Wei). In *Chuanbo yu shehui xuekan* 10, 197–212.

Allert, Tilman. 2009. *The Hitler Salute: On the Meaning of a Gesture* (Jefferson Chase (trans.)). New York: St Martin's Press.

Antonioni, Michelangelo. 1972. *Chung Kuo, Cina* [documentary film]. RAI.

Bey, Hakim. 1991. *T.A.Z.: The Temporary Autonomous Zone, Ontological Anarchy, Poetic Terrorism*. New York: Autonomedia.

Bonnin, Michel. 2010. *Shiluo de yidai: Zhongguo de shangshan xiaxiang yundong 1968–1980* (*The Lost Generation: China's Rustication Movement 1968–1980*). Ouyang Yin (ed.). Beijing: The Encyclopaedia of China Publishing House.

Cai, Xiang. 2008. "Qishi niandai: modai huiyi" (The seventies: memories of the last generation). In Bei Dao and Li Tuo (eds.), *Qishi niandai* (*The Seventies*). Hong Kong: Oxford University Press, 331–347.

Chan, Anita. 1985. *Children of Mao: Personality Development and Political Activism in the Red Guard Generation*. London: Macmillan.

Chen, Tina Mai. 2001. "Dressing for the Party: clothing, citizenship, and gender-formation in Mao's China." *Fashion Theory* 5(2), 143–171.

Croll, Elisabeth. 1995. *Changing Identities of Chinese Women: Rhetoric, Experience, and Self-perception in Twentieth-century China*. Hong Kong: Hong Kong University Press.

De Certeau, Michel. 1984. *The Practice of Everyday Life*. Berkeley, CA: University of California Press.

Demick, Barbara. 2009. *Nothing to Envy: Ordinary Lives in North Korea*. New York: Spiegel and Grau.

Deng, Gang. 2008. "Wo cengjing shi shan lang haizei" (I used to be a mountain wolf and sea robber). In Bei Dao and Li Tuo (eds.), *Qishi niandai* (*The Seventies*). Hong Kong: Oxford University Press, 359–381.

Denzin, Norman. 1978. "The comparative life history method." In Norman Denzin (ed.), *The Research Act*. New York: McGraw Hill, 214–255.

Dong, Guoqiang, and Andrew G. Walder. 2011. "Local politics in the Chinese Cultural Revolution: Nanjing under military control." *The Journal of Asian Studies* 70, 425–447.

Evans, Harriet. 1997. *Woman and Sexuality in China: Female Sexuality and Gender since 1949*. Cambridge: Polity.

Fei, Hsiao-Tung. 1992. *Xingxing chong xingxing* (*Going and Going*). Ningxia: People's Publishing House.

Figes, Orlando. 2007. *The Whisperers: Private Life in Stalin's Russia*. New York: Metropolitan Books.

Finnane, Antonia. 2008. *Changing Clothes in China: Fashion, History, Nation*. New York: Columbia University Press.

Fisher, Jill A. 2002. "Tattooing the body, marking culture." *Body & Society* 8(4), 91–107.

Fitzpatrick, Sheila, and Alf Lüdtke. 2009. "Energizing the everyday: on the breaking and making of social bonds in Nazism and Stalinism." In Michael Geyer and Sheila Fitzpatrick (eds.), *Beyond Totalitarianism: Stalinism and Nazism Compared*. New York: Cambridge University Press, 167–301.

Foucault, Michel. 1981. "*Omnes et singulatim*: towards a criticism of 'political reason'." In Sterling M. McMurrin (ed.), *The Tanner Lectures on Human Values*. Cambridge: Cambridge University Press, 223–254.

Guillain, Robert. 1957. *The Blue Ants: 600 Million Chinese under the Red Flag* (Mervyn Savill (trans.)). London: Secker and Warburg.

Guo, Dehong, Wang Haiguang and Han Gang. 2009. *Zhonghua renmin gongheguo zhuanti shi gao (3): shi nian fengyu (Thematic History of the People's Republic of China (3): Ten Years of Turmoil)*. Sichuan: People's Publishing House.

He, Shu. 2010. *Wei Mao zhuxi er zhan: wenge shiqing Chongqing da wudou shilu (Fighting for Chairman Mao: Records of Chongqing Armed Conflict during the Cultural Revolution)*. Hong Kong: Joint Publishing.

Hellbeck, Jochen. 2006. *Revolution on My Mind: Writing a Diary under Stalin*. Cambridge, MA: Harvard University Press.

Honig, Emily, and Hershatter Gail. 1988. *Personal Voices: Chinese Women in the 1980s*. Stanford, CA: Stanford University Press.

Ip, Hung-Yok. 2003. "Fashioning appearances: feminine beauty in Chinese Communist revolutionary culture." *Modern China* 29(3), 329–361.

Jarvis, Lucy. 1973. *The Forbidden City* [documentary film]. N.B.C. Television.

Jin, Chunming. 1995. *"Wenhua dageming" shigao (A Manuscript of the History of the "Great Cultural Revolution")*. Sichuan: People's Publishing House.

Jin, Dalu. 2011. *Feichang yu zhengchang: Shanghai wenge shiqi de shehui shenghuo (Ordinary and Extraordinary: Lives and Society in Shanghai in the Cultural Revolution)*. Shanghai: Ci Shu Publishing House.

Klemperer, Victor. 2000. *The Language of the Third Reich: Lti, Lingua Tertii Imperii: A Philologist's Notebook* (Martin Brady (trans.)). London: Athlone Press.

Knopp, Guido. 2002. *Hitler's Children* (Angus McGeoch (trans.)). Stroud: Sutton.

Kuhn, Philip A. 1999. *Jiao hun: 1768 nian Zhongguo yaoshu da konghuang (Calling the Soul: Fear of the Chinese Witchcraft in 1768)* (Chen Qian and Liu Yongyi (trans.)). Shanghai: Joint Publishing Company.

Kunz, Jean Lock. 1996. "From Maoism to ELLE: the impact of political ideology on fashion trends in China." *International Sociology* 11(3), 317–335.

Lee, H.Y. 1978. *The Politics of the Cultural Revolution*. Berkeley, CA: University of California Press.

Lei, Yi. 2000. "Richang shenghuo yu lishi yanjiu" (Everyday life and historical studies). *Shixue lilun yanjiu* 3, 121–27.

Li, Danhui, and Shi Yun. 2008. *Nan yi jixu de "jixu geming" – cong pi Lin dao pi Deng (1972–1976) (Difficult to Continue the "Continuous Revolution": From Criticizing Lin to Criticizing Deng (1972–1976))*. Hong Kong: Chinese University of Hong Kong Press.

Li, Ling. 2008. "70 niandai: woxinzhong de suipian" (The seventies: fragments in my heart). In Bei Dao and Li Tuo (eds.), *Qishi niandai* (*The Seventies*). Hong Kong: Oxford University Press, 235–256.

Li, Xun. 2015. *Geming zaofan niandai: Shanghai wenge yundong shi gao* (*Days of the Revolutionary Rebels: A Manuscript of the History of the Cultural Revolution Movement in Shanghai*). Hong Kong: Oxford University Press.

Liu, Dong. 2005. "Heitian de gushi – 'wenge' shidai de dixia shouchao ben" (Stories of the dark days: underground manuscripts of the Cultural Revolution era). *Kaifang shidai* 6, 144–157.

Liu, Qingfeng (ed.). 1996. *Wenhua da geming: lishi zhenxiang yu yanjiu* (*The Great Cultural Revolution: Historical Facts and Research*). Hong Kong: Chinese University Press.

Liu, Zhijun. 2002. "Ying pian 'gugong' yin chu de kuaguo qingyuan" (The transnational love brought about by the film "Forbidden City"). *Zong Heng* 7, 39–41.

Ma, Hong. 1979. "Zenyang liyong Xianggang wei jiasu woguo sige xiandaihua jianshe fuwu" (How to take advantage of Hong Kong to speed up the realization of the four modernizations). *Jingji yanjiu cankao ziliao* 39, 15–16.

MacFarquhar, Roderick. 1981. *The Origins of the Cultural Revolution (Vols. 1 and 2)*. Cambridge: Cambridge University Press.

MacFarquhar, Roderick, and Michael Schoenhals. 2006. *Mao's Last Revolution*. Cambridge, MA: Harvard University Press.

Mei, Zhencai. 2007. "Wenge shi cijian zheng lishi" (The Cultural Revolution poetry witnesses history). In Song Yongyi (ed.), *Wenhua da geming: lishi zhenxiang yu jiti jiyi* (*The Cultural Revolution: The Real History and Collective Memory*). Hong Kong: Tianyuan shuwu, 635.

Obukhova, Elena, Ezra W. Zuckerman and Jiayin Zhang. 2014. "When politics froze fashion: the effect of the Cultural Revolution on naming in Beijing." *American Journal of Sociology* 120(2), 555–583.

Perry, Elizabeth J., and Xun Li. 1997. *Proletarian Power: Shanghai in the Cultural Revolution*. Boulder, CO: Westview Press.

Pickowicz, Paul G., and Andrew G. Walder (eds.). 2006. *The Chinese Cultural Revolution as History*. Stanford, CA: Stanford University Press.

Qing, Qiuzi. 2006. *Zheteng shinian* (*Ten Years of Up-side-down*). Anhui: Literature and Art Publishing House.

Rosen, Stanley. 1981. *The Role of Sent-down Youth in the Chinese Cultural Revolution: The Case of Guangzhou*. Berkeley, CA: University of California Press.

Ryder, Norman B. 1965. "The cohort as a concept in the study of social change." *American Sociological Review* 30(6), 843–861.

Scott, James C. 2008. "Everyday forms of resistance." *The Copenhagen Journal of Asian Studies* 4(1), 33–62.

Shan, Shaojie. 2001. *Mao Zedong de zhizheng chunqiu* (*The Ruling Years of Mao Zedong*). Taipei: Lianjing Publishing and Public Utility.

Shang, Yewen. 1972. "Fuwu ye yao genghao de wei gongnongbing fuwu" (The service industry must serve the workers, peasants and soldiers better), *Renmin ribao*, 5 April.

Siu, Helen 1989. *Agents and Victims in South China: Accomplices in Rural Revolution*. New Haven, CT: Yale University Press.

Sun, Peidong. 2010. "Kujiaoshang de jieji douzheng: wenge shiqi Guangdong de 'qizhuang yifu' yu guojia guixun" (Class struggle on the leg opening: "bizarre clothes" and state discipline in Guangdong during the Cultural Revolution). *Kaifang shidai* 6, 84–101.

Sun, Peidong. 2012. "Zongtizhuyi beijing xia de shishang: 'wenge' shiqi Guangdong minzhong zhuozhuang shishang fenxi" (Fashion under totalism: an analysis of everyday clothes and fashion in Guangdong in the Cultural Revolution). *Kaifang shidai* 4, 92–113.

Sun, Peidong. 2013. *Shishang yu zhengzhi: wenge shiqi Guangdong minzhong richang zhuozhuang shishang* (*Fashion and Politics: Everyday Clothes and Fashion in Guangdong, 1966–1976*). Beijing: People's Publishing House.

Tang, Shaojie. 2003. *Yi ye zhi qiu: Qinghua daxue 1968 nian "bairi da wudou"* (*An Autumn Leaf: The "Hundred Days of Armed Struggle" at Tsinghua University in 1968*). Hong Kong: Chinese University of Hong Kong Press.

Teiwes, Frederick C., and Warren Sun. 2007. *The End of the Maoist Era: Chinese Politics during the Twilight of the Cultural Revolution, 1972–1976*. New York: M.E. Sharpe.

Thornton, Patricia M. 2002. "Framing dissent in contemporary China: irony, ambiguity and metonymy." *The China Quarterly* 171, 661–681.

Tilly, Charles. 1991. "Domination, resistance, compliance … discourse." *Sociological Forum* 6(3), 593–602.

Walder, Andrew G. 2009. *Fractured Rebellion: The Beijing Red Guard Movement*. Cambridge, MA: Harvard University Press.

Wang, Nianyi. 1988. *Dadongluan de niandai: 1949–1976 nian de Zhongguo* (*A Time of Great Upheavals: China from 1949 to 1976*). Henan: People's Publishing House.

Wang, Shaoguang. 1995a. *Failure of Charisma: The Cultural Revolution in Wuhan*. Oxford: Oxford University Press.

Wang, Shaoguang. 1995b. "Tuokuan wenge yanjiu de shiye" (Broaden the horizon of Cultural Revolution research). *21st Century* 5, 92–102.

Wang, Shaoguang, Huang Wansheng, Shan Shilian, Cai Xiang, Jin Dalu, Xu Junzhong and Lao Tian. 2013. "70 niandai Zhongguo" (China in the seventies). *Kaifang shidai* 1, 5–95.

Xu, Bei. 2006. "Wenge shiqi de wuzhi wenhua he richang shenghuo zhixu" (Material culture and the order of everyday life during the Cultural Revolution). *Modern China Studies* 3, 23–34.

Xu, Lan. 1999. "Nüda de laodong shenghuo" (Working life at the women's university). In Yan Mingshi (ed.), *Yan shui qing: jinian Yanan Zhongguo nüzi daxue chengli liushi zhounian* (*Warm Feelings towards the Yan River: A Commemoration of the Sixtieth Anniversary of the Establishment of the Chinese Women's University in Yanan*). Beijing: Chinese Women's Publishing House, 252–254.

Yan, Yunxiang. 2010. "The Chinese path to individualization." *The British Journal of Sociology* 61 (3), 489–512.

Yang, Mayfair Mei-hui. 1999. *Spaces of Their Own: Women's Public Sphere in Transnational China*. Minneapolis, MN: University of Minnesota Press.

Zhai, Yongming. 2008. "Qing chun wu nai" (Helpless youth). In Bei Dao and Li Tuo (eds.), *Qishi niandai* (*The Seventies*). Hong Kong: Oxford University Press, 257–279.

Zhang, Baojun, and Zhao Ziyong. 1997. "Wenhua dageming shiqi neidi yu Xianggang de jingji guanxi" (Economic relations between mainland China and Hong Kong during the Cultural Revolution). *Zhongguo dangshi yanjiu* 2, 45–50.

Zhang, Hanzhi. 1994. *Feng yu qing: yi fuqin, yi zhuxi, yi Guan Hua* (*Love through Thick and Thin: Remembering Father, Remembering the Chairman and Remembering Guan Hua*). Shanghai: Literature and Art Publishing House.

Zhang, Hong. 2004. "Geming nü zhuang" (Revolutionary women's clothes). *Nanfeng chuang* 9, 86.

Zhu, Dake. 2006. "Ling yu xiu de hongse fengqing" (Red style on collars and sleeves). *Hua cheng* 4, 107–110.

The Silent Revolution: Decollectivization from Below during the Cultural Revolution

Frank Dikötter[*]

Abstract
This article uses fresh archival evidence to point at a rarely noticed phenomenon, namely the undermining of the planned economy by a myriad of dispersed acts of resistance during the last years of the Cultural Revolution. Villagers reconnected with the market in some of the poorest places in the hinterland as well as in better-off regions along the coast. This silent, structural revolution often involved the quiet acquiescence, if not active cooperation, of local cadres. In conclusion, the article suggests that if there was an architect of economic reforms, it was the people and not Deng Xiaoping: as with his counterparts in Central Europe and the Soviet Union, Deng had little choice but to go along with the flow.

Keywords: China; Cultural Revolution; planned economy; decollectivization; market

As Istvan Rév, a historian of Hungary, noted some years ago, social scientists are attracted by political movements that have concrete, articulated aims. Historical actors must possess "political consciousness," or else they are unlikely to be granted much significance. "They must be able to write manifestoes, to leave written documents behind them; they must be capable of giving a compact political analysis to the scientist who comes to interview them." The strategies of survival that can to be found in the countryside in planned economies – pilfering, lying, slacking, stealing, bartering, trading – are seen to be "pre-political," or merely reactive, if not downright "reactionary" in trying to revive the old order. They are assumed to have few long-lasting consequences. But, as Rév pointed out, through endless acts of resistance, villagers in the countryside forced the regime to change. "From a closer look, all the important and long-lasting economic and social reforms in all the Central European countries appear as nothing but the legalization of already existing illegal and semilegal practices. What seems to be the work of the professional reformers (experimentation with and revitalization of the market, the coexistence of the small and the big

* University of Hong Kong. Email: dikotter@mac.com.

© The China Quarterly, 2016   doi:10.1017/S0305741016000746

in agriculture, the convergence of the first and the second economies, the granting of concessions to small-scale private enterprises, the liberalization of the planning mechanism) is in fact the consequence of continuous atomized resistance."[1]

What Rév means by "atomized resistance" is that in the Soviet Union and in Central Europe, once communist parties had liquidated everything that stood in between the state and the individual, from civic associations and worker unions to private clubs, almost everything became a potential political issue. Instead of smashing all opposition, it became dispersed, "hidden but present everywhere."[2] The use of terror to atomize society into isolated individuals did not result in complete control by the state over all, but in the creation of endless potential enemies. Bringing a chicken to market or slacking at work was no longer an economic act but a subversive, political one. Concern with the family was not a sign of love but a worrisome remnant of bourgeois ideology. Every act of survival in the countryside came to be understood as an anti-party, capitalist practice. In other words, the expansion of coercion and terror created more, not less, room for resistance. But the state was not equipped to fight millions of individual acts of subversion, and in any event was too inflexible to defend itself against challenges from all directions. It had to bend or risk breaking. It went along, reforming the system by legalizing the practices surreptitiously introduced by the villagers.

Much of this transformation from below has escaped the gaze of social scientists, and not only because atomized resistance lacked overt political organization. It also left few traces. Resistance in Central Europe was silent, whether villagers quietly hid the grain, stole food from the fields on the sly or traded it on the black market. "The technique of the resistance is the nonevent, the means is the nonobject, the actors are anonymous."[3]

Kate Zhou has observed a very similar phenomenon in China. Throughout the 1980s, as her pioneering book *How the Farmers Changed China* demonstrates, farmers leeched away the economic dominance of the state and replaced it with their own initiative and ingenuity. There was no organized confrontation, which no communist party anywhere would have tolerated, but a myriad of daily acts of quiet defiance and endless subterfuge instead, which left the cadres defenceless. Without leaders, without overt opposition and without an explicit ideology, villagers undertook a silent structural revolution, as the aggregate effect of many millions of ordinary people changed the economic and political landscape for ever. In short, if there was an architect of economic reforms, it was the people and not Deng Xiaoping 邓小平, who had little choice but to go along with the flow, as did his counterparts in Central Europe and the Soviet Union.[4]

1 Rév 1987, 341–45; I would like to thank Patricia M. Thornton for having brought the work of Istvan Rév to my attention.
2 Ibid., 347.
3 Ibid., 349.
4 Zhou 1996, 15.

One of the difficulties that historians of communism face is finding evidence of a revolution that produced no sounds. But, as the work of Gábor T. Rittersporn and others has illustrated in the case of the Soviet Union, there is plenty of telling material that can be teased out of the archives.[5] In the case of China, while access to Party archives on the Mao era is checkered, there are still more than enough clues to indicate that a silent revolution started a decade earlier than Kate Zhou has suggested, namely during the Cultural Revolution.

In fact, as Kate Zhou herself has indicated in her book, resistance against collect-ivization started as early as the 1950s, and reached a peak during Mao's Great Famine. In an odd twist, the attempt to replace individual rewards with moral incen-tives during the Great Leap Forward produced a nation of entrepreneurs. People did not simply wait to starve to death. In a society in disintegration, they resorted to every means available to survive. So destructive was radical collectivization that at every level the population tried to circumvent, undermine or exploit the master plan, covertly giving full scope to the profit motive that the Party tried to eliminate. As the catastrophe unfolded, claiming tens of millions of victims, the very survival of an ordinary person came to depend on the ability to lie, charm, hide, steal, cheat, pilfer, forage, smuggle, trick, manipulate or otherwise outwit the state.[6]

Much of this covert behaviour came under scrutiny during the "socialist edu-cation" campaign from 1962 to 1966, as the state tried to shore up the socialist economy and stamp out anything that smacked of "capitalism." But, with the onset of the Cultural Revolution, parts of the countryside again used the chaos to reclaim some of the freedoms they had lost under communism, expanding their private plots, taking produce to market, opening underground factories or leaving the people's communes to seek their fortune in the city. The trend was substantial enough in some villages to amount to decollectivization.

But yet again, the pendulum swung back, as revolutionary committees in 1968 effectively turned the country into a military dictatorship, using the threat of war with the Soviet Union a year later to impose much greater control over the coun-tryside. The "learn from Dazhai" campaign heralded a return to the Great Leap Forward by promising prosperity and abundance to all those who laboured the land collectively. In their eagerness to radically collectivize the economy, some cadres abolished private plots altogether and even slaughtered private animals. In Zhejiang province as a whole, a quarter of all production teams reverted to the extreme collectivization of the Great Leap Forward by handing over respon-sibility for accounting to the brigade, the second tier of organization in the coun-tryside, placed between the people's commune and the team. It meant that the villagers lost control over income distribution. Simply gathering firewood or rais-ing a buffalo was now denounced as "capitalist."[7] In Gansu province, private

5 Rittersporn 2014.
6 Zhou 1996; Dikötter 2010.
7 Zhejiang Provincial Archives, 8 September 1971, J116-25-159, 160–62; Zhejiang Provincial Archives, 17 March 1972, J116-25-250, 73–76.

plots covering a total surface of more than 77,000 hectares were returned to the collectives, which accounted for roughly a third of all private holdings. In some counties, one report noted, "all private plots have been entirely taken back."[8]

The tool used by the revolutionary committees to enforce the Dazhai 大寨 model was a widespread campaign against graft, speculation and waste, usually referred to as the "three antis." Across the country, the campaign was directed at millions of ordinary people who had quietly exploited the chaos of the Cultural Revolution to advance their own economic freedoms. From poor villagers who had enlarged their private plots to ordinary people who had bought some vegetables from the black market, the campaign crushed those accused of "following the capitalist road." Numbers can be numbing but they indicate the extent of the persecution. In Hubei, such "capitalist roaders" represented 447,000 out of the 736,000 victims harassed by the authorities from February 1970 to October 1971. They made up 169,000 of the total of 225,000 suspects taken to task in the three first months of the campaign in Gansu.[9]

This campaign was paralleled by an equally wide-ranging strike against "counter-revolutionary activities," defined in such a way as to encompass almost anything deemed to be "destructive." Much more evidence is needed to capture the precise contours of the "one strike" and "three antis" campaigns, which varied enormously from place to place, but in provinces like Hubei and Gansu they implicated roughly one in every 50 people. Very few of the culprits were shot, and many got away with a reprimand or a spell in a re-education camp. In sharp contrast to the purges that claimed several million victims in the early years of the People's Republic when the regime tried to eliminate all organizations standing in between the state and the individual, the point of the "one strike" and "three antis" campaigns was not to physically eliminate real or imagined enemies but rather to intimidate the greatest number of people possible. The objective was to produce a docile population by turning almost every act and every utterance into a potential crime.

The result was "atomized resistance," to borrow Istvan Rév's expression. But not only did the regime create millions of new enemies by turning virtually every minor act of defiance into a political crime, it also suffered a huge blow with the death of Lin Biao 林彪 in September 1971. The Lin Biao incident drastically undermined the role of the military and forced Mao to turn to those Party officials denounced as "capitalist roaders" during the height of the Cultural Revolution; however, the power and prestige they once wielded was gone. If the Great Leap Forward had destroyed the credibility of the Party, the Cultural Revolution undermined its very organization.

***

8 Gansu Provincial Archives, 1 September 1969, 129-4-179, 95–104.
9 Hubei Provincial Archives, 25 November 1970, SZ139-2-290, n.p.; Hubei Provincial Archives, 17 September 1971, SZ139-2-114, n.p.; Gansu Provincial Archives, 6 May 1970, 129-6-45, 46–47.

The extent to which ordinary villagers reconnected with the market in the last five years of the Chairman's reign is amply illustrated by evidence from the archives. Even in the very heart of the revolution, amidst the dusty, sandstone-coloured hills of northern Shaanxi where the Communist Party had established its head-quarters during the Second World War, capitalism seemed rampant by 1974. The "Yan'an spirit" championed selfless dedication to the greater good, but on the ground, local people embraced the market in order to pull themselves out of poverty. One village in Yan'an 延安 even abandoned any attempt to wrench food from the arid and parched soil and specialized in selling pork instead. In order to fulfil their quota of grain deliveries to the state, they used the profit from their meat business to buy back corn from the market. Local cadres super-vised the entire operation. Few in the village seemed to have any interest in pol-itics. More than three years after the demise of Lin Biao, posters of the erstwhile heir apparent still fluttered in the wind. Slogans painted on outside walls were fading, and dated mostly from 1969.[10]

Yan'an was not alone in taking to the market. Entire people's communes in Luonan 洛南, less than two hours away from Xi'an by bus, had divided up all collective assets and handed responsibility for production back to individual fam-ilies. Many villagers abandoned two decades of monoculture, imposed by a state keen on producing grain to feed the cities and barter on the international market, and cultivated crops that performed well on the black market. Some rented out their plots and went to the city instead, working in underground factories and sending back remittances to the village. Other freedoms flourished. The head of one production team, instead of adorning his front door with slogans exalting Chairman Mao, displayed couplets composed by a Tang dynasty emperor. Traditional geomancy, decried as superstition since liberation, seemed to matter more than the latest Party directives, which everybody ignored. Spirit mediums and fortune tellers did the rounds.[11]

In Pucheng 蒲城, further to the north of Xi'an, some cadres also stood back and allowed the villagers to go about their business. Here, too, propitious cou-plets in traditional calligraphy largely displaced loud slogans in brash red, and here too, Party officials expressed little interest in reading newspapers, let alone keeping up with the Party line. "Not one Party meeting has been called, and not one of the prescribed works of Marx, Lenin and Chairman Mao has been studied," deplored one report. In some production brigades, telephone confer-ences were not a realistic prospect, since the lines had been cut down and were used by the villagers to dry sweet potatoes. Instead of working for the collectives, people with any kind of expertise offered their services to the highest bidder. There were doctors who gave private consultations for a fee. There were self-employed artisans. Chen Hongru 陈鸿儒, classified as a "rich peasant" and a "counter-revolutionary" to boot, worked as a carpenter on the black market,

---

10 Shaanxi Provincial Archives, 24 January 1975, 123-71-209, 1–7.
11 Shaanxi Provincial Archives, 6 January 1975, 123-71-209, 8–15.

helping out production teams during the busy season for no less than 25 work points a day, more than twice the amount a hard-working male adult could earn in a collective.[12]

This all took place in Shaanxi, where millions went hungry, some of them eating mud or stripping bark from trees. Necessity is the proverbial mother of invention, and the overlap between sheer destitution and the entrepreneurial spirit could be found elsewhere. In many cases, as the example of Yan'an illustrates, the local cadres took a lead by distributing the land to the farmers. Sometimes, a deal was struck between representatives of the state and those who tilled the land, as the fiction of collective ownership was preserved by turning over a percentage of the crop to Party officials. Bribery often greased the wheels of free enterprise, as the villagers paid the cadres to look the other way.

The return to market principles was facilitated by divisions at the top. Throughout the Cultural Revolution, partisan wrangling and factional infighting among the leadership had resulted in constant changes in government policy. On the ground, villagers were often subject to the ebb and flow of radical politics, as the precise contours of the collective economy, from the size of private plots to the number of animals that a family could own, shifted from one campaign to the next. They were also at the mercy of the local cadres, who had some scope to interpret or negotiate the constantly changing rules of the game.

This became particularly prominent after the North China Agricultural Conference in the summer of 1970, as Zhou Enlai 周恩来 tried to move away from the destructive effects of extreme collectivization. In subsequent months, numerous articles appeared in the press stressing the right of villagers to tend private plots, the importance of local peasant markets and the contribution of cash crops to the collective economy. These measures did not go beyond what was introduced after the catastrophe of the Great Leap Forward. Private plots, for instance, were extremely limited in size and could only be cultivated by villagers in their spare time once all collective duties had been completed, while a great variety of products could not be traded in local markets, including all those over which the state had a monopoly, from cotton, edible oil, meat and grain to tobacco and timber. Still, the more extreme interpretations of the "learn from Dazhai" campaign were softened. On 26 December 1971, precisely seven years after Chen Yonggui 陈永贵 had shared a meal with Chairman Mao to launch the slogan, "In agriculture, learn from Dazhai" (*nongye xue dazhai* 农业学大寨), the *People's Daily* even cautioned against "blindly learning from Dazhai."[13]

The countryside was allowed to diversify its production and establish small industries, a policy also heralded by the premier at the 1970 North China Agricultural Conference. The idea was that China should "walk on two legs," as rural enterprises would support agricultural development, for instance by

---

12 Shaanxi Provincial Archives, 6 February 1975, 123-71-209, 34–48.
13 Zweig 1989, 61–62. In communist parlance, these measures were referred to as the "sixty articles."

producing farming tools, chemical fertilizers and cement. But this, too, was hardly a new departure. In Dazhai, the peasants working under Chen Yonggui operated a brick kiln, a noodle factory and a bauxite mine, as agriculture and industry
merged to advance the collective cause. The whole idea of "walking on two legs"
dated from the Great Leap Forward, when Chairman Mao thought that his
country could overtake its competitors by relocating industry to the countryside,
liberating the productive potential of every peasant in huge people's communes.
The rural enterprises that the state encouraged remained firmly under collective
leadership.[14]

Given these conflicting messages from the top, very different approaches
appeared throughout the countryside, as overzealous cadres continued to impose
radical collectivization and ban private plots in some places, whilst elsewhere villagers were allowed more scope for private initiatives. But, most of all, as the
standing of the Party suffered a blow in the aftermath of the Lin Biao affair,
some cadres started deliberately twisting and bending various state directives,
taking them far beyond what the leadership intended. As one village official
put it, the rural cadres, "after the continuous flip-flop of government policies
and after their repeated humiliations in public during struggle sessions," lost
interest in politics. They devoted their energy to production instead. Some of
them opened up every portion of collective property to negotiation, from control
over the pigsty, the fish pond and the forest, to the exact dimensions of individual
plots. They allowed a black market to thrive in the knowledge that their own livelihoods, including the food they ate, depended on free trade. They encouraged the
villagers to leave the collectives and strike out on their own.[15]

***

Much as need ruled large parts of the country, prompting villagers to rely on their
own wits to pull themselves out of destitution, opportunity also played an important role. Some villages were better off than others. They capitalized on their
advantages to improve their collective lot, whether these advantages were proximity to transportation routes, abundant fish and wildlife, a regular water supply,
fertile soil, a level terrain for farming or access to sources of energy such as coal
and wood.

Wealthy regions joined those mired in poverty in a silent revolution that sub-
verted the planned economy. In villages along the southern coast, people raised
ducks, kept bees, grew fish, baked bricks and cut timber, always in the name of
the collective. By late 1971, in the county of Xinchang 新昌, Zhejiang, which
housed a population of roughly a quarter of a million people, some two-thirds
of all villagers were independent – or "go-it-aloners" in the parlance of the

14 See "Economic situation in China," 1971, Public Records Office, London, FCO 21-841; see also Kueh
     2006.
15 Huang 1989, 109–110. There are clear parallels with Zhou 1996, 55. See also Thaxton 2008, 278;
     Kelliher 1992.

time. Much of this was done with the tacit consent of the local authorities, who rented the land to individual households in exchange for a portion of the crop.[16] A year before Mao Zedong's death, the habit of leaving the collectives to try one's luck on private land or in underground factories was described as "widespread" throughout the province. Wenzhou 温州 took the trend to the extreme, as private capitalism flourished in the city and its isolated delta despite repeated harassment from the government.

Nowhere was this trend more evident than in Guangdong, a subtropical province with plenty of light, heat and water, as well as abundant waterways and a long coastline ideal for economic growth. Markets were everywhere. In Qingyuan 清远, virtually every commodity normally banned from the market by virtue of a government monopoly was openly on sale, including grain, peanuts, oil and tobacco. Business was swift. It took a team of five youths sent by the village elders no more than half an hour to dispose of 200 kilos of grain.[17]

Further inland, in the county of Puning 普宁, some 30 markets covered the needs of more than a million people. They attracted local farmers, artisans and traders, each with their vendible goods on hand, back or cart. Pedlars offered colourful illustrations from traditional operas, books from the imperial and republican eras and collections of traditional poetry that had escaped the clutches of the Red Guards. There were itinerant doctors offering their services. Storytellers used wooden clappers to mark the most dramatic moments of their stories. Blind people sang traditional folk songs for a few alms. Touts stood outside local restaurants selling ration coupons. Many hundreds came by bicycle from other parts of the province each day. In some markets, organized gangs travelled up and down the coast, going all the way to Shanghai to trade in prohibited goods. A few went as far as Jiangxi to procure tractors in response to requests from local villages keen to mechanize.[18]

Here, too, the local cadres were reluctant to interfere. Some even encouraged the villagers to abandon grain production despite it being mandated by the state and pursue more profitable crops instead. Government agents failed to stamp out illegal trading, as "they are only concerned with collecting fees, and do not care about government policy," the authors of one detailed investigation deplored. Small pedlars could be suppressed, the report continued, but "the cadres and the villagers will have no vegetables to eat."[19]

The market exploited the difference between the fixed price set by the command economy for agricultural products and the higher amounts ordinary people were prepared to pay. A difference of 100 per cent was common, but some commodities, for instance soy beans, reached 500 per cent, meaning that the state

---

16 The expression was *jietian daohu*, meaning to "lend the land to individual households": Zhejiang Provincial Archives, 8 September 1971, J116-25-159, 155; White 1998, 120–21.
17 Guangdong Provincial Archives, 1 November 1975, 294-A2.14-6, 52.
18 Guangdong Provincial Archives, 20 December 1973, 296-A2.1-51, 44–53; Guangdong Provincial Archives, 20 March 1974, 294-A2.13-8, 1–28.
19 Guangdong Provincial Archives, 20 December 1973, 296-A2.1-51, 44–53.

procured them at 0.44 yuan per kilo when the same amount could fetch 2.2 yuan on the market.[20] As Istvan Rév has noted for Central Europe, the higher the prices on the black market, the less incentive there is to hand over produce to the state. The more successful villagers were, the more incentive they had to resist. "It was the invisible hand of resistance, the micro actions, having a profound effect on the macro sphere of politics."[21]

The market in Puning, like elsewhere, thrived because the command economy could not deliver sufficient goods to meet the demands of ordinary people. Widespread shortages forced prices up, stimulating private enterprise. Timber was a case in point. By 1973, fir was ten times more expensive than it had been at the beginning of the Cultural Revolution in 1966. Across the county, there were thousands of unfinished houses, abandoned for lack of timber. Some people were willing to pay a premium on the black market. Across the mountains in the north of Guangdong province, there was the random felling of trees. The trade was not limited to a few farmers bringing planks to market on their bicycle carts: there were hundreds of factories in Lechang 乐昌, Qingyuan and Huaiji 怀集 illegally trading in timber, up to 70,000 cubic metres in 1973 according to one estimate.[22]

Guangdong had another asset that helped some people sidestep the planned economy. Not far away from the Pearl River Delta, counties like Kaiping 开平 and Taishan 台山 were traditionally dominated by emigration overseas. Before liberation, whole villages had displayed ostentatious mansions built by returned migrants, including thousands of large, fortified towers influenced by foreign architecture and furnished with everything from flushing toilets and marble tiles to Gothic battlements and turrets. Relations between these emigrant communities and the Communist Party were bad, and in 1952 many bore the brunt of a bloody campaign of land reform. Years later, at the height of the Cultural Revolution, when people lived and died by their class background, many were denounced as "spies," "traitors" and "counter-revolutionaries," further disrupting links with overseas communities. But, after 1970, goods and remittances once again started to pour across the border. By 1974, the amount of money reaching the villagers from overseas was twice as high as in 1965. Families with overseas connections had been the first to suffer from the onslaught of the Cultural Revolution, and now they were the first to emerge from uniform poverty. They used foreign remittances to tackle a housing crisis created by years of neglect if not wilful assault on anything bearing the hallmark of imperialism. In Taishan and elsewhere in the region, they bought up steel, timber and concrete. Chen Jijin 陈季金 shared a mud hovel with his family of eight. He was

---

20 Ibid.
21 Rév 1987, 348.
22 Report from Guangdong Provincial Revolutionary Committee, 26 November 1973, Shandong Provincial Archives, A47-2-247, 37–39; Guangdong Provincial Archives, 20 December 1973, 296-A2.1-51, 44–53.

waiting for a remittance of 20,000 yuan to build a new house – a sum representing the combined annual salaries of 30 qualified factory workers.[23]

The number of parcels received from abroad also went up. In Guangzhou, the provincial capital, more than 200,000 packages had accumulated in 1972, but the backlog was cleared by the end of the year. They contained mainly clothes and edible oil, reflecting local market shortages. Other commodities included beans, bulbs, matches and medicine. Some of them found their way onto the black market.[24]

***

A measure of decollectivization could also be seen in other provinces. In Sichuan, a huge inland province which had suffered terribly during the Great Leap Famine before being wrecked during the Cultural Revolution, the land was rented to the farmers in the early 1970s. The desire to own land was driven from below and only ratified by local authorities much later.[25]

Returning the land to the cultivators was but one aspect of a silent revolution in the countryside. Some wealthier villages not only planted profitable crops for the market but also began establishing local factories. This was common in many parts of Guangdong. In Chaoan 潮安, just outside Shantou 汕头, where entire villages had been reduced to poverty after embroidery was declared to be "feudal" at the height of the Cultural Revolution, historic links with the overseas community were revived after the Ministry of Light Industry lifted the trading restrictions in 1972.[26] Two years later, up to half of the women in some villages once again specialized in drawn work and embroidery. Their output was worth 1.3 million yuan on the foreign market. Others turned to manufacturing hardware and tools. But while some of these village enterprises were collectively owned, many merely used the appearance of a collective to run a business entirely along private lines. A good example was Dongli Village 东里村, where all but 40 of the 420 families were members of a nail factory. They worked from home and were paid by the piece. All the profits went straight to the individual workers, who were also responsible for finding the raw material. Some bought it from street pedlars, others obtained recycled iron from the black market, and a few went to Shantou to buy in bulk. A good worker made 5 to 10 yuan a day, the equivalent of what an ordinary farmer made by working in a commune for an entire month.[27]

The village enterprises contributed to the market in more than one way. They not only sold their wares through intermediaries but also used their earnings to buy grain and fodder for their pigs, along with imported goods that the planned

23 Guangdong Provincial Archives, 26 September 1975, 253-2-183, 95–99.
24 Ibid.; Report from the Ministry for Trade, 13 December 1972, Hebei Provincial Archives, 919-3-100, 37.
25 Bramall 1995.
26 Report from the Ministry for Light Industry, 13 December 1972, Hebei Provincial Archives, 919-3-100, 17–21.
27 Guangdong Provincial Archives, 20 March 1974, 294-A2.13-8, 1–28.

economy could not provide, such as fish oil or aspirin. They sent purchasing agents to compete with the state sector for the scarce resources needed to run their businesses, buying up coal, steel and iron.[28]

These examples come from Guangdong, but rural enterprises were not limited to the south. In parts of Jiangsu, contracts were concluded between the production team and individual households as early as 1969, in blatant violation of the radical policies of the time. This process often began in regions where the land was unsuitable for agriculture. Along the coast, for instance, some villagers at first abandoned the sandy soil and switched to raising fish instead. They then gradually turned their attention to industry. In Chuansha 川沙, where villagers were mandated by the state to grow cotton, the industrial portion of total production increased from 54 per cent in 1970 to 74 per cent five years later, a rate of growth far superior to the years of "economic reform" after 1978. In contrast, in Songjiang 松江 county local leaders continued to obey the state's call for grain.[29]

The growth of cottage industries in the Yangtze Delta followed old manufacturing habits and trading routes that predated liberation. They were revived as soon as the hand of the state weakened. Much as Shantou had a long tradition in exporting embroideries to overseas markets, for many centuries the villages around Shanghai had specialized in household goods, ceramics, cloth, silk and other handicrafts. Mechanization spread from the late 19th century onwards, as simple devices for reeling silk, for instance, were incorporated into the village mills, diversifying production even further. Sophisticated guilds, chambers of commerce and banks in Shanghai, often with overseas connections, coordinated a flourishing trade. The Shanghai Silk Reeling Industry Trade Association, to name but one, promoted the production and commerce of silk in Shanghai, Jiangsu, Anhui and Zhejiang prior to being disbanded by the communists in 1949.

The extent to which rural industry reconnected with its past in the early 1970s is shown by statistics: in Jiangsu province as a whole, industry represented a mere 13 per cent of total output in the countryside in 1970, but a phenomenal 40 per cent by 1976. These factories were often collective, if in name only. Tangqiao Village 塘桥村, with help from the cadres, established a metalworking factory with 25 employees in 1970. A year later, it set up a power plant as well as a cardboard box factory, several other metal shops and an animal feed processing plant. A brick factory followed in 1972, all of it in blatant defiance of the state's demand that the countryside grow grain and "learn from Dazhai." The village leaders now attracted political attention and started opening new enterprises under the umbrella of a "comprehensive factory." The facade of planned unity was abandoned the moment Chairman Mao died in 1976.[30]

---

28 Ibid.
29 White 1998, 94.
30 Ibid., 112–15.

There were also underground factories that dispensed altogether with the pretence of collective ownership. These, too, were run by village leaders. They had appeared during the Great Leap Forward, although many folded during the catastrophe that followed. The sociologist Fei Xiaotong 费孝通 wrote of these clandestine enterprises that "peasants did not mind what the nature of ownership was. The only thing they did mind was to keep up their livelihood." Some of them were run by individuals, who merely used the name – and often the accountant – of the collective. In other words, they attached themselves to production teams and relied on state officials for protection.[31]

Officials in the higher echelons of power could do very little about the trend. In Shanghai, Zhang Chunqiao 张春桥 fulminated about the "sprouts of capitalism in the countryside." Others railed against the attack on the "dictatorship of the proletariat." There were periodic campaigns to "cut the tail of capitalism" but they were met with widespread sabotage, as villagers slaughtered their animals and diverted collective resources for their own use. Private firms went underground, at least temporarily till the storm blew over. In reality, outside some of the cities where the radical followers of the Chairman were well entrenched, large parts of the countryside were no longer within their reach.[32]

***

When the garden economy created by private plots and rented land produced a surplus, villagers sometimes got on their bicycles and went to the city to sell their vegetables, fruit, chickens, ducks and fish. A few took their produce from door to door, others gathered outside department stores, by railway stations or near the factory gates, sitting on curbs and spreading out their wares on the ground or on small card tables. They were regularly chased away by public security services, but they kept on coming back. Sometimes, the local authorities turned a blind eye, as people met at an agreed time to trade goods at makeshift bazaars.[33]

Villagers went even further in restoring the links that had tied the countryside to the cities. They migrated in large numbers, despite the restrictions imposed by the household registration system. During the Great Leap Forward, tens of millions of villagers had resettled in the cities, working in underground factories or on construction projects. Many were sent home during the famine but they kept on coming back, carrying out the dirty, dangerous or demeaning jobs that city dwellers were unwilling to do. By the early 1970s, many villages had a well-established tradition of migration, knowing how to evade agents of the state, where to seek employment in the city and how to look after family members left behind. Sometimes, the cadres themselves encouraged a form of chain migration by agreeing to take care of children and the elderly, as remittances from workers in the city contributed to the survival of the entire village. The migrants

---

31 Fei Xiaotong, as quoted in White 1998, 118.
32 White 1998, 120–21.
33 For good examples, see Thaxton 2008.

continued to submit their quota of grain, either through relatives or by paying a fee directly to the village leader.[34]

Many millions evaded government control in the wake of the Lin Biao affair, seeping through the holes of the household registration system to settle inside the very heart of the city or along its periphery. Circles of relative wealth appeared around the cities, as pedlars and farmers moved to fringe areas where they culti- vated vegetables or manufactured small goods to sell to urban residents. Some gave up on agriculture to set up food stalls or open small restaurants near the local markets.

Many lived in a twilight zone, constantly evading government control and run- ning the risk of being sent back to their home villages, but large numbers man- aged to acquire the right to stay in the city. Not all of them were peasants. There were rural cadres keen to acquire urban residency, workers who had been sent to the Third Front and erstwhile city dwellers banned to the countryside after 1968. They pulled strings, offered bribes and pleaded with the authorities. Many of them were recruited by state enterprises, thereby allowing factory leaders to cut labour costs. Those who were formally allowed to stay brought over friends and relatives from the village.

The numbers were staggering and counteracted the efforts the state had made to curb the urban population in 1968–1969. In Shaanxi, major cities across the province grew by a quarter of a million people in 1970, and again by a third of a million the following year, reaching a total of 3.6 million. Once natural population growth and changes to the planned economy had been taken into ac- count, it appeared that many were villagers, soldiers and cadres who had mana- ged to bypass the restrictions imposed by the household registration system.[35]

It was the same elsewhere. In Hubei, the urban population grew by a mere third of a million between 1965 and 1970, but by half a million in the following two years. In 1972 alone, more than 300,000 people managed to acquire urban residency. A fifth of these permits were deemed to have been obtained fraudulent- ly. There were also tens of thousands of people without any right of abode, in- cluding children and women married to urban residents. On top of this, in 1971 and 1972 half a million farmers settled in the periphery, on the very edge of urban areas, many of them moving in and out of the city during the day or working overnight shifts.[36]

Even in Beijing the authorities found it difficult to control the movement of people. By 1973, there were clusters of unemployed people openly wandering about the streets. Some were seeking work, others had secretly returned from their exile in the countryside, while whole groups of migrants were in transit, on their way to Heilongjiang. By one estimate, some 200,000 to 300,000 people

---

34 Shaanxi Provincial Archives, 20 August 1973, 123-71-70, 1–6.
35 Ibid.
36 Hubei Provincial Archives, 20 October 1972, SZ75-6-77, 12; Hubei Provincial Archives, 26 November 1973, SZ75-6-107, 58–59. See also Bonnin 2013.

passed through the capital every day. The burden was such that a year later, the public security bureau employed more than 10,000 agents around the clock to try to keep the capital free of undesirable elements.[37]

Not only were more and more people ready to ignore the restrictions imposed on their freedom of movement by the household registration system but they were also happy to travel for free. In Harbin, the provincial capital of Heilongjiang, the local authorities estimated that 1.3 million people travelled without a ticket in 1973. A more precise example comes from Lanzhou, the capital of Gansu: during a random check carried out on 14 October 1973, two out of every three travellers were unable to produce a ticket on demand. About a third of a million people also scrambled on board freight trains in Lanzhou that same year. The express train from Shanghai to Urumqi, on the other hand, was "frequently" blocked by large groups of people who forced it to slow down and then boarded without a ticket. In parts of the country, travelling for free became a habit, as people argued that the "people's trains" were designed for "the people." In the station in Zhengzhou, a major railway hub in Henan, over a 1,000 travellers rushed to get on a train without a ticket each and every day.[38]

There was little that a weakened state could do to curtail the movement of millions of people – but there was a safety valve. In May 1970, the regime formally allowed some migrants to settle in Heilongjiang. With mountains covered in virgin larch, purple linden and red tree, the region had abundant natural resources that had already attracted people fleeing starvation in the wake of the Great Leap Forward. But, for the most part, the province remained an uninhabited wilderness. The state hoped that more riches would be tapped through voluntary resettlement – besides massive labour camps. The majority of migrants came from Shandong and Hebei, and many did not wait for the new state policy. In Zhaoyuan 招远 county alone, more than 2,000 people pulled up stakes in the single month of July 1969 and left in search of a better life in Heilongjiang. Some villages were almost emptied, as up to one-third of the locals voted with their feet, including the accountant and all the Party leaders.[39]

Conclusion

Throughout the country, from 1971 onwards people started quietly reconnecting with the past, whether they were local leaders who focused on economic growth or villagers who reconstituted popular markets that had existed long before liberation. Sometimes, a farmer merely pushed the boundaries of the planned

---

37   "Letter from embassy," 23 May 1973, Public Record Office, London, FCO 21-1089, 2; Report from the Ministry of Public Security, 30 August 1974, Shandong Provincial Archives, A47-2-247, 103–06.

38   Report from the State Council, 3 March 1974, Shandong Provincial Archives, A47-2-247, 26–29.

39   The directive was repeated in the following years; see Order from State Council, 5 June 1973, Hebei Provincial Archives, 919-3-100, 14–15; Report from the State Planning Committee, 25 July 1974, Shandong Provincial Archives, A47-2-247, 85–87; Shandong Provincial Archives, 19 August 1969, A47-21-100, 38–39.

economy by bringing some corn to market or by spending more time on a private plot. In other cases, they were bolder – opening underground factories or speculating in commodities normally controlled by the state. But everywhere, in one way or another, millions upon millions of villagers surreptitiously reconnected with traditional practices, emboldened to take matters into their own hands by the failure of the Cultural Revolution. Even before Mao died in September 1976, large parts of the countryside had "gone capitalist."

The extent and depth of these liberal practices are difficult to gauge, as so much was done on the sly, but they thrived even more after the death of Mao. By 1979, many county leaders in Anhui had no choice but to allow families to cultivate the land. As one local leader put it, "household contracting was like an irresistible wave, spontaneously topping the limits we had placed, and it could not be suppressed or turned around." In Sichuan, too, local leaders found it difficult to contain the division of the land. Zhao Ziyang 赵紫阳, who had arrived in Sichuan in 1975 to take over as the head of the provincial Party committee, decided to go with the flow.[40]

By 1980, tens of thousands of local decisions had placed 40 per cent of Anhui production teams, 50 per cent of Guizhou teams and 60 per cent of Gansu teams under household contracts. Deng Xiaoping had neither the will nor the ability to fight the trend. As Kate Zhou has written, "When the government lifted restrictions, it did so only in recognition of the fact that the sea of unorganized farmers had already made them irrelevant."[41]

In the winter of 1982–1983, the people's communes were officially dissolved. It was the end of an era. The covert practices that had spread in the countryside in the last years of the Cultural Revolution now flourished, as villagers returned to family farming, cultivated crops that could be sold for a profit on the market, established privately owned shops or went to the cities to work in factories. Rural decollectivization, in turn, liberated even more labour in the countryside, fuelling a boom in village enterprises. Rural industry provided most of the country's double-digit growth, offsetting the inefficient performance of state-owned enterprises. In this great transformation, the villagers took centre stage. The rapid economic growth did not start in the cities with a trickle-down effect to the countryside, but flowed instead from the rural to the urban sector. The private entrepreneurs who transformed the economy were millions upon millions of ordinary villagers, and they effectively outmanoeuvred the state. If there was a great architect of economic reform, it was the people.[42] But, as in Central Europe and the Soviet Union, there was a price to pay. By undermining the planned economy, villagers not only forced the regime to adapt, they also allowed it to last.

40　Yang 1996, 157.
41　White 1998, 96; Zhou 1996, 8.
42　Zhou 1996, 231–34.

Biographical note

Frank Dikötter is Chair Professor of Humanities at the University of Hong Kong. Before moving to Asia in 2006, he was professor of the modern history of China at SOAS, University of London. He has published ten books about the history of China, including *Mao's Great Famine*, which won the BBC Samuel Johnson Prize for Non-Fiction in 2011 and was translated into 13 languages. *The Tragedy of Liberation: A History of the Chinese Revolution 1945– 1957* was shortlisted for the Orwell Prize in 2014. *The Cultural Revolution: A People's History, 1962–1976* is the last volume in his trilogy on the Mao era and was published in early May 2016.

摘要: 这篇论文利用了新的资料库證据，来證明文革晚期存在著繁多零散的抵抗行动，最终颠覆了规划经济。在这个鲜有人留意到的现象里，村民重新和市场连繫起来，　这些村民由腹地里最贫困的地方以至沿岸较富庶的地方都有。这场静默的革命直捣社会的架构，地方干部对此往往无奈默许，甚至推波助澜。总括而言，论文提出背後真正策划经济改革的，是人民，而不是邓小平，和中欧和苏联的领导一样，他不过是别无选择下，随大势所趋行事。

关键词: 中国; 文革; 规划经济; 非集体化; 市场

References

Bonnin, Michel. 2013. *The Lost Generation: The Rustification of China's Educated Youth (1968– 1980)*. Hong Kong: Chinese University of Hong Kong Press.

Bramall, Chris. 1995. "Origins of the agricultural 'miracle': some evidence from Sichuan." *The China Quaterly* 143, 731–755.

Huang, Shu-min. 1989. *The Spiral Road: Change in a Chinese Village through the Eyes of a Communist Party Leader*. Boulder, CO: Westview Press.

Kelliher, Daniel. 1992. *Peasant Power in China: The Era of Rural Reform, 1979–1989*. New Haven, CT: Yale University Press.

Kueh, Y. Y. 2006. "Mao and agriculture in China's industrialization: three antitheses in a 50-year perspective." *The China Quarterly* 187, 700–723.

Rév, Istvan. 1987. "The advantages of being atomized: how Hungarian peasants coped with collectivization." *Dissent* 34(3), 341–45.

Rittersporn, Gábor T. 2014. *Anguish, Anger, and Folkways in Soviet Russia*. Pittsburgh, PA: University of Pittsburgh Press.

Thaxton, Ralph. 2008. *Catastrophe and Contention in Rural China: Mao's Great Leap Famine and the Origins of Righteous Resistance in Da Fo Village*. Cambridge: Cambridge University Press.

White, Lynn T. 1998. *Unstately Power: Local Causes of China's Economic Reforms*. Armonk, NY: M.E. Sharpe.

Yang, Dali. 1996. *Calamity and Reform in China: State, Rural Society, and Institutional Change since the Great Leap Famine*. Stanford, CA: Stanford University Press.

Zhou, Kate. 1996. *How the Farmers Changed China: Power of the People*. Boulder, CO: Westview Press.

Zweig, David. 1989. *Agrarian Radicalism in China, 1968–1981*. Cambridge, MA: Harvard University Press.

Index

Note: Page numbers in italic indicate figures or illustrations; page numbers followed by *n* indicate a footnote with relevant number.

Afghanistan, Soviet invasion (1979) 18, 29
agriculture 200–202, 203–6, 209
Anhui province 212
anti-corruption campaign 3–4, 92
apologies
  from former Red Guards 85–6, 158
  Song Binbin 136–7, 138–9, 141, 145–6, 150
army uniforms 182, *190*
art
politics and 122, 131–2
see also Rent Collection Courtyard
Assman, Jan 10
Australia, and Maoism 35

Baader, Andreas 45–6, 51
Backer, Larry Catá 100
Badiou, Alain 115
Bakken, Børge 128
Barmé, Geremie 139
Baxandall, Phineas 8
Beauvoir, Simone de 44
Beijing, migrants 210–211
Beijing Commune 104, 111
Beijing Normal University Middle School
  anniversary celebrations 143
  violence 136, 138–9, 143
  work team 138, 143
  see also Bian Zhongyun
Beijing Red Guards 109–110
Beijing Workers' Representative Assembly 114
Bernstein, Thomas P. 16
Bian Zhongyun
  death 138–9
  "false Party member" accusation 138
  Jiyi (*Remembrance*) symposium 137, 139, 144–5
  official apology ceremony 141
  published accounts and documentaries 139–40
  responsibility for her death still uncertain 142, 144–5
  Song Binbin apology 136–7, 138–9, 141
  Though I Am Gone (documentary) 140
  timing of the apology 145
  Wang Jingyao's refusal to forget and forgive 141, 145

big-character posters 41, 100, 104, 143, 182
Black Panther Party 40
bloodline theory 86
Bo Xilai 80–81, 82, 83, 149–50
Bo Yibo 106
Bodnar, John E. 10
Bracey, John 48

cadres
  clothing as marker of social identity 180–81
  Cultural Revolution overthrow 18–19
  encouragement of collectivization resistance 202–3, 204, 205, 212
  May 7 schools (reform through labour) 19
  rehabilitation 17, 22, 23
  three-in-one revolutionary committees 112
Cai Guoqiang 123–5
Cao Diqiu 109–110
Capanna, Mario 48–9
capitalism 58, 66–7, 69, 73
CCP (Communist Party of China)
  calls for reform 78–9
  Constitution 68–9
  continuing success 61
  Deng Xiaoping reforms 22
  diluted "catch all party" 100
  and the NPC (National People's Congress) 83–4
  vanguard of the working class 68–9
  weakened by Cultural Revolution 18–19
  Zhou Enlai reform 19, 22
censorship 83, 84, 90*n72*, 133, 145–6, 146*n41*
Central Committee
  "All Party members should firmly uphold the socialist legal system" (1986) 79

Document No.9 (2013) 7, 87–8
Instructions on coping with strikes (1957) 91
see also Resolution on certain questions in the history of our Party (1981)

Central Discipline Inspection
  Commission (CDIC) 3, 4
Certeau, Michel de 178
Charter 08 79, 80
chedi fouding (thoroughly negate)
  campaign 36, 51, 55*n1*, 64, 115, 137,
  147
Chen Boda 110–111, 112
Chen Hongru 202–3
Chen Jijin 206–7
Chen, Tina Mai 185
Chen Xiaolu 147, 151
Chen Yi 147*n47*
Chen Yizi 9
Chen Yonggui 203, 204
Chen Yun 142
Chengdu
  Jianchuan Museum 163
  zhiqing exhibition 160–61, 165, 166–7
China Digital Times 146*n41*
China Youth News 85
Chongqing
  anti-Mafia campaigns 80–81
  zhiqing 169
Chongqing model 80–81, 83, 149–50
cinema 160, 166*n54*
class, bloodline theory 86
class struggle 131–2
clothing
  army uniforms 182, *190*
  bridalwear 186
  collars 179–80, 185–6
  colour manipulation 182–3
  coping with material scarcity 178–81
  criticism of the unconventional 182–3
  cun zai (bad person) *183*

Dacron 193
  dresses and skirts 187
  fertilizer trousers 180–81
  foreign influence 187–91, *188*, *189*,
    190, 192
  gunnysack shirts 180
  as marker of social identity 180–81
  stereotyped homogeneity 176
  wedding clothes 79–80, 186, 191
  women and fashion 184–7, *189*, *191*
collars, and clothing resistance 179–80,
  185–6
collectivization 200–201, 204
  see also decollectivization

communist legacies 8
communist parties
  collapse 70–71
  and the working class 58, 59–61, 65, 70
  see also CCP (Communist Party of
    China)
Communist Party (Soviet Union) 17, 21,
  99, 100
Communist Youth League (CYL) 107
Constitution (1975) 86–7, 91, 92
Constitution (1982)
  amendments 80
  freedom of the individual 85
  media campaign 84–5
  online campaign (2002) 85
  property rights 80, 85
  relationship between NPC and CCP
    83–4
  removal of right to strike 78, 85
  voting rights 79
constitutionalism
  constituted power vs constituent power
    77, 81, 82, 92
  definition 76*n1*
  Liao's 1980 reform proposals 78–9
  Reform consensus forum (2012) 83–4
  Reform consensus petition (2012) 84
  rise of demands for reform 76–80
  socialist vs universal constitutionalism
    87–9
constitutionalist alliance 76–7, 80, 87–
  90, 91–2
constitutionalist revolution 81, 91–2
consumer goods 26
corruption *see* anti-corruption
  campaign
criticism-self-criticism 48
"Criticize Lin Biao and Confucius"
  campaign 19–20
cultural amnesia 8
cultural legacies 9
cultural memory 10–11
Cultural Revolution
  affective dimensions 120–22, 123, 129–
    30, 131
  earlier nostalgia for 148*n51*
  Maoist rebel faction counter-narrative
    137–8, 145–8
  official campaign to 'negate' 55*n1*,
    115, 137
  possibility of a repeat 2–4

yousuo buzu (what had not worked)
campaign 62–4
see also Resolution on certain
questions in the history of our Party
(1981)
Curcio, Renato 46
Dacron 193
Dazhai campaign 200–201, 203
de Certeau, Michel 178
deaths, Cultural Revolution 4
decentralization 9, 20
decollectivization
cadre attitude 202–3, 204, 205, 212
covert reaction to extreme
collectivization 200, 202–4, 209–212
Guangdong province 205–7
rural enterprises 207–9
Deng Xiaoping
Beijing Normal University Middle
School and 138, 141–2
criticize Deng campaign 22
economic reforms 2, 7, 17, 27, 61
education reforms 22
era compared with Gorbachev's 17,
21, 22
June 1989 crackdown (Tiananmen
Square) 161
personal authority 17, 22–3
refusal to lead *yousuo buzu* (what had
not worked) campaign 62–4
rehabilitation of officials 17, 22, 23
revival of party-state institutions 17,
20, 22, 23
sidelined by Mao (1976) 20, 22
to blame for Cultural Revolution
violence 137
and the working class 65, 72
Deng Xiaoping Theory 90
depoliticization
parliamentary parties 69–71
of working classes 67–9
dictatorship, Chinese attachment to 30
dictatorship of the proletariat campaign
63
Ding Huimin 169
Ding Yizhuang 170
Disch, Lisa 102
Document No.9 (Central Committee
General Office) (2013) 7, 87–8
dress resistance
by women 184–7

colour manipulation 182–3
everyday clothing 191–2
foreign influence 187–91, *188*, *189*,
190, 192
individualization 183–4
reaction against material scarcity 178–
81
dresses, officially sanctioned wear 187
Dutschke, Rudi 39

economic reform
China's success compared with Soviet
failure 17–18
explanation for 168
from private entrepreneurs 212
legacy of Cultural Revolution 16–17
rural reforms 9
under Deng Xiaoping 2, 17, 27
see also constitutionalism
economy, China's relative backwardness
(1950-76) 18, 24–7, *25*, *26*, 65*n14*
education
compulsory courses 90
Deng Xiaoping reforms 22
egalitarian politics 56, 57, 59–61, 63, 68,
73
Elbaum, Max 38, 49
elections
1980 79
Cultural Revolution goals 100, 102–3
embroidery 207
Ensslin, Gudrun 46, 51

family
bloodline theory 86
children of CCP leadership 86, 141–2
Fang, Lizhi 8
fashion, women's clothing 184–7
father of the nation 89–90
Feng Jinglan 139
Feng Xiang 90–91, 93
films 160, 166*n54*
Finnane, Antonia 185
Foucault, Michel 48
Foxconn 66, 68, 69, 72*n25*
France
Gauche Prolétarienne (GP) 43–4, 44,
48
Maoist influence 36, 43–4, 48, 49
security response to Maoist groups 45
Franceschini, Alberto 46
freedom, four great freedoms 87, 92

freedom of association 79, 87
freedom of the press 79, 83, 84, 87
freedom of speech 83, 87
freedom of thought 79

Gang of Four 20, 71
Gansu province 200–201, 211
Gao, Xingjian 1, 2
gay liberation movements 47
GDP per capita (1950-76) 24–6, *25*, *26*, 65*n14*
Gehrig, Sebastian 45
Geismar, Alain 48
geomancy 202
Germany *see* West Germany
Global Times 6
Gold, Thomas B. 9
Gong Gangmo 80, 81
Gorbachev, Mikhail
  bureaucratic opposition 30
  glasnost, perestroika and reforms 17, 21, 70
  newcomer status 22–3
  withdrawal from Afghanistan 18
Gou, Terry 72*n25*
governmentality 122
Great Leap Forward 25, 27, 200, 204, 209
Grumbach, Tiennot 43
Grzymala-Busse, Anna 8
Gu Hongzhang 170
Guangdong province
  clothing 180–82, 183–4, 187–91, *188*, *189*, *190*, 192
  decollectivization 205–7
  rural enterprises 207–8
  Western influence 176–7

hair styles 186
Halbwachs, Maurice 10
Hanshew, Karrin 50–51
Harbin
  parade 190–92, *190*
  travelling for free 211
Hardt, Michael 115
He Weifang 80–81
Heilongjiang province
  Harbin parade 190–92, *190*
  Heihe Zhiqing Museum 163
  migrants 211
  three-in-one revolutionary committee model 112

travelling for free 211
Hing, Alex 44
Hinton, Carma 139, 144
Hirst, William 10
historical legacy 8–12, 16–17
historiography 148–50
Hong Kong, influence on Guangdong residents 188–9, *188*, 191
housing 26–7, 206–7
Hu Jie 140
Hu Jintao 3, 83, 89, 115
Hu Jiwei 78
Hu Yaobang 78, 142
Hu Zhitao 139
Hua Bingxiao 88
Hua Guofeng 22, 23
Huaxia publishing house 161–2
Hubei province 201, 210
human rights
  Bo Xilai case 82
  in *Spring and Autumn Annals* 83
Hundred Flowers movement 103

I Wor Kuen (US) 44, 48
India, Maoist Naxalite movement 36, 48
individualization, clothing choice 183–4
industry
  industrial units (*danwei*) 64–6
  inefficiency 26
  rural enterprises 207–9
  underground factories 202, 209
internet
  censorship 90*n72*, 133, 145–6, 146*n41*
  Chongqing anti-mafia campaign 81
  Document No. 9 87–8
  Jiyi (*Remembrance*) symposium 137, 139, 144–5
  Mao as father of the nation 89–90
  Maoist rebel faction comments 146–7
  zhiqing websites 162
Internet Information Bureau 145–6
Ip, Hung-Yok 184–5
Italy
  collapse of party system 71
  Communist Party (PCI) decline 70–71
  "hot autumn" strikes 60
  Maoist influence 36, 37, 39, 40, 49
  Red Army Brigades 45, 46
  security response to Maoist groups 45
  students 40

Jasmine Revolution 79

Jiang Qing 109, 127
Jiang Shihua 165–6, 169
Jiang Zemin
  and corruption 3, 4
  "three represents" 99, 100, 101
Jiangsu province 208
Jin Dalu 170
Jin Guangyao 170
Jiyi (*Remembrance*) symposium 137,
  139, 144–5
July, Serge 48

K-Gruppen (Germany) 43, 44, 48
Kang Sheng 112–13
Katz, Richard 70
Khrushchev, Nikita 2, 28
Koenen, Gerd 39, 41
Kuai Dafu 106, 108
Kubik, Jan 8
Kühn, Andreas 43, 48
Kunz, Jean Lock 184
Kunzelmann, Dieter 41–2

labour market 64, 65, 66, 68
landlords 124, 128, 129, 130, 131
Langhans, Dieter 42
Lao Gui 169
Lee, Hong Yung 9
Lee Kuan Yew 50
Lee Siew Choh 50
left-wing politics 36, 38, 49
legacy 8–12, 16–17
Li Hongyun 143
Li Qiang 80
Li Qisheng 130
Li Rui 78, 83
Li Shaoyan 126
Li Xiannian 180
Li Yang 146
Li Zhuang 80–81, 81
Liao Gailong 78–9
Libération 48
Liberation Daily 182–3
liberation movements 38
Lim, Louisa *The People's Republic of
  Amnesia* 1
Lin Biao 3
  "Criticize Lin Biao and Confucius"
    campaign 19–20
  Lin Biao affair (1971) 19, 180, 201
  on Mao's great democracy 105

promotion of foreign revolution 37–8,
  39
Linhart, Robert 49
literature
  great criticism campaign 193
  zhiqing 159, 161–2, 166
Liu Jin 139, 142–3, 144
Liu Shaoqi 3, 27, 28, 114, 137, 141–2
Liu Wencai 124, 128, 129, 131
Liu Xiaobo 79
Liu Xiaofeng 89–90
Liu Xiaomeng 170
Liu Zaifu 78
Long Taicheng 125*n16*, 127
Lorenz, Peter 46
Lotta, Raymond 42
Luonan 202

Ma Li 129, 130*n36*
Mair, Peter 70
Manier, David 10
Manor House Museum (Anren) 123–31
Mao Zedong
  and Beijing Commune 111
  call to the workers 91
  and capitalism 66
  critique of Party organizations 107
  dictatorship of the proletariat
    campaign 63
  dispute with Deng Xiaoping 61–2
  father of the nation 89–90
  fear of being unseated 2
  international admirers 34–5
  little red book 38, 40, 46
  quotations and poems 34, 42, 43, 46,
    57
  responsibility for Cultural Revolution
    violence 141
  revival of ties with the West 18
  and revolutionary committees 114, 115
  support for his policies 2
  theory of permanent revolution 92*n81*
  and worker preparatory committees
    114
  yousuo buzu (what had not worked)
    campaign 62–4
Mao Zedong Thought 90
Maoism 120–23
Maoist rebel faction 137–8, 145–8, 149,
  150
Marbury versus Madison ruling 81

market economy 202–4, 205–6
market reforms 8, 20, 29–30
markets, agricultural 205, 209
martial arts (*qigong*) 160
Marx, Karl 66, 67, 105
Marxism 16, 90
Marxism-Leninism 102
May 7 cadre schools 19
May 16 Notification 99–100
medical science 128
memory
  carrier groups 140–41, 144
  Cultural Revolution 9–10, 154–5
  Jiyi (*Remembrance*) symposium 137,
    139, 144, 144–5
  political control 166–8
  see also zhiqing (educated youth)
Meyer, Till 46
middle schools
  Red Guards 113
  see also Beijing Normal University
    Middle School
migrant workers
  internal 66, 209–211
  new labour 93
  overseas returnees 206–7
museums, *zhiqing* museums 163

Nanfang zhoumo (*Nanfang Weekend*/
  Southern Weekend) 84, 85, 146
Negri, Antonio 71, 93, 115
Newton, Huey 40
Niccolai, Roberto 46
Nie Yuanzi 100, 104
Nixon, Richard 29, 180
Nora, Pierre 9, 10, 11
NPC (National People's Congress)
  call for bicameralism 78
  and the CCP (Communist Party of
    China) 83–4
  creation 102–3
  discredited following anti-rightist
    campaign 103
  student candidates 79

O'Brien, Kevin 103
O'Neil, Dennis 39–40, 41, 42, 47
Open Times 89–90

Paris Commune 100, 103–5, 111, 112,
  114–15
Party Congress (1966) 100

Party Congress (1978) 78
Party Congress (1997) 78
party-state institutions 17, 30–31
peasants 126–7, 128–31
Peking Review 34–5, 42
Peng Xiaomeng 142
People's Daily (*Renmin ribao*) 7, 100,
  105, 111, 120, 128, 203
People's Liberation Army (PLA) 2, 3, 9,
  20, 112
permanent revolution 92*n81*
Pitkin, Hannah 101
PLA (People's Liberation Army) 2, 3, 9,
  20, 112
planned economy
  atomized resistance 202–4, 207–211
  opportunities for subversion 204–7
  rural survival strategies 198–9
Poland, Solidarity movement 59*n7*, 60,
  70, 71
political parties
  decline 56, 72–3
  depoliticization 69–71
  see also CCP (Communist Party of
    China); communist parties
political representation
  contemporary China 100, 101
  Cultural Revolution experimentation
    100–101, 104–5
  Jiang Zemin's "three represents" 99,
    100, 101
  Mao's great democracy 105
  May 16 Notification 99–100
  Paris Commune model 100, 103–4,
    111–12
  post-Mao era 101
  Red Guard Congresses 101, 113
  in revolutionary socialism 101–3
  in Shanghai 109–110
  student committees 107–9
  work teams 106–7
  Workers' Representative Assemblies
    113–14
  see also revolutionary committees
post-structuralism 48
poverty 27
Priestland, David 49
property rights 80, 85, 87
public opinion 86, 192
Pucheng 202–3
Pun, Ngai 66

rationing 26
Reagan, Ronald 35, 49
reconciliation 143–5
Red Army Faction (RAF) (Germany)
  45–6, 50–51
Red Flag 104
Red Guard Congresses 101, 113
Red Guards
  Conservatives (senior leaders) 86, 157
  documentaries 139–40
  dual experiences 144
  end with rustication movement 155
  factional strife 109, 113, 156–7
  formation 57n4, 108
  loyalty to Mao 107
  Mao and 91
  media apologies from former Red
    Guards 85–6, 158
  negative phenomenon 157–8
  Old Red Guards 142
  Old Red Guards as victims 147
  Rebels (students) 86, 157
  representative assemblies 113
  in Shanghai 109–110
  violence 86n51, 138–9, 141–2
reform *see* constitutionalism; economic
  reform
rehabilitation of officials 17, 22, 23
Renmin ribao see *People's Daily*
  (*Renmin ribao*)
Rent Collection Courtyard 123–32
  cost per statue 127
  emotional effect 125–7, 129–30
  enmity and resistance 130
  ethnographic fieldwork 126–7, 130–31
  faces 125n16
  Manor House Museum original 123–
    31
  reform era transformation 132
  Venice Biennale reconstruction (1999)
    123–5
representative politics *see* political
  representation
resistance
  against state collectivization 200, 202–
    212
  atomized daily resistance 199–200
  workers' tactics 67n19
  see also dress resistance
Resolution on certain questions in the
  history of our Party (1981) 6n1, 7, 8

and 1982 Constitution 79
contestation 148, 151
Maoist rebel faction responses 146,
  147
negating the Cultural Revolution
  55n1, 137
silence on responsiblity for violence
  142
restaurants, *zhiqing* restaurants 162
Rév, Istvan 198–9, 206
Revolutionary Action Movement
  (RAM) (US) 40, 47, 48, 51
revolutionary committees
  collectivization campaign 200–201
  composition 19, 101
  elections vs appointment 112–13
  lack of delegation and accountability
    101, 114–15
  military domination 19
  Party control 115
  16 points (August 1966) 107–8, 112,
    115
  three-in-one model 112, 114
  worker representatives 114
Revolutionary Union (US) 42, 44
right-wing politics 35–6
River Elegy (film) 160
Rolin, Olivier 43
Ross, Andrew 48
rule of law 78, 83–4
rural camps, reform through labour 19
rural economy, survival strategies 198–9
rural enterprises 207–9, 212
rural living standards 27
rural reform 9
rustication movement 155–6
  see also zhiqing (educated youth)

Santayana, George 1, 2
Sartre, Jean-Paul 44
Scarlet Guards 110
Schleyer, Hanns Martin 50–51
Schmitt, Carl 120, 121
schools
  revolutionary committees 107–9
  see also Red Guards; students
Scott, James 178
sculpture, *Rent Collection Courtyard*
  123–32
Seale, Bobby 40
self-help 48

sent-down youth 156*n9*
    see also zhiqing (educated youth)
Seth, Sanjay 48
seven black categories 86
Shaanxi province 203, 210
shame 1, 143
Shanghai
    Beijing Red Guards in (1966) 109–110
    Commune (January storm 1967) 60,
        71, 101, 111–12, 114
    rural enterprises 208, 209
    silk industry 208
    zhiqing commemoration 167
    zhiqing compensation appeals 169
    Zhiqing Museum 163
    zhiqing researchers 170
Shanghai Revolutionary Committee 101
Shi Weimin 170
shirts, gunnysack shirts 180
Sichuan province 112, 207, 212
silk industry 208
Singapore, Barisan Socialis pro-Maoism
    50
"16 points" (August 1966) 107–8, 112,
    115
socialism 59–60
socialist constitutionalism 87–9
Song Binbin
    apology 136–7, 138–9, 141
    Beijing Middle School violence 136,
        138–9
    carrier group membership 142
    eminent graduate 143*n33*
    reaction to apology 136–7, 145–6, 150
    Red Guard documentary 139
    Red Guard and victim of Cultural
        Revolution 144
    timing of the apology 145
Southern Weekend see Nanfang zhoumo
Soviet Union
    Afghanistan invasion (1979) 18, 29
    atomized rural resistance 199
    collapse 16, 21, 30
    economic failure vs China's success
        17–18, 21
    economy 18, 23–4, 27
    glasnost and reforms 17, 21, 70
    nuclear test ban treaty (1964) 28
    Sino-Soviet split 18, 28–9
Spring and Autumn Annals 77, 82–3, 84,
    85, 86, 90

Stalin, Joseph (Josif Dzhugashvili) 2
strikes 78, 85, 87, 91, 92–3
students
    committees 107–9
    constitutionalism demands 79
    Maoist influence 40–41
    NPC candidates 79
    tensions with work teams 106–7
    see also Red Guards
supernatural powers (*teyi gongneng*)
    160, 202

Tangqiao Village 208
Tatlin, Vladimir 125
television, and collective memory 9–10
terrorist violence, inspired by Maoism
    45–7, 50–51
Thatcher, Margaret 35
"three antis" campaigns 201
"three represents" 99, 100, 101
Tiananmen Square
    mass meeting (1966) 144
    protests (1976) 22
    protests (1989) 11, 66, 67*n20*, 80, 160,
        161
Tianjin, revolutionary committee 112–
    13
timber 206
Tong Zhiwei 81, 88
transport, travelling for free 211
trousers, fertilizer trousers 180–81
Tsinghua High School 107, 108
Tsinghua University 106

United States
    China's strategic realignment with 18,
        28–9
    civil rights movement 39–40
    I Wor Kuen 44, 48
    Maoist influence 36, 38, 39–40, 41, 42,
        44, 45, 47, 49–50
    Marbury versus Madison ruling 81
    nuclear test ban treaty (1964) 28
    Revolutionary Action Movement
        (RAM) 40, 47, 48, 51
    Revolutionary Union 42, 44
    security response to Maoist groups 45
    students 41
    working class 39–40
universal constitutionalism 87–9
universities
    compulsory courses 90

Maoist influence in Western
  institutions 48
  see also students
urban areas, rural migrants 209–211

victimhood 144, 147–8, 150–51
Vietnam War 38, 42
violence
  Beijing Normal University Middle
    School 136, 138–9, 143
  "Criticize Lin Biao and Confucius"
    campaign 19–20
  Mao Zedong's mistakes 141
  Red Guards 86*n51*
  responsibility for 137, 141, 142
  Western Maoism and 45–7, 50–52

Walder, Andrew 4, 106
Wang Guanyi 129
Wang Hongwen 110
Wang, Hui 36, 70
Wang Jingyao 140, 145
Wang Qishan 3
Wang Shaoguang 100
Wang Youqin 140–41
  Victims of the Cultural Revolution 139
Wang Zhi'an 130
wedding clothes 79–80, 186, 191
Weibo 81, 87–8, 90*n72*
  see also internet
Wen Jiabao 149, 149–50
West Germany
  2 June Movement 46
  green movement 36
  K-Gruppen 43, 44, 48
  Kommune 1 42
  Kommunistischer Bund
    Westdeutschland (KBW) 43, 47
  Maoist influence 37, 39, 40–42, 43, 45–
    6, 47, 48
  Red Army Faction (RAF) 45–6, 50–51
  security response to Maoist groups 45
  students 40–41, 41, 45
  terrorism 45–6, 50–51
Westad, Odd Arne 16
Western Maoism
  and grassroots parties 42–5
  international spread 34–7
  later disillusionment and despair 49–
    50, 51
  legitimization of political violence 51–
    2

since the 1970s 47–51
  and terrorist violence 45–7, 50–51
and Western counterculture 37–42, 47
Williams, Robert 47
Wittenberg, Jason 9
Wolin, Richard 48
women
  clothing and fashion 184–7
  women's rights 47
work teams 106–7, 138, 143
Workers' Congresses 101
Workers' Representative Assemblies
  113–14
workers' universities 64
workers/working class
  CCP as vanguard of the working class
    68–9
  and communist parties 58, 59–61, 65,
    70
  depoliticization 67–9
  Mao Zedong opinion 91
  Maoist experiments 64–6, 72
  political role 57–61, 71
  resistance protests 67*n19*
  theoretical study groups 64, 66
  US 39–40

Xi Jinping
  anti-corruption campaign 3–4
  *Approachable: The Charm of Xi
    Jinping's Words* 2
  cult of Xi *dada* 2–3
  opposition to his July 2010 lecture 83
  and power of the people 115–16
  on two historical periods of socialist
    past (2013) 7–8, 138, 148, 168
  zhiqing experience 164, 169
Xiao Shu 89
Xiaoxiang Morning News 85
Xie Mingan 170
Xie Tao 83
Xinjiang province 112, 167, 169
Xu Caihou 3
Xu Chongde 88
Xu Fa 170
Xu Jilin 100
Xu Wenli 79
Xu Youyu 146, 149–50, 170

Yan'an 186, 202
Yang, Guobin 156, 159
Yang Le 9–10

Ye Weili 139, 143
Young, Ethan 39, 41, 44, 45, 49–50
young people
    ignorance of Cultural Revolution 1
    Western and US counterculture and
        Maoism 37–42
    see also zhiqing (educated youth)
yousuo buzu (what had not worked)
    campaign 62–4
Yu Keping 115–16
Yu Luoke 86*n50*
Yunnan province, *zhiqing* experience
    165–6

Zhang Bojun 103
Zhang Chunqiao 103, 109, 110, 111,
    112, 113–14
Zhang Hanzhi 185–6
Zhang Lifan 88
Zhang Qianfan 84, 88, 90, 91
Zhang Xuezhong 90
Zhang Youyu 91
Zhao Chu 89
Zhao Fan 170
Zhao Shudong 127
Zhao Ziyang 78, 212
Zhejiang province 200, 204–5
Zheng Zhisi 104
zhiqing (educated youth)
    cinema 166*n54*
    clothing resistance 185

common identity 156, 157, 165, 166
compensation claims 168–70
conflicting memories 170–71
critical memories 165–6
delayed generation 159
exhibitions 160–61, 165
literary accounts 159, 161–2, 166
memories 154–5
motivations for remembering 158
mutual assistance 165–6, 169–70
numbers affected 155
paradoxical nostalgia 163–4
political control of memorial activities
    166–8
rustication experience as political
    capital 164
surge in *zhiqing* nostalgia 159–63
zhiqing restaurants 162, 164
zhiqing websites 162
Zhou Enlai
    Communist Party rebuilding 19, 22
    and decollectivization 203
    and Red Guards 108
    revolutionary committee appointments
        112–13
    and Shanghai Commune 112
    and Shanghai workers 110
    US negotiations 29
Zhou, Kate, *How the Farmers Changed
    China* 199–200, 212
Zhou Yongkang 3–4